CONSUMER GUIDE®

COMP▮▮▮▮▮▮▮▮▮ TO

USED CARS

1988 EDITION

Copyright © 1988 Publications International, Ltd. All rights reserved. This publication may not be reproduced or quoted in whole or in part by mimeograph or any other printed means or for presentation on radio, television, videotape, or film without written permission from: Louis Weber, CEO, Publications International, Ltd., 7373 N. Cicero, Lincolnwood, Illinois 60646. Permission is never granted for commercial purposes. Printed in USA.

Contents

Contents

Contents

Contents

Contents • Introduction

Introduction

The average used car sells for about $6000, the average new one for about $13,000, but purchase price is only one reason Americans buy more used cars than new cars each year. Used cars cost less to drive in the long run because depreciation has already taken its toll. You don't go into debt as deeply, and insurance bills are smaller.

Still, finding a dependable used car isn't easy. It takes time, effort and patience. Don't be swayed by a car's appearance or a salesman's smooth talk. If you're impulsive or uninformed you're headed for trouble. That's where this guide comes in.

We list cars alphabetically and save space by combining some "corporate cousins," such as the Buick Skyhawk and Oldsmobile Firenza. Each listing includes three price ranges for each model year based on wholesale amounts paid by dealers at auctions, plus retail selling prices at used-car lots. Each range allows for variations in mileage, condition and extra equipment. We define our ranges this way: **Good**—a low-mileage car that needs little or no repair or reconditioning. **Average**—may need $500 to $1000 in appearance and mechanical work before it deserves a "Good" rating. **Poor**—a high-mileage car that needs extensive reconditioning, both in appearance and mechanical work. These ranges are intended as guidelines in determining fair market value. Actual selling prices can vary widely, depending on locale, supply and demand, and a car's condition.

Introduction

We also list available engines and principal dimensions for each model's major body styles. The fuel economy figures are projections of what we expect a car in good running condition to get in city and suburban driving.

We include major safety recalls ordered by the National Highway Traffic Safety Administration (NHTSA). All safety recalls for a particular car may not be listed, since some cover as few as a dozen autos and some may have been announced after this book was published. We don't emphasize service-related recalls; instead, the text describing each entry mentions major service and repair problems to watch for. For an up-to-date list of recalls supplementing our listings, call the NHTSA toll-free **Auto Safety Hotline:** 1-800-424-9393 (426-0123, if you live in Washington D.C.). The operator will list the recalls for any model you specify. NHTSA will also send you free a detailed recall history of any model.

No matter where you shop, there are some universal used-car hunting rules. Uneven rows of odometer numerals can be a sign of odometer tampering. Wet weather and artificial lights hide bad paint finishes. Watch for mismatched colors, uneven body panels or paint overspray. Knock on fenders and doors to detect spots where filler has been used. Don't buy a car whose catalytic converter has been removed. Inspect underhood fluids, belts, hoses and wires. Check for leaks in the engine compartment and under the car. Go for a test drive in the city and on the freeway. Evaluate engine response, steering accuracy, brake feel and stopping power. Heavy blue smoke from the tailpipe means oil is being burned and an engine overhaul may be imminent. Black smoke reveals fuel-system problems that may not be easy to fix. White smoke that persists after warmup could be a sign of internal coolant leakage, maybe a blown head gasket. Any car worth more than a few hundred dollars deserves analysis by a professional mechanic before you buy.

Federal law requires used car dealers to post on each vehicle a window sticker indicating whether the vehicle is offered "As Is-No Warranty," "Implied Warranty Only," or "Warranty." The mandatory sticker includes definitions of each warranty condition. You might also be offered an extra-cost service contract. These contracts often are tricky, so be certain you need the coverage.

Acura Integra 1986-88

1987 Acura Integra LS 5-door

Sporty 3- and 5-door hatchbacks, introduced in late spring 1986, are the lower-priced offerings from American Honda's new car division. Though similar to Honda's other U.S. models, Integras have a distinctive personality. A high-revving, 1.6-liter double overhead cam 4-cylinder engine (four valves per cylinder) delivers eager acceleration at high rpm, though torque is lacking at lower speeds. Both 5-speed manual and 4-speed overdrive automatic transmissions are available. Mileage is good with the 5-speed. So is performance, even though the tiny engine has to work hard to get it. Wide tires and firm suspension produce fine agility and cornering power, but a rather shaky ride. Hard acceleration makes the engine growl deeply, while the tires roar at highway speeds. Front seat space is okay, though the wheelarches cramp the feet. The 3-door's back seat is tight. Split folding rear seatbacks allow ample cargo capacity. Nice interior holds a good amount of standard equipment, even on the base RS series.

Price Range	GOOD	AVERAGE	POOR
1986 Integra	$9000–10,800	$8500–9800	$7500–8300
1987 Integra	9700–11,800	9300–11,000	9000–9500
1988 Integra	10,500–13,000	10,000–12,500	—

Dimensions	WHEEL-BASE, IN.	LGTH., IN.	HT., IN.	WIDTH, IN.	AVG. WT., LBS.	CARGO VOL. CU.FT.	FUEL TANK, GAL.
3d sdn	96.5	168.5	53.0	65.6	2326	16.0	13.2
5d sdn	99.2	171.3	53.0	65.6	2390	16.0	13.2

Engines	L/CID	BHP	MPG	AVAIL.
dohc I-4 FI	1.6/97	113–118	25–30	86–88

KEY: L/CID = liters/cubic inch displacement; **BHP** = brake horsepower; **MPG** = estimated average miles per gallon; **ohc** = overhead cam; **dohc** = double overhead cam; **ohv** = overhead valve; **I** = in-line engine; **V** = V engine; **flat** = horizontally opposed engine; **D** = diesel; **T** = turbocharged; **bbl.** = barrel (carburetor); **FI** = fuel injection.

RECALL HISTORY

None to date.

Acura Legend 1986-88

American Honda's upscale mid-size, front-drive sedan debuted in March 1986 to challenge European luxury models. Though it feels much like an enlarged Accord, the smooth overhead-cam, 24-valve, 2.5-liter V-6 can deliver snappy acceleration—but with the sound of luxury. A coupe joined the lineup in spring 1987, setting on a 2-inch shorter wheelbase with different rear suspension and bigger, more powerful V-6 engine. For 1988, the sedan gets some of the coupe equipment, including the larger 2.7-liter V-6 and anti-lock brakes (on mid- and top-line models). The 5-speed manual shift beats the 4-speed automatic for performance and mileage. Automatic also shifts harshly and its lockup torque converter cuts in and out too often. Suspension is softer than most Eurosedans for a supple, controlled ride, but Legend grows bouncy at high speed and can even bot-

1987 Acura Legend 4-door

tom out on rough roads. Cruising is quiet and easy. Light, variable-assist power steering delivers prompt responses and handling is capable and reassuring, with moderate body lean and a secure grip around tight turns. Rear seat head and leg room allow three to sit comfortably. Standard cloth upholstery lacks the expected luxury look, but the optional leather offered after '86 adds a bit of class. Ranking as the most expensive Japanese sedan sold in the U.S., Legend is far from cheap on the used car market. Many new sedans were discounted heavily, which could reduce their secondhand prices; but the coupe has quickly become a hot seller.

Price Range	GOOD	AVERAGE	POOR
1986 Legend	$17,000–18,000	$16,000–17,000	$15,000–16,000
1987 Legend	19,000–20,000	18,000–19,000	17,000–18,000
1988 Legend	21,000–27,000	20,000–25,000	—

Dimensions	WHEEL-BASE, IN.	LGTH., IN.	HT., IN.	WIDTH, IN.	AVG. WT., LBS.	CARGO VOL., CU. FT.	FUEL TANK, GAL.
2d cpe	106.5	188.0	53.9	68.7	3100	NA	NA
4d sdn	108.6	189.4	54.7	68.3	3077	NA	18.0

Engines	L/CID	BHP	MPG	AVAIL.
ohc V-6 FI	2.5/152	151	20–25	86–87
ohc V-6 FI	2.7/163	161	19–24	87–88

KEY: L/CID = liters/cubic inch displacement; **BHP** = brake horsepower; **MPG** = estimated average miles per gallon; **ohc** = overhead cam; **dohc** = double overhead cam; **ohv** = overhead valve; **I** = in-line engine; **V** = V engine; **flat** = horizontally opposed engine; **D** = diesel; **T** = turbocharged; **bbl.** = barrel (carburetor); **FI** = fuel injection.

RECALL HISTORY

None to date.

AMC Concord 1978-83

American Motors' facelifted replacement for the Hornet was dropped in 1983, so parts and service are easy to find. Expect mediocre mileage with any engine; dull performance except from the 304-cid V-8 (1978–1979 only). Most used models team AMC's anvil-tough 258-cid six with a Chrysler-built "Torque Command" 3-speed automatic—the best drivetrain for this rather overweight, oversized compact. Cramped rear seat and tight trunk are offset by a good durability/repair record and safe, if uninspired, road

1979 AMC Concord 4-door

manners. Look for oil leaks in 1981–83 258-cid engine with plastic valve cover. Plastic bushing in gear shift linkage prone to wear; replacement required. Most models are well equipped. Not a best buy for economy or roominess, but this nice, quiet car beats some rivals in long-term reliability.

Price Range	GOOD	AVERAGE	POOR
1978 Concord	$800–1000	$650–900	$500–700
1979 Concord	1100–1500	900–1300	650–900
1980 Concord	1400–2000	1200–1700	950–1200
1981 Concord	1750–2500	1500–2200	1250–1600
1982 Concord	2100–2900	1900–2600	1500–2000
1983 Concord	2500–3200	2300–3000	1800–2400

Dimensions	WHEEL-BASE, IN.	LGTH., IN.	HT., IN.	WIDTH, IN.	AVG. WT., LBS.	CARGO VOL., CU. FT.	FUEL TANK, GAL.
2d sdn/3d cpe	108.0	186.0	51.6	71.0	2765	11.4	22.0
4d sdn	108.0	186.0	51.1	71.0	2835	11.4	22.0
5d wgn	108.0	186.0	51.3	71.0	2870	56.9	22.0

Engines	L/CID	BHP	MPG	AVAIL.
ohc I-4 2 bbl.	2.0/121	80	20–23	78–79
ohv I-4 2 bbl.	2.5/151	89	20–23	80–82
ohv I-6 2 bbl.	3.8/232	90	16–19	78–79
ohv I-6 2 bbl.	4.2/258	110	16–18	78–83
ohv V-8 2 bbl.	5.0/304	125	13–15	78–79

KEY: L/CID = liters/cubic inch displacement; **BHP** = brake horsepower; **MPG** = estimated average miles per gallon; **ohc** = overhead cam; **dohc** = double overhead cam; **ohv** = overhead valve; **I** = in-line engine; **V** = V engine; **flat** = horizontally opposed engine; **D** = diesel; **T** = turbocharged; **bbl.** = barrel (carburetor); **FI** = fuel injection.

RECALL HISTORY

None to date.

AMC Eagle 1980-88

1981 AMC Eagle 5-door

Despite paltry sales, this unique but aging 4-wheel-drive passenger car, set on a modified Concord platform with proven AMC bodyshells and running gear, remains in the lineup after Chrysler's takeover. Though not intended for heavy-duty boulder bashing, Eagles ride 3 inches higher than 2WD counterparts to clear off-road obstacles. Sedans and wagons of 1980 were joined the next year by two short-wheelbase, 2-door derivatives of the Gremlin/Spirit: the SX/4 coupe and Kammback sedan. Back seats are cramped in both, and they were dropped by '84. AMC's trusty 258-cid six, standard on 1985-88 versions, powers most used models; Pontiac's 151-cid "Iron Duke" four was the base engine from 1981-83, an AMC-built four in 1984 only. Offered first with full-time 4WD, a switchable 2/4WD mechanism called Selec-Trac was optional for '81, standard beginning in 1982. Selec-Trac economy is only fair, little better than full-time 4WD, but it cuts tire/driveline wear. A 5-speed manual transmission became optional in '82. For 1985, the 4-speed manual shift was dropped and standard 4WD, now called Select Drive, gained "shift-on-the-fly" capability. Only the base station wagon, with automatic shift and a bigger load of standard equipment, remains for 1988. Eagles offer acceptable on-road behavior and very good ride (for 4WD). Performance is adequate with a six, but a four will suffice only on smaller Eagles. Construction quality is generally high; pleasant interior details border on the gaudy. However, 4WD requires increased maintenance, is more likely to need repair, and costs more to fix. Ball joints seem to wear quickly and excessive ring/pinion clearance leads to driveline clunks and noise. Check for paint and driveline flaws on 1980-81 models. Though mediocre as a passenger car, 4WD attracts snowbelt residents and buyers who like to leave the road now and then. Industry eyes now turn toward the new Eagle Premier, a stylish full-size sedan built to lure Taurus buyers.

Price Range	GOOD	AVERAGE	POOR
1980 Eagle	$1800–2600	$1600–2100	$1400–1800
1981 Eagle	2000–3200	1800–2700	1500–2300
1982 Eagle	2500–4000	2200–3700	1900–2800
1983 Eagle	3500–5000	3000–4500	2500–3600
1984 Eagle	5200–6100	4500–5400	3800–4500
1985 Eagle	6800–7600	6400–7200	5800–6600
1986 Eagle	8200–9300	7800–8700	7100–8000
1987 Eagle	9900–11,000	8900–10,500	8500–9500
1988 Eagle	11,000–13,000	10,000–12,000	

Dimensions	WHEEL-BASE, IN.	LGTH., IN.	HT., IN.	WIDTH, IN.	AVG. WT., LBS.	CARGO VOL., CU. FT.	FUEL TANK, GAL.
2d sdn	97.2	166.6	55.2	72.3	3075	28.7	21.0
3d cpe	97.2	166.6	55.2	73.0	3125	25.0	21.0
2d sdn	109.3	183.2	55.8	73.0	3415	11.4	22.0
4d sdn	109.3	180.9	54.4	72.3	3335	12.2	22.0
5d wgn	109.3	180.9	54.6	72.3	3384	57.0	22.0

Engines	L/CID	BHP	MPG	AVAIL.
ohv I-6 2 bbl.	4.2/258	110–112	15–19	80–88
ohv I-4 2 bbl.	2.5/151	90	18–22	81–83
ohv I-4 2 bbl.	2.5/150	NA	18–22	84

KEY: L/CID = liters/cubic inch displacement; BHP = brake horsepower; MPG = estimated average miles per gallon; ohc = overhead cam; dohc = double overhead cam; ohv = overhead valve; I = in-line engine; V = V engine; flat = horizontally opposed engine; D = diesel; T = turbocharged; bbl. = barrel (carburetor); FI = fuel injection.

RECALL HISTORY

1980: half shaft assemblies on front-wheel-drive mechanism could fracture near inboard attachment point. **1982:** fluid in 4- and 5-speed manual transmissions was replaced because it was too thin and could damage the transmission.

AMC Spirit 1979-83

1980 AMC Spirit 2-door

After Gremlin bit the dust in 1978, the Spirit took its place, with the same body/chassis design and choice of engines. The sawed-off 2-door sedan, with rear side windows enlarged, was joined by an attractive 3-door Liftback coupe. Though plusher and better-built that its predecessor, the Spirit endures the same cramped interior, listless ride, and mediocre fuel economy. A 5-speed manual gearbox, offered from 1982 on, is best for mileage. For 1980, AMC replaced the VW/Audi four base engine with Pontiac's 151-cid "Iron Duke" four—a much better powerplant. Comprehensive factory rust-protection measures and use of corrosion-resistant metal also make 1980 and newer models a wiser choice. Changing little through the years but for its grille, minor trim and options, production halted when AMC began to build the front-drive Renault Encore. Watch for oil leaks on 1981–83 six-cylinder engines with the plastic valve cover. Also, a plastic bushing in the gear shift linkage wears out and must be replaced.

Price Range	GOOD	AVERAGE	POOR
1979 Spirit	$900–1400	$750–1150	$500–700
1980 Spirit	1200–1600	1000–1400	750–1050
1981 Spirit	1600–1900	1250–1700	1000–1300
1982 Spirit	1900–2400	1700–2200	1300–1700
1983 Spirit	2600–3000	2200–2700	1800–2300

Dimensions	WHEEL-BASE, IN.	LGTH., IN.	HT., IN.	WIDTH, IN.	AVG. WT., LBS.	CARGO VOL. CU. FT.	FUEL TANK, GAL.
2d sdn	96.0	167.0	51.6	72.0	2620	27.3	21.0
3d cpe	96.0	168.4	51.5	71.9	2665	25.5	21.0

Engines	L/CID	BHP	MPG	AVAIL.
ohc I-4 2 bbl.	2.0/121	80	21–24	79
ohv I-4 2 bbl.	2.5/151	89	21–24	80–82
ohv I-6 1 bbl.	3.8/232	90	16–19	79
ohv I-6 2 bbl.	4.2/258	110	16–19	79–83
ohv V-8 2 bbl.	5.0/304	125	13–15	79

KEY: L/CID = liters/cubic inch displacement; **BHP** = brake horsepower; **MPG** = estimated average miles per gallon; **ohc** = overhead cam; **dohc** = double overhead cam; **ohv** = overhead valve; **I** = in-line engine; **V** = V engine; **flat** = horizontally opposed engine; **D** = diesel; **T** = turbocharged; **bbl.** = barrel (carburetor); **FI** = fuel injection.

RECALL HISTORY

None to date.

Audi 4000/Coupe 1979-87

Great road car offers excellent driving position, good visibility and riding comfort, secure handling with responsive controls. Durable and reliable, the smaller Audi has rated average or higher in every category except electrical problems, which appear more often than usual. A 2-door with 5-cylinder Audi 5000 engine was offered in 1980-81 with automatic or manual ("5 + 5") shift. Five-cylinder fastback Coupe, based on sedan bodyshell, debuted in 1981. VW's diesel four, available in 1982-83, had a history of oil burn-

1980 Audi 4000 4-door

Audi

ing and leaks. Both the diesel and 1.7-liter gas engine were dropped for '84, making a slightly larger VW four (from the Rabbit GTI) standard. The 4-wheel-drive 4000S Quattro, 5-cylinder powered, also bowed in '84 as standard equipment on all models expanded to include air conditioning, cruise control, power steering and alloy wheels. More aerodynamic styling arrived for '85 and the base 2-door sedan departed, so all 4000 models added an "S." In 1986, the 4WD version changed to 4000CS Quattro, while all gained a longer warranty. Late in the 1987 model year, the Coupe GT added a new standard 2.3-liter 5-cylinder engine, rated 130 horsepower, plus extra standard equipment including a sunroof. Though parts and service are costly, this premium German sedan has many virtues, including decent economy and fine craftsmanship. In addition, it's not been plagued by charges of sudden acceleration, like its controversial bigger brother. For 1988 an all-new, roomier Audi 80 and 90 series replaces the 4000.

Price Range	GOOD	AVERAGE	POOR
1979 4000	$1600–2100	$1400–1900	$1200–1500
1980 4000	2000–2600	1700–2200	1400–1800
1981 4000/Coupe	2700–3400	2300–3100	1900–2500
1982 4000/Coupe	3200–4400	2800–3800	2300–3000
1983 4000/Coupe	4500–6000	4000–5200	3500–4500
1984 4000/Coupe	6700–8800	6000–8200	5400–7000
1985 4000S/Coupe	9500–11,500	8300–10,500	7500–9000
1986 4000S/Coupe	11,000–13,000	10,000–12,000	9000–10,000
1986 4000CS Quattro	14,000–15,000	13,000–14,000	11,500–13,000
1987 4000S/Coupe	13,500–15,000	12,000–14,000	11,000–12,500
1987 4000CS Quattro	18,000–19,000	16,000–18,000	15,000–16,000

1985 Audi Coupe GT

CONSUMER GUIDE®

Audi

Dimensions	WHEEL-BASE, IN.	LGTH., IN.	HT., IN.	WIDTH, IN.	AVG. WT., LBS.	CARGO VOL., CU. FT.	FUEL TANK, GAL.
2d cpe	99.8	176.7	53.7	66.3	2500	11.2	15.8
2d sdn	99.8	176.6	53.7	66.2	2250	12.0	15.8
4d sdn	99.8	176.6	53.7	66.2	2337	12.0	15.8

Engines	L/CID	BHP	MPG	AVAIL.
ohc I-4 FI	1.6/97	76–78	25–27	79–81
ohc I-4D FI	1.6/97	52	33–37	82–83
ohc I-4TD FI	1.6/97	68	30–34	83
ohc I-4 FI	1.7/105	74	24–27	82–83
ohc I-5 FI	2.1/131	100	20–23	80–83
ohc I-4 FI	1.8/109	102	22–26	84–87
ohc I-5 FI	2.2/136	110–115	20–25	84–87
ohc I-5 FI	2.3/141	130	19–24	87

KEY: L/CID = liters/cubic inch displacement; **BHP** = brake horsepower; **MPG** = estimated average miles per gallon; **ohc** = overhead cam; **dohc** = double overhead cam; **ohv** = overhead valve; **I** = in-line engine; **V** = V engine; **flat** = horizontally opposed engine; **D** = diesel; **T** = turbocharged; **bbl.** = barrel (carburetor); **FI** = fuel injection.

RECALL HISTORY

1980–81: electrical connector in fuse panel on some 4000 models could overload, interrupting supply of electricity to fuel pump, causing car to stall or preventing it from starting. **1981:** brake calipers on 4000 models could allow fluid to seep out, which could eventually lead to brake failure. **1984:** under adverse conditions, brake hose may crack and leak fluid, resulting in increased stopping distance. **1985-86:** idle stabilizer valve on 5-cylinder models with automatic transmission may have excessive wear, resulting in speed fluctuations and "unsatisfactory driveability." **1986:** rear or right front seatbelt locks may not engage properly; belts could separate in event of heavy brake application or impact.

Audi 5000 1978-83

Audi's replacement for the trouble-prone 100LS had average to below-average repair record in 1978–79; weak in driveline, engine, electricals, exhaust and air conditioning. Suspension on '78s also needed more repairs than normal. Rear wheel bearings on 1980 models prone to early failure. A diesel variant of the five-cylinder gas engine debuted in 1980. Turbocharged gas engine appeared in mid-1980, turbo diesel two years later. Performance is smooth and brisk from turbos, fair on others. Mileage ranges from fair to good, depending on engine. Roomy interiors offer excel-

Audi

1981 Audi 5000S 4-door

lent driving position and good visibility. Decor is a bit austere, but materials are good quality. Complex front-drive mechanicals and expensive parts/service means the larger Audi isn't cheap to buy or to operate. Some common problems have included electrical troubles with the rear lights, hot starting difficulties, transmission failure due to leaky internal seals. Electrical relay problems in 1981 models can run down battery. Charges of sudden acceleration in later 5000 models also apply to this series, which was recalled to install a shift-lock device.

Price Range	GOOD	AVERAGE	POOR
1978 5000	$1600–2000	$1200–1800	$1000–1300
1979 5000	1900–2500	1500–2100	1250–1600
1980 5000	2300–3400	2000–2900	1700–2300
1981 5000	3000–4000	2500–3500	2200–2800
1982 5000	3800–5000	3300–4600	2800–3600
1983 5000	5000–6200	4400–5500	3600–4400

Dimensions	WHEEL-BASE, IN.	LGTH., IN.	HT., IN.	WIDTH, IN.	AVG. WT., LBS.	CARGO VOL., CU. FT.	FUEL TANK, GAL.
4d sdn	105.5	188.9	54.7	69.6	2825	15.0	19.8

Engines	L/CID	BHP	MPG	AVAIL.
ohc I-5D FI	2.0/121	67	28–32	80–82
ohc I-5TD FI	2.0/121	84	25–28	83
ohc I-5 FI	2.1/131	100	18–21	78–83
ohc I-5T FI	2.1/131	130	16–20	80–83

KEY: L/CID = liters/cubic inch displacement; **BHP** = brake horsepower; **MPG** = estimated average miles per gallon; **ohc** = overhead cam; **dohc** = double overhead cam; **ohv** = overhead valve; **I** = in-line engine; **V** = V engine; **flat** = horizontally opposed engine; **D** = diesel; **T** = turbocharged; **bbl.** = barrel (carburetor); **FI** = fuel injection.

RECALL HISTORY

1978–82: driver's side floor mat on gas-powered models with automatic transmission could slide under accelerator pedal and hook onto vibration damper, causing throttle to remain partly open during deceleration. **1978–83:** brake pedal on cars with automatic transmission had insufficient height differential from gas pedal, so driver could inadvertently step on both pedals at same time. **1978-83:** voluntary recall to install automatic shift lock (no charge); see 1984-87 Audi listing for details. **1983:** under adverse conditions, brake hose may crack and leak fluid, resulting in increased stopping distance.

Audi 5000 1984-87

Introduced in spring 1984 as the world's most aerodynamic sedan, the impressively restyled 5000 drew a lot more raves than its predecessor. Later on, many of those cheers turned to boos amid charges of sudden, unintended acceleration when the automatic transmission was shifted from Park into Drive or Reverse. Sedans were first powered only by a carryover 5-cylinder engine. A turbocharged sedan and 5-door wagon arrived the next fall. For 1985, the normally aspirated engine grew slightly, and the rust warranty was raised to six years. An enlarged, more powerful turbo came the next year. Also new for '86 was the 5000CS Turbo

1984 Audi 5000S Turbo 4-door

Audi

Quattro 4-wheel-drive sedan and wagon, with standard anti-lock braking system (ABS). ABS became optional on all other 5000 models for 1987. Later in the 1987 model year a new 2.3-liter engine, delivering 20 more horsepower, took over from the prior 2.2. Creating a fine blend of form and function, Audi's slick design surrounds an interior that holds five in comfort, with a trunk at least as spacious as most other mid-size sedans. Capable front-drive handling and a firm, well-controlled ride carry on the 5000's reputation for fine road manners. Performance is brisk with 5-speed manual shift, passable with 3-speed automatic. Turbo acceleration isn't so much swifter unless it's a 5-speed, which was unavailable on turbos until 1986. A higher level of workmanship and reliability than before should have enhanced the value of the new versions on the used car market, but those safety allegations have kept buyers wary and prices down. A recall of 1978-86 models to install a shiftlock device, which prevents the transmission from being shifted into Drive or Reverse unless the brake pedal is depressed, was announced early in 1987. That didn't resolve the dispute. Court battles and a NHTSA investigation continue. In addition, hot starting problems and difficulties with rear lights have been common. Transmission failure due to leaky internal seals is another trouble spot. By spring 1988, a new Audi 100 and 200 series will retire the 5000 badge—but not necessarily restore the corporate image.

Price Range	GOOD	AVERAGE	POOR
1984 5000S	$6500–8500	$5500–7500	$4500–5600
1985 5000S	9000–11,000	7000–9500	5500–7000
1986 5000S	12,000–14,000	10,000–12,000	8000–10,000
1986 5000CS Quattro	18,000–21,000	17,000–19,000	15,000–17,500
1987 5000S	15,000–18,000	12,000–15,000	11,000–13,000
1987 5000CS Quattro	25,000–28,000	22,000–15,000	21,000–23,000

Dimensions	WHEEL-BASE, IN.	LGTH., IN.	HT., IN.	WIDTH, IN.	AVG. WT., LBS.	CARGO VOL., CU. FT.	FUEL TANK, GAL.
4d sdn	105.8	192.7	54.7	71.4	2844	16.8	21.1
5d wgn	105.8	192.7	55.7	71.4	3042	38.5	21.1

Engines	L/CID	BHP	MPG	AVAIL.
ohc I-5 FI	2.1/131	100	18–23	84
ohc I-5T FI	2.1/131	140	17–22	84–85
ohc I-5 FI	2.2/136	110	18–23	85–87
ohc I-5T FI	2.2/136	158	16–21	86–87
ohc I-5 FI	2.3/141	130	19–24	87

KEY: L/CID = liters/cubic inch displacement; **BHP** = brake horsepower; **MPG** = estimated average miles per gallon; **ohc** = overhead cam; **dohc** = double overhead cam; **ohv** = overhead valve; **I** = in-line engine; **V** = V engine; **flat** = horizontally opposed engine; **D** = diesel; **T** = turbocharged; **bbl.** = barrel (carburetor); **FI** = fuel injection.

RECALL HISTORY

1984: under adverse conditions, brake hose may crack and leak fluid, resulting in increased stopping distance. **1984-86:** install automatic shiftlocking device in models with automatic transmission, in an attempt to eliminate possibility that car may accelerate suddenly while shifting into Drive or Reverse; problem of sudden acceleration has yet to be resolved. **1984-87 Turbo:** repeated "topping off" of gas tank may cause fuel vapors to build up and escape into engine compartment, where they could be ignited by turbocharger heat if under heavy load for extended period; modify fuel filler neck and/or install valve in vent line of charcoal evaporative canister. **1985-86:** misadjustment of fuel distributor allows fuel to escape and be absorbed by air filter; if engine backfires, fuel could ignite and result in underhood fire. **1985-86:** idle stabilizer valve on cars with automatic transmission may be excessively worn, causing speed fluctuations or engine surging that could result in loss of control. **1986:** rear or right front seatbelt locks may not engage properly; belts could separate in event of heavy brake application or impact. **1986-87:** possible that rear brake caliper could bend and overheat, causing spongy pedal or, in extreme cases, failure of one of the two braking systems.

BMW 320i 1978-83

BMW's best-seller proved a highly reliable contender for upscale buyers' attention. The compact and refined 2-door sedan is quieter, softer riding and more comfortable inside than its predecessor, and handles even better on rough surfaces. Performance from the 2.0-liter four is snappy. Gas mileage is quite good, especially on the highway. Performance didn't even suffer when engine size was cut to 1.8 liters for 1980. Trunk space is generous, the front cabin spacious, the rear adequate for grownups. Heating and ventilation improved so much that many buyers passed up the optional add-on air conditioner. Poor electrical grounding may cause battery charging problems on 1978-80 models. Low fuel pressure could bring cold starting woes on some 1980-83 versions.

BMW

1981 BMW 320i 2-door

Price Range	GOOD	AVERAGE	POOR
1978 320i	$3800–4200	$3400–3900	$3000–3500
1979 320i	4400–4800	4100–4600	3600–4200
1980 320i	5100–5700	4800–5300	4100–4800
1981 320i	5900–6300	5600–6000	5000–5600
1982 320i	6800–7400	6400–6800	6000–6400
1983 320i	8000–8500	7500–8000	7000–7600

Dimensions	WHEEL-BASE, IN.	LGTH., IN.	HT., IN.	WIDTH, IN.	AVG. WT., LBS.	CARGO VOL., CU. FT.	FUEL TANK, GAL.
2d sdn	100.9	177.5	54.3	63.4	2650	16.2	15.3

Engines	L/CID	BHP	MPG	AVAIL.
ohc I-4 FI	2.0/121	110	19–26	78–79
ohc I-4 FI	1.8/108	101	20–26	80–83

KEY: L/CID = liters/cubic inch displacement; **BHP** = brake horsepower; **MPG** = estimated average miles per gallon; **ohc** = overhead cam; **dohc** = double overhead cam; **ohv** = overhead valve; **I** = in-line engine; **V** = V engine; **flat** = horizontally opposed engine; **D** = diesel; **T** = turbocharged; **bbl.** = barrel (carburetor); **FI** = fuel injection.

RECALL HISTORY

1977: possibility bolt connecting main wiring harness from positive battery post to terminal under fuse panel is improperly torqued, which could lead to temporary current interruption and electrical system breakdown. **1977:** possibility high flow rate in fuel system may, under extreme altitude and/or temperature conditions, or fuel contamination, produce fuel vapor bubbles that result in rough running or stalling. **1977–79:** possibility defective damper springs on throttle return spring could prevent throttle from returning to idle position upon release. **1978:** possibility defective rubber seal between tire valve stem and rim may allow slow air seepage around base, which could result in under-inflated tire.

BMW 318i/325 1983-87

1986 BMW 325e 4-door

Though closely resembling the 320i, its 3-Series successor wears all-new sheetmetal on a different chassis. It hit U.S. shores late in the 1983 model year, powered by the same 1.8-liter 4-cylinder engine as before, but with higher compression ratio and electronic fuel injection. Even with a sticker price up by $3000, the new small Bimmer sold as briskly as the old one, carrying on as the "yuppie" favorite. In spring 1984 the 6-cylinder 325e arrived, the first 3-Series BMW sold in the U.S. with other than four cylinders. The 164-cid (2.7-liter) in-line six is BMW's efficient "eta" engine, also used in the 528e. A 4-door sedan was added in the '85 model year, with either engine available. For '86, the 4-cylinder powerplant disappeared, leaving only the 325 six. Two new models also bowed: a 325e luxury 4-door sedan and a 325es enthusiast's 2-door. All 1986-87 models have standard Bosch anti-lock braking (ABS) and the optional 4-speed automatic transmission gained 3-mode electronic control. Rear seat room is barely adequate for adults in either body style. Standard seats are too firm and poorly shaped for comfort. Since the smooth, refined four has to rev high to develop much power, it moves best with a 5-speed. The torquey six peaks at lower engine

BMW

speeds, so it's a better match for the automatic transmission and typical American driving. With either engine, the small BMW offers commendable handling and quality, but at a hefty price. However, surging at idle has been a problem on some 1984-85 models and the rear muffler bracket up through 1985 tends to break off. New 325i convertible arrived late in the 1987 model year, accompanied by a high-performance M3 2-door with dual overhead cam 2.3-liter four churning out 192 horsepower. Joining them for '88 will be a 325ix with 4-wheel-drive.

Price Range	GOOD	AVERAGE	POOR
1983 318i	$8800–9300	$8200–8900	$7800–8300
1984 318i	10,000–10,500	9500–10,000	8800–9500
1984 325e	12,300–13,000	11,600–12,500	11,000–11,700
1985 318i	11,800–12,400	11,000–11,800	10,200–11,000
1985 325e	14,000–15,000	13,000–14,000	12,000–13,000
1986 325/e/es	16,500–18,000	15,000–16,500	14,000–15,000
1987 325/e/es	19,000–22,000	17,500–20,000	17,000–18,500

Dimensions	WHEEL-BASE, IN.	LGTH., IN.	HT., IN.	WIDTH, IN.	AVG. WT., LBS.	CARGO VOL., CU. FT.	FUEL TANK, GAL.
2d/4d sdn	101.2	176.8	54.3	64.8	2560	15.0	15.3

Engines	L/CID	BHP	MPG	AVAIL.
ohc I-4 FI	1.8/108	101	23–29	83–85
ohc I-6 FI	2.7/164	121	20–25	84–87
ohc I-6 FI	2.5/152	168	18–23	88

KEY: L/CID = liters/cubic inch displacement; **BHP** = brake horsepower; **MPG** = estimated average miles per gallon; **ohc** = overhead cam; **dohc** = double overhead cam; **ohv** = overhead valve; **I** = in-line engine; **V** = V engine; **flat** = horizontally opposed engine; **D** = diesel; **T** = turbocharged; **bbl.** = barrel (carburetor); **FI** = fuel injection.

RECALL HISTORY

1984 318i: possibility engine defect could cause car to accelerate suddenly when put into gear. **1984 318i:** possibility heater control valve connector may bind while closing, causing solenoid to draw extra current and overheat, which could result in instrument panel fire. **1984 318i:** idle control valve may backfire into intake manifold, become damaged and remain open, which results in abnormally high idle speed. **1985-86:** two parts of steering column could separate if force of collision strikes steering gearbox; special plates should be installed to replace attaching pins. **1986-87:** added load of high-mount brake light could allow its switch to overheat and lead to melting of plastic parts, causing switch to jam in either on or off position.

Buick Century/ Regal 1978-81

1978 Buick Century Special 2-door

Twin downsized intermediates, close kin to the Olds Cutlass Salon and Cutlass Supreme, shrunk by about 10 inches and lost a lot of weight for better fuel mileage. Passenger room, however, is about the same as their predecessors. Century sedans from 1978–80 had distinctive "aeroback" sloped tail; for '81, the 2-door sedan disappeared and the 4-door was replaced by a notchback design. Regal was a 2-door coupe from 1978–80, but heavily reworked for 1981 with a more sloped nose and higher tail—a shape that continued on later models. Overall repair history with a V-6 is average for 1978–80, but much worse on '81s. Premature body wear, squeaks and rattles are the major woes. V-8 models are similar, but '80s also have suspension woes. Some models with the V-6 and small V-8s were equipped with the undersized Turbo Hydra-matic 200C transmission, which has a record of early failure. Avoid the Sport Coupes in either series; their standard turbocharged V-6 needed many repairs. All told, both are better buys than rivals from Chrysler, Dodge, Ford and Mercury.

Price Range	GOOD	AVERAGE	POOR
1978 Century	$1400–1700	$900–1400	$600–1000
1978 Regal	1700–2100	1300–1700	900–1300
1979 Century	1800–2200	1200–1800	800–1200
1979 Regal	2100–2500	1700–2200	1300–1700

Buick

Price Range

	GOOD	AVERAGE	POOR
1980 Century	2200–2700	1500–2200	1100–1600
1980 Regal	2600–3100	2100–2600	1700–2100
1981 Century	2800–3500	2200–2900	1500–2300
1981 Regal	3000–3800	2700–3200	2100–2800

Dimensions

	WHEEL-BASE, IN.	LGTH., IN.	HT., IN.	WIDTH, IN.	AVG. WT., LBS.	CARGO VOL., CU. FT.	FUEL TANK, GAL.
2d cpe	108.1	200.0	53.4	71.6	3200	17.1	18.1
2d sdn	108.1	196.0	54.1	71.2	3200	17.4	18.1
4d sdn	108.1	196.0	55.0	71.2	3332	17.4	18.1
5d wgn	108.1	200.0	55.7	71.2	3450	78.2	18.1

Engines

	L/CID	BHP	MPG	AVAIL.
ohv V-6 2 bbl.	3.2/196	90–105	20–21	78–79
ohv V-6 2 bbl.	3.8/231	105–115	18–21	78–81
ohv V-6 T 4 bbl.	3.8/231	170–175	17–18	79–80
ohv V-8 2 bbl.	4.3/265	120	17–19	80–81
ohv V-8 2 bbl.	4.9/301	140	15–17	79
ohv V-8 4 bbl.	4.9/301	140–150	15–17	79–81
ohv V-8 2 bbl.	5.0/305	145	15–16.5	78
ohv V-8 4 bbl.	5.0/305	160	14–16	78

KEY: L/CID = liters/cubic inch displacement; **BHP** = brake horsepower; **MPG** = estimated average miles per gallon; **ohc** = overhead cam; **dohc** = double overhead cam; **ohv** = overhead valve; **I** = in-line engine; **V** = V engine; **flat** = horizontally opposed engine; **D** = diesel; **T** = turbocharged; **bbl.** = barrel (carburetor); **FI** = fuel injection.

RECALL HISTORY

1978: possibility fan blade spider (hub portion) may fatigue and break apart, throwing off two-blade segment. **1978:** faulty wheel bearings could damage front wheel spindles and, in extreme cases, result in loss of control. **1978–80:** deficient rear axle shafts on certain cars have end buttons that are too thin or could wear excessively, causing shaft/wheel assembly to separate from vehicle. **1978–80:** enlargement of wheel cylinder pilot hole in rear brake backing plate could allow wheel cylinder to rotate, causing loss of brake fluid. **1978–81:** two bolts in lower control arm of rear suspension could break from corrosion, resulting in loss of control. **1979:** models with 301-cid engine may have excessive emissions. **1979:** possibility rear stoplights could become inoperative and cruise control remain engaged after brakes are released, because of incorrect assembly.

Buick Century 1982-88

When launched in mid-1982, Century was part of a new generation of A-car front-drive intermediates that includes

1987 Buick Century Limited 2-door

the Olds Cutlass Ciera (which shares the same engines), Chevrolet Celebrity, and Pontiac 6000. All are longer, plusher, more costly derivatives of GM's ill-fated X-car family. Engine choices include the base 2.5-liter four, optional gas V-6s, plus a 4.3-liter diesel V-6. Buick's 3.0-liter V-6 was replaced in '86 by a Chevrolet-built 2.8 as the first engine option above base. A 3.8-liter V-6 and 4-speed overdrive automatic came late in '84, and that 3.8 gained port fuel injection and Computer Controlled Coil Ignition for 1986. A 3-speed automatic is standard with all other engines. The base four is barely adequate for sedans, weaker yet in the station wagon added for 1984. A small V-6 boosts performance only mildly, but every little bit helps. The 3.8-liter V-6 feels almost like a V-8 (and uses almost as much gas in the city); it gained 25 horsepower in 1986. For 1987, the "Generation II" base four added 6 horsepower, while the 2.8 V-6 got fuel injection and 13 more horsepower. Twin balance shafts went into the 1988 "Tech IV" four, for smoother and quieter running. Beware of the diesel. Even though its repair record is better than some, diesels are far from perfect and have poor resale value. Watch for engine/transaxle vibrations due to deterioration of upper engine torque strap. Passenger and trunk space rival that of larger rear-drive GM mid-sizes and the roomy wagon holds more cargo than a Regal. Well-designed and constructed, a Century generally costs more to maintain than mechanically simpler rear-drives.

Buick

Price Range

	GOOD	AVERAGE	POOR
1982 Century	$3600–4300	$3200–3900	$2700–3300
1983 Century	4600–5200	3900–4700	3000–3900
1984 Century	5300–6000	4700–5400	3800–4600
1985 Century	6500–7800	5900–7100	5000–6300
1986 Century	7900–9200	7200–8400	6000–7400
1987 Century	9100–10,500	8500–9800	7700–8700
1988 Century	10,700–12,500	10,000–11,500	—

Dimensions

	WHEEL-BASE, IN.	LGTH., IN.	HT., IN.	WIDTH, IN.	AVG. WT., LBS.	CARGO VOL., CU. FT.	FUEL TANK, GAL.
2d cpe	104.9	189.1	54.6	69.4	2625	16.2	15.7
4d sdn	104.9	189.1	54.6	69.4	2710	16.2	15.7
5d wgn	104.9	191.2	54.2	69.4	2906	74.4	15.7

Engines

	L/CID	BHP	MPG	AVAIL.
ohv I-4 FI	2.5/151	90–98	20–25	82–88
ohv V-6 2 bbl.	2.8/173	112	18–24	85–86
ohv V-6 FI	2.8/173	125	19–24	87–88
ohv V-6 2 bbl.	3.0/181	110	17–23	82–85
ohv V-6 FI	3.8/231	125	16–23	84–85
ohv V-6 FI	3.8/231	150	17–23	86–88
ohv V-6D FI	4.3/262	85	23–29	82–85

KEY: L/CID = liters/cubic inch displacement; **BHP** = brake horsepower; **MPG** = estimated average miles per gallon; **ohc** = overhead cam; **dohc** = double overhead cam; **ohv** = overhead valve; **I** = in-line engine; **V** = V engine; **flat** = horizontally opposed engine; **D** = diesel; **T** = turbocharged; **bbl.** = barrel (carburetor); **FI** = fuel injection.

RECALL HISTORY

1982: possibility brake hoses don't meet federal standards for strength, which could result in loss of brake fluid and partial loss of braking ability. **1982:** hose clamps on fuel tank filler pipe could fracture, causing leaks and possibility of fire. **1983:** brake proportioning valve could break and separate from master cylinder, causing fluid leak and partial loss of braking ability. **1984:** 2-door models with optional bucket seats may have seatback locks that don't meet federal safety requirements. **1984:** fuel system of 2.5-liter four engine may leak at injection feed pipe connection, which could result in under-hood fire that may spread to passenger compartment. **1984 wagon:** some were assembled with incorrect rear brake system and may exceed required maximum stopping distance. **1986:** on cars with 2.8-liter engine and 108-amp generator, "Bat" terminal on rectifier end frame may contact carburetor fuel inlet pipe; erosion of terminal boot could result in underhood fire. **1986:** on cars with luggage rack and opera lamp options, an incorrect wiring harness may cause the center high-mounted stop lamp to remain lit when headlights or parking lights are on; and opera lamps may come on when brakes are applied.

Buick Electra 1978-84

1982 Buick Electra Park Avenue 4-door

Slightly longer than a LeSabre, the plusher Electra (like the similar C-bodied Olds Ninety-Eight) sits on the same platform as Cadillac's DeVille. Though much smaller than their "land yacht" forerunners, these rear-drive sedans are almost as roomy and more economical (but far from mileage champs, even with the V-6 that became the base engine for 1980). Most are V-8 powered, which is more appropriate for a car of this size. Avoid the Olds-built diesel V-8, offered from 1980 on, which sells for less but suffered serious mechanical flaws. Electra gets high marks for durability and reliability, a top rating for room and comfort. Main differences over the slightly smaller B-body cars lie in the luxurious trappings. If you don't need this kind of posh travel, LeSabre might be a better choice.

Price Range	GOOD	AVERAGE	POOR
1978 Electra	$2200–2800	$1700–2300	$1000–1600
1979 Electra	2800–3400	2200–2800	1400–2100
1980 Electra	3200–3800	2600–3300	1600–2600
1981 Electra	3900–4800	3300–4000	1900–3200
1982 Electra	5000–6200	4400–5200	2500–4300
1983 Electra	6500–7800	5700–7000	3000–5500
1984 Electra	8400–9800	7500–8900	4500–7500

Buick

Dimensions	WHEEL-BASE, IN.	LGTH., IN.	HT., IN.	WIDTH, IN.	AVG. WT., LBS.	CARGO VOL., CU. FT.	FUEL TANK, GAL.
2d cpe	119.0	221.1	57.2	76.3	3945	20.5	27.0
4d sdn	119.0	221.1	57.2	76.3	3973	20.5	27.0

Engines	L/CID	BHP	MPG	AVAIL.
ohv V-6 4 bbl.	4.1/252	125	15–18	80–83
ohv V-8 2 bbl.	4.9/301	135	14–17	79
ohv V-8 4 bbl.	5.0/307	140–150	14–17	80–84
ohv V-8 4 bbl.	5.7/350	160–170	15–16	78–79
ohv V-8 D FI	5.7/350	105–125	23–27	80–84
ohv V-8 4 bbl.	6.6/403	185	12–14	78

KEY: L/CID = liters/cubic inch displacement; **BHP** = brake horsepower; **MPG** = estimated average miles per gallon; **ohc** = overhead cam; **dohc** = double overhead cam; **ohv** = overhead valve; **I** = in-line engine; **V** = V engine; **flat** = horizontally opposed engine; **D** = diesel; **T** = turbocharged; **bbl.** = barrel (carburetor); **FI** = fuel injection.

RECALL HISTORY

1978: possibility fan blade spider (hub portion) may fatigue and break apart, throwing off two-blade segment. **1979:** possibility stoplights could become inoperative and cruise control stay engaged after brake is released, because of incorrect assembly. **1979–80:** outboard front seatbelt anchor bolts could break off during normal use. **1982:** governor in injection pump on diesel V-8 could fail, preventing throttle from returning to idle or engine from being shut off. **1984:** rubber fuel return hose on certain models with 5.0-liter gas V-8 could crack and allow slow gasoline leak as engine runs.

Buick Electra 1985-88

The name remained but the front-drive Electra, like its companion Olds Ninety-Eight, is dramatically smaller than previous full-size, rear-drive models. Interior dimensions didn't shrink much, yet despite Buick's six-passenger claim, it's really a roomy four-seater with ample (not full-size) trunk space. Models include a coupe (until 1988) and sedan in base or plush Park Avenue trim, plus an enthusiast's T Type. A 3.0-liter V-6 was standard the first year, a 4.3-liter diesel V-6 optional. But most Electras were sold with the fuel-injected 3.8-liter V-6, which gained 15 horsepower and became the sole engine for '86. For 1987, it received low-friction roller lifters and 10 more horsepower. Latest Electras carry the new GM "3800" version with balance shaft, which cranks out 165 horsepower.

1985 Buick Electra T Type 4-door

Computer-controlled anti-lock braking (ABS) became optional on late '86 versions, later standard on T Type. Posh appointments are reminiscent of the old Electra, and the new version has sold well. Performance with 3.8 V-6 beats the old V-8. Handling and roadability have improved, too; fuel mileage has changed little. We like the modern Electra's manageable size and improved road manners.

Price Range	GOOD	AVERAGE	POOR
1985 Electra	$10,000–11,000	$9000–10,000	$8000–9000
1986 Electra	11,500–13,000	10,500–11,500	9500–10,500
1987 Electra	13,500–16,000	12,500–14,000	11,500–12,500
1988 Electra	16,000–18,500	14,000–17,000	—

Dimensions	WHEEL-BASE, IN.	LGTH., IN.	HT., IN.	WIDTH, IN.	AVG. WT., LBS.	CARGO VOL., CU. FT.	FUEL TANK, GAL.
2d cpe	110.8	197.0	54.3	72.1	3225	15.7	18.0
4d sdn	110.8	197.0	54.3	72.1	3275	15.7	18.0

Engines	L/CID	BHP	MPG	AVAIL.
ohv V-6 2 bbl.	3.0/181	110	16–20	85
ohv V-6 FI	3.8/231	125–165	17–21	85–88
ohv V-6 D FI	4.3/262	85	20–24	85

KEY: L/CID = liters/cubic inch displacement; **BHP** = brake horsepower; **MPG** = estimated average miles per gallon; **ohc** = overhead cam; **dohc** = double overhead cam; **ohv** = overhead valve; **I** = in-line engine; **V** = V engine; **flat** = horizontally opposed engine; **D** = diesel; **T** = turbocharged; **bbl.** = barrel (carburetor); **FI** = fuel injection.

RECALL HISTORY

1986: power steering hose could overheat and rupture due to insufficient clearance from exhaust manifold, possibly causing underhood fire. **1986:** contacts on push-pull headlight switch may

Buick

be intermittent, causing headlamps to flicker or go out suddenly. **1986:** fluid may seep from anti-lock brake system onto pump motor and certain relays may have been exposed to water contamination; could result in total loss of rear brakes and loss of power assist to front brakes. **1987 Park Avenue:** fusible link could melt under high-resistance load and ignite plastic windshield washer bracket, causing underhood fire; replace with nonflammable bracket.

Buick LeSabre 1978-85

1978 Buick LeSabre Custom 4-door

More luxurious and expensive than the similar B-bodied Chevrolet Caprice and Pontiac Bonneville/Parisienne, the full-size LeSabre remains in high demand. So does its near twin, the Olds Delta 88. Mileage is acceptable with a V-6 engine, but many buyers chose one of the more powerful gas V-8s. The 350-cid engine that Olds converted to diesel had reliability problems that resulted in lawsuits against GM, and it departed during the 1985 model year. Another engine to avoid is the turbocharged V-6 in the 1978-80 Sport Coupe, because of its history of mechanical bugs. Gas engines in 1978-80 models had driveability problems related to emissions controls. GM's "200" automatic transmission was one more trouble spot. Even so, LeSabre has a lot of pluses, including a spacious interior and luggage area—a fine choice for families that need lots of room. Most examples are plushly furnished and have been well maintained. For 1986, the LeSabre nameplate went on a new, much smaller front-drive model.

Price Range	GOOD	AVERAGE	POOR
1978 LeSabre	$1800–2300	$1300–1800	$900–1300
1979 LeSabre	2100–2600	1600–2100	1000–1600
1980 LeSabre	2500–3000	1900–2500	1200–1800
1981 LeSabre	3000–3800	2400–3200	1500–2300
1982 LeSabre	3800–4700	3200–3900	1800–3100
1983 LeSabre	5000–5800	4000–5300	2500–3900
1984 LeSabre	6300–7500	5500–6800	3300–5200
1985 LeSabre	8000–9000	7000–8100	4800–6900

Dimensions	WHEEL-BASE, IN.	LGTH., IN.	HT., IN.	WIDTH, IN.	AVG. WT., LBS.	CARGO VOL., CU. FT.	FUEL TANK, GAL.
2d cpe	115.9	218.1	56.0	76.3	3492	20.8	27.0
4d sdn	115.9	218.1	56.7	76.3	3531	20.8	27.0
5d wgn	115.9	220.3	58.5	79.8	4085	87.2	22.0

Engines	L/CID	BHP	MPG	AVAIL.
ohv V-6 2 bbl.	3.8/231	105–115	16–18	78–85
ohv V-6 T 4 bbl.	3.8/231	170	15–17	78–80
ohv V-6 4 bbl.	4.1/252	125	16–19	80–84
ohv V-8 2 bbl.	4.9/301	135–140	16–18	78–79
ohv V-8 4 bbl.	4.9/301	140	15–17	80
ohv V-8 4 bbl.	5.0/307	140	14–17	81–85
ohv V-8 4 bbl.	5.7/350	155	15–16	79–80
ohv V-8 D FI	5.7/350	105	23–27	80–85

KEY: L/CID = liters/cubic inch displacement; **BHP** = brake horsepower; **MPG** = estimated average miles per gallon; **ohc** = overhead cam; **dohc** = double overhead cam; **ohv** = overhead valve; **I** = in-line engine; **V** = V engine; **flat** = horizontally opposed engine; **D** = diesel; **T** = turbocharged; **bbl.** = barrel (carburetor); **FI** = fuel injection.

RECALL HISTORY

1978: possibility fan blade spider (hub portion) may fatigue and break apart, throwing off two-blade segment. **1979:** models with 301-cid engine may have excessive emissions. **1979:** brake lights could become inoperative and cruise control remain engaged after brakes are released. **1979–80:** possibility outboard front seatbelt anchor belts could break off during normal use. **1981:** some models with gas engines have wrong brake pedal support bracket, which could reduce braking effectiveness. **1982:** injection pump governor on diesel V-8 could fail, preventing throttle from returning to idle or engine from being shut off. **1984:** rubber fuel hose on certain models with 5.0-liter V-8 could crack and allow slow gasoline leak as engine runs.

Buick LeSabre 1986-88

1986 Buick LeSabre Limited 4-door

Downsized front-drive Buick is 22 inches shorter and 400 pounds lighter than its full-size predecessor. Like its cousin, the Olds Delta 88, LeSabre rides the same platform as the Electra and Olds Ninety-Eight. A 2-door coupe and 4-door sedan came in Custom or Limited trim at first; lower-cost base models joined for the second season. The initial 3.0-liter V-6 lacked oomph. The 3.8 V-6 (first optional, then standard for '87) performs a lot better, but guzzles nearly as much gas as the older V-8s. A more powerful GM "3800" 3.8-liter V-6 is standard on the '88 T Type, optional on other LeSabres. Anti-lock braking and "T" handling suspension became optional in 1987, but the suspension option didn't last a second year. A 4-speed overdrive automatic transmission is standard. LeSabre offers a steady, absorbent ride, plus responsive handling for a domestic family car. There's room for six in a pinch, but four will be much more comfortable. LeSabre isn't quite as plush as the otherwise similar Electra, but its price isn't as hefty either. Unlike other Buick models, LeSabre sold well during 1987, which could affect its used-car price. For the last remaining full-size, rear-drive LeSabre, check the Estate Wagon listing below.

Price Range	GOOD	AVERAGE	POOR
1986 LeSabre	$10,000–11,500	$9000–10,000	$8200–8900
1987 LeSabre	12,000–13,500	10,500–12,000	9500–10,500
1988 LeSabre	13,500–15,000	12,000–14,000	—

Dimensions	WHEEL-BASE, IN.	LGTH., IN.	HT., IN.	WIDTH, IN.	AVG. WT., LBS.	CARGO VOL., CU. FT.	FUEL TANK, GAL.
2d cpe	110.8	196.2	54.7	72.1	3163	15.7	18.0
4d sdn	110.8	196.2	55.5	72.1	3203	16.4	18.0

Engines	L/CID	BHP	MPG	AVAIL.
ohv V-6 FI	3.0/181	125	17–22	86
ohv V-6 FI	3.8/231	150–165	15–20	86–88

KEY: L/CID = liters/cubic inch displacement; **BHP** = brake horsepower; **MPG** = estimated average miles per gallon; **ohc** = overhead cam; **dohc** = double overhead cam; **ohv** = overhead valve; **I** = in-line engine; **V** = V engine; **flat** = horizontally opposed engine; **D** = diesel; **T** = turbocharged; **bbl.** = barrel (carburetor); **FI** = fuel injection.

RECALL HISTORY

1986: contacts on push-pull headlight switch may be intermittent, causing headlamps to flicker or go out suddenly. **1987:** fusible link could melt under high-resistance load and ignite plastic windshield washer bracket, causing underhood fire; replace with nonflammable bracket. **1987:** fluid may seep from anti-lock brake system onto pump motor and certain relays may have been exposed to water contamination; could result in total loss of rear brakes and loss of power assist to front brakes.

Buick LeSabre/ Electra Estate 1986-88

Twin station wagons are the last holdovers from Buick's full-size, rear-drive lineup. Others disappeared after 1985. Both use Oldsmobile's 5.0-liter V-8 with 4-barrel carburetor and 4-speed automatic transmission. They differ only in trim and equipment, with Electra the plusher of the pair. Chevrolet Caprice and Pontiac Safari wagons are similar. Only a van is likely to match the generous cargo volume, 5000-pound towing capacity and spacious six-passenger interior (eight with a third seat, which became standard for 1988). On the down side, the V-8 guzzles gas to haul all this bulk around and the clumsy, boatlike handling makes these behemoths tedious to drive in urban areas. Among the last of their breed, they shine brightest on the open road. Large families may still find them tempting. Latest versions have even more standard equipment to add to their allure.

Buick

1980 Buick Electra Estate 5-door

Price Range	GOOD	AVERAGE	POOR
1986 Electra Estate	$12,000–13,000	$11,000–12,000	$9500–11,000
1986 LeSabre Estate	10,000–11,000	9000–10,000	8000–9000
1987 Electra Estate	14,000–15,000	13,000–14,000	12,000–13,000
1987 LeSabre Estate	12,000–13,000	11,000–12,000	10,000–11,000
1988 Electra Estate	16,500–17,500	15,000–16,500	—
1988 LeSabre Estate	13,000–15,000	12,000–14,000	—

Dimensions	WHEEL-BASE, IN.	LGTH., IN.	HT., IN.	WIDTH, IN.	AVG. WT., LBS.	CARGO VOL., CU. FT.	FUEL TANK, GAL.
5d wgn	115.9	220.5	59.3	79.3	4120	87.9	22.0

Engines	L/CID	BHP	MPG	AVAIL.
ohv V-8 4 bbl.	5.0/307	140	15–19	86–88

KEY: L/CID = liters/cubic inch displacement; **BHP** = brake horsepower; **MPG** = estimated average miles per gallon; **ohc** = overhead cam; **dohc** = double overhead cam; **ohv** = overhead valve; **I** = in-line engine; **V** = V engine; **flat** = horizontally opposed engine; **D** = diesel; **T** = turbocharged; **bbl.** = barrel (carburetor); **FI** = fuel injection.

RECALL HISTORY

1986: contacts on push-pull headlight switch may be intermittent, causing headlamps to flicker or go out suddenly.

Buick Regal 1982-87

When Buick merged the rear-drive Century sedan and wagon and the Regal coupe under one model name, the new Regal became the company's best-seller. Two years later, though, that title was taken over by the front-drive

1982 Buick Regal 2-door

Century, also introduced in '82. Regal's station wagon was cancelled after 1983, the sedan the next year; only the stylish coupe survived. Styling, interior details and engine choices changed in most years, but not by much. The base 3.8-liter V-6 provides rather leisurely motion with decent gas mileage. For a bit more power, the 4.1-liter V-6 doesn't guzzle much more fuel. An Oldsmobile-built 5.0-liter V-8 became optional for 1986. A turbocharged V-6 in the Sport Coupe, later in T Type and Grand National models, packs more punch than many V-8s. That turbo gained 35 horsepower with a new intercooler for '86 but, sadly, has more repair troubles than normally aspirated engines. Neither diesel engine has a good repair record or resale value; diesels were abandoned during '85. Regals are attractively and comfortably furnished. Reliability records were above average in most years. Not so popular as they used to be, used Regals still command fairly high prices. The performance-oriented Grand National has also attracted some collector interest. An all-new, shorter front-drive Regal with flush glass and sleek, rounded body arrived for the 1988 model year.

Price Range	GOOD	AVERAGE	POOR
1982 Regal	$4000–4900	$3500–4200	$2500–3400
1983 Regal	5000–5600	4100–5000	3200–4000
1984 Regal	5900–6800	5100–6000	3800–5000
1985 Regal	7000–8000	6200–7200	4400–6100
1986 Regal	8800–10,000	7600–8800	6000–7500
1987 Regal	10,000–11,000	9000–10,000	8000–9000

Buick

Dimensions	WHEEL-BASE, IN.	LGTH., IN.	HT., IN.	WIDTH, IN.	AVG. WT., LBS.	CARGO VOL., CU. FT.	FUEL TANK, GAL.
2d cpe	108.1	200.6	55.3	71.6	3250	16.2	18.1
4d sdn	108.1	196.0	56.2	71.1	3275	15.6	18.2
5d wgn	108.1	196.7	57.1	71.1	3410	71.8	18.2

Engines	L/CID	BHP	MPG	AVAIL.
ohv V-6 2 bbl.	3.8/231	110	16–19	82–87
ohv V-6T 4 bbl.	3.8/231	175–180	12–15	82–84
ohv V-6T FI	3.8/231	200–245	13–17	85–87
ohv V-6 4 bbl.	4.1/252	125	14–17	82–84
ohv V-6D FI	4.3/262	85	25–28	82–85
ohv V-8 4 bbl.	5.0/307	140	14–17	86–87
ohv V-8D FI	5.7/350	105	23–27	82–83

KEY: L/CID = liters/cubic inch displacement; **BHP** = brake horsepower; **MPG** = estimated average miles per gallon; **ohc** = overhead cam; **dohc** = double overhead cam; **ohv** = overhead valve; **I** = in-line engine; **V** = V engine; **flat** = horizontally opposed engine; **D** = diesel; **T** = turbocharged; **bbl.** = barrel (carburetor); **FI** = fuel injection.

RECALL HISTORY

1982: injection pump governor on diesel V-8 could fail, preventing throttle from returning to idle or engine from being shut off. **1982:** fuel inlet pipe at carburetor could crack and leak, creating possibility of underhood fire. **1984:** 2-door models with optional bucket seats may have seatback locks that fail to meet federal safety requirements. **1984:** steering gear-to-frame bolt on a few cars may not have been tightened to spec and could come loose from frame. **1984-85:** on cars without full aluminum rear bumper reinforcement, rear bumper may fracture during rear-end collision, puncture fuel tank and cause leak, with potential for fire. **1985:** tie rods on some models may have loose adjuster clamps, which could allow tie rod to loosen and separate, with loss of steering control. **1986:** on models with removable Hatchroof (T-tops), driver's side shoulder belt anchor plate may be upside-down in lock pillar; in a crash, belt may pull loose, increasing likelihood of injury.

Buick Riviera 1979-85

Riviera advanced to the front-drive generation when GM redesigned its luxury coupes for 1979. Sharing mechanicals with Toronado and Cadillac Eldorado, the Riv is a near relative of the Olds in looks and price. All-independent suspension gives better handling with smoother, more controlled ride than larger previous rear-drive Rivs. In-

1983 Buick Riviera T Type 2-door

terior is ample for four adults, though less roomy in the rear. Best engine bets are the Buick 4.1-liter V-6 and Olds 5.0-liter V-8; naturally, the V-8 is the choice for performance, if not economy. Stay away from the trouble-prone diesel, which has little value on the used car market. Riviera's turbocharged V-6 is a unique offering on sporty models, but its complexity can bring more frequent (and costly) repairs. Rarest and most expensive of all is the 1982–85 convertible. Neither cheap nor a model of efficiency, Riviera remains a solid personal-luxury cruiser made in the USA.

Price Range	GOOD	AVERAGE	POOR
1979 Riviera	$3300–4000	$2500–3300	$1600–2400
1980 Riviera	4200–4900	3400–4200	2400–3300
1981 Riviera	5000–5600	4300–5000	3000–4200
1982 Riviera	6000–6700	5200–6000	3500–5100
1982 Convertible	9000–10,000	8000–9000	6500–8000
1983 Riviera	7800–8500	6600–7800	4500–6500
1983 Convertible	11,000–12,000	10,000–11,000	9000–10,000
1984 Riviera	9500–10,000	8500–9500	6000–8500
1984 Convertible	12,500–14,000	11,500–12,500	10,500–11,500
1985 Riviera	11,500–12,500	10,500–11,500	8500–10,500
1985 Convertible	15,500–17,000	14,000–15,500	12,500–14,000

Dimensions	WHEEL-BASE, IN.	LGTH., IN.	HT., IN.	WIDTH, IN.	AVG. WT., LBS.	CARGO VOL., CU. FT.	FUEL TANK, GAL.
2d cpe	114.0	206.6	54.3	72.8	3700	15.8	21.1
2d conv.	114.0	206.6	54.3	72.8	3725	12.7	21.1

Buick

Engines	L/CID	BHP	MPG	AVAIL.
ohv V-6T 4 bbl.	3.8/231	170–190	12–15	79–85
ohv V-6 4 bbl.	4.1/252	125	14–17	81–84
ohv V-8 4 bbl.	5.0/307	140	14–18	80–85
ohv V-8D FI	5.7/350	105	23–27	81–85
ohv V-8 4 bbl.	5.7/350	160–170	17–18	79–80

KEY: L/CID = liters/cubic inch displacement; **BHP** = brake horsepower; **MPG** = estimated average miles per gallon; **ohc** = overhead cam; **dohc** = double overhead cam; **ohv** = overhead valve; **I** = in-line engine; **V** = V engine; **flat** = horizontally opposed engine; **D** = diesel; **T** = turbocharged; **bbl.** = barrel (carburetor); **FI** = fuel injection.

RECALL HISTORY

1980: possibility on diesel cars that wire in EGR harness could be pinched, causing electrical short that could result in fire. **1981:** left front control arm nuts could loosen and come off, reducing or losing steering control. **1982:** injection pump governor on diesel V-8 may fail and throttle valve could stick, preventing engine from returning to idle speed or being shut off.

Buick Riviera 1986-88

Trimmed down in a total restyle, Riviera kept its familiar front-drive and independent rear suspension, but lost 19 inches in length and 6 inches of wheelbase. Plenty of publicity went to the new Graphic Control Center (GCC), which uses a touch-sensitive video screen to control climate and stereo, as well as show engine gauges, diagnostic data and a trip computer. All you do is touch specified points on the screen and displays appear. We've had trouble retrieving the GCC display we wanted, touching the wrong

1986 Buick Riviera T Type 2-door

spot on the screen; but it does eliminate a lot of switches and buttons. The second-year GCC added small pushbuttons, in response to complaints. Options for '88 even include an electronic compass and cellular telephone directory. Still, it's a complex high-tech gadget that makes you take your eyes off the road, and costs a bundle to repair. The transverse-mounted 3.8-liter V-6 with sequential fuel injection is peppy. Riviera is agile too, with good high-speed stability. Unfortunately, the soft base suspension allows ample body lean in corners and the power steering lacks feel. Handling of the sporty T Type is a lot more impressive, but it rides roughly. Plush interior seats four. Trunk space is tight. The V-6 gained 10 horsepower, roller valve lifters and hydraulic mounts for 1987. A new version for 1988 added 15 more horsepower, while anti-lock braking became optional. A special hood ornament and instrument panel trim plate note the fact that 1988 is the Riv's 25th anniversary. Though far superior to earlier Rivieras in acceleration, handling and stability, the current version doesn't offer quite as much as we'd expect for its lofty price tag. Lagging early sales suggested a lack of appeal to both traditional Riv buyers and the new, younger target market; but they improved a bit during 1987. All told, other premium luxury coupes such as the Lincoln Mark VII LSC offer more value.

Price Range	GOOD	AVERAGE	POOR
1986 Riviera	$14,000–15,000	$13,000–14,000	$12,000–13,000
1987 Riviera	16,500–18,000	15,000–17,000	14,000–15,000
1988 Riviera	19,000–22,000	18,000–20,000	—

Dimensions	WHEEL-BASE, IN.	LGTH., IN.	HT., IN.	WIDTH, IN.	AVG. WT., LBS.	CARGO VOL., CU. FT.	FUEL TANK, GAL.
2d cpe	108.0	187.2	53.5	71.7	3307	13.9	18.0

Engines	L/CID	BHP	MPG	AVAIL.
ohv V-6 FI	3.8/231	140–165	18–22	86–88

KEY: L/CID = liters/cubic inch displacement; BHP = brake horsepower; MPG = estimated average miles per gallon; ohc = overhead cam; dohc = double overhead cam; ohv = overhead valve; I = in-line engine; V = V engine; flat = horizontally opposed engine; D = diesel; T = turbocharged; bbl. = barrel (carburetor); FI = fuel injection.

RECALL HISTORY

None to date.

Buick Skyhawk and Oldsmobile Starfire 1978-80

1978 Buick Skyhawk 3-door

Racy hatchback variant of Chevrolet's Monza coupe, descended from the ill-fated Vega, offered more style than substance. Front cabin is a tight squeeze, the rear barely fit for adults. Good handling is offset by choppy ride, due to short wheelbase and limited wheel travel. Fold-down back seats add cargo space, but sloping roof cuts it down. Skyhawks came only with a Buick 231-cid V-6. Starfires could also have a 151-cid "Iron Duke" four, or a Chevrolet 305-cid V-8 in the sport Firenza model. Best mileage comes from the "Duke." The V-6 had a worse-than-average repair record, including early timing chain failures. It's fairly obvious that stuffing a V-8 into a chassis designed for lightweight 4-cylinder engines might prove troublesome. And the Firenza had major troubles: the heavy engine makes the whole drivetrain sag, producing serious vibrations at highway speeds. Attractively styled, these cars also suffered clutch, transmission, brake and rust woes. Don't let the shapely form sway your decision.

Price Range	GOOD	AVERAGE	POOR
1978 Skyhawk	$1100–1400	$750–1000	$500–750
1978 Starfire	1000–1300	700–950	500–750

Price Range	GOOD	AVERAGE	POOR
1979 Skyhawk	1200–1500	900–1200	600–900
1979 Starfire	1150–1450	800–1100	550–800
1980 Skyhawk	1400–1800	1100–1500	750–1050
1980 Starfire	1400–1700	1100–1500	750–1050

Dimensions	WHEEL-BASE, IN.	LGTH., IN.	HT., IN.	WIDTH, IN.	AVG. WT., LBS.	CARGO VOL., CU. FT.	FUEL TANK, GAL.
3d cpe	97.0	179.3	50.2	65.4	2850	27.8	18.5

Engines	L/CID	BHP	MPG	AVAIL.
ohv I-4 2 bbl.	2.5/151	85–90	20–23	78–80
ohv V-6 2 bbl.	3.8/231	105–115	17–19	78–80
ohv V-8 2 bbl.	5.0/305	130–145	15–17	78–80

KEY: L/CID = liters/cubic inch displacement; **BHP** = brake horsepower; **MPG** = estimated average miles per gallon; **ohc** = overhead cam; **dohc** = double overhead cam; **ohv** = overhead valve; **I** = in-line engine; **V** = V engine; **flat** = horizontally opposed engine; **D** = diesel; **T** = turbocharged; **bbl.** = barrel (carburetor); **FI** = fuel injection.

RECALL HISTORY

1978: left engine mount could be deformed by bottoming out of suspension, which could damage steering linkage or Pitman arm, interfering with steering. **1978:** steering intermediate shaft coupling may have been machined oversize where it attaches to steering gear shaft, not properly tightening on shaft when clamp and pinch bolt were installed; could result in loss of steering control. **1979:** replacement of fuel feeder hose, which may chafe against EGR valve, causing rupture, fuel leakage, potential fire hazard.

1978 Oldsmobile Starfire GT 3-door

Buick Skyhawk and Oldsmobile Firenza 1982-88

1982 Buick Skyhawk 2-door

Front-drive subcompacts are part of the J-car family that includes Chevy Cavalier, Pontiac J2000 and Cadillac Cimarron. Both makes include a 4-door sedan and station wagon (added for '83). Buick also has a 2-door notchback coupe, Olds a 3-door hatchback. For 1986, each line expanded to include all four body styles, but the hatchback was dropped for '88 as a result of poor sales. The original carbureted 1.8-liter four was stroked to 2.0 liters for 1983 and gained throttle-body fuel injection for better performance and mileage. An overhead cam, fuel-injected 1.8 four, imported from GM of Brazil, became an option in '83; many dealers chose it over the Chevy-built 2.0. The Brazilian 1.8 is a bit stingier with gas, but a weak performer. A turbocharger tweaked the 1.8 in the sporty T Type to 150 horsepower for '84, but few buyers cared. Olds responded the next year by making a Chevy 2.8-liter V-6 standard in its GT hatchback. For 1987, all three 4-cylinder engines and the V-6 were reworked. The optional Pontiac overhead-cam four grew from 1.8 to 2.0 liters, gaining plenty of power in both turbo and normally aspirated versions. A new Getrag-designed 5-speed manual gearbox appeared for '87 on the Skyhawk turbo and Firenza GT. Both lines were trimmed to a single price level for 1988, and the V-6 departed; but Skyhawk added a new S/E coupe with concealed headlamps, blackout exterior and GT suspension. Intended to compete with Honda's Accord, J-cars have lagged in economy, acceleration and value, among other key areas. Assembly quality is above average. But since most models are equipped as little luxury cars, a similar (if less plush) Cavalier or Pontiac 2000 offers nearly as much for a smaller investment.

Price Range	GOOD	AVERAGE	POOR
1982 Skyhawk	$3000–3500	$2500–3000	$2000–2500
1982 Firenza	3000–3600	2500–3100	2000–2600
1983 Skyhawk	3600–4200	3000–3800	2500–3000
1983 Firenza	3700–4300	3000–3900	2500–3000
1984 Skyhawk	4200–4800	3800–4500	3000–3800
1984 Firenza	4300–4900	3900–4600	3000–3800
1985 Skyhawk	5400–6000	4700–5600	4000–4700
1985 Firenza	5500–6200	4800–5700	4100–4800
1986 Skyhawk	6300–7200	5500–6500	4800–5500
1986 Firenza	6400–7400	5600–6600	4900–5600
1987 Skyhawk	7300–8500	6700–7600	5800–6600
1987 Firenza	7500–9000	6900–8000	5900–6800
1988 Skyhawk	8200–9500	7700–8900	—
1988 Firenza	8500–10,000	8000–9200	—

Dimensions	WHEEL-BASE, IN.	LGTH., IN.	HT., IN.	WIDTH, IN.	AVG. WT., LBS.	CARGO VOL., CU. FT.	FUEL TANK, GAL.
2d cpe	101.2	175.3	54.0	65.0	2395	12.6	13.6
3d cpe	101.2	179.3	50.8	65.0	2415	38.5	14.0
4d sdn	101.2	177.3	54.0	65.0	2450	13.5	13.6
5d wgn	101.2	177.1	53.9	65.0	2475	63.4	14.0

Engines	L/CID	BHP	MPG	AVAIL.
ohv I-4 2 bbl.	1.8/112	88	21–25	82
ohv I-4 FI	2.0/121	86–90	22–26	83–88
ohc I-4 FI	1.8/112	84	23–27	83–86
ohc I-4 T FI	1.8/112	150	21–27	84–86
ohc I-4 FI	2.0/121	96	22–26	87–88
ohc I-4 T FI	2.0/121	165	20–25	87
ohv V-6 FI	2.8/173	120–130	19–25	85–87

KEY: L/CID = liters/cubic inch displacement; **BHP** = brake horsepower; **MPG** = estimated average miles per gallon; **ohc** = overhead cam; **dohc** = double overhead cam; **ohv** = overhead valve; **I** = in-line engine; **V** = V engine; **flat** = horizontally opposed engine; **D** = diesel; **T** = turbocharged; **bbl.** = barrel (carburetor); **FI** = fuel injection.

RECALL HISTORY

1982: hose clamps on fuel tank filler pipe could fracture, causing fuel leaks and possibility of fire. **1983:** brake proportioning valve

Buick

could break and separate from master cylinder, causing fluid leak and partial braking loss. **1983-84:** metal floor pan anchor bar of manually adjustable driver's seat could fatigue and break, allowing seat to tip backward without warning. **1984:** 2-door models with optional bucket seats may have seatback locks that don't meet federal safety requirements. **1985:** plastic trim cover on air cleaner of ohv 2.0-liter engine could fall off and land on exhaust manifold, creating fire hazard. **1986 Skyhawk:** taillamp lens does not conform to standard, and could be inadequate in times of reduced visibility. **1986 Firenza wagon:** right rear taillamp assembly might be incorrectly assembled, resulting in reduced illumination. **1987:** some parking brake lever mechanisms may not engage properly when applied; vehicle could roll unexpectedly.

Buick Skylark and Oldsmobile Omega 1978-79

1978 Buick Skylark Custom 2-door

Twin offshoots of the popular old Chevy Nova differ mainly in grilles, taillamps and trim. Both are available in 2-door, 4-door and 3-door hatchback form. Hatchbacks hold more cargo but also deliver more squeaks and rattles. Buick's 231-cid V-6 is easy enough on gas, but suffered a worse-than-average repair record in early years. The 305-cid Chevrolet V-8 is fairly economical and durable. Cracked leaves in rear springs are a common flaw, revealed by a buckboard-like ride and tendency for the rear end to "dog-track" sideways. Not a space-efficient design by today's standards, but pretty good for its time. Many were sold, so quite a few should still be around.

1978 Buick Skylark Custom 2-door

Price Range	GOOD	AVERAGE	POOR
1978 Skylark	$1200–1500	$900–1200	$650–900
1978 Omega	1200–1450	900–1100	650–900
1979 Skylark	1250–1600	1000–1250	800–1000
1979 Omega	1250–1650	1000–1300	750–1000

Dimensions	WHEEL-BASE, IN.	LGTH., IN.	HT., IN.	WIDTH, IN.	AVG. WT., LBS.	CARGO VOL., CU. FT.	FUEL TANK, GAL.
2d/3d sdn	111.0	200.2	53.2	72.7	3425	13.0	21.0
4d sdn	111.0	200.3	54.2	72.7	3500	13.0	21.0

Engines	L/CID	BHP	MPG	AVAIL.
ohv V-6 2 bbl.	3.8/231	105–110	17–19	78–79

KEY: L/CID = liters/cubic inch displacement; **BHP** = brake horsepower; **MPG** = estimated average miles per gallon; **ohc** = overhead cam; **dohc** = double overhead cam; **ohv** = overhead valve; **I** = in-line engine; **V** = V engine; **flat** = horizontally opposed engine; **D** = diesel; **T** = turbocharged; **bbl.** = barrel (carburetor); **FI** = fuel injection.

RECALL HISTORY

1978: rear axle shaft may have flaw in metal that could cause tire and wheel assembly to separate from vehicle. **1978:** fan blade spider (hub portion) may fatigue and break apart, throwing off two-blade segment. **1979:** correction of improperly routed power steering hose, which may rupture and leak power steering fluid, creating potential fire hazard.

Buick Skylark 1980-85

GM's X-car front-drive compacts debuted to rave reviews, but soon lost appeal because of a deplorably long list of safety recalls, plus new-model bugs, mechanical failures and sloppy workmanship. Relatives include the Olds

Buick

1980 Buick Skylark Limited 4-door

Omega, Chevy Citation and Pontiac Phoenix. Both 2- and 4-door Skylarks offer surprisingly generous interior and cargo room. Four adults sit with space to spare. Standard "Iron Duke" 4-cylinder engine gained throttle-body fuel injection for '82, which improved economy and driveability. The more powerful 2.8-liter V-6 has a better durability record and doesn't burn much more gas, but check for oil leaks and cooling ills. Pre-1982 automatic transaxles tend to leak. A serious problem exists with rear brake lockup caused by incorrect brake proportioning valve and overly aggressive rear brake linings. Front brakes may also experience faster-than-normal wear. Engine/transaxle vibrations may appear due to deterioration of upper engine torque strap. A high-output V-6, added for 1981, gained port-type fuel injection as an '85 option. Buick dropped the 2-door in its final season. GM's first stab at smaller front-drive cars was a worthy idea, but carried out poorly. They improved after 1981, but not enough to recommend any models as used cars.

Price Range	GOOD	AVERAGE	POOR
1980 Skylark	$1600–2000	$1200–1600	$900–1200
1981 Skylark	2000–2500	1600–2000	1300–1600
1982 Skylark	2600–3200	2000–2500	1700–2000
1983 Skylark	3200–3800	2700–3200	2200–2700
1984 Skylark	3900–4500	3400–3900	2800–3400
1985 Skylark	4600–5100	4000–4600	3500–4000

Dimensions	WHEEL-BASE, IN.	LGTH., IN.	HT., IN.	WIDTH, IN.	AVG. WT., LBS.	CARGO VOL., CU. FT.	FUEL TANK, GAL.
2d cpe	104.9	181.1	53.0	69.1	2531	14.3	14.6
4d sdn	104.9	181.1	53.0	69.1	2562	14.4	15.1

CONSUMER GUIDE®

Engines	L/CID	BHP	MPG	AVAIL.
ohv I-4 2 bbl.	2.5/151	84–90	21–24	80–81
ohv I-4 FI	2.5/151	90–92	22–25	82–85
ohv V-6 2 bbl.	2.8/173	110–115	20–22	80–85
ohv V-6 2 bbl.	2.8/173	130–135	18–21	81–84
ohv V-6 FI	2.8/173	125	18–21	85

KEY: L/CID = liters/cubic inch displacement; **BHP** = brake horsepower; **MPG** = estimated average miles per gallon; **ohc** = overhead cam; **dohc** = double overhead cam; **ohv** = overhead valve; **I** = in-line engine; **V** = V engine; **flat** = horizontally opposed engine; **D** = diesel; **T** = turbocharged; **bbl.** = barrel (carburetor); **FI** = fuel injection.

RECALL HISTORY

1980: rear brakes tend to lock in moderate to hard braking, which can cause car to spin unexpectedly. **1980:** clutch cable could interfere with brake pipe and eventually cause pipe to break, causing loss of fluid and partial loss of braking capability. **1980:** fuel hoses could contact right drive axle boot, which could wear hole in hose, causing fuel leaks and possibility of engine fire. **1980:** front coil spring may be too large in diameter and could be forced over lower spring seat of strut assembly, which could damage brake hose and suspension. **1980:** automatic transmission cooler line hoses could fail under certain conditions, creating potential for fire. **1980:** possibility steering gear mounting plate could crack at high mileage, which would allow steering gear attachment to come loose; under certain conditions, could result in crash. **1981:** cars with V-6 engine and power steering may have incorrectly routed power steering hose that could deteriorate and leak, possibly causing fire. **1981:** engine ground cable could break and reduce performance of electrical system, dimming headlights and slowing wipers. **1982:** brake hoses might not meet federal standards for strength; loss of fluid could result in partial braking loss. **1982:** hose clamps on fuel tank filler pipe and vent pipe could fracture, causing fuel leaks that could create fire possibility. **1983:** brake proportioning valve could break and separate from master cylinder, causing fluid leak and partial braking loss. **1984:** fuel system of 2.5-liter four may leak at injection feed pipe connection, resulting in underhood fire that could spread to passenger compartment. **1984:** rear control arm attaching bolts may fracture; if all four fail on one side, could result in control arm dropping enough to cut rear brake hose. **1984:** on 2-door models with optional bucket seats, defective inertia locks may allow seat to fold forward in event of crash. **1985:** on cars with 2.8-liter fuel-injected V-6, throttle linkage retaining clip might interfere with throttle body casting, causing throttle to remain open after driver has removed foot from gas pedal.

Buick Somerset Regal/ Somerset/Skylark 1985-88

1986 Buick Skylark Limited 4-door

All-new Somerset Regal luxury coupe, introduced for 1985 partly to take the place of GM's discredited (and discontinued) X-cars, was aimed at the "yuppie" market. So were its N-body companions, the Olds Calais and Pontiac Grand Am. A 4-door sedan was added for '86 and given the familiar Skylark name; the 2-door coupe dropped the "Regal" and became, simply, Somerset. Base engine is a 2.5-liter four. Performance is a lot more lively from the optional 3.0-liter V-6, but that one comes only with automatic, not the 5-speed manual shift. It drinks a bit more gas as well. The four was reworked extensively for '87, adding contra-rotating balance shafts when hooked to the 5-speed gearbox. These are well-made cars, quiet and easy to handle, that hold four adults in comfort and style. They don't come cheap. Manual shift and the Somerset name were dropped for 1988 and all 2.5-liter fours got twin balance shafts, but the big news is the new optional "Quad 4" (16-valve) double overhead cam engine.

Price Range	GOOD	AVERAGE	POOR
1985 Somerset Regal	$6800–7400	$6300–6800	$5800–6300
1986 Somerset	7800–8700	7300–8100	6800–7400
1986 Skylark	7900–8500	7400–8000	6900–7400
1987 Somerset	9000–10,000	8500–9300	7800–8500
1987 Skylark	9100–9900	8600–9200	7900–8500
1988 Skylark	10,000–11,000	9500–10,500	8500–9500

Dimensions	WHEEL-BASE, IN.	LGTH., IN.	HT., IN.	WIDTH, IN.	AVG. WT., LBS.	CARGO VOL., CU. FT.	FUEL TANK, GAL.
2d cpe	103.4	180.0	52.1	67.7	2530	13.5	13.6
4d sdn	103.4	180.1	52.1	66.6	2568	13.4	13.6

Engines	L/CID	BHP	MPG	AVAIL.
ohv I-4 FI	2.5/151	92–98	22–25	85–88
ohv V-6 FI	3.0/181	125–135	18–22	85–88

KEY: L/CID = liters/cubic inch displacement; **BHP** = brake horsepower; **MPG** = estimated average miles per gallon; **ohc** = overhead cam; **dohc** = double overhead cam; **ohv** = overhead valve; **I** = in-line engine; **V** = V engine; **flat** = horizontally opposed engine; **D** = diesel; **T** = turbocharged; **bbl.** = barrel (carburetor); **FI** = fuel injection.

RECALL HISTORY

1985: throttle return spring on 2.5-liter engine could fail, preventing throttle from returning to closed (idle) position when accelerator pedal is released. **1985-86:** small cracks may develop in body pillar around door striker bolt hole, which could make door hard to close and allow it to open during collision; install reinforcement plates.

Cadillac Cimarron 1982-88

Highest-priced addition to front-drive subcompact J-car lineup differs from Chevy Cavalier and Pontiac J2000 only in styling details and longer list of standard equipment. (Check the Cavalier entry for basic facts.) Sold only as a 4-door sedan, Cimarron was GM's response to BMW and

1985 Cadillac Cimarron D'Oro 4-door

Cadillac

comparable small European sport sedans. Priced in that league, but not nearly so agile or peppy, it's been a weak seller and an embarrassment to Cadillac. Biggest shortcoming, beyond the copycat styling, was the anemic 4-cylinder engine, which was enlarged and given throttle-body fuel injection for 1983. Real improvement arrived only with the Chevrolet-made 2.8-liter V-6 that became optional on '85½ models. A Generation II version of the V-6 became standard for '87, along with a Getrag-designed 5-speed manual gearbox. Next year, the V-6 added a speed-density fuel control system to improve idling and tires grew to 14-inch size. In any form, though, Cimarron amounts to little more than a costly Cavalier.

Price Range	GOOD	AVERAGE	POOR
1982 Cimarron	$3700–4000	$3300–3700	$2600–3300
1983 Cimarron	4800–5500	4500–4900	3800–4400
1984 Cimarron	6500–7000	5800–6500	5200–6000
1985 Cimarron	7500–8500	7000–7800	6400–7000
1986 Cimarron	9500–10,500	8500–9500	7800–8800
1987 Cimarron	13,000–14,000	11,500–13,000	10,500–11,500
1988 Cimarron	15,000–16,000	14,000–15,000	—

Dimensions	WHEEL-BASE, IN.	LGTH., IN.	HT., IN.	WIDTH, IN.	AVG. WT., LBS.	CARGO VOL., CU. FT.	FUEL TANK, GAL.
4d sdn	101.2	173.1	52.0	65.0	2583	12.0	13.6

Engines	L/CID	BHP	MPG	AVAIL.
ohv I-4 2 bbl.	1.8/112	88	20–23	82
ohv I-4 FI	2.0/121	85–88	21–24	83–86
ohv V-6 FI	2.8/173	120–135	18–23	85–88

KEY: L/CID = liters/cubic inch displacement; **BHP** = brake horsepower; **MPG** = estimated average miles per gallon; **ohc** = overhead cam; **dohc** = double overhead cam; **ohv** = overhead valve; **I** = in-line engine; **V** = V engine; **flat** = horizontally opposed engine; **D** = diesel; **T** = turbocharged; **bbl.** = barrel (carburetor); **FI** = fuel injection.

RECALL HISTORY

1982: hose clamps on fuel tank filler pipe and vent pipe could fracture, causing fuel leaks with fire potential. **1983-84:** metal floor pan anchor bar of manually adjustable driver's seat could fatigue and break, allowing seat to tip backward without warning. **1985:** plastic trim cover on air cleaner of RPD LQS 2.0-liter engine could fall off and land on exhaust manifold, creating fire hazard. **1986:** contacts on push-pull headlight switch may be intermittent, causing headlamps to flicker or go out suddenly.

Cadillac DeVille/ Fleetwood/Brougham 1978-88

1979 Cadillac Coupe de Ville

Rear-drive C-body Cadillacs are nearly as roomy as their gigantic forerunners, still carrying on the American tradition of big luxury cars. Repair record started out good, slipped to average for 1979-80, then much worse the next year. Olds-built diesel V-8 of 1979-81 promised top mileage but delivered trouble, including crankshaft and head gasket failures, cracked heads, oil leaks and injection pump problems. Stay away from the diesel, and from the 368-cid variable-displacement V-8-6-4 gasoline engine offered only for '81. That complex powerplant drew many complaints about erratic operation and sudden stalling, which led to several class-action lawsuits. Big array of standard electrical accessories is tempting, but troublesome. Other trouble spots: the 4.1-liter HT4100 fuel-injected V-8 with an aluminum cylinder block has suffered coolant and oil leaks, the Digital Electronic Fuel Injection (DEFI) system can be difficult and costly to repair, and some diesels were equipped with undersized Turbo Hydra-matic 200C transmissions, which have a record of early failure. Only the super plush, near-classic Fleetwood Brougham survived into 1985, when smaller front-drive Fleetwoods arrived.

Cadillac

The Brougham coupe was dropped in mid-1985, so all late models are sedans. An Oldsmobile 5.0-liter V-8 replaced the Caddy 4.1 in 1986, adding some needed pulling power; it received a new electronic spark control system for '88. All told, we'd choose a Buick Electra or Olds 98 with reliable gas engine. But big Caddies have diehard fans, and are expected to hang on for a few more years.

Price Range	GOOD	AVERAGE	POOR
1978 DeVille	$2400–2800	$2000–2400	$1500–2000
1978 Fleetwood	2600–3000	2200–2600	1500–2100
1979 DeVille	3300–3800	2800–3300	2300–2800
1979 Fleetwood	3800–4200	3400–3800	2700–3300
1980 DeVille	4000–4500	3500–4000	3000–3500
1980 Fleetwood	4900–5300	4300–4900	3700–4300
1981 DeVille	4700–5100	4300–4800	3800–4300
1981 Fleetwood	5500–6100	5000–5700	4400–5000
1982 DeVille	6200–6700	5500–6200	4800–5500
1982 Fleetwood	7200–8000	6500–7200	5700–6500
1983 DeVille	7800–8500	7200–8000	6500–7200
1983 Fleetwood	9200–10,000	8500–9500	7500–8500
1984 DeVille	9300–10,000	8500–9500	7800–8500
1984 Fleetwood	11,500–12,500	10,500–11,500	9500–10,500
1985 Brougham	14,000–15,500	12,800–14,000	12,000–12,800
1986 Brougham	17,500–18,500	16,000–17,500	15,000–16,000
1987 Brougham	20,000–21,000	19,000–20,000	18,000–19,000
1988 Brougham	22,000–23,000	21,000–22,000	—

Dimensions	WHEEL-BASE, IN.	LGTH., IN.	HT., IN.	WIDTH, IN.	AVG. WT., LBS.	CARGO VOL., CU. FT.	FUEL TANK, GAL.
2d cpe	121.5	221.0	54.6	75.4	4200	19.6	24.5
4d sdn	121.5	221.0	56.7	75.3	4250	19.6	24.5

1985 Cadillac Fleetwood Brougham 4-door

Cadillac

Engines	L/CID	BHP	MPG	AVAIL.
ohv V-6 4 bbl.	4.1/252	125	13–17	81–82
ohv V-8 FI	4.1/249	125–135	13–17	82–86
ohv V-8 4 bbl.	5.0/307	140	15–19	86–88
ohv V-8D FI	5.7/350	105–125	21–23	79–85
ohv V-8 4 bbl.	6.0/368	150	12–15	80–81
ohv V-8 FI	6.0/368	140	12–15	81
ohv V-8 4 bbl.	7.0/425	180	13–14	78–79
ohv V-8 FI	7.0/425	195	12–14	78–79

KEY: L/CID = liters/cubic inch displacement; BHP = brake horsepower; MPG = estimated average miles per gallon; ohc = overhead cam; dohc = double overhead cam; ohv = overhead valve; I = in-line engine; V = V engine; flat = horizontally opposed engine; D = diesel; T = turbocharged; bbl. = barrel (carburetor); FI = fuel injection.

RECALL HISTORY

1978: installation of new floor mat to prevent gas pedal from catching. **1979:** outboard front seatbelt anchor bolts could break off during normal use. **1982:** injection pump governor on diesel V-8 may fail and throttle valve could stick, preventing engine from returning to idle or being shut off. **1986:** on cars with 5.0-liter V-8, a wiring harness under the instrument panel may not be properly secured in its retainer, and could interfere with accelerator lever, preventing throttle from returning to closed (idle) position when pedal is released.

Cadillac DeVille/ Fleetwood 1985-88

Two famous Cadillac badges appeared on dramatically trimmed-down, front-drive models for 1985. Two feet shorter and 600 pounds lighter than their predecessors, both DeVille and Fleetwood carry a transverse-mounted V-8 engine. Buick Electra and Olds Ninety-Eight, the other two GM C-bodies, shrunk at the same time. Both performance and mileage are better than before. Handling is more responsive and the well-controlled ride isn't so marshmallow-soft. Despite Cadillac's claim of six-passenger capacity, these are roomy four-seaters. Both 2-door coupe and 4-door Sedan DeVille versions are available. Fleetwood for '86 was actually an option package, not a separate model. The 4.1-liter V-8, with a history of coolant and oil leaks, gained a few horsepower for 1986 as the 4.3-liter diesel (a no-cost '85 option) disappeared and anti-

Cadillac

1985 Cadillac Fleetwood 4-door

lock braking became optional. The renowned Sixty Special name returned for '87 on a stretched (115.8-inch wheelbase) version of the Fleetwood d'Elegance sedan, with standard anti-lock brakes. A 25-horsepower boost arrived for 1988 from the enlarged 4.5-liter V-8, which delivers snappy low-speed acceleration. Though less spacious than before, inside and in the trunk, DeVille and Fleetwood are Cadillac's best-sellers, offering familiar luxury but with more capable handling.

Price Range	GOOD	AVERAGE	POOR
1985 DeVille	$12,000–13,000	$11,400–12,200	$10,000–11,400
1985 Fleetwood	13,500–14,500	12,500–13,500	11,500–12,500
1986 DeVille	15,000–16,500	14,000–15,000	13,000–14,000
1987 DeVille	18,000–19,000	17,000–18,000	16,000–17,000
1987 Fleetwood	22,000–24,000	20,000–22,000	19,000–20,000
1988 DeVille	21,000–22,000	20,000–21,000	—
1988 Fleetwood	24,000–26,000	22,000–24,000	—

Dimensions	WHEEL-BASE, IN.	LGTH., IN.	HT., IN.	WIDTH, IN.	AVG. WT., LBS.	CARGO VOL., CU. FT.	FUEL TANK, GAL.
2d cpe	110.8	195.0	55.0	71.7	3324	15.7	18.0
4d sdn	110.8	195.0	55.0	71.7	3396	15.7	18.0
Sixty Special	115.8	201.5	55.0	71.7	NA	15.7	18.0

Engines	L/CID	BHP	MPG	AVAIL.
ohv V-8 FI	4.1/249	125–130	16–20	85–87
ohv V-6D FI	4.3/262	85	21–24	85
ohv V-8 FI	4.5/273	155	16–20	88

KEY: L/CID = liters/cubic inch displacement; **BHP** = brake horsepower; **MPG** = estimated average miles per gallon; **ohc** = overhead cam; **dohc** = double overhead cam; **ohv** = overhead valve; **I** = in-line engine; **V** = V engine; **flat** = horizontally opposed engine; **D** = diesel; **T** = turbocharged; **bbl.** = barrel (carburetor); **FI** = fuel injection.

RECALL HISTORY

1986: contacts on push-pull headlight switch may be intermittent, causing headlamps to flicker or go out suddenly. **1986-87 DeVille:** fluid may seep from anti-lock brake system onto pump motor and certain relays may have been exposed to water contamination; could result in total loss of rear brakes and loss of power assist to front brakes.

Cadillac Eldorado 1979-85

1984 Cadillac Eldorado Biarritz convertible

Downsized Eldorado guzzles less fuel than its elephantine ancestors, but it's still no miser at the gas pump. Olds-built diesel V-8 offers impressive mileage, but dismal reliability/durability record is reason enough to stay away. Beware, too, of the complex variable-displacement V-8-6-4 gas engine sold in 1981. It brought anguish to many owners and dealers when new, and would be no better today (see listing for the Cadillac DeVille for a rundown of diesel and V-8-6-4 engine problems). The 249-cid gasoline V-8 that powered Eldos through 1985 just manages to propel the car's still-hefty weight. Despite lengthy body, rear seat and cargo space aren't so generous. Eldorados cost more than Rivieras and Toronados, which are the same basic car. The ultra-posh Biarritz convertible, added for 1984, commands far more dollars yet. What do you get over a Riv or Toro? Slightly better workmanship and materials—plus the famed Cadillac crest.

Cadillac

Price Range	GOOD	AVERAGE	POOR
1979 Eldorado	$4300–4700	$3900–4400	$3000–3800
1980 Eldorado	5300–5800	4900–5400	4200–4800
1981 Eldorado	6600–7000	6000–6600	5000–5900
1982 Eldorado	8500–9000	7800—8500	6900–7700
1983 Eldorado	10,500–11,000	10,000–10,500	9000–10,000
1984 Eldorado	12,700–13,700	12,000–12,800	10,800–11,900
1984 Convertible	18,000–20,000	17,000–18,500	16,000–17,000
1985 Eldorado	15,000–16,000	14,000–15,000	13,400–14,000
1985 Convertible	22,000–24,000	20,000–22,000	19,000–20,000

Dimensions	WHEEL-BASE, IN.	LGTH., IN.	HT., IN.	WIDTH, IN.	AVG. WT., LBS.	CARGO VOL., CU. FT.	FUEL TANK, GAL.
2d cpe	114.0	204.5	54.3	70.6	3734	15.0	20.3
2d conv.	114.0	204.5	54.3	70.6	3913	NA	20.3

Engines	L/CID	BHP	MPG	AVAIL.
ohv V-6 2 bbl.	4.1/252	125	14–17	81–82
ohv V-8 FI	4.1/249	125	14–17	82–85
ohv V-8D FI	5.7/350	105–125	22–22.5	79–85
ohv V-8 FI	5.7/350	160–170	13–16	79–80
ohv V-8 FI	6.0/368	145	13–16	81

KEY: L/CID = liters/cubic inch displacement; BHP = brake horsepower; MPG = estimated average miles per gallon; ohc = overhead cam; dohc = double overhead cam; ohv = overhead valve; I = in-line engine; V = V engine; flat = horizontally opposed engine; D = diesel; T = turbocharged; bbl. = barrel (carburetor); FI = fuel injection.

RECALL HISTORY

1980: possible that improperly torqued attaching screws on transmission shift control might cause unattended car to slip into gear and roll. **1981:** left front upper control arm nuts could loosen and come off, reducing steering control and eventually causing car to crash. **1982:** injection pump governor on diesel V-8 may fail and throttle valve could stick, preventing engine from returning to idle speed or being shut off. **1984:** optional bucket seats may have seatback locks that fail to meet federal safety requirements.

Cadillac Eldorado/ Seville 1986-88

Twin personal-luxury front-drive Cadillacs suffered a huge sales loss after shrinking by over 16 inches in total redesign. Nearly identical mechanically, the Eldo coupe and Seville sedan carried a transverse-mounted 4.1-liter V-8 and rode the same chassis as the Buick Riviera and Olds

1986 Cadillac Eldorado Biarritz 2-door

Toronado. Performance is brisker than before due to the size and weight loss. Ride control and stability are improved too. But they're now 4-passenger cars, which is part of the reason for their diminished appeal. The other cause: both cars look too much like cheaper GM models, even though each is loaded with luxury features and technical refinements. Real walnut veneer trim is standard on Seville and the top-rung Eldorado Biarritz. Options include a cellular phone. All those extras place this pair at a higher price level than their oversize predecessors. Eldo sold better in second year, but lack of buyer interest sparked another dramatic restyle for '88, including an extended squared-off rear end, sharp-edge front fenders, and "power dome" hood. Seville alterations are mainly up front, but both models also gained the new Cadillac 4.5-liter V-8 engine.

Price Range	GOOD	AVERAGE	POOR
1986 Eldorado	$18,000–19,500	$17,000–18,000	$16,000–17,000
1986 Seville	19,000–20,500	18,000–19,500	17,000–18,000
1987 Eldorado	20,000–21,500	19,000–20,000	18,000–19,000
1987 Seville	21,500–23,500	20,000–21,500	19,000–20,000
1988 Eldorado	22,000–24,000	21,000–22,500	—
1988 Seville	25,000–27,500	24,000–25,500	

Dimensions	WHEEL-BASE, IN.	LGTH., IN.	HT., IN.	WIDTH, IN.	AVG. WT., LBS.	CARGO VOL., CU. FT.	FUEL TANK, GAL.
2d cpe	108.0	188.2	53.7	71.3	3365	14.1	18.0
4d sdn	108.0	188.2	53.7	70.9	3428	14.1	18.0

Engines	L/CID	BHP	MPG	AVAIL.
ohv V-8 FI	4.1/249	130	16–20	86–87
ohv V-8 FI	4.5/273	155	16–20	88

Cadillac

KEY: L/CID = liters/cubic inch displacement; **BHP** = brake horsepower; **MPG** = estimated average miles per gallon; **ohc** = overhead cam; **dohc** = double overhead cam; **ohv** = overhead valve; **I** = in-line engine; **V** = V engine; **flat** = horizontally opposed engine; **D** = diesel; **T** = turbocharged; **bbl.** = barrel (carburetor); **FI** = fuel injection.

RECALL HISTORY

1986: floor mat could become mispositioned and prevent gas pedal from returning to idle position, causing possible loss of control. **1986-87:** poor electrical contacts in Twilight Sentinel control could result in intermittent headlight circuit, causing sudden loss of lights.

Cadillac Seville 1978-79

1978 Cadillac Seville 4-door

First-generation Cadillac compact, introduced in 1975, was basically a major revision of the old Chevy Nova. Despite first-year difficulties, plus brake and electrical faults in each year (no surprise considering the number of standard gadgets), Seville sold well. Beware of the diesel that appeared in 1979, since many owners complained about poor starting and clogged fuel systems, not to mention problems with cracked cylinder heads, crankshaft and head gasket failures, oil leaks and injection pump troubles. We'd take Seville over a Lincoln Versailles. But you have to expect high maintenance costs if you choose one of these early versions.

Price Range	GOOD	AVERAGE	POOR
1978 Seville	$4000–4500	$3300–4000	$2500–3200
1979 Seville	5000–5500	4500–5000	4000–4500

Dimensions	WHEEL-BASE, IN.	LGTH., IN.	HT., IN.	WIDTH, IN.	AVG. WT., LBS.	CARGO VOL., CU. FT.	FUEL TANK, GAL.
4d sdn	114.3	204.0	54.6	71.8	4300	13.8	21.0

Engines	L/CID	BHP	MPG	AVAIL.
ohv V-8D FI	5.7/350	125	20–23	79
ohv V-8 FI	5.7/350	170–180	12–15	78–79

KEY: L/CID = liters/cubic inch displacement; **BHP** = brake horsepower; **MPG** = estimated average miles per gallon; **ohc** = overhead cam; **dohc** = double overhead cam; **ohv** = overhead valve; **I** = in-line engine; **V** = V engine; **flat** = horizontally opposed engine; **D** = diesel; **T** = turbocharged; **bbl.** = barrel (carburetor); **FI** = fuel injection.

RECALL HISTORY

1978: replacement of fuel feeder hose, which could deteriorate, resulting in fuel leakage and potential underhood fire.

Cadillac Seville 1980-85

1983 Cadillac Seville Elegante 4-door

Striking 1980 restyle gave the showpiece of the Cadillac line its distinctive "bustleback" rear end and modern front-drive layout. Running gear and chassis are shared with E-body luxury coupes: Eldorado, Buick Riviera and Olds Toronado. Based on its poor repair record and dismal resale value, we advise against the troublesome Oldsmobile diesel V-8 that was standard for 1980, optional later. Also beware of Cadillac's innovative but flawed variable-displacement 368-cid gas engine, offered only during the '81 model year (see the listing for the Cadillac DeVille for a discussion on these engines). Both the carbureted Buick-made 252-cid V-6 offered in 1981–82 and the newer 249-cid aluminum-block Caddy V-8 have proven far more reliable. Electronically controlled fuel injection seems to cause the most trouble, as do the many electric doodads found on most Sevilles. Though more sensible than the rear-drive behemoths of past years, Seville isn't one of our favorite used luxury sedans.

Price Range	GOOD	AVERAGE	POOR
1980 Seville	$6300–6800	$5800–6300	$5000–5800
1981 Seville	7500–8000	7000–7500	6500–7000
1982 Seville	9500–10,000	9000–9500	8000–8900
1983 Seville	11,500–12,000	10,800–11,500	9800–10,700
1984 Seville	13,700–14,700	12,900–13,700	11,900–12,800
1985 Seville	16,200–17,000	15,500–16,500	14,500–15,500

Dimensions	WHEEL-BASE, IN.	LGTH., IN.	HT., IN.	WIDTH, IN.	AVG. WT., LBS.	CARGO VOL., CU. FT.	FUEL TANK, GAL.
4d sdn	114.0	204.8	54.3	70.9	4000	14.5	20.3

Engines	L/CID	BHP	MPG	AVAIL.
ohv V-6 4 bbl.	4.1/252	125	13–16	81–82
ohv V-8 FI	4.1/249	125	12–16	82–85
ohv V-8 D FI	5.7/350	105	20–23	80–85
ohv V-8 FI	5.7/350	160	12–15	80
ohv V-8 FI	6.0/368	145	12–15	80–81

KEY: L/CID = liters/cubic inch displacement; **BHP** = brake horsepower; **MPG** = estimated average miles per gallon; **ohc** = overhead cam; **dohc** = double overhead cam; **ohv** = overhead valve; **I** = in-line engine; **V** = V engine; **flat** = horizontally opposed engine; **D** = diesel; **T** = turbocharged; **bbl.** = barrel (carburetor); **FI** = fuel injection.

RECALL HISTORY

1980: possible that improperly torqued attaching screws on transmission shift control might cause unattended car to slip into gear and roll. **1981:** left front upper control arm nuts could loosen and come off, reducing steering control and possibly causing crash. **1982:** injection pump governor on diesel V-8 may fail and throttle valve could stick, preventing engine from returning to idle speed or being shut off.

Chevrolet Astro 1985-88

Chevrolet's rear-drive entry into the small van market is taller, tougher and more truck-like than its Dodge/Plymouth rivals, with gross rating up to 5500 pounds. A

1985 Chevrolet Astro

2.5-liter four-cylinder engine and 4-speed manual shift were standard the first year; options included a 4.3-liter V-6, automatic and 5-speed manual transmissions. Passenger vans for 1986–88 are powered by the V-6, which gained fuel injection and 5-speed manual. The four remains standard on cargo vans. Big on cargo space, Astro can also be fitted to tow up to 6000 pounds. The passenger version seats up to eight. Servicing isn't so easy. For anything beyond fluid checks, you have to battle a removable cover. Acceleration is okay with the four, better with V-6, though V-6 economy drops to fair. Rear-wheel drive is great for hauling, but Astro rides and handles more like a van than a car. If you don't need its brawn, a front-drive van from Chrysler might work just as well.

Price Range	GOOD	AVERAGE	POOR
1985 Astro	$8100–8700	$7500–8300	$7000–7500
1986 Astro	9200–10,000	8500–9200	8000–8500
1987 Astro	10,300–11,500	9500–10,300	9000–9500
1988 Astro	11,000–12,500	10,000–11,000	—

Dimensions	WHEEL-BASE, IN.	LGTH., IN.	HT., IN.	WIDTH, IN.	AVG. WT., LBS.	CARGO VOL., CU. FT.	FUEL TANK, GAL.
5d van	111.0	176.8	71.7	77.0	3084	151.1	17.0

Engines	L/CID	BHP	MPG	AVAIL.
ohv I-4 FI	2.5/151	92–96	19–24	85–88

Chevrolet

Engines	L/CID	BHP	MPG	AVAIL.
ohv V-6 4 bbl.	4.3/262	147	14–19	85
ohv V-6 FI	4.3/262	150–155	15–19	86–88

KEY: L/CID = liters/cubic inch displacement; **BHP** = brake horsepower; **MPG** = estimated average miles per gallon; **ohc** = overhead cam; **dohc** = double overhead cam; **ohv** = overhead valve; **I** = in-line engine; **V** = V engine; **flat** = horizontally opposed engine; **D** = diesel; **T** = turbocharged; **bbl.** = barrel (carburetor); **FI** = fuel injection.

RECALL HISTORY

None to date.

Chevrolet Camaro 1978-81

1980 Chevrolet Camaro Z28 2-door

Handsome second-generation ponycar received its second facelift for 1978. Since a V-8 Camaro weighs nearly as much as a Caprice, gas mileage isn't thrilling, but a gently driven six can manage 17-18 mpg. Handling ranks far above average, ride does not. Collectors like the performance-packed Z28's tenacious handling and vigorous movement. Despite long wheelbase, back seat is tight and best occupied by children, or used to supplement the skimpy trunk. Slightly below-average repair record slipped way down by 1980. Most model years suffer squeaks, rattles, premature rust and deteriorating paint. The 305 V-8 engine has a history of premature camshaft failures and valve guide wear.

Price Range	GOOD	AVERAGE	POOR
1978 Camaro	$2100–2600	$1500–2200	$1200–1600
1979 Camaro	2300–3000	1800–2600	1500–1900
1980 Camaro	2700–3600	2100–3100	1700–2200
1981 Camaro	3400–4500	2800–3900	2300–2900

Dimensions	WHEEL-BASE, IN.	LGTH., IN.	HT., IN.	WIDTH, IN.	AVG. WT., LBS.	CARGO VOL., CU. FT.	FUEL TANK, GAL.
2d cpe	108.0	197.6	49.2	74.4	3400	9.2	21.0

Engines	L/CID	BHP	MPG	AVAIL.
ohv V-6 2 bbl.	3.8/229	110–115	18–21	80–81
ohv I-6 1 bbl.	4.1/250	100–115	18–20	78–79
ohv V-8 2 bbl.	4.4/267	115–120	16–18	80–81
ohv V-8 2 bbl.	5.0/305	130–145	15–18	78–79
ohv V-8 4 bbl.	5.0/305	155–165	14–16	80–81
ohv V-8 4 bbl.	5.7/350	155–175	12–15	78–81

KEY: L/CID = liters/cubic inch displacement; **BHP** = brake horsepower; **MPG** = estimated average miles per gallon; **ohc** = overhead cam; **dohc** = double overhead cam; **ohv** = overhead valve; **I** = in-line engine; **V** = V engine; **flat** = horizontally opposed engine; **D** = diesel; **T** = turbocharged; **bbl.** = barrel (carburetor); **FI** = fuel injection.

RECALL HISTORY

1979: brake lights could become inoperative and cruise control could stay activated after brakes are released, because of incorrect lubricant used in assembly. **1980:** lower ball joints may not have been tightened to steering knuckle, which could result in separation. **1981:** possible that rear seatbelt retractors would not restrain smaller passengers in a crash.

Chevrolet Camaro 1982-88

Smaller third-generation sporty coupe gained a bit of room in back, but still not enough for grownups. Lift-up hatch and fold-down rear seatback add cargo space. Base engine through 1986 was Pontiac's 2.5-liter "Iron Duke" four, but most Camaros carry an optional 2.8-liter V-6 or 5.0 V-8. Standard in the plush Berlinetta, the V-6 gained port fuel injection for 1985. Hooked to 5-speed manual shift, it offers the best performance/economy balance. Four 305-cid V-8 versions have been sold: a base 4-barrel; Cross-Fire with twin injectors in 1982-83; high-output carbureted, starting late-1983 (given fuel injection for '88); and tuned port injection from '85 on. For 1987-88 the top-rung IROC-Z could even have a 5.7-liter Corvette V-8 (automatic transmission only), while the 4-cylinder engine left the lineup. The Z28

Chevrolet

1986 Chevrolet Camaro Berlinetta 3-door

was dropped for '88 so the IROC-Z became a model on its own, rather than an option; and the base Camaro added some of the Z28's styling touches and standard equipment. Avoid the Cross-Fire, which delivered more trouble than performance. Other optional V-8s perform as promised, but guzzle plenty of fuel. All-coil suspension improves Camaro's agility. Ride is acceptable, except on stiffly sprung Z28. Snug driving position has tight headroom. Skip first-year models and expect many squeaks and rattles on most Z28s (especially '82s). Neither Camaro nor similar Pontiac Firebird is cheap, but trim styling attracts plenty of interest.

Price Range	GOOD	AVERAGE	POOR
1982 Camaro	$3900–5500	$3300–5000	$2800–3800
1983 Camaro	4500–7000	4000–6500	3500–5000
1984 Camaro	5400–8000	4800–7500	4000–6000
1985 Camaro	6300–9300	5600–8500	4800–6500
1986 Camaro	8000–11,000	7000–10,000	6000–8000
1987 Camaro	9000–12,500	8300–11,500	7000–9000
1988 Camaro	11,000–15,000	9800–13,000	—

Dimensions	WHEEL-BASE, IN.	LGTH., IN.	HT., IN.	WIDTH, IN.	AVG. WT., LBS.	CARGO VOL., CU. FT.	FUEL TANK, GAL.
3d cpe	101.0	187.8	49.8	72.8	3100	30.9	16.0
2d conv	101.0	192.0	50.3	72.8	3351	5.2	15.5

Engines	L/CID	BHP	MPG	AVAIL.
ohv I-4 FI	2.5/151	88–92	19–23	82–86
ohv V-6 2 bbl.	2.8/173	107–112	17–21	82–84
ohv V-6 FI	2.8/173	135	17–21	85–88

Chevrolet

Engines	L/CID	BHP	MPG	AVAIL.
ohv V-8 4 bbl.	5.0/305	150–190	13–16	82–87
ohv V-8 FI	5.0/305	165–175	12–15	82–83
ohv V-8 FI (TPI)	5.0/305	195–200	15–19	85–88
ohv V-8 FI	5.0/305	170	15–19	88
ohv V-8 FI	5.7/350	225–230	14–18	87

KEY: L/CID = liters/cubic inch displacement; **BHP** = brake horsepower; **MPG** = estimated average miles per gallon; **ohc** = overhead cam; **dohc** = double overhead cam; **ohv** = overhead valve; **I** = in-line engine; **V** = V engine; **flat** = horizontally opposed engine; **D** = diesel; **T** = turbocharged; **bbl.** = barrel (carburetor); **FI** = fuel injection.

RECALL HISTORY

1982: thermal vacuum switch in evaporative emission control system of carbureted 5.0-liter V-8 engine may be broken. **1982:** rear seatbelts may not meet federal safety standards. **1982 Z28:** fuel-injected engine may have faulty fuel vent valve that could force fuel out filler neck if cap was removed while tank was more than ¾ full. **1983:** fiberglass hoods on certain models could separate and outer panel could fold back and block driver's view while car is moving. **1983–85:** dislocation of a spring cover will not allow shoulder seatbelt to retract after being extended; extra slack could increase severity of injuries in the event of an accident. **1984:** certain rear brake hoses fail to conform to standard and might separate from fittings, resulting in loss of fluid and partial loss of braking. **1984:** optional bucket seats may have seatback locks that don't meet federal safety requirements. **1986:** contacts on push-pull headlight switch may be intermittent, causing headlamps to flicker or go out suddenly.

Chevrolet Caprice/ Impala 1978-88

Downsized a decade ago and little changed since, the full-size Chevy is one of our favorite big cars. Roomy inside with a spacious trunk, plus good ride and handling, it's a fine choice for the larger family. Economy is okay with a six, but cars of this weight need more power. Best all-purpose engine is the 305-cid V-8, but it squeezes out 20 mpg only in moderate cruising. Beware of the diesel V-8 with its poor reliability and resale value. Major problems include crankshaft and head gasket failures, cracked cylinder heads, oil leaks and injection pump problems. The 305 V-8 has a history of premature camshaft failure, and 1978–

Chevrolet

1986 Chevrolet Caprice Classic 4-door

80 305 and 350 V-8s can experience early valve guide wear due to a faulty EGR valve. Some V-6 and 267-cid V-8s were equipped with undersized Turbo Hydra-matic 200C transmissions, which have a record of early failure. Nonetheless, repair history has been above average most years. The famous Impala name was finally dropped after 1985, replaced by a base Caprice sedan. Impalas carry less equipment, so they're cheaper as used cars. For 1988 the coupe disappeared, while standard equipment expanded to include such items as stereo radio and tinted glass. We rate these tops among lower-priced full-size cars.

Price Range	GOOD	AVERAGE	POOR
1978 Caprice	$1700–2000	$1300–1700	$1000–1300
1978 Impala	1300–1700	900–1300	700–900
1979 Caprice	2100–2400	1800–2100	1300–1800
1979 Impala	1600–1900	1300–1600	900–1300
1980 Caprice	2500–2800	2000–2500	1500–2000
1980 Impala	2100–2400	1600–2100	1200–1600
1981 Caprice	3200–3600	2700–3200	2100–2700
1981 Impala	2400–2700	2000–2400	1600–2000
1982 Caprice	3700–4200	3300–3800	2800–3300
1982 Impala	3100–3400	2700–3100	2200–2700
1983 Caprice	4900–5400	4400–5000	3600–4400
1983 Impala	3900–4400	3600–3900	3000–3600
1984 Caprice	6000–6500	5500–6000	5000–5500
1984 Impala	5000–5300	4500–5000	3900–4500
1985 Caprice	7200–8100	6700–7500	6200–6800
1985 Impala	6200–6600	5800–6200	5200–5800
1986 Caprice	7700–9800	7200–9000	6800–7900
1987 Caprice	9000–11,500	8300–10,500	7700–9500
1988 Caprice	11,500–14,000	10,000–12,500	—

Chevrolet

Dimensions	WHEEL-BASE, IN.	LGTH., IN.	HT., IN.	WIDTH, IN.	AVG. WT., LBS.	CARGO VOL., CU. FT.	FUEL TANK, GAL.
2d cpe	116.0	212.1	56.0	75.3	3675	20.3	21.0
4d sdn	116.0	212.1	56.0	75.4	3775	20.3	21.0
5d wgn	116.0	214.7	58.0	79.3	4175	89.1	22.0

Engines	L/CID	BHP	MPG	AVAIL.
ohv V-6 2 bbl.	3.8/229	110–115	17–20	80–84
ohv V-6 2 bbl.	3.8/231	110	16–18	81–84
ohv I-6 1 bbl.	4.1/250	110–115	17–19	78–79
ohv V-6 FI	4.3/262	130–140	17–20	85–88
ohv V-8 2 bbl.	4.4/267	115–120	16–18	80–82
ohv V-8 4 bbl.	5.0/305	130–145	15–17	78–79
ohv V-8 4 bbl.	5.0/305	150–170	14–16	80–88
ohv V-8 4 bbl.	5.0/307	140	15–18	87–88
ohv V-8 4 bbl.	5.7/350	170	13–15	78–79
ohv V-8 D FI	5.7/350	105	23–27	80–85

KEY: L/CID = liters/cubic inch displacement; **BHP** = brake horsepower; **MPG** = estimated average miles per gallon; **ohc** = overhead cam; **dohc** = double overhead cam; **ohv** = overhead valve; **I** = in-line engine; **V** = V engine; **flat** = horizontally opposed engine; **D** = diesel; **T** = turbocharged; **bbl.** = barrel (carburetor); **FI** = fuel injection.

RECALL HISTORY

1978: front bench seats may fail to conform to federal safety standard; adjuster assembly lock bars may not remain engaged when specified forces are applied to seat, increasing likelihood of injury in case of accident. **1979:** brake lights could become inoperative and cruise control could remain engaged after brakes are released, because of improper assembly. **1979:** outboard seatbelt anchor bolts could break off during normal use, increasing chance of injury. **1980:** inspection and possible repair of front brake pipe,

1987 Chevrolet Caprice Classic 5-door

Chevrolet

which may come in contact with edge of oil pan, causing rupture and resulting in loss of braking ability. **1981:** cars with gas engines could have incorrect brake pedal support bracket, which could reduce braking effectiveness. **1982:** injection pump governor on diesel V-8 could fail, preventing throttle from returning to idle or engine from being shut off. **1982:** thermal vacuum switch in evaporative emission control system may be broken. **1985:** a hose in fuel feed and return pipe assemblies may contact pointed end of radiator shroud attaching screw, which could cause gasoline leak and risk of underhood fire. **1985:** battery cable on cars with 4.3-liter V-6 engine may contact upper control arm or exhaust manifold shield, which could eventually wear through insulation; could result in underhood fire.

Chevrolet Cavalier 1982-88

1982 Chevrolet Cavalier 3-door

Front-drive subcompact J-car, close kin to Pontiac's J2000, was the best-selling car in America in 1984. Acceleration and driveability with the original 1.8-liter four were poor, especially with automatic. An enlarged 2.0-liter version with fuel injection helped '83 models, but mileage and performance still fail to excite. Fairly quiet ordinarily, the engine grows harsh at higher rpm. Capable handling/ roadholding becomes even more athletic with optional sport suspension. New for '86 was a sporty Z24 performance package with optional 2.8-liter V-6, targeting the youth market. A sharp limited-production convertible added in '84 costs far more than its mates. New sheetmetal was added in a major 1988 restyle aimed at the aero Beretta/ Corsica look, and the 3-door hatchback was dropped. Trouble spots: 1984 models with fuel injection may be hard to start in cold weather if proper startup procedure isn't followed, due to glitch in engine computer programming; deterioration of upper engine torque strap causes engine/ transaxle vibrations; and the manual shift linkage of the 5-speed transaxle is troublesome. Generation II engines for '87 hooked up with a new 5-speed manual transaxle designed by Getrag. One of Detroit's better recent products, Cavalier strikes us as a better value now than when it was new.

Price Range	GOOD	AVERAGE	POOR
1982 Cavalier	$2200–3000	$1800–2600	$1300–1800
1983 Cavalier	3300–3800	2800–3400	2200–2800
1984 Cavalier	4000–4400	3500–4100	3000–3500
1984 Convertible	6800–7400	6300–6800	5900–6300
1985 Cavalier	5000–5500	4500–5000	4000–4500
1985 Convertible	8000–8500	7500–8000	7000–7500
1986 Cavalier	6000–7000	5400–6600	4800–5500
1986 Convertible	9300–10,000	8800–9500	8300–8800
1987 Cavalier	7000–9000	6300–8300	5800–7000
1987 Convertible	12,500–14,000	11,500–13,000	11,000–11,500
1988 Cavalier	8000–10,500	7000–9500	—
1988 Convertible	13,000–14,500	12,500–13,500	—

Dimensions	WHEEL-BASE, IN.	LGTH., IN.	HT., IN.	WIDTH, IN.	AVG. WT., LBS.	CARGO VOL., CU. FT.	FUEL TANK, GAL.
2d cpe/conv.	101.2	170.9	52.0	66.0	2380	13.2	14.0
3d cpe	101.2	173.5	51.9	66.0	2445	38.5	14.0
4d sdn	101.2	172.4	53.9	66.3	2425	13.6	14.0
5d wgn	101.2	173.0	54.4	66.3	2490	64.0	14.0

Engines	L/CID	BHP	MPG	AVAIL.
ohv I-4 2 bbl.	1.8/112	88	21–25	82
ohv I-4 FI	2.0/121	85–90	22–26	83–88
ohv V-6 FI	2.8/173	120–130	19–24	86–88

KEY: L/CID = liters/cubic inch displacement; BHP = brake horsepower; MPG = estimated average miles per gallon; ohc = overhead cam; dohc = double overhead cam; ohv = overhead valve; I = in-line engine; V = V engine; flat = horizontally opposed engine; D = diesel; T = turbocharged; bbl. = barrel (carburetor); FI = fuel injection.

Chevrolet

RECALL HISTORY

1982: hose clamps on fuel tank filler pipe and vent pipe could fracture, causing leaks that could create possibility of fire. **1983:** brake proportioning valve could break and separate from master cylinder, causing fluid leak and partial loss of braking ability. **1983-84:** metal floor pan anchor bar of manually adjustable driver's seat could fatigue and break, allowing seat to tip backward without warning. **1984:** 2-door models with optional bucket seats may have seatback locks that fail to meet federal safety requirements. **1985:** on cars with 2.0-liter engine, without underhood insulation blanket, air cleaner plastic trim cover could detach and fall onto exhaust manifold, possibly causing fire. **1985:** plastic trim cover on air cleaner of 2.0-liter engine could fall off and land on exhaust manifold, creating fire hazard. **1986:** contacts on push-pull headlight switch may be intermittent, causing headlamps to flicker or go out suddenly. **1987:** some parking brake lever mechanisms may not engage properly when applied; vehicle could roll away unexpectedly. **1987:** accelerator cable on 2.0-liter engine may contain water which could freeze while car is parked, causing restriction in cable when throttle is first opened, not returning to idle position; could result in loss of control.

Chevrolet Celebrity 1982-88

Part of GM's mid-size A-car quartet, Celebrity uses the same engines as Pontiac's 6000. Interior space and running gear are the same as compact Citation, but Celebrity is

1982 Chevrolet Celebrity 2-door

Chevrolet

trimmed and equipped better. Power steering/brakes and automatic transmission were standard in 1982–83; automatic optional later. Most used cars have all three. A roomy 5-door wagon debuted for 1984. So did a Eurosport handling/appearance package. Base 2.5-liter four lacks power to haul a full load. A high-output fuel-injected V-6 became optional for '85, but carbureted version is the best choice. Diesel power departed after '85. Generation II engines, reworked for 1987, both have fuel injection and a new Getrag-designed 5-speed manual shift became available with the V-6. Balance shafts were added to the Tech IV engine for '88. Celebrity is more spacious than a bigger Malibu, with front-wheel-drive traction and responsive handling. Mileage is no better, though. Workmanship has been good, so these cars have bettered the dismal recall record of their X-car parents. There have been some driveability problems with the computerized engine control system in 1982 models, and deterioration of the upper engine torque strap causes engine/transaxle vibration. Verdict: a capable, pleasant and modern family car.

Price Range	GOOD	AVERAGE	POOR
1982 Celebrity	$3300–3700	$2800–3300	$2500–2800
1983 Celebrity	3900–4500	3500–3900	3000–3500
1984 Celebrity	5000–5500	4500–5000	3800–4500
1985 Celebrity	6000–6600	5500–6000	4800–5500
1986 Celebrity	7300–8000	6700–7400	5900–6700
1987 Celebrity	8500–9300	7800–8800	7000–7800
1988 Celebrity	10,000–11,500	9500–10,500	—

Dimensions	WHEEL-BASE, IN.	LGTH., IN.	HT., IN.	WIDTH, IN.	AVG. WT., LBS.	CARGO VOL. CU. FT.	FUEL TANK, GAL.
2d cpe	104.9	188.3	53.9	69.3	2663	16.2	15.7
4d sdn	104.9	188.3	53.9	69.3	2702	16.2	15.7
5d wgn	104.9	190.8	54.3	69.3	2856	75.1	15.7

Engines	L/CID	BHP	MPG	AVAIL.
ohv I-4 FI	2.5/151	90–98	20–24	82–88
ohv V-6 2 bbl.	2.8/173	112	18–22	82–86
ohv V-6 FI	2.8/173	125–130	18–23	85–88
ohv V-6D FI	4.3/262	85	24–28	82–85

KEY: L/CID = liters/cubic inch displacement; **BHP** = brake horsepower; **MPG** = estimated average miles per gallon; **ohc** = overhead cam; **dohc** = double overhead cam; **ohv** = overhead valve; **I** = in-line engine; **V** = V engine; **flat** = horizontally opposed engine; **D** = diesel; **T** = turbocharged; **bbl.** = barrel (carburetor); **FI** = fuel injection.

Chevrolet

RECALL HISTORY

1982: hose clamps on fuel tank filler pipe and vent pipe could fracture, causing fuel leaks that could create possibility of fire. **1982:** possible that brake hoses don't meet federal standards for strength; loss of fluid could result in partial loss of braking capability. **1983:** brake proportioning valve could break and separate from master cylinder, causing fluid leak and partial loss of braking ability. **1984:** fuel system of 2.5-liter engine may leak at throttle body injection feed pipe connection, which could result in fire. **1984:** 2-door models with optional bucket seats may have seatback locks that fail to meet federal safety requirements. **1985:** throttle linkage retaining clip on fuel-injected V-6 might interfere with throttle body casting, which could cause throttle to remain open after driver has released accelerator pedal. **1985:** clutch cable on some cars with 4-speed manual transmission is not properly secured and may contact master cylinder brake pipe; over time, could result in wear, fluid leakage and partial loss of braking action. **1986:** contacts on push-pull headlight switch may be intermittent, causing headlamps to flicker or go out suddenly.

Chevrolet Chevette and Pontiac 1000 1978-87

Simple little rear-drive subcompact, based on GM's T-car design from Opel in Germany, has unsophisticated suspension and a buzzy, low-power four-cylinder engine with a bad reputation for oil burning and valve-cover leaks. Pon-

1986 Chevrolet Chevette 5-door

tiac T1000 version arrived in 1981; renamed 1000 two years later. An Isuzu 1.8-liter diesel became optional in late '81, delivering 40-plus mpg economy but feeble acceleration. Steering is quick, handling mediocre, road manners safe if dull. Hatchback adds utility, but cramped interior and jumpy ride discourage long drives. Average repair history, but brake problems in all years and air conditioner was flawed through '78. Front suspension/alignment problems are common due to sagging chassis cross support. Body squeaks and rattles with age, yet seems to hold up well. Parts and service easy to find. Okay around town, but Chevette can't match newer front-drive subcompacts.

Price Range	GOOD	AVERAGE	POOR
1978 Chevette	$700–900	$500–700	$350–500
1979 Chevette	900–1100	700–900	500–700
1980 Chevette	1200–1400	900–1200	700–900
1981 Chevette	1400–1600	1100–1400	900–1100
1981 T1000	1450–1750	1250–1500	1000–1250
1982 Chevette	1900–2200	1500–1900	1200–1500
1982 T1000	2000–2250	1700–2000	1350–1700
1983 Chevette	2300–2600	1900–2300	1600–1900
1983 1000	2400–2700	2100–2400	1700–2100
1984 Chevette	2700–3000	2300–2700	2000–2300
1984 1000	2800–3100	2500–2800	2100–2500
1985 Chevette	3300–3700	3000–3300	2500–3000
1985 1000	3350–3750	3100–3400	2600–3000
1986 Chevette	3800–4200	3500–3800	3100–3500
1986 1000	3900–4300	3600–3900	3200–3600
1987 Chevette	4600–5100	4100–4700	3800–4100
1987 1000	4700–5100	4300–4800	3900–4300

1986 Pontiac 1000 5-door

Chevrolet

Dimensions	WHEEL-BASE, IN.	LGTH., IN.	HT., IN.	WIDTH, IN.	AVG. WT., LBS.	CARGO VOL., CU. FT.	FUEL TANK, GAL.
3d sdn	94.3	161.9	52.8	61.8	2085	27.1	12.5
5d sdn	97.3	164.9	52.8	61.8	2144	28.8	12.5

Engines	L/CID	BHP	MPG	AVAIL.
ohc I-4 1 bbl./2 bbl.	1.6/98	60–74	25–28	78–87
ohc I-4D FI	1.8/111	51	32–48	82–86

KEY: L/CID = liters/cubic inch displacement; **BHP** = brake horsepower; **MPG** = estimated average miles per gallon; **ohc** = overhead cam; **dohc** = double overhead cam; **ohv** = overhead valve; **I** = in-line engine; **V** = V engine; **flat** = horizontally opposed engine; **D** = diesel; **T** = turbocharged; **bbl.** = barrel (carburetor); **FI** = fuel injection.

RECALL HISTORY

1980–81: rear seatbelt retractors may not meet federal safety requirements for restraining smaller passengers. **1980–82:** fuel inlet housing plug may come loose on some gas engines, causing fuel leak and creating possibility of fire. **1981-84:** on cars with both air conditioning and power steering, crankshaft pulley bolts could fail and cause damage. **1984:** optional bucket seats on 2-door models may have seatback locks that fail to meet federal safety requirements. **1986:** contacts on push-pull headlight switch may be intermittent, causing headlamps to flicker or go out suddenly.

Chevrolet Citation 1980-85

Front-drive Chevy X-car topped sales charts after mid-1979 debut, but plunged fast after steady stream of recalls and disastrous repair record on 1980–81 models. GM and the government have battled for years over how many '80 X-cars should be recalled due to rear brakes that tend to lock, caused by incorrect brake proportioning valve and overly aggressive rear brake linings. Front brakes also tend to experience faster than normal wear. Other early weak points include clutch, manual shift linkage, V-6 carburetors and cooling systems, spotty paint and premature surface rust. Pre-1982 automatic transaxles tend to leak, transmission fluid leakage around driveshaft seals is a problem, and deterioration of the upper engine torque strap can cause engine/transaxle vibrations. "Iron Duke" four returns good mileage, but is sluggish with automatic. V-6 performs much better with acceptable economy. High-output V-6, standard on sporty X-11 and optional on others, moves even better. Roomy interior seats four adults easily;

1980 Chevrolet Citation 5-door

luggage space generous. X-car execution improved after 1982, but changes didn't keep them competitive with newer alternatives. Your best bet? Steer clear of the X-cars.

Price Range	GOOD	AVERAGE	POOR
1980 Citation	$1100–1400	$800–1200	$500–800
1981 Citation	1600–2000	1300–1700	1000–1300
1982 Citation	1900–2300	1650–2000	1400–1700
1983 Citation	2600–3100	2200–2800	1800–2200
1984 Citation	3400–3900	2900–3500	2400–2900
1985 Citation	4300–4800	3800–4400	3300–3800

Dimensions	WHEEL-BASE, IN.	LGTH., IN.	HT., IN.	WIDTH, IN.	AVG. WT., LBS.	CARGO VOL. CU. FT.	FUEL TANK, GAL.
2d cpe	104.9	176.7	53.1	68.3	2479	14.3	14.0
3d sdn	104.9	176.7	53.1	68.3	2467	35.1	14.6
5d sdn	104.9	176.7	53.9	68.3	2507	35.7	14.6

Engines	L/CID	BHP	MPG	AVAIL.
ohv I-4 2 bbl.	2.5/151	90	21–24	80–81
ohv I-4 FI	2.5/151	90	22–25	82–85
ohv V-6 2 bbl.	2.8/173	112–115	20–22	80–85
ohv V-6 2 bbl.	2.8/173	135	18–21	81–84
ohv V-6 FI	2.8/173	130	20–22	85

KEY: L/CID = liters/cubic inch displacement; **BHP** = brake horsepower; **MPG** = estimated average miles per gallon; **ohc** = overhead cam; **dohc** = double overhead cam; **ohv** = overhead valve; **I** = in-line engine; **V** = V engine; **flat** = horizontally opposed engine; **D** = diesel; **T** = turbocharged; **bbl.** = barrel (carburetor); **FI** = fuel injection.

RECALL HISTORY

1980: rear brakes tend to lock in moderate to hard braking, which can cause car to spin unexpectedly. **1980:** clutch control cable

Chevrolet

could interfere with brake pipe and eventually cause pipe to break, causing loss of fluid and partial loss of braking capability. **1980:** fuel hose could contact right drive axle boot, which could wear a hole in the hose, causing fuel leaks and possibility of engine fire. **1980:** longitudinal body bars at rear control arm may not have been adequately welded and could damage brake or fuel lines, resulting in separation of control arm. **1980:** front coil spring may be too large in diameter and could be forced over lower seat of strut assembly, which could damage brake hose and suspension. **1980:** automatic transmission cooler line hoses could fail under certain conditions, creating potential for fire. **1980:** steering gear mounting plate could crack at high mileage, which would allow gear attachment to come loose; under certain conditions, could result in crash. **1981:** cars with V-6 engines may have incorrectly routed power steering hose that could deteriorate and leak, possibly causing fire. **1981:** engine ground cable could break and reduce performance of electrical system, dimming headlights and slowing wipers. **1982:** possible that brake hoses don't meet federal standards for strength; loss of fluid could result in partial loss of braking capability. **1982:** hose clamps on fuel tank filler pipe and vent pipe could fracture, causing fuel leaks that may create possibility of fire. **1983:** brake proportioning valve could break and separate from master cylinder, causing fluid leak and partial loss of braking ability. **1984:** fuel system of 2.5-liter engine may leak at injection feed pipe connection, which could result in underhood fire. **1985:** throttle linkage retaining clip of fuel-injected V-6 might interfere with throttle body casting, which could cause throttle to remain open after driver has released accelerator pedal.

Chevrolet Malibu 1978-83

Practical rear-drive family car seats five with good trunk space, fine visibility and capable road manners. Solid and fairly quiet on the move, Chevy's first downsized mid-size model delivers passable mileage with larger V-6, but the 200-cid version lacks power. Some California cars have a Buick-made 231-cid V-6. Think twice about the problem-prone Olds diesel V-6 and V-8, optional in 1982–83. Repair history is decent, but suspension ills are fairly common on V-8 cars, mediocre paint on 1978–80 models. The 305 V-8 has a history of premature camshaft failure and valve-guide wear and some V-6s and 305-cid V-8s were equipped with the undersized Turbo Hydra-matic 200C transmission which has a record of early failure.

1979 Chevrolet Malibu 4-door

Price Range

	GOOD	AVERAGE	POOR
1978 Malibu	$1200–1700	$900–1300	$600–900
1979 Malibu	1600–2100	1200–1700	900–1200
1980 Malibu	1900–2500	1500–2100	1200–1500
1981 Malibu	2300–2900	1800–2500	1500–1900
1982 Malibu	3100–3900	2800–3500	2200–2800
1983 Malibu	4000–4600	3700–4200	3100–3700

Dimensions

	WHEEL-BASE, IN.	LGTH., IN.	HT., IN.	WIDTH, IN.	AVG. WT., LBS.	CARGO VOL., CU. FT.	FUEL TANK, GAL.
2d cpe	108.1	192.7	54.2	72.3	3125	16.1	17.4
4d sdn	108.1	192.7	54.2	72.3	3275	16.1	17.4
5d wgn	108.1	193.4	54.5	71.9	3450	72.4	18.0

Engines

	L/CID	BHP	MPG	AVAIL.
ohv V-6 2 bbl.	3.3/200	95	20–21	78–79
ohv V-6 2 bbl.	3.8/229	110–115	19–21	80–83
ohv V-6 2 bbl.	3.8/231	105–115	19–21	78–83
ohv V-8 2 bbl.	4.4/267	115–125	17–19	79–82
ohv V-8 4 bbl.	5.0/305	145–160	15–17	78–83
ohv V-6 D FI	4.3/262	83	25–28	82–83
ohv V-8 D FI	5.7/350	105	23–27	82–83

KEY: L/CID = liters/cubic inch displacement; **BHP** = brake horsepower; **MPG** = estimated average miles per gallon; **ohc** = overhead cam; **dohc** = double overhead cam; **ohv** = overhead valve; **I** = in-line engine; **V** = V engine; **flat** = horizontally opposed engine; **D** = diesel; **T** = turbocharged; **bbl.** = barrel (carburetor); **FI** = fuel injection.

RECALL HISTORY

1978: fan blade spider (hub portion) may fatigue and break apart, throwing off two-blade segment. **1978:** possible front bench seats have incorrect head restraints that fail to conform to federal safety standard; in event of accident, could result in head injury to rear

Chevrolet

seat passenger. **1978:** faulty wheel bearings could damage front wheel spindles and result, in extreme cases, in loss of control. **1978–80:** some rear axle shafts have end buttons that are thin or wear excessively, which could result in separation of axle shaft and wheel assembly, resulting in loss of control. **1978–80:** enlarged wheel cylinder pilot hole in rear brake backing plate could allow cylinder to rotate, causing loss of fluid that could lead to loss of rear brake action. **1978–81:** replacement of two bolts in lower control arms of rear suspension that could break from corrosion, resulting in loss of vehicle control. **1980–81:** front brake pipe may contact edge of oil pan, causing rupture and resulting in loss of braking ability. **1982:** injection pump governor on diesel V-8 engine could fail, preventing throttle from returning to idle or engine from being shut off. **1982 Classic:** thermal vacuum switch in evaporative emission control system of gas engine may be broken. **1983:** brake master cylinder pipe could develop leak from rubbing on air cleaner resonator bracket, causing loss of rear-wheel braking.

Chevrolet Monte Carlo 1978-88

1979 Chevrolet Monte Carlo 2-door

Downsized rear-drive luxury coupe is built on Malibu sedan chassis, but curvier body contours reduce interior room. Four can sit comfortably, with generous trunk space. Basic design is shared by G-body Pontiac Grand Prix,

Buick Regal and Olds Cutlass Supreme. Road manners and mileage are nothing special. Limited-production Monte Carlo SS, a descendent of 1960s muscle cars powered by high-output V-8, attracts some collector interest. Repair history average for most years, although the 305 V-8 has a history of premature camshaft failure and valve guide wear. Also some V-6s and 305 V-8s were equipped with the undersized Turbo Hydra-matic 200C transmission which has a record of early failure. Plenty of well-kept Montes are around, but Malibu is more practical and a stylish Regal or Cutlass Supreme coupe has a better repair record.

Price Range	GOOD	AVERAGE	POOR
1978 Monte Carlo	$1500–1800	$1200–1500	$900–1200
1979 Monte Carlo	1900–2200	1600–1900	1300–1600
1980 Monte Carlo	2400–2800	2100–2500	1700–2100
1981 Monte Carlo	3000–3500	2600–3200	2200–2600
1982 Monte Carlo	3900–4300	3500–4000	2900–3500
1983 Monte Carlo	5000–6500	4500–5900	3800–4700
1984 Monte Carlo	5900–8000	5500–7500	4600–5800
1985 Monte Carlo	7200–9000	6600–8500	5700–6900
1986 Monte Carlo	8500–11,000	7800–10,000	7000–8500
1987 Monte Carlo	10,000–12,500	9000–11,500	8500–10,000
1988 Monte Carlo	11,500–15,000	10,500–14,000	—

Dimensions	WHEEL-BASE, IN.	LGTH., IN.	HT., IN.	WIDTH, IN.	AVG. WT., LBS.	CARGO VOL., CU. FT.	FUEL TANK, GAL.
2d cpe	108.0	200.4	54.4	71.8	3139	16.2	19.8

Engines	L/CID	BHP	MPG	AVAIL.
ohv V-6 2 bbl.	3.3/200	94	20–21	79
ohv V-6 2 bbl.	3.8/229	115	19–21	80–84
ohv V-6 2 bbl.	3.8/231	105–115	19–21	78–84
ohv V-6T 4 bbl.	3.8/231	170	15–17	80–81
ohv V-6 FI	4.3/262	130–145	17–21	85–88
ohv V-8 2 bbl.	4.4/267	120–125	16–18	79–82
ohv V-8 2 bbl.	5.0/305	145	15–18	78
ohv V-8 4 bbl.	5.0/305	150–165	14–17	79–88
ohv V-8 4 bbl.	5.0/305	180	16–19	83–88
ohv V-6D FI	4.3/262	85	25–28	82–83
ohv V-8D FI	5.7/350	105	23–27	82–84

KEY: L/CID = liters/cubic inch displacement; **BHP** = brake horsepower; **MPG** = estimated average miles per gallon; **ohc** = overhead cam; **dohc** = double overhead cam; **ohv** = overhead valve; **I** = in-line engine; **V** = V engine; **flat** = horizontally opposed engine; **D** = diesel; **T** = turbocharged; **bbl.** = barrel (carburetor); **FI** = fuel injection.

Chevrolet
RECALL HISTORY

1978: front bench seats may have incorrect head restraints that don't conform to federal safety standard; in event of accident, could result in head injury to rear seat passenger. **1978:** fan blade spider (hub portion) may fatigue and break apart, throwing off two-blade segment. **1978:** faulty wheel bearings could damage front wheel spindles and result, in extreme cases, in loss of control. **1978–80:** some rear axle shafts have end buttons that are thin or wear excessively, which could result in separation of axle shaft and wheel, leading to loss of control. **1978–80:** enlarged wheel cylinder pilot hole in rear brake backing plate could allow cylinder to rotate, causing loss of fluid that could lead to loss of rear brake action. **1978–81:** replacement of two bolts in lower control arms of rear suspension that could break from corrosion, resulting in loss of vehicle control. **1979:** brake lights may become inoperative and cruise control could stay engaged after brakes are released. **1979–80:** front brake pipe may come in contact with edge of oil pan, causing rupture and resulting in loss of braking ability. **1982:** injection pump governor on diesel V-8 could fail, preventing throttle from returning to idle or engine from being shut off. **1982:** thermal vacuum switch in evaporative emission control system of gas engine may be broken. **1983:** brake master cylinder pipe could develop a leak from rubbing on air cleaner resonator bracket, causing loss of rear-wheel braking capability. **1984:** models with optional bucket seats may have seatback locks that fail to meet federal safety requirements. **1986:** contacts on push-pull headlight switch may be intermittent, causing headlamps to flicker or go out suddenly.

Chevrolet Monza 1978-80

By 1978, this sporty subcompact descendant of the best-forgotten Vega had switched to a Pontiac "Iron Duke" four-cylinder base engine, but its repair record was no less dismal. Buick-made V-6s weren't much better. Small V-8s are peppy but heavy, causing drivetrain to sag and creating vibration problems. The 305 V-8 has a history of premature camshaft failure and valve guide wear. Changing V-8 spark plugs is extremely difficult because of the tight fit. Ride is mediocre, but handling and roadholding aren't bad. Cargo area is marginal, back seat hardly counts. Body is rust prone; durability and basic design questionable. Obviously, not much to recommend it; you're taking a chance if you buy a Monza.

1978 Chevrolet Monza 2-door

Price Range

	GOOD	AVERAGE	POOR
1978 Monza	$900–1200	$600–900	$350–600
1979 Monza	1000–1300	700–1000	400–700
1980 Monza	1300–1600	1000–1350	700–1000

Dimensions

	WHEEL-BASE, IN.	LGTH., IN.	HT., IN.	WIDTH, IN.	AVG. WT., LBS.	CARGO VOL., CU. FT.	FUEL TANK, GAL.
2d cpe	97.0	179.2	49.8	65.4	2975	6.6	18.5
3d cpe	97.0	179.2	50.2	65.4	2750	27.8	18.5
3d wgn	97.0	178.0	51.8	65.4	2900	46.6	15.0

Engines

	L/CID	BHP	MPG	AVAIL.
ohv I-4 2 bbl.	2.5/151	85–90	20–22	78–80
ohv V-6 2 bbl.	3.2/196	90–105	18–20	78–79
ohv V-6 2 bbl.	3.8/231	110	17–19	80
ohv V-8 2 bbl.	5.0/305	130–145	15–17	78

KEY: L/CID = liters/cubic inch displacement; **BHP** = brake horsepower; **MPG** = estimated average miles per gallon; **ohc** = overhead cam; **dohc** = double overhead cam; **ohv** = overhead valve; **I** = in-line engine; **V** = V engine; **flat** = horizontally opposed engine; **D** = diesel; **T** = turbocharged; **bbl.** = barrel (carburetor); **FI** = fuel injection.

RECALL HISTORY

1978: steering problem may result from defective left front engine mount, which could deform and interfere with steering linkage. **1978:** steering intermediate shaft coupling may have been machined oversize where it attaches to steering gear shaft; may prevent coupling from properly tightening on shaft when clamp and pinch bolt were installed, which could result in loss of steering control. **1979:** fuel feeder hose may chafe against EGR valve causing rupture, fuel leakage and potential fire hazard. **1980:** possible that rear seat retractors would not restrain smaller passengers in crash.

Chevrolet Nova and Pontiac Phoenix 1978-79

1977 Chevrolet Nova Concours 4-door

Restyled upgrade of the old 1968-74 Nova came in 2- and 4-door sedan form, plus a 3-door hatchback. Handling/roadholding beat the prior generation—no surprise since suspension design comes from Camaro/Firebird. Ride is fairly comfortable, but watch for rear wheel misalignment due to shifted rear leaf springs, a common malady. Best engine bets: Chevy's 250-cid inline six and 350-cid V-8 (though it has a history of premature camshaft failure and valve guide wear), or Buick's 231-cid V-6. Fuel economy isn't great, but these heavy compacts ranked among the best of their era.

Price Range	GOOD	AVERAGE	POOR
1978 Nova	$1200–1600	$950–1200	$700–950
1978 Phoenix	1200–1500	900–1200	700–950
1979 Nova	1500–1800	1200–1550	1000–1200
1979 Phoenix	1500–1750	1150–1500	900–1200

Dimensions	WHEEL-BASE, IN.	LGTH., IN.	HT., IN.	WIDTH, IN.	AVG. WT., LBS.	CARGO VOL. CU. FT.	FUEL TANK, GAL.
2d/3d sdn	110.0	196.7	52.6	72.2	3300	13.0	21.0
4d sdn	111.0	196.7	53.6	72.2	3400	13.0	21.0

1979 Pontiac Phoenix 2-door

Engines	L/CID	BHP	MPG	AVAIL.
Nova				
ohv I-6 1 bbl.	4.1/250	105–110	18–20	78–79
ohv V-8 2 bbl.	5.0/305	140–145	15–17	78–79
Phoenix				
ohv I-4 2 bbl.	2.5/151	85–90	18–21	78–79
ohv V-6 2 bbl.	3.8/231	105	18–20	78–79
ohv V-8 2 bbl.	5.0/305	145	15–18	78–79
ohv V-8 4 bbl.	5.7/350	155–165	13–15	78–79

KEY: L/CID = liters/cubic inch displacement; **BHP** = brake horsepower; **MPG** = estimated average miles per gallon; **ohc** = overhead cam; **dohc** = double overhead cam; **ohv** = overhead valve; **I** = in-line engine; **V** = V engine; **flat** = horizontally opposed engine; **D** = diesel; **T** = turbocharged; **bbl.** = barrel (carburetor); **FI** = fuel injection.

RECALL HISTORY

1978: rear axle shaft may have flaw in metal that could cause tire and wheel assembly to separate from vehicle. **1978:** fan blade spider (hub portion) may fatigue and break apart, allowing two-blade segment to be thrown off.

Chevrolet Nova 1985-88

Produced in California as a joint venture between GM and Toyota, the front-drive Nova is nearly identical to the Toyota Corolla. Sales have been below Chevrolet projec-

Chevrolet

1987 Chevrolet Nova 5-door

tions, even with incentives. A 4-door sedan and 5-door hatchback are powered by a 1.6-liter 4-cylinder engine. A new twin-cam, 16-valve 1.6-liter four (from Toyota's FX16) is available on the 1988 4-door, with 4-wheel disc brakes. Acceleration is okay with 5-speed manual shift, but tedious with automatic. Engine and road noise grow annoying. The ride is pleasantly compliant and Nova is agile and easy to maneuver. Add good fuel mileage and the promise of Toyota-style reliability, and this Japanese-American becomes a worthy subcompact choice, reasonably priced for the small family. First models had a problem with idle shake, but Chevrolet says Nova ranks among the top GM cars in customer satisfaction and has the lowest warranty repair rate. Corolla differs little, so you might look for the one that has the most tempting price.

Price Range	GOOD	AVERAGE	POOR
1985 Nova	$5700–6200	$5300–5800	$4800–5200
1986 Nova	6800–7500	6300–6800	5500–6100
1987 Nova	7800–8300	7200–7800	6500–7200
1988 Nova	8500–9200	8000–8500	—

Dimensions	WHEEL-BASE, IN.	LGTH., IN.	HT., IN.	WIDTH, IN.	AVG. WT., LBS.	CARGO VOL., CU. FT.	FUEL TANK, GAL.
4d sdn	95.7	166.3	53.0	64.4	2162	12.7	13.2
5d sdn	95.7	166.3	52.8	64.4	2204	26.0	13.2

Engines	L/CID	BHP	MPG	AVAIL.
ohc I-4 2 bbl.	1.6/97	70–74	26–30	85–88

KEY: L/CID = liters/cubic inch displacement; **BHP** = brake horsepower; **MPG** = estimated average miles per gallon; **ohc** = overhead cam; **dohc** = double overhead

cam; **ohv** = overhead valve; **I** = in-line engine; **V** = V engine; **flat** = horizontally opposed engine; **D** = diesel; **T** = turbocharged; **bbl.** = barrel (carburetor); **FI** = fuel injection.

RECALL HISTORY

None to date.

Chevrolet Spectrum 1985-88

1985 Chevrolet Spectrum 3-door

Front-drive subcompact, built in Japan by Isuzu, was introduced in the east but sold nationwide beginning in 1986. Available in 3-door hatchback or 4-door sedan form, powered by a 1.5-liter overhead cam four. Fuel mileage, even with optional 3-speed automatic, is terrific; but expect to push hard on the gas pedal to keep up with traffic. Performance is barely adequate even with 5-speed manual shift, but a Turbo option version for 1987-88 sedans should move out a lot more swiftly. The carbureted engine is noisy, even nasty sounding when approaching higher speeds. Early versions also stumbled and hesitated during warm-up. Inside, headroom is generous and even the back seat has decent leg room. Seats are comfortably upholstered. Handling is nothing special, due to skinny tires and soft suspension. Though competitively priced, Spectrum

Chevrolet

doesn't quite measure up to a Civic, Corolla or Nova. Isuzu sells a nearly identical car called the I-Mark.

Price Range	GOOD	AVERAGE	POOR
1985 Spectrum	$4700–5100	$4400–4800	$3900–4400
1986 Spectrum	6000–6500	5500–6000	5000–5500
1987 Spectrum	6800–7900	6300–7300	5800–6500
1988 Spectrum	7500–8500	7000–8000	—

Dimensions	WHEEL-BASE, IN.	LGTH., IN.	HT., IN.	WIDTH, IN.	AVG. WT., LBS.	CARGO VOL. CU. FT.	FUEL TANK, GAL.
3d sdn	94.5	156.0	52.0	63.6	1933	29.7	11.1
4d sdn	94.5	159.0	52.0	63.6	1961	11.3	11.1

Engines	L/CID	BHP	MPG	AVAIL.
ohc I-4 2 bbl.	1.5/90	70–75	31–37	85–88
ohc I-4T FI	1.5/90	105–110	28-34	87–88

KEY: L/CID = liters/cubic inch displacement; **BHP** = brake horsepower; **MPG** = estimated average miles per gallon; **ohc** = overhead cam; **dohc** = double overhead cam; **ohv** = overhead valve; **I** = in-line engine; **V** = V engine; **flat** = horizontally opposed engine; **D** = diesel; **T** = turbocharged; **bbl.** = barrel (carburetor); **FI** = fuel injection.

RECALL HISTORY

1985-86: fuel pump diaphragm may perforate, allowing fuel to leak into underhood area, which could create a fire hazard.

Chevrolet Sprint 1985-88

Front-drive mini-compact, built by Suzuki of Japan, debuted as the lightest production car sold in the U.S. at 1500 pounds. It also offered the highest gas mileage estimates. Smooth 3-cylinder engine is surprisingly peppy, boosted by quick and nimble handling. Though fine for the city, the light weight is a problem on the road. Sprint grows noisy at higher speeds, bounces over bumps, and suffers in crosswinds. In a collision, too, Sprint might be victimized by a heavier car. Bumpers until '87 were rated for only 2.5-mph crashes, so even a minor fender-bender could be costly. Early models came only in 3-door hatchback form with 5-speed manual shift, but a longer 5-door and automatic joined the line by 1986. The economy Sprint ER earned top 1986 EPA ratings of 55 mpg city, 60 mpg

1986 Chevrolet Sprint Plus 5-door

highway, and won the mileage race again in 1987. The new Metro, which replaces the ER for 1988, should prove equally miserly. At the other end of the scale, an aerodynamic-bodied 1987-88 Turbo model promises sparkling performance in a tiny package—still with impressive economy. Verdict: hard to beat for low-cost transportation, but not the best choice for extensive highway driving.

Price Range	GOOD	AVERAGE	POOR
1985 Sprint	$3900–4200	$3500–3900	$3000–3500
1986 Sprint	4500–4800	4000–4500	3500–4000
1987 Sprint	5400–6500	4900–6000	4200–5000
1988 Sprint	6200–7500	5500–7000	—

Dimensions	WHEEL-BASE, IN.	LGTH., IN.	HT., IN.	WIDTH, IN.	AVG. WT., LBS.	CARGO VOL. CU. FT.	FUEL TANK, GAL.
3d sdn	88.4	141.1	53.1	60.3	1533	18.1	8.0
5d sdn	92.3	145.1	53.1	60.3	1569	20.2	8.0

Engines	L/CID	BHP	MPG	AVAIL.
ohc I-3 2 bbl.	1.0/61	46–48	42–56	85–88
ohc I-3T FI	1.0/61	70	35–40	87–88

KEY: L/CID = liters/cubic inch displacement; **BHP** = brake horsepower; **MPG** = estimated average miles per gallon; **ohc** = overhead cam; **dohc** = double overhead cam; **ohv** = overhead valve; **I** = in-line engine; **V** = V engine; **flat** = horizontally opposed engine; **D** = diesel; **T** = turbocharged; **bbl.** = barrel (carburetor); **FI** = fuel injection.

RECALL HISTORY

None to date.

Chrysler Cordoba 1978-79

1978 Chrysler Cordoba 2-door

Chrysler's first personal-luxury coupe handles nicely with a sporty feel. Performance is average, fuel economy distressing; 14–17 mpg ratings are tough to match even with smallest V-8. A near twin to Dodge Charger/Magnum, it's about as roomy as comparable Ford models, but heavier and less spacious than GM's late '70s mid-size coupes. Durability record is flawed by carburetor and engine problems, mainly in valves and seals. Catalytic converter rustout is also common. All Cordobas have automatic transmission. Already outmoded when new, Cordoba is hardly a top choice today.

Price Range	GOOD	AVERAGE	POOR
1978 Cordoba	$1250–1500	$1000–1250	$650–1000
1979 Cordoba	1500–1800	1200–1500	800–1200

Dimensions	WHEEL-BASE, IN.	LGTH., IN.	HT., IN.	WIDTH, IN.	AVG. WT., LBS.	CARGO VOL., CU. FT.	FUEL TANK, GAL.
2d cpe	114.9	215.8	52.1	77.1	3786	16.3	21.0

Engines	L/CID	BHP	MPG	AVAIL.
ohv V-8 2 bbl.	5.2/318	135	14–17	78–79
ohv V-8 4 bbl.	5.2/318	155	13–16	78–79
ohv V-8 2 bbl.	5.9/360	150	13–16	78–79
ohv V-8 4 bbl.	5.9/360	195	12–15	78–79
ohv V-8 4 bbl.	6.6/400	235	11–14	78–79

KEY: **L/CID** = liters/cubic inch displacement; **BHP** = brake horsepower; **MPG** = estimated average miles per gallon; **ohc** = overhead cam; **dohc** = double overhead cam; **ohv** = overhead valve; **I** = in-line engine; **V** = V engine; **flat** = horizontally opposed engine; **D** = diesel; **T** = turbocharged; **bbl.** = barrel (carburetor); **FI** = fuel injection.

RECALL HISTORY

None to date.

Chrysler Cordoba 1980-83

1980 Chrysler Cordoba Crown 2-door

Mid-size upscale coupe lost length and weight in 1980 revision. Based on the Aspen/Volare chassis, it's about as roomy as before, but hardly spacious in back seat and trunk. Economy improved, but not by much. Thirsty 360-cid V-8 departed after 1980. Optional 318-cid V-8 is a good choice, but it tends to guzzle, too. Standard slant six gives sluggish pickup and, because of its marginal power, can drink even more gas. Cordobas run very quietly, but handling is mushy with strong understeer in tight corners. Standard power steering is too light and lacks feel. Rust and problems with windows, doors and locks occur more often than average on 1980 models, but fit and finish improved in final years. The Carter Thermoquad carburetor on the V-8s can be troublesome and front suspension misalignment and idler arm wear are common on 1982–83 models.

Chrysler

1982 Chrysler Cordoba 2-door

Price Range	GOOD	AVERAGE	POOR
1980 Cordoba	$1800–2100	$1500–1800	$1200–1500
1981 Cordoba	2400–2800	2000–2400	1600–2000
1982 Cordoba	3300–3800	2800–3400	2200–2800
1983 Cordoba	4200–4700	3800–4200	3000–3700

Dimensions	WHEEL-BASE, IN.	LGTH., IN.	HT., IN.	WIDTH, IN.	AVG. WT., LBS.	CARGO VOL. CU. FT.	FUEL TANK, GAL.
2d cpe	112.7	210.1	53.3	72.7	3446	16.7	18.0

Engines	L/CID	BHP	MPG	AVAIL.
ohv I-6 1 bbl.	3.7/225	85–100	16–19	80–83
ohv V-8 2 bbl.	5.2/318	130–135	16–18	80–83
ohv V-8 4 bbl.	5.2/318	155–165	14–17	80–82
ohv V-8 4 bbl.	5.9/360	185	13–16	80

KEY: L/CID = liters/cubic inch displacement; **BHP** = brake horsepower; **MPG** = estimated average miles per gallon; **ohc** = overhead cam; **dohc** = double overhead cam; **ohv** = overhead valve; **I** = in-line engine; **V** = V engine; **flat** = horizontally opposed engine; **D** = diesel; **T** = turbocharged; **bbl.** = barrel (carburetor); **FI** = fuel injection.

RECALL HISTORY

1980: inspection and repair of sticking throttle, which may cause engine to idle too fast; and for exhaust fumes leaking into passenger compartment. **1981:** improper grounding of carburetor solenoid could result in flooding and loss of engine power. **1981:** automatic speed control switch could stick in "resume" position, preventing system from being deactivated with normal brake pedal application.

Chrysler E Class 1983-84

Stretched version of front-drive K-car sits on a three-inch-longer wheelbase. E-body sedans also debuted in 1983 as

1983 Chrysler E Class 4-door

Chrysler New Yorker and Dodge 600. Standard and sturdy 2.2-liter four-cylinder engine delivers only so-so acceleration, but decent mileage even with automatic: about 20 mpg in the city, 25 on the highway. Fuel injection was to become standard on all fours in '84, but many were sold with carburetors. Performance from the turbocharged 2.2, introduced for 1984, is lively, but its exhaust is loud. The 2.6-liter four is quieter than either 2.2, though lacking in driveability and performance. Handling is dull, the chassis soft, with too much body roll and bouncing on the road. Four can sit easily; six can manage. Electronic Voice Alert is standard. Carrying less equipment than a New Yorker, thus priced lower, E Class was revised for '85 and renamed Plymouth Caravelle (see that entry). Well-designed, manageable in size with tolerable road manners, it's a good choice—though non-turbo engines are rather short on power. Chrysler's 5-year/50,000-mile powertrain and rust warranties cannot be assigned to second owners. Loose upper MacPherson strut mounts have been a problem on some E Class cars.

Price Range	GOOD	AVERAGE	POOR
1983 E Class	$4300–4800	$3800–4300	$3200–3800
1984 E Class	5400–6000	4900–5500	4300–4800

Dimensions	WHEEL-BASE, IN.	LGTH., IN.	HT., IN.	WIDTH, IN.	AVG. WT., LBS.	CARGO VOL., CU. FT.	FUEL TANK, GAL.
4d sdn	103.1	185.6	52.9	68.3	2590	17.1	13.1

Chrysler

Engines	L/CID	BHP	MPG	AVAIL.
ohc I-4 2 bbl./FI	2.2/135	94–99	20–25	83–84
ohc I-4T FI	2.2/135	140	18–24	84
ohc I-4 2 bbl.	2.6/156	93–101	19–24	83–84

KEY: L/CID = liters/cubic inch displacement; **BHP** = brake horsepower; **MPG** = estimated average miles per gallon; **ohc** = overhead cam; **dohc** = double overhead cam; **ohv** = overhead valve; **I** = in-line engine; **V** = V engine; **flat** = horizontally opposed engine; **D** = diesel; **T** = turbocharged; **bbl.** = barrel (carburetor); **FI** = fuel injection.

RECALL HISTORY

1983: brake fluid hose could leak from rubbing against exhaust bracket, resulting in partial brake failure. **1983:** electric fuel filler door release could have electrical arcing at filler cap, which could ignite fuel vapors.

(Chrysler) Imperial 1981-83

1981 Imperial 2-door

Neoclassic "bustleback" personal-luxury coupe was supposed to boost Chrysler's image, but prestige-car prospects didn't rush to buy. Rear-drive design evolved from Cordoba coupe. Imperial sold as "one-price" model with no extra-cost options, but customers could choose colors, sound systems and other details. All use a fuel-injected 318-cid V-8 hooked to TorqueFlite automatic. Silent, sedate performance and road manners are as expected in a luxury car,

1982 Imperial "Frank Sinatra Edition" 2-door

but soft suspension turns ragged on rougher roads. Superb front seat offers ample room, but confined in back. Gadget-filled, but built to higher standards than lesser Chrysler products; above average in fit and finish. The electronic fuel injection system could be troublesome, however, and front suspension misalignment and idler arm wear is common in 1982–83 models. Even with antiquated styling, Imperial is a good used-car choice. Not many are around, and those have some collector potential.

Price Range	GOOD		AVERAGE		POOR
1981 Imperial	$4500–5000		$4000–4500		$3500–4000
1982 Imperial	6000–6500		5500–6000		4800–5500
1983 Imperial	7600–8250		7000–7800		6200–7000

Dimensions	WHEEL-BASE, IN.	LGTH., IN.	HT., IN.	WIDTH, IN.	AVG. WT., LBS.	CARGO VOL. CU. FT.	FUEL TANK, GAL.
2d cpe	112.7	213.3	53.2	72.7	3975	16.1	18.0

Engines	L/CID	BHP	MPG	AVAIL.
ohv V-8 FI	5.2/318	140	13–17	81–83

KEY: L/CID = liters/cubic inch displacement; **BHP** = brake horsepower; **MPG** = estimated average miles per gallon; **ohc** = overhead cam; **dohc** = double overhead cam; **ohv** = overhead valve; **I** = in-line engine; **V** = V engine; **flat** = horizontally opposed engine; **D** = diesel; **T** = turbocharged; **bbl.** = barrel (carburetor); **FI** = fuel injection.

RECALL HISTORY

1981: automatic speed control switch could stick in "resume" position, preventing system from being deactivated by normal brake pedal application.

Chrysler Laser 1984-86

1984 Chrysler Laser 3-door

Hatchback sport coupe is another offspring of the front-drive K-car. Dodge Daytona is similar, but less luxurious. Base engine, a fuel-injected 2.2-liter four, delivers pretty good mileage but mild performance (especially with automatic). Potent turbocharged version offers acceleration that rivals V-8 cars, plus equally impressive handling. The turbo's exhaust is loud, though, and its stiff suspension turns a city drive into a jarring adventure. New for 1986 was a 2.5-liter enlargement of the base four, with balancing shafts to cut vibration. All engines perform best with 5-speed manual shift, but clumsy linkage and stiff clutch make automatic a better choice for most drivers. Analog instruments are fine, but top-line XE has a digital display that's not easy to read. Fold-down rear seats create generous cargo area, but are small for people. Long, heavy doors and low front seats make entry/exit a chore. Check out '84s carefully. We weren't so impressed with the assembly quality of some.

Price Range	GOOD	AVERAGE	POOR
1984 Laser	$5600–6400	$4900–5900	$4300–4900
1985 Laser	6700–7700	6000–7000	5400–6100
1986 Laser	7700–9100	7000–8500	6500–7200

1986 Chrysler Laser 3-door

1986 Chrysler Laser XT 3-door

Dimensions	WHEEL-BASE, IN.	LGTH., IN.	HT., IN.	WIDTH, IN.	AVG. WT., LBS.	CARGO VOL., CU. FT.	FUEL TANK, GAL.
3d cpe	97.1	175.0	50.3	69.3	2612	32.8	14.0

Engines	L/CID	BHP	MPG	AVAIL.
ohc I-4 FI	2.2/135	97–99	20–25	84–86
ohc I-4T FI	2.2/135	142—146	19–24	84–86
ohc I-4 FI	2.5/153	100	20–24	86

KEY: L/CID = liters/cubic inch displacement; **BHP** = brake horsepower; **MPG** = estimated average miles per gallon; **ohc** = overhead cam; **dohc** = double overhead cam; **ohv** = overhead valve; **I** = in-line engine; **V** = V engine; **flat** = horizontally opposed engine; **D** = diesel; **T** = turbocharged; **bbl.** = barrel (carburetor); **FI** = fuel injection.

RECALL HISTORY

1984: inadequate structural integrity of hood latch system could cause separation of hood panel from latch mechanism, allowing hood to open while car is in motion. **1985 Turbo:** fuel hose routed to fuel system pressure regulator may have inadequately tightened hose clamp; fuel leakage could result in underhood fire. **1986:** battery cap vents may be partially or completely blocked with plastic flashing; buildup of internal gas pressure, especially during charging, could result in case rupture, and release of gases and/or acid that could cause injury.

Chrysler LeBaron 1980-81

1981 Chrysler LeBaron Medallion 4-door

Reshaped sheetmetal gave luxury mid-size spinoff of the Aspen/Volare a squarer, more formal look for 1981, and 2-door coupe moved to a shorter wheelbase. Basic design and mechanicals remained unchanged. Repair data scanty, but Chrysler probably had fixed quality control problems by this time, including tendency of prior LeBarons to rust prematurely. Standard slant six engine is more economical, but overmatched here. Mileage is worse with optional 318-cid V-8, but midrange pickup is much better. Other minuses: limp ride and handling, awkward driving position, and excessive road noise. Still, buyers moving down from a larger car might want to give old LeBaron a try. Very limited-production Fifth Avenue Edition sedan, sold during 1980, resumed life as a New Yorker two years later. Basic design still survives as the Fifth Avenue, so parts and service aren't a problem.

Price Range	GOOD	AVERAGE	POOR
1980 LeBaron	$1900–2400	$1500–2100	$1200–1500
1981 LeBaron	2600–3200	2100–2800	1700–2100

Dimensions	WHEEL-BASE, IN.	LGTH., IN.	HT., IN.	WIDTH, IN.	AVG. WT., LBS.	CARGO VOL., CU. FT.	FUEL TANK, GAL.
2d cpe	108.7	201.7	53.4	72.4	3285	14.8	18.0
4d sdn	112.7	205.7	55.3	72.4	3390	15.6	18.0
5d wgn	112.7	206.0	55.5	72.4	3580	73.3	18.0

Engines	L/CID	BHP	MPG	AVAIL.
ohv I-6 1 bbl.	3.7/225	85–100	16–19	80–81

Engines	L/CID	BHP	MPG	AVAIL.
ohv V-8 2 bbl.	5.2/318	130–135	16–18	80–81
ohv V-8 4 bbl.	5.2/318	155–165	14–17	80–81

KEY: L/CID = liters/cubic inch displacement; **BHP** = brake horsepower; **MPG** = estimated average miles per gallon; **ohc** = overhead cam; **dohc** = double overhead cam; **ohv** = overhead valve; **I** = in-line engine; **V** = V engine; **flat** = horizontally opposed engine; **D** = diesel; **T** = turbocharged; **bbl.** = barrel (carburetor); **FI** = fuel injection.

RECALL HISTORY

1980: front brake hose could contact tires in extreme turns, resulting in hose failure and loss of front braking. **1981:** loss of grounding at carburetor solenoid could result in flooding and loss of engine power. **1981:** automatic speed control switch could stick in "resume" position, preventing system from being deactivated by normal pedal application.

Chrysler LeBaron 1982-88

Latest LeBaron and similar Dodge 400 were the first of several spinoffs from the compact front-drive K-car, sending Chrysler into the luxury mid-size market. LeBaron differs from less costly Aries/Reliant mainly in plusher interior and front-end look, with Imperial-style vertical grille. A 5-door Town & Country wagon with mock-wood side trim was added for mid-1982. So was a revived convertible, Chrysler's first since 1971. The first K-vertibles were

1982 Chrysler LeBaron 2-door

Chrysler

conversions done by an outside contractor; late '82s and beyond are made by Chrysler and more tightly constructed. Electronic Voice Alert system became standard for '83. Fuel injection began its phase-in on the 2.2-liter four the next year, as a turbocharged version became optional. For 1986, a 2.5-liter four with balancing shafts replaced the Mitsubishi 2.6, which had been standard in convertibles, optional in others. Heavier ragtops suffer in performance and economy and have less back seat space, plus a looser ride on bumpy roads. A turbo delivers plenty of punch, and mileage isn't bad if driven lightly. LeBaron gives no more function than a cheaper K-car, but a lot more flash for a higher price. Town & Country is the most costly of the three convertible models. Coupe and convertible changed radically for 1987, built on a stretched Daytona platform with long hood, hidden headlamps, short deck and Coke-bottle side shape. But sedan and wagon carry on former design. Loose upper MacPherson strut mounts were a problem on some units up to the 1984 model year.

Price Range	GOOD	AVERAGE	POOR
1982 LeBaron	$3400–4200	$3000–3800	$2500–3000
1982 Convertible	5000–5500	4500–5000	4000–4500
1983 LeBaron	4300–5200	3900–4700	3300–3900
1983 Convertible	5800–6700	5400–6200	4800–5600
1984 LeBaron	5100–6000	4600–5400	4000–4600
1984 Convertible	6900–8000	6500–7500	5600–6600
1985 LeBaron	6300–7700	5900–7200	5200–6000
1985 Convertible	8200–9500	7800–9000	7000–8000
1986 LeBaron	7700–9500	7200–9000	6500–7500
1986 Convertible	9750–11,500	9200–10,750	8700–9500
1987 LeBaron sdn/wgn	9000–10,500	8400–10,000	7800–9000
1987 Coupe	10,500–11,500	9800–10,500	9000–9900
1987 Convertible	12,000–14,500	11,000–12,500	10,500—11,500
1988 LeBaron sdn/wgn	11,000–12,500	10,000–11,500	—
1988 Coupe	11,500–13,000	11,000–12,000	—
1988 Convertible	14,000–18,000	13,000–14,000	—

Dimensions	WHEEL-BASE, IN.	LGTH., IN.	HT., IN.	WIDTH, IN.	AVG. WT., LBS.	CARGO VOL., CU. FT.	FUEL TANK, GAL.
2d cpe	100.1	181.2	52.5	68.4	2465	15.0	13.0
2d conv.	100.1	181.2	54.1	68.4	2530	13.1	13.0
4d sdn	100.1	181.2	52.9	68.4	2540	15.0	13.0
5d wgn	100.1	179.8	52.7	68.4	2655	68.6	13.0

1985 Chrysler LeBaron Town & Country 5-door

Dimensions	WHEEL-BASE, IN.	LGTH., IN.	HT., IN.	WIDTH, IN.	AVG. WT., LBS.	CARGO VOL., CU. FT.	FUEL TANK, GAL.
Cpe (87–88)	100.3	184.9	50.9	68.4	2590	14.0	14.0
Conv. (87–88)	100.3	184.9	52.2	68.4	2786	14.0	14.0

Engines	L/CID	BHP	MPG	AVAIL.
ohc I-4 2 bbl./FI	2.2/135	84–99	20–24	82–88
ohc I-4T FI	2.2/135	142–146	18–23	84–88
ohc I-4 FI	2.5/153	96–100	19–24	86–88
ohc I-4 2 bbl.	2.6/156	93–101	18–23	82–85

KEY: L/CID = liters/cubic inch displacement; **BHP** = brake horsepower; **MPG** = estimated average miles per gallon; **ohc** = overhead cam; **dohc** = double overhead cam; **ohv** = overhead valve; **I** = in-line engine; **V** = V engine; **flat** = horizontally opposed engine; **D** = diesel; **T** = turbocharged; **bbl.** = barrel (carburetor); **FI** = fuel injection.

RECALL HISTORY

1983: brake fluid hose could leak from rubbing against exhaust bracket, resulting in partial brake failure. **1984:** engine compartment fuel reservoir may leak fuel at seam and inlet hose connection, which could cause engine compartment fire. **1985:** seatbelts omitted from some models with optional front seat center cushion and folding armrest. **1985 Turbo:** fuel hose routed to pressure regulator may have inadequately tightened hose clamp; fuel leakage could result in underhood fire. **1986:** battery cap vents may be partially or completely blocked with plastic flashing; buildup of internal gas pressure, especially while charging, could result in case rupture and release of gases and/or acid, which might cause injury. **1986:** resistor in electronic instrument panel cluster may be subjected to current overload, which could start an instrument panel fire. **1987 Convertible:** improperly positioned floor may restrict return of gas pedal to idle.

Chrysler LeBaron GTS 1985-88

1985 Chrysler LeBaron GTS Turbo 5-door

Attractive, cleverly designed hatchback sedan on stretched
K-car platform aims to blend function and fun. Dodge
Lancer is its mid-size twin. Performance is tame with base
2.2-liter four and automatic, but suspension is firm and
capable. Optional 1985 suspension packages improve handling even more. A turbocharged 2.2 can rival some V-8s
in go-power. For 1986, a 2.5-liter four became optional,
with balancing shafts to reduce vibration and noise. With
any engine, though, GTS is rather loud for an upscale car.
Mileage and performance are best with 5-speed manual
shift, but Chrysler's balky linkage makes us prefer automatic. Four adults sit easily, with plenty of cargo room
and a fold-down rear seat. Chrysler's quality control and
drivetrain refinement haven't matched the promise of the
GTS design, so we can't give it an unqualified yes as a
used car.

Price Range	GOOD	AVERAGE	POOR
1985 LeBaron GTS	$6800–7600	$6200–7200	$5500–6200
1986 LeBaron GTS	8100–9500	7500–9000	6900–7700
1987 LeBaron GTS	9400–11,000	8800–10,500	8000–9000
1988 LeBaron GTS	10,500–12,000	10,000–11,000	—

Dimensions	WHEEL-BASE, IN.	LGTH., IN.	HT., IN.	WIDTH, IN.	AVG. WT., LBS.	CARGO VOL., CU. FT.	FUEL TANK, GAL.
5d sdn	103.1	180.4	53.0	68.5	2660	40.7	14.0

Engines	L/CID	BHP	MPG	AVAIL.
ohc I-4 FI	2.2/135	96–99	20–24	85–88
ohc I-4T FI	2.2/135	146	18–22	85–88
ohc I-4 FI	2.5/153	100	19–23	86–88

KEY: L/CID = liters/cubic inch displacement; **BHP** = brake horsepower; **MPG** = estimated average miles per gallon; **ohc** = overhead cam; **dohc** = double overhead cam; **ohv** = overhead valve; **I** = in-line engine; **V** = V engine; **flat** = horizontally opposed engine; **D** = diesel; **T** = turbocharged; **bbl.** = barrel (carburetor); **FI** = fuel injection.

RECALL HISTORY

1986: battery cap vents may be partially or completely blocked with plastic flashing; buildup of internal gas pressure, especially while charging, could result in case rupture and release of gases and/or acid, which might cause injury.

Chrysler Newport/ New Yorker 1979-81

Introduced two years after GM's downsized big cars, the full-size R-body Chrysler wasn't a hot seller. Despite a loss of 800 pounds from previous models, it's still a heavy (and roomy) car. The body is smaller, yet bulky, sitting atop a chassis and running gear derived from earlier mid-sizes. Fuel economy reached an estimated 17 mpg with the standard 225-cid six, but don't expect to do that well—or to get much pulling power. The big 360-cid V-8 was dropped after 1980. The intake manifold on 1979–80 models with

1979 Chrysler Newport 4-door

Chrysler

the slant six could crack, causing rough idle problems. Lax workmanship on '79s makes later models a better choice. Visibility is limited in the opera-window New Yorker. We rank these well below Ford/GM rivals for ride, handling and silence. Big-car fans can do better elsewhere. Dodge St. Regis and Plymouth Gran Fury are similar.

Price Range	GOOD	AVERAGE	POOR
1979 Newport	$1600–1800	$1300–1600	$1000–1300
1979 New Yorker	2000–2400	1750–2000	1500–1750
1980 Newport	2000–2300	1750–2000	1400–1750
1980 New Yorker	2600–3100	2300–2800	2000–2300
1981 Newport	2400–2800	2000–2500	1600–2000
1981 New Yorker	4000–4500	3400–4000	2900–3500

Dimensions	WHEEL-BASE, IN.	LGTH., IN.	HT., IN.	WIDTH, IN.	AVG. WT., LBS.	CARGO VOL., CU. FT.	FUEL TANK, GAL.
4d sdn	118.5	220.2	54.5	77.6	3600	21.3	21.0
4d sdn	118.5	221.5	54.5	77.6	3850	21.3	21.0

Engines	L/CID	BHP	MPG	AVAIL.
ohv I-6 2 bbl.	3.7/225	85–110	15–18	79–81
ohv V-8 2 bbl.	5.2/318	130–135	15–17	79–81
ohv V-8 4 bbl.	5.2/318	155–165	14–17	79–81
ohv V-8 2 bbl.	5.9/360	150	13–16	79–80
ohv V-8 4 bbl.	5.9/360	195	12–15	79–80

KEY: L/CID = liters/cubic inch displacement; **BHP** = brake horsepower; **MPG** = estimated average miles per gallon; **ohc** = overhead cam; **dohc** = double overhead cam; **ohv** = overhead valve; **I** = in-line engine; **V** = V engine; **flat** = horizontally opposed engine; **D** = diesel; **T** = turbocharged; **bbl.** = barrel (carburetor); **FI** = fuel injection.

1979 Chrysler New Yorker Fifth Avenue 4-door

RECALL HISTORY

1981: improper grounding of carburetor solenoid could result in carburetor flooding and loss of engine power. **1981:** automatic speed control switch could stick in "resume" position, preventing system from being deactivated by normal brake pedal application.

Chrysler New Yorker/ Fifth Avenue 1982-88

1985 Chrysler Fifth Avenue 4-door

Revised New Yorker took over from the 1980–81 LeBaron as Chrysler's "full-size" rear-drive luxury sedan. Better equipped and higher priced, it's closer to mid-size in length and interior space. Launched in regular or Fifth Avenue trim, the name became New Yorker Fifth Avenue for 1983, to distinguish it from the front-drive New Yorker introduced that year (see separate entry). Next year, its moniker was shortened to Fifth Avenue. Whatever the name, it's been a strong seller, aided by competitive price and a load of standard equipment. Standard 225-cid slant six, too small for a car of this size, was dropped after 1983. Proven 318-cid V-8 with standard TorqueFlite automatic delivers smooth, quiet, easy motion. Drawbacks include limp ride and humdrum handling, dated dash layout, and poor mileage (which warranted a "guzzler tax" for 1986–87).

Chrysler

Chrysler's 5-year/50,000-mile warranty is transferable to used-car buyers for a small fee. Although problems were few, front suspension misalignment and idler arm wear were common in 1982–83 models. These well-equipped cars were bargains when new, grew more popular each year, and rate as good values used. Latest version are built at former AMC plant in Wisconsin, following Chrysler takeover.

Price Range	GOOD	AVERAGE	POOR
1982 New Yorker	$5000–5700	$4500–5000	$4000–4500
1982 N.Y. (Fifth Ave.)	5500–6200	5000–5500	4500–5000
1983 N.Y. Fifth Ave.	6700–7200	6200–6700	5600–6100
1984 Fifth Avenue	8500–9000	8000–8600	7500–8000
1985 Fifth Avenue	10,000–10,500	9400–10,000	8800–9400
1986 Fifth Avenue	11,500–12,000	11,000–11,500	10,500–11,000
1987 Fifth Avenue	13,500–14,500	13,000–14,000	12,250–13,000
1988 Fifth Avenue	16,000–17,000	15,000–16,000	—

Dimensions	WHEEL-BASE, IN.	LGTH., IN.	HT., IN.	WIDTH, IN.	AVG. WT., LBS.	CARGO VOL., CU. FT.	FUEL TANK, GAL.
4d sdn	112.7	206.7	55.3	74.2	3747	15.6	18.0

Engines	L/CID	BHP	MPG	AVAIL.
ohv I-6 1 bbl.	3.7/225	90	16–18	82–83
ohv V-8 2 bbl.	5.2/318	130–140	15–18	82–88
ohv V-8 4 bbl.	5.2/318	165	14–17	82

KEY: L/CID = liters/cubic inch displacement; BHP = brake horsepower; MPG = estimated average miles per gallon; ohc = overhead cam; dohc = double overhead cam; ohv = overhead valve; I = in-line engine; V = V engine; flat = horizontally opposed engine; D = diesel; T = turbocharged; bbl. = barrel (carburetor); FI = fuel injection.

RECALL HISTORY

None to date.

Chrysler New Yorker 1983-87

Plushest of the three stretched front-drive K-cars introduced for 1983, New Yorker is priced higher than the E Class or Dodge 600 as a used car. Most comments for Chrysler E Class apply to the New Yorker. Base 2.2-liter engine was dropped for 1985, making the 2.6 standard. For 1986, a new Chrysler 2.5-liter four with twin balancing

1983 Chrysler New Yorker 4-door

shafts replaced the 2.6 as base powerplant. Usual sedate performance would be a lot healthier with optional turbocharged 2.2, but it's noisy and coarse in a car this posh. Reasonably sized and mannerly on the road, New Yorker isn't a bad choice for mid-size luxury. For 1988 the New Yorker name goes on a brand-new, longer mid-size version of Chrysler's C-body, related to Dodge Dynasty and powered by a Mitsubishi-built 3.0-liter V-6.

Price Range	GOOD	AVERAGE	POOR
1983 New Yorker	$5500–6000	$5000–5600	$4200–4900
1984 New Yorker	6800–7500	6200–6800	5400–6100
1985 New Yorker	8700–9200	8000–8800	7500–8000
1986 New Yorker	10,000–10,750	9500–10,200	8800–9500
1987 New Yorker	11,500–12,500	11,000–12,000	10,500–11,000

Dimensions	WHEEL-BASE, IN.	LGTH., IN.	HT., IN.	WIDTH, IN.	AVG. WT., LBS.	CARGO VOL., CU. FT.	FUEL TANK, GAL.
4d sdn	103.3	185.1	53.4	68.4	2795	17.0	14.0

Engines	L/CID	BHP	MPG	AVAIL.
ohc I-4 2 bbl.	2.2/135	94–99	20–25	83–84
ohc I-4T FI	2.2/135	142–146	18–24	84–87
ohc I-4 FI	2.5/153	100	20–25	86–87
ohc I-4 2 bbl.	2.6/156	101	19–24	· 83–85

KEY: L/CID = liters/cubic inch displacement; **BHP** = brake horsepower; **MPG** = estimated average miles per gallon; **ohc** = overhead cam; **dohc** = double overhead cam; **ohv** = overhead valve; **I** = in-line engine; **V** = V engine; **flat** = horizontally opposed engine; **D** = diesel; **T** = turbocharged; **bbl.** = barrel (carburetor); **FI** = fuel injection.

RECALL HISTORY

1983: brake fluid hose could leak from rubbing against exhaust bracket, resulting in partial brake failure. **1985 Turbo:** fuel hose routed to pressure regulator may have inadequately tightened clamp; fuel leakage could result in underhood fire. **1986:** battery cap vents may be partially or completely blocked with plastic flashing; buildup of internal gas pressure, especially while charging, could result in case rupture and release of gases and/or acid, which might cause injury. **1986:** resistor in electronic instrument panel cluster may be subjected to current overload, which could start an instrument panel fire.

Dodge Aries 1981-88

1981 Dodge Aries 5-door

Front-wheel-drive K-car and its twin, the Plymouth Reliant, sold well enough to help keep Chrysler afloat. Replacing the flawed Aspen/Volare, this well-designed compact soon rivaled Chevrolet Citation and other GM X-cars for the family market. Recall and reliability/durability records are better, though quality control hasn't always been tops (especially in early years). Loose upper MacPherson strut mounts were a problem on some cars up to the 1984 model year. Standard 2.2-liter four has proven very sturdy and easy to service, however. Performance and economy aren't much different with the 2.6-liter Mitsubishi option; but Chrysler's 2.5-liter four, introduced for '86, may be quieter than either one. Fuel injection finally reached the base engine in 1986. Manual shift (on 2.2 engine only) produces best mileage, but clumsy shift linkage makes automatic a better choice. Road/engine noise is excessive,

Dodge

handling humdrum (at best), but K-cars offer good traction and a decent ride. Interior seats 4-5 adults easily, though over-reclined front bench seat isn't pleasing and low-trim models look cheap. Front bucket seats, standard for 1987, improve driver's comfort. Major 1985 facelift gave more rounded corners and new front/rear styling. Aries "America" for 1988 is reduced to a single (LE) price series with limited options to keep price down; and the automatic transmission adds a lockup torque converter. Unfortunately, Chrysler's 5-year/50,000-mile warranty cannot be transferred to new owners. K-car verdict: good choice for reliable, low-cost family motoring.

Price Range	GOOD	AVERAGE	POOR
1981 Aries	$1800–2500	$1400–2100	$1100–1500
1982 Aries	2300–3000	1800–2600	1500–2000
1983 Aries	3100–3800	2700–3400	2300–2800
1984 Aries	4000–4900	3400–4200	2900–3400
1985 Aries	4800–5800	4300–5200	3800–4300
1986 Aries	6000–7100	5500–6400	5000–5600
1987 Aries	7200–8100	6500–7500	6000–6800
1988 Aries	7000–7500	6500–7000	—

Dimensions	WHEEL-BASE, IN.	LGTH., IN.	HT., IN.	WIDTH, IN.	AVG. WT., LBS.	CARGO VOL., CU. FT.	FUEL TANK, GAL.
2d sdn	100.3	176.1	52.5	68.4	2317	15.0	14.0
4d sdn	100.3	176.1	52.5	68.4	2323	15.0	14.0
5d wgn	100.3	176.1	53.1	68.4	2432	67.7	14.0

1986 Dodge Aries 2-door

Dodge

Engines	L/CID	BHP	MPG	AVAIL.
ohc I-4 2 bbl.	2.2/135	88–96	21–28	81–85
ohc I-4 FI	2.2/135	93–97	22–27	86–88
ohc I-4 FI	2.5/153	96–100	21–26	86–88
ohc I-4 2 bbl.	2.6/156	93–101	20–26	81–85

KEY: L/CID = liters/cubic inch displacement; BHP = brake horsepower; MPG = estimated average miles per gallon; ohc = overhead cam; dohc = double overhead cam; ohv = overhead valve; I = in-line engine; V = V engine; flat = horizontally opposed engine; D = diesel; T = turbocharged; bbl. = barrel (carburetor); FI = fuel injection.

RECALL HISTORY

1981: faulty stoplight switch could prevent brake lights from working. **1981:** automatic speed control switch could stick in "resume" position, preventing system from being deactivated by normal brake pedal application. **1982:** bolts used to attach front suspension ball joints to steering knuckles could eventually crack, allowing ball joint to separate from knuckle. **1983:** brake fluid hose could leak from rubbing against exhaust bracket, resulting in partial loss of braking capability. **1984–85:** fuel reservoir for 2.2-liter engine may leak at seam and inlet hose connection, which could cause engine compartment fire. **1986:** battery cap vents may be partially or completely blocked with plastic flashing; buildup of internal gas pressure, especially while charging, could result in case rupture and release of gases and/or acid, which might cause injury.

Dodge Aspen and Plymouth Volare 1978-80

Compact replacements for the old Dart/Valiant slipped way down in reliability, with overall repair records far below average. Quality control is the culprit, producing troubles in suspension, steering, brakes, body, ignition and fuel systems. First (1976) models had many official recalls, but final versions seem less flawed. Roomy and decent riding, with good visibility, Aspen/Volare aren't as fuel- or space-efficient as a Ford Fairmont, but rank with other compacts. Two-doors, on shorter wheelbase, are cramped in back. Stay away from performance models like Aspen R/T and Volare Road Runner, which may have been abused and weakened. Aspen and Volare differ only in grilles and minor trim. Basically well-designed, a nice example can make an acceptable used car, but inspect carefully.

1979 Dodge Aspen Sport Wagon

Price Range

	GOOD	AVERAGE	POOR
1978 Aspen	$1150–1400	$900–1200	$550–900
1978 Volare	1100–1400	850–1150	500–850
1979 Aspen	1400–1700	1100–1500	750–1100
1979 Volare	1400–1600	1050–1400	700–1050
1980 Aspen	1600–2000	1300–1700	1000–1300
1980 Volare	1500–1900	1250–1600	950–1250

Dimensions

	WHEEL-BASE, IN.	LGTH., IN.	HT., IN.	WIDTH, IN.	AVG. WT., LBS.	CARGO VOL., CU. FT.	FUEL TANK, GAL.
2d cpe	108.7	192.7	53.5	72.8	3239	16.6	18.0
4d sdn	112.7	201.2	55.3	72.8	3294	16.6	18.0
5d wgn	112.7	201.2	55.7	72.8	3514	73.1	18.0

Engines

	L/CID	BHP	MPG	AVAIL.
ohv I-6 1 bbl.	3.7/225	100	17–20	78–80
ohv I-6 2 bbl.	3.7/225	110	16–19	78–79
ohv V-8 2 bbl.	5.2/318	135	15–18	78–80
ohv V-8 4 bbl.	5.2/318	155	14–17	78
ohv V-8 2 bbl.	5.9/360	170	14–17	78
ohv V-8 4 bbl.	5.9/360	195	13–16	78–79

KEY: L/CID = liters/cubic inch displacement; **BHP** = brake horsepower; **MPG** = estimated average miles per gallon; **ohc** = overhead cam; **dohc** = double overhead cam; **ohv** = overhead valve; **I** = in-line engine; **V** = V engine; **flat** = horizontally opposed engine; **D** = diesel; **T** = turbocharged; **bbl.** = barrel (carburetor); **FI** = fuel injection.

RECALL HISTORY

1978: possible that front suspension pivot bar support plate may fatigue due to high torque inputs on bushings, under severe service; if failure progresses through pivot bar mounting hole, vehicle directional control may be adversely affected. **1979:** small number of cars, for possibility three fuel line hoses are made of neoprene

Dodge

rubber compound, which may deteriorate with continued exposure to underhood temperature; could result in fuel leakage and underhood fire. **1980:** front brake hose could contact tires during extreme turn, resulting in hose failure and loss of front braking.

Dodge Caravan 1984-88

1984 Dodge Caravan

Caravan and the identical Plymouth Voyager were the first new-breed compact vans made by an American company. Unique front-drive design uses transverse-mounted K-car powertrains. Base passenger vans seat five (up to eight with optional third seat). Center and rear seats remove to create up to 125 cubic feet of cargo space—in a vehicle no longer than a K-car. Not many buyers choose the Mini Ram cargo version. Standard 2.2-liter engine is okay with 5-speed manual, sluggish with automatic, noisy either way. Optional Mitsubishi 2.6-liter four (sold only with automatic) is quieter, smoother and a bit more powerful. Mileage could be better, though. Many owners barely reach 20 mpg with the 2.6 engine (well below EPA estimates). A stretched Grand Caravan, on 119-inch wheelbase, arrived in spring 1987. Its LE edition is powered by a Mitsubishi 3.0-liter V-6 engine, also optional in other '88 vans that otherwise carry the new 2.5-liter four. Caravan's road manners and driving position are more like a car than a van, with front-drive traction and stable ride. Load and towing capacities are limited. Early models had trouble with the sliding door, brakes, interior rattles and driveability (2.6-liter engine). Even so, it's earned high praise from owners and we agree. Many first-year buyers had to wait weeks for delivery, and the vans still sell briskly. We recommend Caravan as tops among modern passenger vans.

Price Range	GOOD	AVERAGE	POOR
1984 Caravan	$7500–8200	$7000–7800	$6200–7000
1985 Caravan	9000–9500	8300–9100	7700–8300
1986 Caravan	10,000–11,000	9400–10,500	8800–9500
1987 Caravan	11,500–12,300	10,500–11,500	10,000–10,750
1988 Caravan	12,000–13,250	11,000–12,000	—

Dimensions	WHEEL-BASE, IN.	LGTH., IN.	HT., IN.	WIDTH, IN.	AVG. WT., LBS.	CARGO VOL., CU. FT.	FUEL TANK, GAL.
4d van	112.0	175.9	64.2	69.6	2911	125.0	15.0
4d van	119.1	190.5	65.0	69.6	3304	150.0	15.0

Engines	L/CID	BHP	MPG	AVAIL.
ohc I-4 2 bbl.	2.2/135	95–101	17–20	84–87
ohc I-4 2 bbl.	2.6/156	104	16–20	84–87
ohc I-4 FI	2.5/153	96–102	18–22	87–88
ohc V-6 FI	3.0/187	136–144	16–20	87–88

KEY: L/CID = liters/cubic inch displacement; BHP = brake horsepower; MPG = estimated average miles per gallon; ohc = overhead cam; dohc = double overhead cam; ohv = overhead valve; I = in-line engine; V = V engine; flat = horizontally opposed engine; D = diesel; T = turbocharged; bbl. = barrel (carburetor); FI = fuel injection.

RECALL HISTORY

1984–85: roadway stone could become lodged in weight-sensing brake proportioning valve, which might change brake feel and increase stopping distance during hard braking; protective cover should be installed. **1984–85:** fuel supply tube between pump and filter on 2.2-liter engine may be subject to vibration fatigue, cracking at fuel pump end, which could cause fuel leakage and create potential for fire. **1986 7-8 passenger van:** first rear seats were installed with incorrect left side riser; in case of accident, seats may become detached, causing serious injuries.

Dodge Challenger and Plymouth Sapporo 1978-83

Sporty rear-drive coupe, made in Japan by Mitsubishi, sold by Chrysler dealers under two names. Mechanically identical, both are well-equipped but cramped inside, with

Dodge

1981 Dodge Challenger 2-door

ungenerous trunks. Good driving position lacks headroom. Early Challenger had jazzy paint and silly side windows but looked cleaner, more like Sapporo, after 1981. Decent ride and agile handling come from all-coil suspension with live rear axle. Early models powered by 98-cid four from Dodge Colt. Bigger 156-cid "balancer" four gives more useful power and torque, though it's a rough runner and burns more fuel. Repair record suggests reliability/durability better than average.

Price Range	GOOD	AVERAGE	POOR
1978 Chall./Sapp.	$1300–1600	$1100–1300	$900–1100
1979 Chall./Sapp.	1600–1900	1300–1600	1000–1250
1980 Chall./Sapp.	1900–2200	1700–2000	1300–1700
1981 Chall./Sapp.	2600–2900	2300–2600	1900–2300
1982 Chall./Sapp.	3300–3700	3000–3400	2600–3000
1983 Chall./Sapp.	4300–4700	4000–4400	3500–4000

1983 Plymouth Sapporo Technica 2-door

Dodge

Dimensions	WHEEL-BASE, IN.	LGTH., IN.	HT., IN.	WIDTH, IN.	AVG. WT., LBS.	CARGO VOL., CU. FT.	FUEL TANK, GAL.
2d cpe	99.6	180.0	52.8	65.9	2750	12.4	15.8

Engines	L/CID	BHP	MPG	AVAIL.
ohc I-4 2 bbl.	1.6/98	77	24–28	78–79
ohc I-4 2 bbl.	2.6/156	93	21–26	78–83

KEY: L/CID = liters/cubic inch displacement; **BHP** = brake horsepower; **MPG** = estimated average miles per gallon; **ohc** = overhead cam; **dohc** = double overhead cam; **ohv** = overhead valve; **I** = in-line engine; **V** = V engine; **flat** = horizontally opposed engine; **D** = diesel; **T** = turbocharged; **bbl.** = barrel (carburetor); **FI** = fuel injection.

RECALL HISTORY

1978: inspection and possible repair of potentially leaking fuel pumps, which could pose fire hazard. **1980:** light bulb socket in ashtray could overheat and ignite, possibly spreading fire to other instrument panel components.

Dodge Charger/Magnum 1978-79

Sleeker Magnum XE joined Charger SE, the last remaining personal-luxury coupe in the Dodge lineup, for 1978. Only Magnum survived into 1979. Most comments for the related 1978-79 Chrysler Cordoba (see that entry) apply to this Dodge pair. That includes their gloomy repair record, cramped back seat, and appetite for fuel.

1978 Dodge Charger SE 2-door

Dodge

1979 Dodge Magnum XE 2-door

Price Range	GOOD	AVERAGE	POOR
1978 Charger SE	$1500–1800	$1200–1500	$850–1200
1978 Magnum XE	1350–1650	1050–1350	800–1050
1979 Magnum XE	1500–1800	1200–1500	1000–1200

Dimensions	WHEEL-BASE, IN.	LGTH., IN.	HT., IN.	WIDTH, IN.	AVG. WT., LBS.	CARGO VOL., CU. FT.	FUEL TANK, GAL.
2d cpe	114.9	215.8	52.1	77.7	3786	16.3	21.0

Engines	L/CID	BHP	MPG	AVAIL.
ohv V-8 2 bbl.	5.2/318	145–150	14–17	78–79
ohv V-8 4 bbl.	5.2/318	155	13–16	78
ohv V-8 2 bbl.	5.9/360	155–245	13–16	78–79
ohv V-8 4 bbl.	5.9/360	250	12–15	78–79
ohv V-8 4 bbl.	6.6/400	190–250	11–14	78

KEY: L/CID = liters/cubic inch displacement; **BHP** = brake horsepower; **MPG** = estimated average miles per gallon; **ohc** = overhead cam; **dohc** = double overhead cam; **ohv** = overhead valve; **I** = in-line engine; **V** = V engine; **flat** = horizontally opposed engine; **D** = diesel; **T** = turbocharged; **bbl.** = barrel (carburetor); **FI** = fuel injection.

RECALL HISTORY

None to date.

Dodge Colt and Plymouth Champ 1979-84

Mitsubishi-built subcompact, the first front-drive car imported by Chrysler, sold under separate Dodge and Plymouth names through 1982. Both 1983–84 versions carried the Colt badge. Compact drivetrain with transverse

1979 Plymouth Champ Custom 3-door

engine makes the most of limited space. Two four-cylinder engines were offered: 1.4 or 1.6 liters. The 1.6 delivers swifter movement without much mileage loss. A turbocharged version powered the sport GTS Turbo in '84. Economy is fine with manual shift. Many carry the unusual Twin-Stick dual-range manual transmission, with eight forward speeds. Back seat tight for adults, but folds down to add cargo space. Longer 5-door hatchback was added to 3-door for 1982. Repair rate good, except for very troublesome air conditioners on 1979–80 models. Also, some 1981–83 models suffered steering wheel shimmy problems due to defective strut bar bushings. Less refined than a Honda Civic, but good values as used cars.

Price Range	GOOD	AVERAGE	POOR
1979 Colt/Champ	$1050–1400	$800–1050	$500–800
1980 Colt/Champ	1300–1700	1100–1500	900–1100
1981 Colt/Champ	1600–1900	1300–1700	1000–1300
1982 Colt/Champ	2000–2500	1650–2200	1400–1700
1983 Colt	2600–3100	2300–2800	1900–2300
1984 Colt	3400–3900	3000–3600	2500–3000

Dimensions	WHEEL-BASE, IN.	LGTH., IN.	HT., IN.	WIDTH, IN.	AVG. WT., LBS.	CARGO VOL., CU. FT.	FUEL TANK, GAL.
3d sdn	90.6	156.9	50.0	62.4	1865	22.9	10.6
5d sdn	93.7	161.0	50.0	62.6	1951	22.9	10.6

Dodge

1982 Dodge Colt RS 3-door

Engines	L/CID	BHP	MPG	AVAIL.
ohc I-4 2 bbl.	1.4/86	64	28–34	79–84
ohc I-4 2 bbl.	1.6/97	72	27–33	79–84
ohc I-4T FI	1.6/97	102	24–28	84

KEY: L/CID = liters/cubic inch displacement; **BHP** = brake horsepower; **MPG** = estimated average miles per gallon; **ohc** = overhead cam; **dohc** = double overhead cam; **ohv** = overhead valve; **I** = in-line engine; **V** = V engine; **flat** = horizontally opposed engine; **D** = diesel; **T** = turbocharged; **bbl.** = barrel (carburetor); **FI** = fuel injection.

RECALL HISTORY

1980: light bulb socket in ashtray could overheat and ignite, possibly spreading fire to other instrument panel components.

Dodge/Plymouth Colt 1985-88

Aerodynamically restyled, Mitsubishi-built Colt sits on all-new platform with independent rear suspension. Dodge and Plymouth editions are identical, sold in 3- or 5-door hatchback and 4-door sedan form. Base 1.5-liter engine produces weak performance (especially with automatic) but excellent mileage: close to 30 mpg in town, 40 or more on the highway with 5-speed. A manual 4-speed transmission is standard on the base 3-door; others have the 5-speed. If you crave a pint-sized hot rod, check out the 1.6-liter turbo four, available since 1984 on the GTS 3-door or upscale Premier sedan. Suspension is better on those models

1985 Dodge Colt 4-door

as well, though even a base Colt is agile and easy to maneuver. Hatchbacks suffer from tight interiors, but four adults can ride in sedans without squeezing. The 5-door was deleted for '86. Appearance restyle for 1987 included new fenders, grille, full-width hood and flush aero headlamps. Good-looking DL station wagon, powered by 75-horsepower, 1.5-liter engine with multi-point fuel injection, joined for 1988. Though noisy, Colt isn't a bad late-model choice for economical driving.

Price Range	GOOD	AVERAGE	POOR
1985 Colt	$3900–5100	$3600–4700	$3000–3700
1986 Colt	4800–6000	4300–5300	3500–4400
1987 Colt	5800–7250	5200–6500	4700–5300
1988 Colt	6700–8800	6000–8000	—

Dimensions	WHEEL-BASE, IN.	LGTH., IN.	HT., IN.	WIDTH, IN.	AVG. WT., LBS.	CARGO VOL., CU. FT.	FUEL TANK, GAL.
3d sdn	93.7	157.3	50.8	63.8	1876	26.4	11.9
4d sdn	93.7	169.1	50.8	63.8	1989	10.9	11.9
5d sdn	93.7	157.3	53.5	63.8	1966	25.9	11.9
5d wgn	93.7	169.3	53.7	63.8	2227	60.2	NA

Engines	L/CID	BHP	MPG	AVAIL.
ohc I-4 2 bbl.	1.5/90	68	26–38	85–88
ohc I-4 FI	1.5/90	75	26–34	88
ohc I-4T FI	1.6/97	102–105	24–28	85–88

KEY: L/CID = liters/cubic inch displacement; **BHP** = brake horsepower; **MPG** = estimated average miles per gallon; **ohc** = overhead cam; **dohc** = double overhead

Dodge

cam; **ohv** = overhead valve; **I** = in-line engine; **V** = V engine; **flat** = horizontally opposed engine; **D** = diesel; **T** = turbocharged; **bbl.** = barrel (carburetor); **FI** = fuel injection.

RECALL HISTORY

None to date.

Dodge/Plymouth Colt Vista 1984-88

1985 Plymouth Colt Vista 5-door

Versatile, Mitsubishi-made front-drive wagon arrived in North America for '84. A full-time 4-wheel-drive version was added in mid-1985, then given shift-on-the-fly capability the next year. Aero headlamps and new grille appeared in 1988 reworking. Clever 5-door design makes efficient use of space, with good visibility. Seven passengers fit easily, though the back is best for smaller folks. Center and rear seats tilt forward to add cargo area, or backward to create a double bed (1987–88 rear seat folds flat). Acceleration ranges from sluggish to downright anemic, depending on load; worse with automatic. Twin-Stick manual shift with eight forward speeds was standard in '84, but dropped the next year in favor of a 5-speed. Mileage is a big plus. We managed nearly 24 mpg with automatic, including a lot of city driving. The 2.0-liter four (which added fuel injection in late '87) is gruff and noisy, though, even when cruising. Verdict: nice concept, but Honda Civic and Toyota Tercel wagons beat Colt Vista in quality.

1987 Dodge Colt Vista 4WD 5-door

Price Range	GOOD	AVERAGE	POOR
1984 Colt Vista	$5300–5700	$4800–5300	$4300–4800
1985 Colt Vista	6200–7000	5800–6600	5300–5800
1986 Colt Vista	7300–8300	6800–7800	6300–6900
1987 Colt Vista	8700–9900	8100–9200	7500–8300
1988 Colt Vista	10,500–11,750	9750–10,750	—

Dimensions	WHEEL-BASE, IN.	LGTH., IN.	HT., IN.	WIDTH, IN.	AVG. WT., LBS.	CARGO VOL., CU. FT.	FUEL TANK, GAL.
5d wgn	103.3	174.6	57.3	64.6	2557	63.9	13.2
4WD wgn	103.3	174.6	59.4	64.6	2888	63.9	14.5

Engines	L/CID	BHP	MPG	AVAIL.
ohc I-4 2 bbl.	2.0/122	88	22–26	84–87
ohc I-4 FI	2.0/122	96	21–26	88

KEY: L/CID = liters/cubic inch displacement; **BHP** = brake horsepower; **MPG** = estimated average miles per gallon; **ohc** = overhead cam; **dohc** = double overhead cam; **ohv** = overhead valve; **I** = in-line engine; **V** = V engine; **flat** = horizontally opposed engine; **D** = diesel; **T** = turbocharged; **bbl.** = barrel (carburetor); **FI** = fuel injection.

RECALL HISTORY

None to date.

Dodge Daytona 1984-88

Companion to Chrysler Laser hatchback sport coupe, also derived from front-drive K-car, is aimed more at younger, performance-oriented drivers. Most comments on Laser

Dodge

1984 Dodge Daytona Turbo Z

(see that entry) apply here. Base engine is Chrysler's fuel-injected four, with turbo version optional. For the ultimate, look for a muscular Daytona Turbo Z with ground-effects front air dam, side skirts, and unique rear spoiler. Performance-equipped Daytonas, including the recent turbo Pacifica, look the part and can roll with the hot ones. A new C/S (for Carroll Shelby) handling package was offered on '86 models. New 1987 styling included pop-up headlamps, a 2.5-liter four became the base engine, and the rough-riding Shelby Z added a 174-horsepower Turbo II four. Even a base '88 Daytona might have a C/S Performance Package with Turbo I engine. Early assembly quality was questionable, and you can't transfer Chrysler's 5-year/50,000-mile powertrain and rust warranties. For luxury, look to Laser; for excitement, a used Daytona might serve you well.

Price Range	GOOD	AVERAGE	POOR
1984 Daytona	$5300–6400	$4900–5900	$4400–4900
1985 Daytona	6400–7700	5900–7200	5400–6000
1986 Daytona	7500–8800	7000–8300	6300–7200
1987 Daytona	8900–11,000	8200–10,500	7750–9500
1988 Daytona	10,500–13,000	9500–12,000	—

Dimensions	WHEEL-BASE, IN.	LGTH., IN.	HT., IN.	WIDTH, IN.	AVG. WT., LBS.	CARGO VOL. CU. FT.	FUEL TANK, GAL.
3d cpe	97.0	175.0	50.3	69.3	2546	32.8	14.0

Engines

Engines	L/CID	BHP	MPG	AVAIL.
ohc I-4 FI	2.2/135	97–99	20–25	84–86
ohc I-4T FI	2.2/135	146–149	19–24	84–88
ohc I-4T FI	2.2/135	174	17–22	87–88
ohc I-4 FI	2.5/153	96–100	20–24	86–88

KEY: L/CID = liters/cubic inch displacement; **BHP** = brake horsepower; **MPG** = estimated average miles per gallon; **ohc** = overhead cam; **dohc** = double overhead cam; **ohv** = overhead valve; **I** = in-line engine; **V** = V engine; **flat** = horizontally opposed engine; **D** = diesel; **T** = turbocharged; **bbl.** = barrel (carburetor); **FI** = fuel injection.

RECALL HISTORY

1984: inadequate structural integrity of hood latch system could cause separation of hood panel from latch mechanism, allowing hood to open while car is in motion. **1985 Turbo:** clamp on fuel hose routed to pressure regulator may be inadequately tightened; fuel leakage could result in underhood fire. **1986:** battery cap vents may be partially or completely blocked with plastic flashing; buildup of internal gas pressure, especially while charging, could result in case rupture and release of gases and/or acid, which might cause injury.

Dodge Diplomat 1980-88

Last rear-drive Dodge, related to Chrysler LeBaron with chassis derived from Aspen/Volare, first came in coupe, sedan and wagon form. Only the sedan remained for 1982, as Plymouth also began to produce a nearly identical sedan, the Gran Fury. Slow sellers generally, Diplomats are popular mainly as police cars and taxis, though a plusher SE model has a distinctive grille and outside trim.

1981 Dodge Diplomat 2-door

Dodge

Sole drivetrain after 1983 is Chrysler's old reliable 318-cid V-8, coupled to the tough TorqueFlite automatic transmission. Measuring between mid- and full-size, Diplomat trails Ford and GM big cars in roominess, intermediates in economy. Soft suspension gives typical boulevard ride, which grows turbulent over bumps. Smooth drivetrain is tempting, but better used-car values are around.

Price Range	GOOD	AVERAGE	POOR
1980 Diplomat	$1900–2500	$1600–2200	$1200–1600
1981 Diplomat	2500–3100	2100–2800	1700–2100
1982 Diplomat	2900–3600	2500–3200	2000–2500
1983 Diplomat	3800–4500	3300–4000	2800–3300
1984 Diplomat	4900–5400	4400–4900	3800–4400
1985 Diplomat	5900–6500	5400–6000	4800–5400
1986 Diplomat	7200–8000	6700–7400	6000–6700
1987 Diplomat	8500–9500	7750–8750	7000–7750
1988 Diplomat	10,500–11,750	9900–11,000	—

Dimensions	WHEEL-BASE, IN.	LGTH., IN.	HT., IN.	WIDTH, IN.	AVG. WT., LBS.	CARGO VOL., CU. FT.	FUEL TANK, GAL.
2d cpe	108.7	201.2	53.5	74.2	3260	16.0	18.0
4d sdn	112.7	205.7	55.3	74.2	3425	15.6	18.0
5d wgn	112.7	205.5	55.4	74.2	3515	72.3	18.0

Engines	L/CID	BHP	MPG	AVAIL.
ohv I-6 1 bbl.	3.7/225	85–90	16–19	80–83
ohv V-8 2 bbl.	5.2/318	120–140	15–19	80–88
ohv V-8 4 bbl.	5.2/318	165	14–17	80–82

1986 Dodge Diplomat 4-door

KEY: L/CID = liters/cubic inch displacement; BHP = brake horsepower; MPG = estimated average miles per gallon; ohc = overhead cam; dohc = double overhead cam; ohv = overhead valve; I = in-line engine; V = V engine; flat = horizontally opposed engine; D = diesel; T = turbocharged; bbl. = barrel (carburetor); FI = fuel injection.

RECALL HISTORY

1981: carburetor solenoid could lose grounding, resulting in loss of engine power due to flooding. **1981:** automatic speed control switch could stick in "resume" position, preventing system from being deactivated by normal brake application. **1986:** battery cap vents may be partially or completely blocked with plastic flashing; buildup of internal gas pressure, especially during charging, could result in case rupture, and release of gases and/or acid that could cause injury.

Dodge Lancer 1985-88

1986 Dodge Lancer ES Turbo 5-door

Roomy hatchback 5-door sedan differs little from Chrysler LeBaron GTS, which rides the same lengthened K-car platform. Road manners are capable, even with base suspension. Sporty ES model has special handling suspension that allows crisp cornering with less body roll. Engine choices include base 2.2-liter four, 2.2 turbo, and after 1985 a 2.5-liter four with balancing shafts. None of the three are quiet. High-performance Lancer Shelby, produced in limited numbers during 1987, became a regular model for

Dodge

1987 Dodge Lancer ES Turbo 5-door

'88. Painted red or white, Shelby comes with driving lights
in the front spoiler and a 174-horsepower Turbo II engine
under the hood. Most comments in LeBaron GTS entry
also apply to Lancer.

Price Range	GOOD	AVERAGE	POOR
1985 Lancer	$6600–7700	$6200–7200	$5600–6200
1986 Lancer	7900–8800	7300–8300	6800–7500
1987 Lancer	9000–10,000	8400–9500	8000–8700
1988 Lancer	10,000–11,250	9500–10,500	—

Dimensions	WHEEL-BASE, IN.	LGTH., IN.	HT., IN.	WIDTH, IN.	AVG. WT., LBS.	CARGO VOL., CU. FT.	FUEL TANK, GAL.
5d sdn	103.1	180.4	53.0	68.5	2660	40.7	14.0

Engines	L/CID	BHP	MPG	AVAIL.
ohc I-4 FI	2.2/135	93–99	20–24	85–88
ohc I-4T FI	2.2/135	146	18–22	85–88
ohc I-4T FI	2.2/135	174	17–22	88
ohc I-4 FI	2.5/153	96–100	19–23	86–88

KEY: L/CID = liters/cubic inch displacement; **BHP** = brake horsepower; **MPG** =
estimated average miles per gallon; **ohc** = overhead cam; **dohc** = double overhead
cam; **ohv** = overhead valve; **I** = in-line engine; **V** = V engine; **flat** = horizontally
opposed engine; **D** = diesel; **T** = turbocharged; **bbl.** = barrel (carburetor); **FI** = fuel
injection.

RECALL HISTORY

1985: seatbelts omitted from some cars with optional front seat
center cushion and folding armrest. **1985 Turbo:** clamp on fuel
hose routed to pressure regulator may be inadequately tightened;

fuel leakage could result in underhood fire. **1986:** battery cap vents may be partially or completely blocked with plastic flashing; buildup of internal gas pressure, especially while charging, could result in case rupture and release of gases and/or acid, which might cause injury.

Dodge Mirada 1980-83

1981 Dodge Mirada CMX 2-door

Upmarket mid-size coupe differs from similar Chrysler Cordoba (see that car's entry) mainly in styling touches. Optional CMX package has "cabriolet" vinyl roof that simulates top-up convertible. Slightly cheaper used than Cordoba, but mechanicals are the same. Standard slant six engine is slow. 1980 models have history of rust, window/door problems, and the Carter Thermoquad carburetors on V-8s were troublesome.

Price Range	GOOD	AVERAGE	POOR
1980 Mirada	$1900–2200	$1600–2000	$1200–1600
1981 Mirada	2500–2900	2200–2600	1800–2200
1982 Mirada	3300–3600	2900–3300	2500–2900
1983 Mirada	4200–4600	3800–4300	3300–3800

Dimensions	WHEEL-BASE, IN.	LGTH., IN.	HT., IN.	WIDTH, IN.	AVG. WT., LBS.	CARGO VOL., CU. FT.	FUEL TANK, GAL.
2d cpe	112.7	209.5	53.2	72.7	3401	16.7	18.0

Dodge

1982 Dodge Mirada CMX 2-door

Engines	L/CID	BHP	MPG	AVAIL.
ohv I-6 1 bbl.	3.7/225	85–90	16–19	80–83
ohv V-8 2 bbl.	5.2/318	120–130	16–18	80–83
ohv V-8 4 bbl.	5.2/318	155–165	14–17	80–82
ohv V-8 4 bbl.	5.9/360	185	13–16	80

KEY: L/CID = liters/cubic inch displacement; **BHP** = brake horsepower; **MPG** = estimated average miles per gallon; **ohc** = overhead cam; **dohc** = double overhead cam; **ohv** = overhead valve; **I** = in-line engine; **V** = V engine; **flat** = horizontally opposed engine; **D** = diesel; **T** = turbocharged; **bbl.** = barrel (carburetor); **FI** = fuel injection.

RECALL HISTORY

1980: inspection and repair of sticking throttles, which may cause engine to idle too fast; and for exhaust fumes leaking into passenger compartment. **1981:** improper grounding of carburetor solenoid could result in flooding and loss of engine power. **1981:** automatic speed control switch could stick in "resume" position, preventing system from being deactivated by normal brake application.

Dodge Omni 1978-88

Omni and its hatchback twin, the Plymouth Horizon, were the first U.S.-made front-drive subcompacts. Cost-cutter America version, launched as an early '87, reduced option choices, cut prices—and doubled sales. Transverse-mounted 4-cylinder engine and independent suspension in space-efficient body imitate the VW Rabbit design. Initial 1.7-liter engine, derived from Rabbit, delivered fine mileage but weak performance. Chrysler's 2.2-liter four, an '81 option, runs quieter and gives better pickup, still

1979 Dodge Omni 5-door

with good economy. For 1983 a 1.6-liter Peugeot-made four replaced the VW base engine and 5-speed manual shift was offered with the 2.2. Next year, a high-output 2.2 was standard in the new GLH (Goes Like Heck), optional in other models. Finally, a 2.2 Turbo became optional in the GLH for 1985–86. The America version kept its carbureted 2.2 for 1987, but gained fuel injection the next year. Any 2.2 is sturdy and lively, at least with a 5-speed. The old 1.7 has suffered valve and oil problems. Lightweight yet stable on the road, Omni holds four adults, though the back is tight and driving position awkward. Interiors tend to be basic. Distressing early repair record improved after 1980. First-year cars had trouble with fuel, electrical and cooling systems, valves, and body hardware. Rubber insulator under 1978–82 carburetor fails, causing vacuum leaks—resulting in stalling and hard starting problems. Power rack-and-pinion steering tends to leak and 1981–83 engines may suffer from hot starting problems. Workmanship can't match Japanese or German rivals, but Omni isn't a bad choice for a reasonable price. Stick with 1981 and later models for best reliability prospects. Assembly quality varies, so inspect carefully.

Price Range	GOOD	AVERAGE	POOR
1978 Omni	$900–1100	$700–900	$450–700
1979 Omni	1100–1300	900–1100	600–900
1980 Omni	1300–1600	1100–1400	900–1100
1981 Omni	1700–2000	1400–1800	1100–1400
1982 Omni	2100–2700	1800–2400	1500–1800

Dodge

Price Range

	GOOD	AVERAGE	POOR
1983 Omni	2700–3200	2500–2900	2100–2500
1984 Omni	3400–3900	3100–3500	2600–3100
1985 Omni	4200–5300	3800–4900	3300–3800
1986 Omni	4900–6300	4500–5900	4000–4500
1987 Omni	5300–5800	4900–5300	4500–4900
1988 Omni	5800–6300	5400–5800	—

Dimensions	WHEEL-BASE, IN.	LGTH., IN.	HT., IN.	WIDTH, IN.	AVG. WT., LBS.	CARGO VOL., CU. FT.	FUEL TANK, GAL.
5d sdn	99.1	164.8	53.0	66.2	2162	36.6	13.0

Engines	L/CID	BHP	MPG	AVAIL.
ohc I-4 2 bbl.	1.7/105	70	25–30	78–82
ohv I-4 2 bbl.	1.6/98	62–64	25–30	83–86
ohc I-4 2 bbl.	2.2/135	84–96	23–28	81–87
ohc I-4 FI	2.2/135	93	23–28	88
ohc I-4 2 bbl.	2.2/135	110	22–28	84–86
ohc I-4 T FI	2.2/135	146	20–26	85–86

KEY: L/CID = liters/cubic inch displacement; **BHP** = brake horsepower; **MPG** = estimated average miles per gallon; **ohc** = overhead cam; **dohc** = double overhead cam; **ohv** = overhead valve; **I** = in-line engine; **V** = V engine; **flat** = horizontally opposed engine; **D** = diesel; **T** = turbocharged; **bbl.** = barrel (carburetor); **FI** = fuel injection.

RECALL HISTORY

1978: front suspension control arm rivets may not be strong enough to withstand high-impact loads, such as hitting a chuckhole at high speed with brakes locked. **1978:** fuel tank might leak when completely filled because rear carpet fasteners may have penetrated tank. **1978:** fuel hose may contact A/C suction hose, causing abrasion and fuel leakage that could result in underhood

1982 Dodge Omni 5-door

fire. **1978:** lower steering shaft coupling may be too large in diameter where it attaches to steering gear shaft; coupling could loosen, causing free play in steering and possible loss of control. **1978-79:** alternator wiring connections may come loose due to engine vibration, disabling charging system. **1979-80:** fuel hoses could become brittle due to high underhood temperatures and crack, causing fuel leak. **1980:** secondary hood latch could bind in open position, making it inoperative. **1981:** automatic speed control switch could stick in "resume" position, preventing system from being deactivated by normal brake pedal application. **1982:** bolts attaching front suspension ball joints to steering knuckles could crack, allowing ball joint to separate from knuckle. **1984-85:** fuel reservoir of 2.2-liter engine may leak at seam and inlet hose connection, which could cause engine compartment fire. **1985:** under certain warm-engine operating conditions, valve in vacuum line between fuel vapor canister and carburetor may allow canister to purge fuel, causing overrich mixture; engine could stall during deceleration. **1985 Turbo:** clamp on fuel hose routed to pressure regulator may be inadequately tightened; fuel leakage could result in underhood fire. **1986:** battery cap vents may be partially or completely blocked with plastic flashing; buildup of internal gas pressure, especially during charging, could result in case rupture, and release of gases and/or acid that could cause injury.

Dodge 024/Charger 1979-87

Sport coupe with slopeback nose is built on a shortened Omni platform. Plymouth TC3/Turismo is similar. First called Omni 024, its name shrunk to 024 for 1981. A Charger 2.2 appeared in mid-1982; for '83, Charger became the official model name. Initial 1.7-liter VW-based four was replaced by Peugeot 1.6 as standard for 1983. Chrysler's 2.2 has been optional since 1981. Performance fans since mid-1983 have been able to order a Shelby Charger, with distinctive blue-silver paint, bigger tires, firmer suspension and high-output 2.2 engine. Shelby Chargers since '85 have been hotter yet, with a standard turbocharged 2.2. The Shelby's high-output engine became optional elsewhere for '84, standard in Charger 2.2 the next year. For 1987, base Chargers carried a carbureted 2.2. Chargers have less rear seat room than Omnis and their unusual design wasn't universally loved, though 1984 and later models look cleaner. Recalls and repair

Dodge

1982 Dodge Charger 2.2 3-door

record are same as Omni (check that entry). Used models range from stripped Misers to nicely equipped Charger 2.2s. For swift running at modest cost, pick out a Charger 2.2 or Shelby—but they're loud, crude and stiff-riding. Don't be surprised by squeaks and rattles with any model. On the whole, they don't rate with Japanese coupes. Charger dropped out after 1987 as production focused on basic Omni America.

1987 Dodge Charger 3-door

Price Range	GOOD	AVERAGE	POOR
1979 Omni 024	$1200–1500	$950–1200	$700–950
1980 Omni 024	1600–1900	1300–1700	1000–1300
1981 024	2000–2250	1500–2000	1200–1500
1982 024	2400–2800	2100–2500	1800–2100
1982 024 Charger	2800–3100	2400–2800	2100–2400
1983 Charger	3200–3600	2800–3300	2400–2800
1983 Shelby	3900–4200	3500–3900	3100–3500
1984 Charger	3900–4500	3600–4100	3100–3600
1984 Shelby	4900–5200	4500–4900	4000–4500
1985 Charger	4700–5200	4400–4900	3900–4400
1985 Shelby	6000–6400	5500–6000	5000–5500
1986 Charger	5500–6200	5100–5800	4600–5100
1986 Shelby	7200–7600	6700–7200	6100–6700
1987 Charger	6500–7000	6000–6600	5500–6000
1987 Shelby	8500–9250	8000–8750	7400–8000

Dimensions	WHEEL-BASE, IN.	LGTH., IN.	HT., IN.	WIDTH, IN.	AVG. WT., LBS.	CARGO VOL., CU. FT.	FUEL TANK, GAL.
3d cpe	96.5	174.8	50.7	66.0	2220	32.4	13.0

Engines	L/CID	BHP	MPG	AVAIL.
ohc I-4 2 bbl.	1.7/105	70	25–30	79–82
ohv I-4 2 bbl.	1.6/98	62–64	25–30	83–86
ohc I-4 2 bbl.	2.2/135	84–96	23–28	81–87
ohc I-4 2 bbl.	2.2/135	110	22–28	84–86
ohc I-4T FI	2.2/135	146	20–26	85–87

KEY: L/CID = liters/cubic inch displacement; **BHP** = brake horsepower; **MPG** = estimated average miles per gallon; **ohc** = overhead cam; **dohc** = double overhead cam; **ohv** = overhead valve; **I** = in-line engine; **V** = V engine; **flat** = horizontally opposed engine; **D** = diesel; **T** = turbocharged; **bbl.** = barrel (carburetor); **FI** = fuel injection.

RECALL HISTORY

See Dodge Omni 1978–88.

Dodge St. Regis and Plymouth Gran Fury 1979-81

Downsized but still full-size pair of R-body sedans differs from Chrysler Newport/New Yorker mainly in nameplate, so see that entry for details. Gran Fury became available in 1980, to satisfy Plymouth dealers who wanted a low-

Dodge

1979 Dodge St. Regis 4-door

priced big car to compete with Caprice and LTD. Plymouth carried less standard equipment than St. Regis, but a long option list. Early workmanship wasn't tops, so choose a 1980–81 version—or look to another model. These two often saw service as police and fleet cars, but never sold well generally. Neither is a high-ranked choice today.

Price Range	GOOD	AVERAGE	POOR
1979 St. Regis	$1500–1800	$1200–1500	$900–1200
1980 St. Regis	2000–2300	1700–2100	1200–1700
1980 Gran Fury	1900–2200	1600–2000	1150–1600
1981 St. Regis	2400–2800	2100–2500	1700–2100
1981 Gran Fury	2200–2600	1900–2300	1600–1900

1980 Plymouth Gran Fury 4-door

Dimensions	WHEEL-BASE, IN.	LGTH., IN.	HT., IN.	WIDTH, IN.	AVG. WT., LBS.	CARGO VOL., CU. FT.	FUEL TANK, GAL.
4d sdn	118.5	220.2	54.5	77.6	3754	21.3	21.0

Engines	L/CID	BHP	MPG	AVAIL.
ohv I-6 2 bbl.	3.7/225	90–110	15–18	79–81
ohv V-8 2 bbl.	5.2/318	120–135	15–17	79–81
ohv V-8 4 bbl.	5.2/318	155	14–17	79–81
ohv V-8 2 bbl.	5.9/360	130–150	13–16	79–80
ohv V-8 4 bbl.	5.9/360	185–195	12–15	79–80

KEY: L/CID = liters/cubic inch displacement; **BHP** = brake horsepower; **MPG** = estimated average miles per gallon; **ohc** = overhead cam; **dohc** = double overhead cam; **ohv** = overhead valve; **I** = in-line engine; **V** = V engine; **flat** = horizontally opposed engine; **D** = diesel; **T** = turbocharged; **bbl.** = barrel (carburetor); **FI** = fuel injection.

RECALL HISTORY

1981: possibility of improper grounding of carburetor solenoid, which could result in loss of engine power because of flooding.
1981: automatic speed control switch could stick in "resume" position, preventing system from being deactivated by normal brake pedal application.

Dodge Shadow and Plymouth Sundance 1987-88

Sporty pair of front-drive P-body subcompacts arrived in summer 1986, in 5-door hatchback form, targeted at affluent young buyers (especially women). A 3-door hatchback came soon after. Built on the same platform as the G-body Daytona, Shadow/Sundance have firmer suspensions and a hefty list of standard equipment. Both 2.2-liter engines are noisy, but the turbo delivers 146 horsepower for snappy performance. Handling beats most small cars, even in base form, with nice high-speed stability and modest roll through fast turns. Quick-ratio power steering has good feel and centers well. ES version (on 3-door Shadow only) rides harshly and is for performance buffs only. As usual, we prefer automatic over the 5-speed manual shift's balky linkage, even though acceleration suffers a bit. Back seat is tight for grownups, but folding rear seatback adds cargo space. For 1988, the high-performance ES gets a new

Dodge

1988 Dodge Shadow ES 5-door

integral lower air dam, fog lamps, fender flares and rear
spoiler; plus a choice of 2.2 turbo or new 2.5-liter engine.
That 2.5 is optional on all models, and delivers a nice
compromise of swiftness and silence. Sundance for '88 adds
a sporty RS package on both body styles.

Price Range	GOOD	AVERAGE	POOR
1987 Shadow	$7600–8200	$7000–7700	$6500–7000
1987 Sundance	7700–8300	7100–7770	6500–7100
1988 Shadow	8100–9000	7600–8500	—
1988 Sundance	8200–9100	7700–8600	—

1988 Plymouth Sundance RS 3-door

Dimensions	WHEEL-BASE, IN.	LGTH., IN.	HT., IN.	WIDTH, IN.	AVG. WT., LBS.	CARGO VOL., CU. FT.	FUEL TANK, GAL.
3d sdn	97.0	171.7	52.7	67.3	2520	33.3	14.0
5d sdn	97.0	171.7	52.7	67.3	2558	33.0	14.0

Engines	L/CID	BHP	MPG	AVAIL.
ohc I-4 FI	2.2/135	97	21–26	87–88
ohc I-4T FI	2.2/135	146	18–22	87–88
ohc I-4 FI	2.5/153	96	20–25	88

KEY: L/CID = liters/cubic inch displacement; **BHP** = brake horsepower; **MPG** = estimated average miles per gallon; **ohc** = overhead cam; **dohc** = double overhead cam; **ohv** = overhead valve; **I** = in-line engine; **V** = V engine; **flat** = horizontally opposed engine; **D** = diesel; **T** = turbocharged; **bbl.** = barrel (carburetor); **FI** = fuel injection.

RECALL HISTORY

None to date.

Dodge 400/600 1982-88

1982 Dodge 400 4-door

Mid-size Dodge 400 was introduced in 1982 as a spinoff from the front-drive compact K-car. Similar to Chrysler LeBaron but for its slat grille, the 400 appeared first as a 2-door coupe, later in sedan and convertible form. Dodge's E-body 600 sedan debuted in 1983, along with the Chrysler E Class/New Yorker. It's a stretched version of the K-car, 3 inches longer in wheelbase. A Eurosedan model, dubbed 600 ES, was offered in 1983–84 with black exterior trim and firmer suspension. Though steadier on the road, crisper in handling, the 600 ES gets a bit jiggly on bumpy surfaces.

Dodge

For 1984, the 400 name was dropped. The coupe and convertible, still on the shorter LeBaron wheelbase, were renamed 600. Base 2.2-liter engine is tough but overtaxed, though mileage is good. Turbocharged edition (available from 1984 on) delivers a lot of exhaust noise along with its thrills. A 2.6-liter Mitsubishi four was optional through 1985, a Chrysler 2.5 later. Some models have Electronic Voice Alert. Costly convertible lags in both performance and economy. 600 SE sedan of 1985–88 is the choice for comfort; latest edition carries standard 2.5-liter engine. Most expensive of the lot is a 600 ES Turbo convertible. Both coupe and convertible were dropped after '86. Up to 1984, loose upper MacPherson strut mounts were a problem on some units.

Price Range	GOOD	AVERAGE	POOR
1982 400	$3400–3700	$3000–3400	$2600–3000
1982 400 Conv.	5100–5500	4600–5100	4000–4600
1983 400	4100–4500	3600–4100	3100–3600
1983 400 Conv.	5800–6200	5400–5900	4750–5400
1983 600	4100–4600	3800–4300	3300–3800
1984 600	4900–5600	4500–5200	4000–4500
1984 600 Conv.	6800–7300	6300–6800	5600–6300
1985 600	6000–6800	5500–6250	5000–5500
1985 600 Conv.	8000–9200	7400–8500	6750–7500
1986 600	7500–8400	6800–7800	6300–690(
1986 600 Conv.	9750–11,500	9250–10,750	8750–9500
1987 600	8800–10,000	8100–9300	7600–8300
1988 600	10,250–11,500	9500–10,500	—

1987 Dodge 600 4-door

Dimensions	WHEEL-BASE, IN.	LGTH., IN.	HT., IN.	WIDTH, IN.	AVG. WT., LBS.	CARGO VOL., CU. FT.	FUEL TANK, GAL.
2d cpe	100.3	180.7	52.7	68.0	2465	15.0	14.0
2d conv.	100.3	180.7	53.7	68.0	2533	13.1	14.0
4d sdn	103.3	186.6	53.1	68.0	2564	17.0	14.0

Engines	L/CID	BHP	MPG	AVAIL.
ohc I-4 2 bbl./FI	2.2/135	84–99	20–25	82–88
ohc I-4 T FI	2.2/135	142–146	18–23	84–88
ohc I-4 FI	2.5/153	96–100	19–24	86–88
ohc I-4 2 bbl.	2.6/156	93–101	18–24	82–85

KEY: L/CID = liters/cubic inch displacement; **BHP** = brake horsepower; **MPG** = estimated average miles per gallon; **ohc** = overhead cam; **dohc** = double overhead cam; **ohv** = overhead valve; **I** = in-line engine; **V** = V engine; **flat** = horizontally opposed engine; **D** = diesel; **T** = turbocharged; **bbl.** = barrel (carburetor); **FI** = fuel injection.

RECALL HISTORY

1983: brake fluid hose could leak from rubbing against exhaust bracket, resulting in partial brake failure. **1985 Turbo:** clamp on fuel hose routed to pressure regulator may be inadequately tightened; fuel leakage could result in underhood fire. **1986:** resistor in electronic instrument panel cluster may be subjected to current overload, which could start an instrument panel fire.

Ford Aerostar 1986-88

Traditional design gives Ford's rear-drive compact van ample passenger and cargo space, plus strong trailer-towing ability (up to 4900 pounds, depending on options). First-year models had a 2.3-liter 4-cylinder base engine, with 2.8 V-6 optional. Both had to struggle to perform. Late in the model year, a stronger, fuel-injected 3.0 V-6 (introduced in Ford Taurus) replaced the 2.8-liter. The V-6 became standard on 1987 passenger models, and in cargo vans for '88. That extra power is needed to haul Aerostar's hefty weight. The 4-cylinder came with 5-speed manual shift only, but V-6 versions may have 4-speed overdrive automatic. Long wheelbase offers a stable, well-controlled ride. Seven people can sit without squeezing (in three-seat edition), but cargo space is limited unless the seats are taken out. Quite a chore, as the rear seat weighs 100 pounds. In the 1988 top-line Eddie Bauer model, a bench seat converts to a bed. Service access is bad news; even fluid checks on the V-6 are hard to make from the front.

Ford

1986 Ford Aerostar XLT

Price Range	GOOD	AVERAGE	POOR
1986 Aerostar	$9000–10,200	$8300–9300	$7800–8400
1987 Aerostar	9800–10,700	9000–10,000	8500–9200
1988 Aerostar	10,750–12,000	10,000–11,250	—

Dimensions	WHEEL-BASE, IN.	LGTH., IN.	HT., IN.	WIDTH, IN.	AVG. WT., LBS.	CARGO VOL. CU. FT.	FUEL TANK, GAL.
4d van	118.9	174.9	72.6	71.7	3500	140.3	17.0

Engines	L/CID	BHP	MPG	AVAIL.
ohc I-4 FI	2.3/140	88	21–26	86–87
ohv V-6 2 bbl.	2.8/171	115	16–20	86
ohv V-6 FI	3.0/182	145	16–21	86–88

KEY: L/CID = liters/cubic inch displacement; **BHP** = brake horsepower; **MPG** = estimated average miles per gallon; **ohc** = overhead cam; **dohc** = double overhead

1987 Ford Aerostar

cam; **ohv** = overhead valve; **I** = in-line engine; **V** = V engine; **flat** = horizontally opposed engine; **D** = diesel; **T** = turbocharged; **bbl.** = barrel (carburetor); **FI** = fuel injection.

RECALL HISTORY

1986: inadequate welding in some underbody areas, including those at rear suspension attachments, may cause suspension to separate; axle could then shift during acceleration or braking and may adversely affect steering control. **1986–87:** replacement of some 3.0-liter V-6 engines because of problem with piston knock in cold weather and during break-in period.

Ford Escort/EXP 1981-88

1985 1/2 Ford Escort GL 5-door

Ford's best-seller, a subcompact front-drive successor to the ill-fated Pinto, first came in 3-door sedan and 5-door wagon form. A 5-door sedan was added for '82. First engine, a newly designed 1.6-liter four, was joined by a High Output version during 1982. Fuel injection became available the next year. A Turbo GT model and diesel engine were offered for '84, but neither sold well; the Mazda-built diesel departed during the '87 model year. Escort was restyled during 1985, receiving a 1.9-liter base engine that gives more zip with only slightly less gas mileage. That engine

Ford

gained fuel injection for 1987. The sporty 3-door GT was
revived for '86 with a more potent fuel-injected engine,
spoiler and more. Snazziest Escorts have usually been
called LX or GLX. Restyled EXP sport coupe, formerly
considered a separate model (see next listing), reappeared
in 1986½ as part of Escort lineup; only the EXP Luxury
coupe continued into 1988. Entry-level Pony was available
only with manual shift until '88. Avoid first-year models,
which were recalled several times. Advantages include
economy, easy maneuverability, comfortable driving position, and tolerable room for four. But you also get timid
performance, a bouncy ride, poor sound insulation, and
so-so workmanship. Problem areas: engine prone to leak
oil around valve cover; ignition timing woes on some engines cause major detonation damage; constant-velocity
driveshaft joints difficult to service. Similar Mercury Lynx
costs more new, but about the same used. Not much to get
excited about, but a fair choice for budget-priced basic
transportation. Fully restyled Escort is expected at mid-
year.

Price Range	GOOD	AVERAGE	POOR
1981 Escort	$2000–2400	$1500–2100	$1100–1500
1982 Escort	2400–2900	2000–2500	1600–2000
1983 Escort	3100–3700	2600–3300	2200–2600
1984 Escort	3500–4500	3200–4600	2700–3200
1985 Escort	4700–5500	4000–4900	3500–4000
1986 Escort	5400–6500	4700–5900	4000–4800
1987 Escort	6000–7600	5400–6700	4900–5700
1987 EXP	6900–7500	6200–6900	5700–6200
1988 Escort	6700–7800	6000–7700	—
1988 EXP	8200–9000	7400–8200	—

1987 Ford Escort EXP Sport Coupe 3-door

Dimensions	WHEEL-BASE, IN.	LGTH., IN.	HT., IN.	WIDTH, IN.	AVG. WT., LBS.	CARGO VOL. CU. FT.	FUEL TANK, GAL.
3d sdn	94.2	163.9	53.3	65.9	2074	32.2	10.0
3d cpe (EXP)	94.2	168.4	50.9	65.9	2291	NA	13.0
5d sdn	94.2	163.9	53.4	65.9	2139	32.0	10.0
5d wgn	94.2	165.0	53.3	65.9	2166	58.8	13.0

Engines	L/CID	BHP	MPG	AVAIL.
ohc I-4 2 bbl.	1.6/98	69–72	27–32	81–85
ohc I-4 2 bbl.	1.6/98	80	26–30	82–85
ohc I-4 FI	1.6/98	84–88	26–30	83–85
ohc I-4T FI	1.6/98	120	22–27	84–85
ohc I-4 2 bbl.	1.9/114	86	26–31	85–86
ohc I-4 FI	1.9/114	90	25–30	87–88
ohc I-4 FI	1.9/114	108–115	22–26	85–88
ohc I-4D FI	2.0/121	52–58	28–35	84–87

KEY: L/CID = liters/cubic inch displacement; **BHP** = brake horsepower; **MPG** = estimated average miles per gallon; **ohc** = overhead cam; **dohc** = double overhead cam; **ohv** = overhead valve; **I** = in-line engine; **V** = V engine; **flat** = horizontally opposed engine; **D** = diesel; **T** = turbocharged; **bbl.** = barrel (carburetor); **FI** = fuel injection.

RECALL HISTORY

1984–85: defective ignition module could make 1.6-liter engine hard to start, run poorly, or stall. **1984–86:** owners warned not to idle engine for more than 5 minutes because overheated catalytic converter could possibly cause fire. **1985:** on cars with 1.9-liter engine and air conditioning, throttle lever may not return to idle position due to misalignment of A/C shutoff switch to throttle lever pin. **1985–86:** stiffness of thick rubber material that covers gearshift on manual transmission may push shift lever out of gear and toward neutral, when operated in cold weather (under 40° F). **1986–88:** check retainer clips on fuel-line spring-lock couplings of fuel-injected engines. **1987:** stainless steel decorative lug nuts on small number of cars could gall and possibly seize on the wheel studs, without providing adequate clamping load on the car wheels; studs could fracture, creating risk of wheel falling off.

Ford EXP and Mercury LN7 1982-85

Twin sporty coupes ride the same wheelbase and front-drive chassis as the boxy Escort/Lynx subcompacts. Main difference is the two-seater hatchback body, with lower

Ford

1982 Ford EXP 3-door

roofline and driving position. Neither version set any sales records, so Mercury dropped its LN7 after 1983. EXP then gained LN7's big "bubbleback" curvy rear window. Ford's turbocharged EXP tried to rival the Pontiac Fiero the next year. Emphasis was on style, but not everyone takes to the "bathtub" cockpit that results from dropped roof and seats. Performance hardly matches the car's speedy looks, and it suffers the same loud engine and exhaust as Escort/Lynx—especially with the high-output powerplant. Stiff chassis gives agile handling but harsh ride, including low-speed thumping and tire noise; engine has been prone to leak oil around the valve cover. Well-equipped but flawed stab at a miniature sports car isn't a good used-car value.

Price Range	GOOD	AVERAGE	POOR
1982 EXP	$2500–2800	$2200–2500	$1800–2200
1982 LN7	2600–3000	2400–2700	2000–2400
1983 EXP	3400–3800	3000–3400	2600–3000
1983 LN7	3500–3900	3100–3500	2700–3100
1984 EXP	3900–4400	3600–4100	3000–3600
1985 EXP	4900–5500	4400–5100	3900–4400

Dimensions	WHEEL-BASE, IN.	LGTH., IN.	HT., IN.	WIDTH, IN.	AVG. WT., LBS.	CARGO VOL., CU. FT.	FUEL TANK, GAL.
3d cpe	94.2	170.3	50.5	65.9	2212	28.8	13.0

Engines	L/CID	BHP	MPG	AVAIL.
ohc I-4 2 bbl.	1.6/98	69–72	27–32	82–85
ohc I-4 2 bbl.	1.6/98	80	26–30	82–85
ohc I-4 FI	1.6/98	84	26–30	83–85
ohc I-4T FI	1.6/98	120	22–27	84–85

1982 Mercury LN7 3-door

KEY: **L/CID** = liters/cubic inch displacement; **BHP** = brake horsepower; **MPG** = estimated average miles per gallon; **ohc** = overhead cam; **dohc** = double overhead cam; **ohv** = overhead valve; **I** = in-line engine; **V** = V engine; **flat** = horizontally opposed engine; **D** = diesel; **T** = turbocharged; **bbl.** = barrel (carburetor); **FI** = fuel injection.

RECALL HISTORY

1981–83: cracks could develop in front door lock pillars, allowing doors to open inadvertently. **1982:** blower motor resistor assembly on models with optional air conditioning could malfunction, causing resistor coil to overheat and possibly causing ignition of evaporator housing. **1982:** possible that 5200 cars do not meet federal fuel spillage requirements in rollovers; corrected by installing revised fuel filler and vent pipe. **1984–85:** defective ignition module could make engine hard to start, run poorly, or stall. **1984–85:** owners warned not to idle engine for more than 5 minutes because overheated catalytic converter could possibly cause fire. **1985:** stiffness of thick rubber material that covers gearshift on manual transmission may push shift lever out of gear and toward neutral, when operated in cold weather (under 40°F).

Ford Fairmont 1978-83

Practical rear-drive family compact introduced the "Fox" body/chassis platform, later used on a number of FoMoCo products. Mercury Zephyr differs only in grille and minor trim. The pair replaces the earlier Maverick/Comet. Main attractions are decent ride, responsive rack-and-pinion steering, good visibility, plus roomy comfort for five (maybe six). More agile than some, roadability rates around aver-

Ford

1979 Ford Fairmont 2-door

1979 Ford Fairmont 5-door

age, but fuel economy very good for this league. Standard 2.3-liter four is rough, noisy and overtaxed, barely thriftier than the reliable 200-cid six, which is a far better choice. Brake and fuel system problems show up a little more often on V-8 models, which offer swifter pickup but drink more gas. Clutch problems plague early manual-shift fours and sixes, MacPherson struts in front suspension tend to wear quickly, radiator may fail prematurely. Watch for leaks in the power rack-and-pinion steering and spring sag on station wagons. Lax workmanship on '78s mars recall history, but repair record improved by 1980. Newer front-drive compacts are more efficiently designed, but Fairmont ranks high for dependability.

Price Range	GOOD	AVERAGE	POOR
1978 Fairmont	$1000–1400	$700–1100	$400–700
1979 Fairmont	1300–1600	900–1300	600–900
1980 Fairmont	1600–2100	1200–1800	900–1200
1981 Fairmont	1800–2500	1400–2000	1100–1500
1982 Fairmont	2200–2800	1900–2500	1600–2000
1983 Fairmont	2700–3300	2300–2900	1900–2300

Dimensions	WHEEL-BASE, IN.	LGTH., IN.	HT., IN.	WIDTH, IN.	AVG. WT., LBS.	CARGO VOL., CU. FT.	FUEL TANK, GAL.
2d cpe/sdn	105.5	195.5	52.9	71.0	2750	16.8	14.0
4d sdn	105.5	195.5	52.9	71.0	2800	16.8	14.0
5d wgn	105.5	195.5	54.2	71.0	2900	79.5	14.0

Engines	L/CID	BHP	MPG	AVAIL.
ohc I-4 2 bbl.	2.3/140	88–93	18–22	78–83
ohv I-6 1 bbl.	3.3/200	85–91	18–21	78–83
ohv V-8 2 bbl.	4.2/255	119	16–19	80–81
ohv V-8 2 bbl.	5.0/302	139–140	15–18	78–79

KEY: L/CID = liters/cubic inch displacement; BHP = brake horsepower; MPG = estimated average miles per gallon; ohc = overhead cam; dohc = double overhead cam; ohv = overhead valve; I = in-line engine; V = V engine; flat = horizontally opposed engine; D = diesel; T = turbocharged; bbl. = barrel (carburetor); FI = fuel injection.

RECALL HISTORY

1978: possibility front disc brake rotors contain cracks, which could affect car's directional control. **1978:** possibility vehicles were equipped with incorrect rear axle assemblies; sedans may have early rear wheel lockup, affecting directional stability; wagon's rear braking effectiveness would be reduced. **1978:** models with 200-cid engine, automatic transmission and thermactor pulse air supply system, for possibility air reed valve may fail; results in reduced fuel economy, power and performance; continued operation may result in engine stalling or overheating of exhaust system, which may lead to scorched rear seats and carpets. **1978:** possible that main wiring assembly may be routed against or near cowl-to-brake pedal support brace; wiring may chafe and one or more wires could become grounded, which might result in loss of power to an accessory or total electrical loss without warning. **1978:** possible that windshield wiper drive linkage may fracture due to metal fatigue, causing wipers to fail without warning. **1978:** possibility vehicles with automatic transmissions and steering column-mounted shift levers were produced with controls that can contact intermediate fuel hose; may result in fuel leakage and potential fire hazard. **1978:** possibility cars with automatic

Ford

transmissions and steering column-mounted shift controls have control rods intended for prior design; could result in deterioration of shift control function with potential for starting in gear or inability to engage "Park" position; if condition occurred on vehicle in which parking brake was not engaged, vehicle might move. **1979:** possibility some cars have brake pushrod to pedal retaining pins that could fall out, resulting in loss of braking capability. **1981:** air injection may need modification to reduce emissions. **1981 V-8:** replace choke pull-down motor to ensure acceptable emissions. **1983:** vehicles with 200-cid engine and C-5 automatic transmission, because of possibility that vibration over long period could cause leak in transmission oil cooler line.

Ford Granada and Mercury Monarch 1978-80

1979 Ford Granada ESS 4-door

Styled with Mercedes in mind, measuring between compact and mid-size, these twins were promoted as bargain-basement substitutes for the real thing. Ford and Mercury editions differ only in grilles, taillights and trim. Overweight design produces tedious handling and poor fuel economy. Ride is pleasant and quiet on smooth roads, poor over rough surfaces. Plush interior is cramped in back; trunk space mediocre. Performance okay with V-8 engine, sluggish with six. Repair record average except for persistent steering/suspension problems, especially power steer-

1979 Mercury Monarch 2-door

ing leaks due to faulty hydraulic cylinder. Variable-venturi carburetor on the 302-cid V-8 was trouble-prone and difficult to repair. Serviceability only fair in tight engine compartment. Rising fuel prices brought early obsolescence and total '81 restyle. Hardly a best bet in an older used car.

Price Range	GOOD	AVERAGE	POOR
1978 Granada	$1200–1500	$900–1200	$700–900
1978 Monarch	1250–1600	950–1250	700–950
1979 Granada	1500–1800	1200–1500	900–1200
1979 Monarch	1500–1800	1150–1550	850–1150
1980 Granada	1900–2400	1600–2000	1200–1600
1980 Monarch	1900–2300	1500–1900	1200–1500

Dimensions	WHEEL-BASE, IN.	LGTH., IN.	HT., IN.	WIDTH, IN.	AVG. WT., LBS.	CARGO VOL., CU. FT.	FUEL TANK, GAL.
2d sdn	109.9	197.7	53.2	71.2	3188	14.8	18.0
4d sdn	109.9	197.7	53.3	71.2	3231	14.8	18.0

Engines	L/CID	BHP	MPG	AVAIL.
ohv I-6 2 bbl.	4.1/250	98	17–19	78–80
ohv V-8 2 bbl.	5.0/302	130–139	15–18	78–80

KEY: L/CID = liters/cubic inch displacement; **BHP** = brake horsepower; **MPG** = estimated average miles per gallon; **ohc** = overhead cam; **dohc** = double overhead cam; **ohv** = overhead valve; **I** = in-line engine; **V** = V engine; **flat** = horizontally opposed engine; **D** = diesel; **T** = turbocharged; **bbl.** = barrel (carburetor); **FI** = fuel injection.

RECALL HISTORY

1978–79: flex-blade cooling on engine with air conditioning may be subject to high stress during normal operation; blades can crack and portions may separate from fan assembly. **1979:** some vehicles may have brake pushrod-to-pedal retaining pins that could fall out, possibly resulting in loss of braking capability.

Ford Granada 1981-82

1981 Ford Granada 4-door

Smaller, lighter Granada and its Mercury Cougar companion became FoMoCo's "true" mid-size offerings after 1979
demise of the LTD II and earlier Cougar. Bulky square-cut
shape, standup grille, increased length and plusher interior were meant to hide similarity to Fairmont/Zephyr
compacts, but all share the same "Fox" chassis and most
inner body structure. Initial 2- and 4-door notchback sedans were joined the next year by a 5-door wagon. Standard
2.3-liter 4-cylinder engine lacks punch and is rough and
noisy. We'd pick the 3.3-liter straight six. A 4.2-liter V-8
was offered only in 1981, Ford's lightweight "Essex" V-6
the next year. The 3.8-liter V-6 gives feeble acceleration
and distressing fuel mileage. Appearance and driving feel

1981 Ford Granada 2-door

Ford

are much like Fairmont—but bigger and heavier. Fairly spacious interior offers nice driving position and good visibility. Handling rates average or worse, ride pleasant but too soft. Repair data scanty, but reliability should match Fairmont's. Basic design continued in production as the restyled LTD. All told, a likable rival to GM mid-sizes; but you get about as much function in a Fairmont, for fewer dollars.

Price Range	GOOD	AVERAGE	POOR
1981 Granada	$2300–2900	$1900–2500	$1500–2000
1982 Granada	3000–3500	2600–3200	2100–2600

Dimensions	WHEEL-BASE, IN.	LGTH., IN.	HT., IN.	WIDTH, IN.	AVG. WT., LBS.	CARGO VOL., CU. FT.	FUEL TANK, GAL.
2d sdn	105.5	196.5	53.0	71.0	2810	16.8	16.0
4d sdn	105.5	196.5	53.0	71.0	2845	16.8	16.0
5d wgn	105.5	196.5	54.2	71.0	3100	74.6	16.0

Engines	L/CID	BHP	MPG	AVAIL.
ohc I-4 2 bbl.	2.3/140	88	18–22	81–82
ohv I-6 1 bbl.	3.3/200	88	18–21	81–82
ohv V-6 2 bbl.	3.8/232	112	17–20	82
ohv V-8 2 bbl.	4.2/255	120	16–19	81

KEY: L/CID = liters/cubic inch displacement; **BHP** = brake horsepower; **MPG** = estimated average miles per gallon; **ohc** = overhead cam; **dohc** = double overhead cam; **ohv** = overhead valve; **I** = in-line engine; **V** = V engine; **flat** = horizontally opposed engine; **D** = diesel; **T** = turbocharged; **bbl.** = barrel (carburetor); **FI** = fuel injection.

RECALL HISTORY

1981: replace choke pull-down motor on V-8 engine to ensure acceptable emissions. **1981:** modify air injection if necessary to meet emissions standards. **1982:** tire placards may show incorrect tire sizes and inflation pressures.

Ford LTD II 1978-79

Mid-size at the time, LTD II ranks as full-size by today's standards. Soft suspension makes the normally smooth, quiet ride grow raucous on rougher roads, impairing handling at the same time. Low seat and long hood hinder visibility. Passengers fit neatly up front, but back is small. Gas mileage marginal with 302-cid V-8, bad with bigger engines. Average repair frequency, but slightly better in brakes, air conditioning and body integrity; far below av-

Ford

1978 Ford LTD II 2-door

erage for ignition and automatic transmission. Also, the difficult-to-repair variable-venturi carburetor on the 302 V-8 was troublesome. Old-fashioned biggie is cheaper than some, but not a desirable value today.

Price Range	GOOD		AVERAGE		POOR	
1978 LTD II	$1200–1500		$900–1200		$700–900	
1979 LTD II	1400–1800		1100–1400		900–1100	

Dimensions	WHEEL-BASE, IN.	LGTH., IN.	HT., IN.	WIDTH, IN.	AVG. WT., LBS.	CARGO VOL., CU. FT.	FUEL TANK, GAL.
2d sdn	121.0	219.6	53.5	79.5	4368	17.1	22.0
4d sdn	121.0	219.6	54.9	79.5	4406	17.1	22.0

Engines	L/CID	BHP	MPG	AVAIL.
ohv V-8 2 bbl.	5.0/302	134	15–17	78–79
ohv V-8 2 bbl.	5.8/351	145–162	12–15	78–79
ohv V-8 2 bbl.	6.6/400	158–180	11–14	78–79
ohv V-8 4 bbl.	7.5/460	195–267	9–12	78

KEY: L/CID = liters/cubic inch displacement; **BHP** = brake horsepower; **MPG** = estimated average miles per gallon; **ohc** = overhead cam; **dohc** = double overhead cam; **ohv** = overhead valve; **I** = in-line engine; **V** = V engine; **flat** = horizontally opposed engine; **D** = diesel; **T** = turbocharged; **bbl.** = barrel (carburetor); **FI** = fuel injection.

RECALL HISTORY

1978 (4-doors): possibility front outboard seatbelt assemblies have shoulder harness retractors that might not lock; also, some retractors may not allow extraction of shoulder belt webbing due to pre-locked condition. **1979 :** replacement of brake pushrod retaining pin, which could fall off and result in loss of braking ability. **1979:** possibility vehicles have Saginaw steering gears with improperly manufactured sector shafts that could cause loss of steering control.

Ford LTD/ LTD Crown Victoria 1979-88

1979 Ford LTD 4-door

Downsizing gave big Ford better handling than prior LTD, with less understeer and body roll. Improved suspension kept the ride comfortable, and interior space remained ample. Fuel mileage doesn't quite match GM rivals, though. Overdrive 4-speed automatic aids economy, but engines on some 1980–81 cars with that transmission have been known to stall suddenly in a hard stop, leaving power brakes and steering unassisted. More problems: rapid brake pad wear is common, springs sag on some station wagons, and the variable-venturi carburetor on the 302 V-8 is troublesome and hard to repair. A 4.2-liter cutdown of the familiar 302-cid V-8 was offered for 1981–82, but we prefer the 302's greater power and torque. That engine changed a lot for 1986, including a switch to port fuel injection. The 351-cid V-8 was phased out after 1980 except in police cars. Crown Victoria was added to the name for 1983, to distinguish this full-size version from the smaller LTD introduced that year. Air conditioning and tinted glass became standard for '87. The first major restyle of its long life came for 1988, including a new grille, hood, bumpers and trunk lid; and the 2-door sedan departed. Verdict: good choice in a big car, but you pay for its comfort at the gas pump.

Ford

1979 Ford LTD Country Squire 5-door

Price Range	GOOD	AVERAGE	POOR
1979 LTD	$1900–2400	$1500–1900	$1100–1500
1980 LTD	2000–2800	1650–2400	1200–1600
1981 LTD	2400–3500	2000–2900	1600–2000
1982 LTD	3300–4500	2900–4000	2300–2900
1983 LTD Crown Vic	5000–6000	4500–5500	4000–4600
1984 LTD Crown Vic	6500–7500	5800–6800	5200–5800
1985 LTD Crown Vic	7900–9000	7200–8300	6500–7400
1986 LTD Crown Vic	9750–11,250	8900–10,500	8300–9200
1987 LTD Crown Vic	12,000–14,000	11,000–13,000	10,000–11,000
1988 LTD Crown Vic	14,000–16,000	12,500–14,000	—

Dimensions	WHEEL-BASE, IN.	LGTH., IN.	HT., IN.	WIDTH, IN.	AVG. WT., LBS.	CARGO VOL., CU. FT.	FUEL TANK, GAL.
2d sdn	114.3	211.0	55.3	77.5	3699	22.4	18.0
4d sdn	114.3	211.0	55.3	77.5	3739	22.4	18.0
5d wgn	114.3	215.0	56.8	79.3	3936	89.5	18.5

Engines	L/CID	BHP	MPG	AVAIL.
ohv V-8 2 bbl.	4.2/255	111–120	15–18	81–82
ohv V-8 FI	5.0/302	130–155	15–18	83–88
ohv V-8 2 bbl.	5.0/302	130–133	14–17	79–82
ohv V-8 2 bbl.	5.8/351	142–145	13–16	79–80

KEY: L/CID = liters/cubic inch displacement; **BHP** = brake horsepower; **MPG** = estimated average miles per gallon; **ohc** = overhead cam; **dohc** = double overhead cam; **ohv** = overhead valve; **I** = in-line engine; **V** = V engine; **flat** = horizontally opposed engine; **D** = diesel; **T** = turbocharged; **bbl.** = barrel (carburetor); **FI** = fuel injection.

RECALL HISTORY

1979 (sedans): may have incorrect rear lamp sockets; tail and backup lamps would fail to comply with federal safety standard.
1979: possibility cars have 6.0-amp circuit breaker rather than 8.5-amp in windshield wiper/washer system; potential for circuit

    CONSUMER GUIDE®

interruption under heavy loads. **1979:** front brake hose may contact and chafe against edges of frame-mounted rebound bumper brackets; may result in hose wear and loss of brake fluid, and subsequent loss of front wheel braking ability, shown by brake warning light and increased pedal travel. **1979:** possible replacement of wrong brake hose that could come in contact with front wheel or tire at extreme turning angle, chafe and rupture, leaking fluid and resulting in loss of front braking ability. **1979:** retaining pin connecting brake pushrod could fall off, resulting in loss of braking. **1979:** possible replacement of power steering gear that could crack and render power steering ineffective. **1979 (302-cid V-8):** flex-blade cooling fan may be improperly riveted; blade could break off fan spider while engine is running. **1979:** coupling rivet pins on lower steering shaft assemblies could work loose, resulting in noticeable free play in steering or loss of control. **1981:** possible that some cars could be started in reverse gear because of faulty neutral safety switch. **1984:** seatbelt anchors may not meet federal safety requirements. **1986–88:** check retainer clips on fuel-line spring-lock couplings of fuel-injected engines. **1987:** steering centerlinks may break at bend location, diminishing control and allowing considerable free play in steering wheel. **1987:** some fuel-injection tube assemblies may be bent, creating potential for fuel leakage and engine fire.

Ford LTD 1983-86

Final version of Ford's rear-drive compact/intermediate design, based on Fairmont/Zephyr chassis, succeeds the 1981–82 Granada/Cougar. Smoother aerodynamic styling with less glitz gives a prestigious look—plus more slippery motion with a good (0.38) coefficient of drag for the sedan. Gas-pressurized front struts and rear shock absorbers improve the ride, but the front end floats too much for real comfort and body roll hinders agile cornering. Base 2.3-liter four delivers agonizingly slow pickup. Optional "Essex" V-6, smooth and quiet, is a better choice, especially with the fuel injection added for 1984. We don't recommend the propane four, since fuel is harder to find and the special tanks add weight. A high performance V-8 became optional late in '84 on the LX sedan. Only the V-6 was available for 1986, LTD's final year. Roomy and comfortable, much improved in fit and finish, this pleasant family car is fairly mannerly on the road. Conservative design may not match front-drive rivals, but for easy motoring, you could do a

Ford

1983 Ford LTD 5-door

lot worse. Mercury Marquis is nearly identical in looks and used-car prices. Although a proven design, MacPherson struts in the front suspension are prone to early failure, the power rack-and-pinion steering tends to leak, and rapid brake pad wear is common.

Price Range	GOOD	AVERAGE	POOR
1983 LTD	$3700–4400	$3200–4000	$2700–3200
1984 LTD	4500–5200	4100–4800	3500–4100
1985 LTD	5700–6600	5100–6200	4600–5100
1986 LTD	7000–7750	6500–7200	6000–6500

1984 Ford LTD LX 4-door

Dimensions	WHEEL-BASE, IN.	LGTH., IN.	HT., IN.	WIDTH, IN.	AVG. WT., LBS.	CARGO VOL., CU. FT.	FUEL TANK, GAL.
4d sdn	105.6	196.5	53.8	71.0	3001	15.1	16.0
5d wgn	105.6	196.5	54.4	71.0	3107	75.4	16.0

Engines	L/CID	BHP	MPG	AVAIL.
ohc I-4 1 bbl.	2.3/140	88–93	17–21	83–85
ohc I-4 propane	2.3/140	—	20–24	83–84
ohv I-6 1 bbl.	3.3/200	87	17–21	83
ohv V-6 2 bbl.	3.8/232	105	16–20	83
ohv V-6 FI	3.8/232	120	17–20	84–86
ohv V-8 FI	5.0/302	165	16–19	84–85

KEY: L/CID = liters/cubic inch displacement; **BHP** = brake horsepower; **MPG** = estimated average miles per gallon; **ohc** = overhead cam; **dohc** = double overhead cam; **ohv** = overhead valve; **I** = in-line engine; **V** = V engine; **flat** = horizontally opposed engine; **D** = diesel; **T** = turbocharged; **bbl.** = barrel (carburetor); **FI** = fuel injection.

RECALL HISTORY

1983: cars with 3.3-liter engine and C-5 automatic transmission, for possibility that vibrations over long period could cause leak in transmission oil cooler line. **1984:** seatbelt anchors may not meet federal safety requirements. **1984–85:** heat shields for catalytic converter outlet pipes were omitted from police-package cars with 5.0-liter fuel-injected engine; after severe duty use, pipes become hot and could ignite certain types of ground cover. **1984–85:** defective ignition module could make 2.3-liter engine hard to start, run poorly or stall. **1985:** rear shell of tandem power brake booster on cars with 3.8- or 5.0-liter engine (except police/taxi) may have thin wall that could crack and come apart after repeated brake use; braking capability would be totally lost without warning.

Ford Mustang 1979-88

Slightly longer than Mustang II, the current generation offers more interior and trunk space, yet weighs about the same as before. Mustang comes in coupe and convertible (since 1983) form, as well as a 3-door hatchback. The similar Mercury Capri (dropped after '86) was sold only as a 3-door. Avoid the weak, noisy base 4-cylinder engine, with its poor repair record. The early turbo four was known to self-destruct before its time, but the reworked turbo available since 1983 has proven more reliable. Be wary of any used turbo, though. Ford's sturdy in-line six replaced the German-made V-6 after 1979, but it's not up to par on

Ford

1979 Ford Mustang 2-door

power. We'd prefer the quieter and torquier 3.8-liter V-6 introduced for 1983, fuel injected the next year. For reliable performance, pick a 302-cid V-8 rather than the 255-cid version. V-8s after 1982 are best, with more power as well as chassis refinements. High-performance GT, reminiscent of early muscle cars, has firmer suspension and wider tires, and a higher price. Also costly today are the convertibles. A potent turbocharged SVO Mustang, introduced for 1984, sold in limited numbers and isn't easy to find on the used car lots. Major restyle hit Mustang for 1987, including new front and rear fascia, aero headlamps, and prominent lower body side moldings. New cylinder heads also helped give the 5.0-liter (302-cid) V-8 an extra 25 horsepower, while the V-6 and turbo disappeared. Watch for leaks in the power rack-and-pinion steering in all models. Verdict: not tops in every area, but good value for the money.

Price Range	GOOD	AVERAGE	POOR
1979 Mustang	$1800–2100	$1500–1800	$1200–1500
1980 Mustang	2200–2600	1900–2300	1500–1900
1981 Mustang	2700–3200	2300–2800	1800–2300
1982 Mustang	3400–4600	3000–4100	2400–3200
1983 Mustang	4000–5600	3600–5100	3000–4000
1983 convertible	7000–8000	6500–7500	6000–6500
1984 Mustang	4800–6600	4500–6000	3800–4900
1984 convertible	8200–9000	7500–8400	6900–7500
1985 Mustang	6000–7800	5300–6900	4800–5600
1985 convertible	9400–10,800	8800–10,000	8000–9000
1986 Mustang	6800–9200	6300–8400	5700–7000
1986 convertible	11,000–12,600	10,000–11,500	9300–10,200

Price Range

Price Range	GOOD	AVERAGE	POOR
1987 Mustang	7800–11,000	7100–9500	6500–8000
1987 convertible	11,750–13,500	11,000–12,500	10,000–11,500
1988 Mustang	9000–12,500	8000–11,000	—
1988 convertible	13,500–16,000	12,500–14,500	—

Dimensions

Dimensions	WHEEL-BASE, IN.	LGTH., IN.	HT., IN.	WIDTH, IN.	AVG. WT., LBS.	CARGO VOL., CU. FT.	FUEL TANK, GAL.
2d cpe	100.5	179.3	52.1	69.1	2700	10.0	15.4
2d conv.	100.5	179.3	52.1	69.1	2975	5.5	15.4
3d cpe	100.5	179.3	52.1	69.1	2800	30.0	15.4
3d SVO	100.5	180.8	52.1	69.1	3250	30.6	15.4

Engines

Engines	L/CID	BHP	MPG	AVAIL.
ohc I-4 1 bbl.	2.3/140	88–93	19–22	79–86
ohc I-4 FI	2.3/140	90	20–24	87–88
ohc I-4 T 1 bbl.	2.3/140	140	16–18	79–81
ohc I-4 T FI	2.3/140	145–205	17–20	83–86
ohv V-6 2 bbl.	2.8/171	109	18–21	79
ohv I-6 1 bbl.	3.3/200	88–91	18–21	79–82
ohv V-6 2 bbl.	3.8/232	105	16–19	83
ohv V-6 FI	3.8/232	120	16–20	84–86
ohv V-8 2 bbl.	4.2/255	111–120	15–18	80–82
ohv V-8 2 bbl.	5.0/302	140–155	13–16	79,82
ohv V-8 4 bbl.	5.0/302	175–210	12–15	83–85
ohv V-8 FI	5.0/302	180–225	13–18	85–88

KEY: L/CID = liters/cubic inch displacement; **BHP** = brake horsepower; **MPG** = estimated average miles per gallon; **ohc** = overhead cam; **dohc** = double overhead cam; **ohv** = overhead valve; **I** = in-line engine; **V** = V engine; **flat** = horizontally opposed engine; **D** = diesel; **T** = turbocharged; **bbl.** = barrel (carburetor); **FI** = fuel injection.

1983 Ford Mustang convertible

Ford
RECALL HISTORY

1979: replacement of plastic fan guard, which may break if it comes in contact with fan. **1979:** correction of improper steering coupling, which could impede steering. **1979 (5.0-liter V-8):** flex-blade cooling fan could crack at high engine speeds and break into fragments. **1979:** replacement of brake pushrod retaining pin, which could fall off and result in loss of braking ability. **1981:** replace choke pull-down motor on 4.2-liter V-8 to ensure acceptable emissions. **1981:** modify air injection as needed to ensure acceptable emissions. **1984:** secondary throttle shaft of carburetor may, with accumulated mileage, be susceptible to dirt contamination and wear of bearing coatings; could allow throttle plates to remain partly open after releasing gas pedal. **1984:** seatbelt anchors may not meet federal safety requirements. **1984-85:** defective ignition module could make 2.3-liter engine hard to start, run poorly or stall. **1985:** rear shell of tandem power brake booster on cars with 3.8- or 5.0-liter engine (except police/taxi) may have thin wall that could crack and come apart after repeated brake use; braking ability would be totally lost without warning. **1986-88:** check retainer clips on fuel-line spring-lock couplings of fuel-injected engines.

Ford Pinto and Mercury Bobcat 1978-80

Unsafe gas tank and fuel filler neck on earlier versions of the rear-drive subcompact cost Ford plenty in both dollars and bad publicity. Later models are adequate, if basic.

1978 Ford Pinto 3-door

Once described as "a car nobody loved, but everybody bought," used examples remain plentiful. Bobcat is plusher of the duo, sporting silly Lincolnesque grille. Short wheelbase and simple suspension add up to rough riding on the bumps. Low seats in tight interior give feeling of sitting in a bathtub. Handles pretty well, though steering is heavy while parking. If you need cargo space, look for a 3-door runabout or wagon rather than the tiny-trunk 2-door sedan. Repair record has been average; upkeep costs lower than average. Still, the 4-cylinder engine has a reputation for premature camshaft wear, loose rack-and-pinion steering mounting bushings may cause steering problems, and bodies are extremely rust-prone. Four-cylinder 1978 models have history of engine, exhaust and automatic transmission troubles, as well as body squeaks.

Price Range	GOOD	AVERAGE	POOR
1978 Pinto	$900–1100	$600–900	$350–600
1978 Bobcat	900–1150	650–900	400–650
1979 Pinto	1000–1300	800–1000	450–800
1979 Bobcat	1050–1350	850–1050	500–850
1980 Pinto	1300–1600	1000–1300	800–1000
1980 Bobcat	1250–1500	1050–1250	800–1050

Dimensions	WHEEL-BASE, IN.	LGTH., IN.	HT., IN.	WIDTH, IN.	AVG. WT., LBS.	CARGO VOL., CU. FT.	FUEL TANK, GAL.
2d sdn	94.5	170.8	50.6	69.4	2070	8.2	13.0
3d sdn	94.5	170.8	50.6	69.4	2070	29.0	13.0
3d wgn	94.8	180.6	52.1	69.4	2550	57.2	14.0

1979 Mercury Bobcat 3-door

Ford

Engines	L/CID	BHP	MPG	AVAIL.
ohc I-4 2 bbl.	2.3/140	82–89	22–25	78–80
ohv V-6 2 bbl.	2.8/171	90–103	18–21	78–79

KEY: L/CID = liters/cubic inch displacement; **BHP** = brake horsepower; **MPG** = estimated average miles per gallon; **ohc** = overhead cam; **dohc** = double overhead cam; **ohv** = overhead valve; **I** = in-line engine; **V** = V engine; **flat** = horizontally opposed engine; **D** = diesel; **T** = turbocharged; **bbl.** = barrel (carburetor); **FI** = fuel injection.

RECALL HISTORY

1978: automatic locking rear seatbelt retractors may fail to lock due to binding of locking pawl, thus failing to meet federal safety standards.

Ford Taurus 1986-88

1987 Ford Taurus 4-door

Ford not only gave its designers freedom to create a memorable vehicle, but surveyed potential customers about design preferences. That effort has paid off. The slick, aerodynamic Taurus found plenty of eager buyers from the start—but even more in its second season. Sales almost doubled for 1987, making Taurus the second best-selling car in the country, after the No. 1 Ford Escort. On the used-car lots, it's bound to make a similar splash. Though corporate cousin Mercury Sable looks similar, the two sedans share no sheetmetal at all, while wagons use the same panels only from the windshield back. We consider these to be the most impressive new domestic cars to arrive in a long while. Both combine contemporary design with a spacious interior, and behave mannerly on the road. Taurus corners nicely, and its moderately firm power steering responds instantly. The firm ride, approaching that of European sedans, is just right on the highway, though you can expect a few bumps on rougher surfaces. Noisy base 4-cylinder engine isn't strong enough for the car, especially with 3-speed automatic transmission. The 3.0-liter V-6, standard on top-level LX and optional on others, promises much brisker passing power (though standing-start pickup is less impressive). A new 3.8 V-6 with balance shaft, optional with 4-speed overdrive automatic on most models for '88, has the same horsepower as the 3.0 but a lot more torque, so performance should be swifter yet. Headroom is ample all around, and adult legs fit in the back. Sedans have a deep, wide trunk. We've had problems with rough idling and slow downshifting with the automatic, as well as inadequate heat distribution (at least on early models). Recalls have been numerous, too, though some affect only a small number of cars. Verdict: the well-designed Taurus is great to look at and a joy to drive. We recommend it over several imports that cost more.

Price Range	GOOD	AVERAGE	POOR
1986 Taurus	$8900–12,000	$8400–11,000	$7800–8700
1987 Taurus	10,300–14,000	9500–12,750	9000–10,500
1988 Taurus	11,500–15,500	10,500–14,500	—

Dimensions	WHEEL-BASE, IN.	LGTH., IN.	HT., IN.	WIDTH, IN.	AVG. WT., LBS.	CARGO VOL. CU. FT.	FUEL TANK, GAL.
4d sdn	106.0	188.4	54.3	70.6	2982	17.0	16.0
5d wgn	106.0	188.4	55.1	70.6	3186	45.7	16.0

Engines	L/CID	BHP	MPG	AVAIL.
ohv I-4 FI	2.5/153	88–90	21–26	86–88
ohv V-6 FI	3.0/182	140	20–25	86–88
ohv V-6 FI	3.8/232	140	NA	88

KEY: L/CID = liters/cubic inch displacement; **BHP** = brake horsepower; **MPG** = estimated average miles per gallon; **ohc** = overhead cam; **dohc** = double overhead cam; **ohv** = overhead valve; **I** = in-line engine; **V** = V engine; **flat** = horizontally opposed engine; **D** = diesel; **T** = turbocharged; **bbl.** = barrel (carburetor); **FI** = fuel injection.

RECALL HISTORY

1986: ignition key on some cars might be removable when the ignition switch is in other than the lock position. **1986:** defective resistor in engine cooling-fan motor circuit could cause air con-

Ford

1987 Ford Taurus 5-door

ditioner problems. **1986:** some cars may have misrouted battery wire that could allow battery current to corrode radiator, possibly leading to radiator leaks. **1986 wagon:** right quarter window may contain tinted glass that was improperly tempered, possibly causing injury in event of accident. **1986-87:** replacement of some 3.0-liter V-6 engines because of problem with piston knock in cold weather during break-in period. **1986-87:** on station wagon with optional rear wiper, under certain conditions, road salt might seep through lower window seal and damage electrical connections; localized thermal stress could then fracture the glass and create risk of injury. **1986-88:** check retainer clips on fuel-line spring-lock couplings of fuel-injected engines. **1987:** lower steering shafts on some cars are too short and could separate, resulting in loss of steering control. **1987:** a few rear spindle assemblies may have been improperly heat treated and could break and separate, causing loss of control without warning.

Ford Tempo 1984-88

Front-drive compact replacement for the rear-drive Fairmont offers distinctive (if controversial) aerodynamic styling over a roomy interior. Mercury Topaz differs only in trim and option list. Chassis is a stretched version of the Escort/Lynx, but with different independent rear suspension. Base 2.3-liter 4-cylinder engine, derived from Ford's in-line six, had a carburetor in 1984, fuel injection the next year. Either way, it lacks the torque to deliver brisk pickup or top mileage when hooked to automatic transmission—which is how most Tempos have been sold. A high-output four, offered only with 5-speed manual shift in the

1984 Ford Tempo 4-door

Sport GL package (GLS series in 1988), performs better without much loss in economy. Not so many of those, or of the Mazda-built diesel engines, are likely to be available. Latest editions should move more swiftly, since both engines get multi-point fuel injection for 1988 and the base version gains 12 horsepower. Four adults fit easily enough in an interior that's rather dark—almost claustrophobic. Low front seats don't allow the most relaxed driving position. Handling is humdrum, but front-drive produces good foul-weather traction. New in 1987 was a part-time 4-wheel-drive option with "shift-on-the-fly" capability; a dashboard switch adds traction when needed. Major '88 aero-look restyle includes new body panels and revised windows on 4-door; two-slot grille and integrated aero headlamps on both bodies. We've been impressed by quality of materials and attention to assembly detail, although rear wheel misalignment is fairly common. Tempo has sold pretty well and is priced reasonably, even with options. If only the early engine had more zip, we'd recommend it without reservation.

Price Range	GOOD	AVERAGE	POOR
1984 Tempo	$3800–4400	$3400–4000	$2700–3400
1985 Tempo	5000–5900	4500–5300	3900–4500
1986 Tempo	6200–6900	5700–6300	5000–5700
1987 Tempo	7700–9000	7000–8000	6400–7200
1988 Tempo	9000–10,500	8000–9500	—

Ford

1985 Ford Tempo 2-door

Dimensions	WHEEL-BASE, IN.	LGTH., IN.	HT., IN.	WIDTH, IN.	AVG. WT., LBS.	CARGO VOL., CU. FT.	FUEL TANK, GAL.
2d sdn	99.9	176.2	52.7	68.3	2381	13.2	15.2
4d sdn	99.9	176.2	52.7	68.3	2438	12.9	15.2

Engines	L/CID	BHP	MPG	AVAIL.
ohv I-4 2 bbl.	2.3/141	84	22–27	84
ohv I-4 FI	2.3/141	86–98	22–27	85–88
ohv I-4 FI	2.3/141	94–100	22–26	85–88
ohc I-4D FI	2.0/121	52	32–36	84–86

KEY: L/CID = liters/cubic inch displacement; **BHP** = brake horsepower; **MPG** = estimated average miles per gallon; **ohc** = overhead cam; **dohc** = double overhead cam; **ohv** = overhead valve; **I** = in-line engine; **V** = V engine; **flat** = horizontally opposed engine; **D** = diesel; **T** = turbocharged; **bbl.** = barrel (carburetor); **FI** = fuel injection.

RECALL HISTORY

1984: front seatbelt webbing on 4-door cars without reclining seats could be cut or severed in a severe frontal crash. **1984:** forward bolt that partly attaches driver's seat back assembly to seat cushion frame may be subject to fatigue fracture; if bolt breaks, seat back will fall backward, which could result in driver losing control. **1984–85:** rear suspension control arm-to-spindle attachment bolts may be subject to fracture during car use; spindle could then disengage, possibly resulting in loss of control. **1984-85:** defective ignition module could make 2.3-liter engine hard to start, run poorly or stall. **1985-86:** stiffness of thick rubber material that covers gearshift on manual transmission may push shift lever out of gear and toward neutral, when operated in cold weather (under 40° F). **1986:** on cars with 2.3-liter engine (non-California) and automatic transmission, intermittent timing in the electronic engine control processor may cause throttle to remain partly open, resulting in unexpected increase in engine speed. **1987:** disturbance in electronic control module of 2.3-liter engine (manual shift) may cause high idling speed, loss of power and, eventually, engine may stop running. **1987:** stainless steel decorative lug nuts on small number of cars might gall and seize on wheel studs, without providing adequate clamping; studs could fracture, creating risk of wheel falling off.

Ford Thunderbird 1978-79

Mid-size T-Bird, far more economical and maneuverable than its oversize predecessor, is little more than an adaptation of LTD II coupe, which differs mainly in styling and equipment. Visibility was much better, trunk bigger, back seat roomier than before. Good repair record shows no serious trouble spots other than paint deterioration and early rust, plus alloy wheels that corrode, making wheel removal extremely difficult. Durability of body, brakes, engines and exhaust systems is above average. Doesn't quite measure up to comparable GM personal-luxury coupes, though, except in size and price.

Price Range	GOOD	AVERAGE	POOR
1978 Thunderbird	$1800–2300	$1400–1800	$1100–1400
1979 Thunderbird	2100–2500	1700–2100	1400–1700

Dimensions	WHEEL-BASE, IN.	LGTH., IN.	HT., IN.	WIDTH, IN.	AVG. WT., LBS.	CARGO VOL., CU. FT.	FUEL TANK, GAL.
2d cpe	114.0	215.5	53.0	78.5	4263	15.6	21.0

1978 Ford Thunderbird 2-door

Ford

1979 Ford Thunderbird 2-door

Engines	L/CID	BHP	MPG	AVAIL.
ohv V-8 2 bbl.	5.0/302	130	15–18	78–79
ohv V-8 2 bbl.	5.8/351	149	14–17	78–79
ohv V-8 2 bbl.	5.8/351	161	13–16	78–79
ohv V-8 2 bbl.	6.6/400	173	12–15	78

KEY: L/CID = liters/cubic inch displacement; **BHP** = brake horsepower; **MPG** = estimated average miles per gallon; **ohc** = overhead cam; **dohc** = double overhead cam; **ohv** = overhead valve; **I** = in-line engine; **V** = V engine; **flat** = horizontally opposed engine; **D** = diesel; **T** = turbocharged; **bbl.** = barrel (carburetor); **FI** = fuel injection.

RECALL HISTORY

1978: front outboard seatbelt assemblies may have shoulder harness retractors that don't lock; also, some retractors may not allow extraction of shoulder belt webbing due to prelocked condition. **1979:** some vehicles may have brake pushrod-to-pedal pins that could fall out, resulting in loss of braking capability. **1979:** some power steering gears may have improperly manufactured sector shafts that could cause loss of steering control.

Ford Thunderbird 1980-82

Stylish mid-size coupe shrunk by more than a foot in length and lost a few pounds for 1980. Both T-Bird and its companion Mercury Cougar XR-7 now rode a stretched Fairmont/Zephyr platform. Fuel economy got a boost, but not enough to beat usual rivals. Slightly tighter interior still seats four adults nicely. Rack-and-pinion steering with revised all-coil suspension improves handling and control, but a Bird still lags in agility. Switch to unit construction made ride noisier, but it's still a refined automobile. Formal roof

1980 Ford Thunderbird 2-door

nearly cuts off over-the-shoulder visibility. Familiar 200-cid inline six gives swifter pickup than expected, but little mileage improvement over a V-8. A 232-cid V-6, offered in 1982, disappoints both ways. Electrical, brake, suspension, and body hardware problems appear more often than usual on 1980–81 V-8 models, and the variable venturi carburetor on the 302 V-8 was trouble-prone and difficult to repair. Apart from a rather bulky baroque form, this Bird is a fairly sensible stab at a type of vehicle that doesn't really excite us. Overall, though, a Buick Regal or Olds Cutlass Supreme might prove more capable. So would the redesigned 1983 T-Bird.

Price Range	GOOD	AVERAGE	POOR
1980 Thunderbird	$2700–3100	$2200–2700	$1800–2200
1981 Thunderbird	3300–3800	2800–3500	2300–2800
1982 Thunderbird	3900–4900	3500–4400	3000–3600

1980 Ford Thunderbird 2-door

Ford

Dimensions	WHEEL-BASE, IN.	LGTH., IN.	HT., IN.	WIDTH, IN.	AVG. WT., LBS.	CARGO VOL. CU. FT.	FUEL TANK, GAL.
2d cpe	108.4	200.4	53.0	74.1	3262	17.7	17.5

Engines	L/CID	BHP	MPG	AVAIL.
ohv I-6 1 bbl.	3.3/200	88	18–21	81–82
ohv V-6 2 bbl.	3.8/232	112	16–20	82
ohv V-8 2 bbl.	4.2/255	111–120	17–20	80–82
ohv V-8 2 bbl.	5.0/302	131	16–19	80–81

KEY: L/CID = liters/cubic inch displacement; **BHP** = brake horsepower; **MPG** = estimated average miles per gallon; **ohc** = overhead cam; **dohc** = double overhead cam; **ohv** = overhead valve; **I** = in-line engine; **V** = V engine; **flat** = horizontally opposed engine; **D** = diesel; **T** = turbocharged; **bbl.** = barrel (carburetor); **FI** = fuel injection.

RECALL HISTORY

1980: some vehicles may be equipped with smaller rear brake assemblies intended for Mustangs. **1981:** replace choke pull-down motor on 4.2- or 5.0-liter engine to ensure acceptable emissions.

Ford Thunderbird 1983-88

1985 Ford Thunderbird Turbo Coupe

Freshly restyled personal-luxury coupe gained more aerodynamic form and lost a bit of bulk. Mercury Cougar, its corporate twin, differs little. Base drivetrain is Ford's 3.8-liter V-6 engine with 3-speed automatic transmission. Options include a fuel-injected V-8 and 4-speed overdrive automatic (standard for '87). Turbo Coupe, powered by a 2.3-

liter turbocharged four with port fuel injection, hit the T-Bird scene for 1983 riding a special handling chassis with bigger tires and "Quadra-Shock" rear suspension. Softer standard chassis allows a lot more lean but cornering ability is still decent, ride steady and relaxed. Refined motoring is seldom marred by noise, except from the harsh turbo engine, which seems out of place in a luxury car of this caliber. Comfortable interiors are plusher yet in upscale Elan and Fila models. All-new sheetmetal altered '87 T-Bird's appearance, while Turbo Coupe got anti-lock brakes and a 190-horsepower intercooled engine. Base V-6 gained multi-point fuel injection and 20 horsepower for '88, along with a balance shaft for smoother running; V-8 versions added dual exhausts. Construction quality seems as good as advertised, although spring sag has been a problem on some models. Not cheap, but we believe the latest T-Birds offer more value than equivalent GM rear-drive coupes.

Price Range	GOOD	AVERAGE	POOR
1983 Thunderbird	$5100–6300	$4700–5800	$4100–5000
1984 Thunderbird	6200–7500	5700–7000	5000–5800
1985 Thunderbird	7600–9000	7000–8300	6400–7200
1986 Thunderbird	9000–11,000	8300–10,000	7700–8500
1987 Thunderbird	10,500–13,000	9800–12,000	9000–10,000
1988 Thunderbird	13,000–16,000	11,500—15,000	—

Dimensions	WHEEL-BASE, IN.	LGTH., IN.	HT., IN.	WIDTH, IN.	AVG. WT., LBS.	CARGO VOL., CU. FT.	FUEL TANK, GAL.
2d cpe	104.0	197.6	53.2	71.1	3069	14.6	20.6

1987 Ford Thunderbird 2-door

Ford • Honda

Engines	L/CID	BHP	MPG	AVAIL.
ohc I-4T FI	2.3/140	145–150	21–26	83–87
ohc I-4T FI	2.3/140	190	18–23	87–88
ohv V-6 2 bbl.	3.8/232	105	17–22	83
ohv V-6 FI	3.8/232	120–140	17–22	84–88
ohv V-8 FI	5.0/302	140–150	16–21	84–88

KEY: L/CID = liters/cubic inch displacement; **BHP** = brake horsepower; **MPG** = estimated average miles per gallon; **ohc** = overhead cam; **dohc** = double overhead cam; **ohv** = overhead valve; **I** = in-line engine; **V** = V engine; **flat** = horizontally opposed engine; **D** = diesel; **T** = turbocharged; **bbl.** = barrel (carburetor); **FI** = fuel injection.

RECALL HISTORY

1984-85: defective ignition module could make 2.3-liter engine hard to start, run poorly or stall. **1985:** improperly anodized internal surfaces of master cylinder may accelerate wear of piston seal, rendering one portion of split-brake system ineffective. **1986-88:** check retainer clips on fuel-line spring-lock couplings of fuel-injected engines. **1987 Turbo Coupe:** problem with cylinder honing at Brazil plant resulted in severe oil consumption on small number of early models with 2.3-liter turbo four.

Honda Accord 1978-81

Enlarged rendition of the Civic concept uses compact front-wheel-drive layout with transverse engine for a spacious interior. Early versions lacked get-up-and-go, but 1979–81 Accords with 1.8-liter four move a lot more swiftly with little economy loss. Handling is stable and responsive. Front seats are comfortable, dash convenient, back tight

1978 Honda Accord 3-door

for adults. Hatchback rear seat folds down. Notchback sedan, introduced for 1979, has small trunk. All are well-equipped, especially sedans and LX coupe. Repair history above average (or better), but 1978s have exhaust system problems, rust is common for 1978–79, overheating attacks many '79s, and 1980–81 models have carburetor flooding problems and brake ills. Regular valve adjustment (about every 15,000 miles) is essential to prevent engine problems. Prices are hefty but workmanship is fine, making Accord a good value. Inspect closely for signs of body corrosion and engine wear before you buy.

Price Range	GOOD	AVERAGE	POOR
1978 Accord	$1500–1900	$1100–1500	$900–1100
1979 Accord	1800–2250	1400–1900	1150–1400
1980 Accord	2400–2700	2000–2500	1600–2000
1981 Accord	3000–3800	2700–3400	2300–2700

Dimensions	WHEEL-BASE, IN.	LGTH., IN.	HT., IN.	WIDTH, IN.	AVG. WT., LBS.	CARGO VOL. CU. FT.	FUEL TANK, GAL.
3d cpe	93.7	162.8	52.3	63.8	2024	8.4	13.0
4d sdn	93.7	171.9	53.3	63.8	2239	13.0	13.2

Engines	L/CID	BHP	MPG	AVAIL.
ohc I-4 3 bbl.	1.6/98	68	29–32	78
ohc I-4 3 bbl.	1.8/107	72	26–30	79–81

KEY: L/CID = liters/cubic inch displacement; **BHP** = brake horsepower; **MPG** = estimated average miles per gallon; **ohc** = overhead cam; **dohc** = double overhead cam; **ohv** = overhead valve; **I** = in-line engine; **V** = V engine; **flat** = horizontally opposed engine; **D** = diesel; **T** = turbocharged; **bbl.** = barrel (carburetor); **FI** = fuel injection.

1981 Honda Accord 4-door

Honda

RECALL HISTORY

1978: repair or replacement of front fenders that could rust prematurely. **1978–79:** repair or replacement of front suspension components that could rust prematurely.

Honda Accord 1982-83

1983 Honda Accord 3-door

Second-edition Accord was longer, lower and wider, gaining passenger and trunk space, but changed little mechanically. Smooth, eager 1.8-liter four delivers snappy pickup and high mileage: toward upper 20s with automatic, around 30 mpg with 5-speed manual shift. Dash is modern and attractive; interior nicely trimmed, but tight in back for adults. Tastefully styled with good road manners and fine reliability, plus repair record far above average. Accords are in high demand—hard to find and expensive. Few problems include hard starting (especially in cold weather), brake rotor warpage, flawed brake backing plates, and typical Honda rust. Also, valve adjustment every 15,000 miles is essential to prevent engine problems. One thing for sure: you won't have trouble finding a buyer when you want to resell.

Price Range	GOOD	AVERAGE	POOR
1982 Accord	$3800–4600	$3400–4100	$2900–3500
1983 Accord	4900–5800	4500–5400	3800–4600

1983 Honda Accord 4-door

Dimensions	WHEEL-BASE, IN.	LGTH., IN.	HT., IN.	WIDTH, IN.	AVG. WT., LBS.	CARGO VOL., CU. FT.	FUEL TANK, GAL.
3d cpe	96.5	165.8	53.3	65.4	2150	NA	15.8
4d sdn	96.5	173.6	54.1	65.4	2170	NA	15.8

Engines	L/CID	BHP	MPG	AVAIL.
ohc I-4 3 bbl.	1.8/107	75	26–30	82–83

KEY: L/CID = liters/cubic inch displacement; **BHP** = brake horsepower; **MPG** = estimated average miles per gallon; **ohc** = overhead cam; **dohc** = double overhead cam; **ohv** = overhead valve; **I** = in-line engine; **V** = V engine; **flat** = horizontally opposed engine; **D** = diesel; **T** = turbocharged; **bbl.** = barrel (carburetor); **FI** = fuel injection.

RECALL HISTORY

1982: wire in charging circuit is of insufficient diameter to handle maximum alternator current; long-term operation under high loads results in heat buildup at terminal area, which could cause short circuit that may damage wire harness and allow battery to become discharged.

Honda Accord 1984-85

Continuation of the previous Accord received new styling and larger engines, but lost none of the pluses of its predecessors—including strong fuel economy. New 1.8-liter four has three valves per cylinder and a single carburetor. (The Prelude version uses twin carbs.) Hatchbacks gained firmer suspension with a rear stabilizer bar for a sportier

Honda

1984 Honda Accord 4-door

feel. New LX sedan's list of standard gear included air conditioning, power windows/locks, and premium stereo. For 1985 a new luxury leader, the SE-i sedan, added fuel injection, power sunroof and leather seats to the LX equipment, all for a price nearly $3000 higher. Made both in Japan and in Ohio, Accord became one of the top 10 sellers by 1984. With demand topping supply, most Accords sold for well above suggested retail price. Used examples aren't cheap either, but buyers seem eager to pay the price. If anything, Honda is doing a better job than before. We can't discern any differences on models made in America. Squealing brakes were a problem on 1984 and some 1985 models due to defective brake backing plates. Also, be ad-

1985 Honda Accord 4-door

vised that regular valve adjustment (every 15,000 miles) is essential to prevent engine problems.

Price Range	GOOD	AVERAGE	POOR
1984 Accord	$5900–7600	$5400–6800	$4800–5700
1985 Accord	7000–9000	6500–8400	5800–7000

Dimensions	WHEEL-BASE, IN.	LGTH., IN.	HT., IN.	WIDTH, IN.	AVG. WT., LBS.	CARGO VOL., CU. FT.	FUEL TANK, GAL.
3d cpe	96.5	167.5	53.3	65.2	2187	27.3	15.8
4d sdn	96.5	175.4	54.1	65.2	2271	13.3	15.8

Engines	L/CID	BHP	MPG	AVAIL.
ohc I-4 3 bbl.	1.8/113	86	24–29	84–85
ohc I-4 FI	1.8/113	101	24–30	85

KEY: L/CID = liters/cubic inch displacement; **BHP** = brake horsepower; **MPG** = estimated average miles per gallon; **ohc** = overhead cam; **dohc** = double overhead cam; **ohv** = overhead valve; **I** = in-line engine; **V** = V engine; **flat** = horizontally opposed engine; **D** = diesel; **T** = turbocharged; **bbl.** = barrel (carburetor); **FI** = fuel injection.

RECALL HISTORY

1984: voltage regulators may contain wrong parts, allowing battery to overcharge, which could result in damage to battery and sudden loss of electrical power.

Honda Accord 1986-88

Latest version of Honda's top seller is a little larger and heavier, more aerodynamically styled, and powered by a bigger (2.0-liter) 4-cylinder engine. Extra length adds leg room in back, so everybody can now enjoy Accord's comfortable ride. Headroom remains tight for tall folks, especially with a sunroof. Roomy trunk has a flat floor and low liftover for easy loading. Performance, while not bad at all, hasn't improved much since added car weight offsets the power increase. With port fuel injection replacing the carburetor, though, the top-line LXi acts more lively than its mates; all the more so in 1988 when it gets a horsepower boost and firmer suspension. Both engines are adequate with automatic, delivering impressive fuel mileage. Though not a sport sedan, Accord handles nicely and is quite agile, absorbing bumps well, though it can get bouncy on rippled pavement. Tire roar on the highway grows annoying, but engine and wind noise are minimal. Generous standard equipment contributes to high prices when new—and at

Honda

1986 Honda Accord DX 4-door

1987 Honda Accord LXi 3-door

the used car lot later. Sedan has proven much more popular than hatchback body. Verdict: one of the most capable, refined family compact cars you're likely to find, well worth its high price. You get all the expected Accord virtues—smooth engine, good mileage, stable handling, pliant ride—plus a more contemporary look, more luggage space, and strong resale value.

Price Range	GOOD	AVERAGE	POOR
1986 Accord	$8000–11,000	$7400–10,000	$6800–8000
1987 Accord	9250–12,500	8600–11,500	8000–9500
1988 Accord	10,500–15,000	9700–14,000	—

Dimensions	WHEEL-BASE, IN.	LGTH., IN.	HT., IN.	WIDTH, IN.	AVG. WT., LBS.	CARGO VOL., CU. FT.	FUEL TANK, GAL.
3d cpe	102.4	174.8	52.6	66.7	2454	19.0	15.8
4d sdn	102.4	178.5	53.3	66.7	2568	14.0	15.8

Engines	L/CID	BHP	MPG	AVAIL.
ohc I-4 2 bbl.	2.0/119	98	24–29	86–88
ohc I-4 FI	2.0/119	110–122	23–28	86–88

KEY: L/CID = liters/cubic inch displacement; **BHP** = brake horsepower; **MPG** = estimated average miles per gallon; **ohc** = overhead cam; **dohc** = double overhead cam; **ohv** = overhead valve; **I** = in-line engine; **V** = V engine; **flat** = horizontally opposed engine; **D** = diesel; **T** = turbocharged; **bbl.** = barrel (carburetor); **FI** = fuel injection.

RECALL HISTORY

None to date.

Honda Civic 1978-79

1978 Honda Civic 5-door

Pioneer front-drive/transverse-engine econocar arrived in the U.S. for 1973. CVCC models have a 1.5-liter (91-cid) engine that uses stratified-charge principle to blend good performance and top gas mileage with low emissions. Handling is a delight, ride not bad for a car so short and light. Workmanship good, but trim on some early models looks cheap. Paint fade, rust, squeaks, rattles, engine and exhaust troubles appear more often than average. CVCCs are less trouble-prone, except for cranky carburetors and air conditioner ills. Head gasket failure on 1978-79 engines was common and front brake rotors are hard to service. Valves must be adjusted every 15,000 miles to prevent engine problems. Avoid semi-automatic transmission, which cuts economy and performance. Shop around for a

Honda

1979 Honda Civic 3-door

Civic in good shape and you'll have a practical car for few dollars.

Price Range	GOOD	AVERAGE	POOR
1978 Civic	$1000–1400	$750–1000	$500–700
1979 Civic	1250–1700	900–1250	600–900

Dimensions	WHEEL-BASE, IN.	LGTH., IN.	HT., IN.	WIDTH, IN.	AVG. WT., LBS.	CARGO VOL., CU. FT.	FUEL TANK, GAL.
2d/3d sdn	86.6	146.9	52.3	59.3	1630	7.0	10.0
5d wgn	89.8	159.5	54.1	59.3	1980	NA	11.0

Engines	L/CID	BHP	MPG	AVAIL.
ohc I-4 2 bbl.	1.2/76	52–59	28–33	78–79
ohc I-4 3 bbl.	1.5/91	64	27–32	78–79

KEY: L/CID = liters/cubic inch displacement; **BHP** = brake horsepower; **MPG** = estimated average miles per gallon; **ohc** = overhead cam; **dohc** = double overhead cam; **ohv** = overhead valve; **I** = in-line engine; **V** = V engine; **flat** = horizontally opposed engine; **D** = diesel; **T** = turbocharged; **bbl.** = barrel (carburetor); **FI** = fuel injection.

RECALL HISTORY

1978: repair or replacement of front fenders that could rust prematurely. **1978–79:** repair or replacement of front suspension components that could rust prematurely.

Honda Civic 1980-83

Honda's economy leader grew slightly in 1980 revision, but the well-built, intelligent design still returns super fuel mileage with sprightly handling. Reworked engine, no longer called CVCC but retaining the stratified-charge cylinder head, is a smooth and mannerly performer. Both 1.3- and 1.5-liter versions yield similar economy. Slick 5-speed overdrive manual shift is better choice than the inept automatic. Notchback 4-door sedan, which joined hatchback and 5-door wagon for 1981, is most costly now. Fine early reliability record except for brake repairs on 1980 models, which might be a weak point on newer Civics too. Carburetor flooding was common on some 1980–81 models due to defective carburetor floats. Valves must be adjusted every 15,000 miles to prevent engine problems. No matter: we recommend them highly as the best of the 1980s minicars.

Price Range	GOOD	AVERAGE	POOR
1980 Civic	$1600–2200	$1250–1900	$1000–1300
1981 Civic	2000–2750	1500–2400	1200–1600
1982 Civic	2500–3500	2100–3100	1700–2300
1983 Civic	3100–4300	2600–3700	2200–2800

1981 Honda Civic 4-door

1981 Honda Civic 5-door

Honda

Dimensions	WHEEL-BASE, IN.	LGTH., IN.	HT., IN.	WIDTH, IN.	AVG. WT., LBS.	CARGO VOL., CU. FT.	FUEL TANK, GAL.
3d sdn	88.6	148.0	53.0	62.2	1832	20.7	10.8
4d sdn	91.3	161.0	53.0	62.2	1950	10.5	12.1
5d wgn	91.3	160.8	54.2	62.2	1956	26.7	10.8

Engines	L/CID	BHP	MPG	AVAIL.
ohc I-4 3 bbl.	1.3/81	58–62	30–35	80–83
ohc I-4 3 bbl.	1.5/91	67–69	28–33	80–83

KEY: L/CID = liters/cubic inch displacement; **BHP** = brake horsepower; **MPG** = estimated average miles per gallon; **ohc** = overhead cam; **dohc** = double overhead cam; **ohv** = overhead valve; **I** = in-line engine; **V** = V engine; **flat** = horizontally opposed engine; **D** = diesel; **T** = turbocharged; **bbl.** = barrel (carburetor); **FI** = fuel injection.

RECALL HISTORY

None to date.

Honda Civic 1984-87

1984 Honda Civic S 3-door

New front-drive platform, five inches longer in wheelbase, gave third-generation Civic considerably more passenger and luggage space, especially on the 4-door sedan and "tall boy" wagon. Entry-level hatchbacks are powered by a new aluminum-block 1.3-liter four with the old CVCC cylinder head. Other models carry an energetic new 1.5-liter aluminum four with three valves per cylinder, which deliv-

ers snappy acceleration along with refinement unheard of
in this league. Revised suspension includes struts and torsion bars up front, but a beam axle in back. Upright wagon
styling allows six-footers to sit comfortably, front or rear.
A 4-wheel-drive wagon debuted in mid-1985. Drive to the
rear wheels on the '87 version engages automatically on
slippery roads. For 1986, a sporty new Civic Si got the
fuel-injected engine from the CRX Si plus a sunroof, spoiler
and air dam. Civic's good handling lets you feel like you're
at the wheel of a sport sedan rather than an econocar. Ride
is stable, if a bit firm for city driving. Poor sound insulation
in hatchbacks lets in too much road/wind noise, but we
can't find much else to complain about. Regular valve adjustment is vital to prevent engine problems. Some 1987
sedans were built in Ohio. In design and execution, this
Civic ranks at the top of our list. Redesigned for 1988 on
longer wheelbase, with 16-valve engine. Honda has also
stopped importing the low-priced 1.3-liter hatchback.

Price Range	GOOD	AVERAGE	POOR
1984 Civic	$3900–5200	$3500–4800	$3000–3700
1985 Civic	4800–6300	4300–5800	3800–4500
1986 Civic	5800–7400	5000–6800	4500–5300
1987 Civic	6400–8800	5800–8300	5300–6500

Dimensions	WHEELBASE, IN.	LGTH., IN.	HT., IN.	WIDTH, IN.	AVG. WT., LBS.	CARGO VOL., CU. FT.	FUEL TANK, GAL.
3d sdn	93.7	150.0	52.6	64.0	1863	14.5	11.9
4d sdn	96.5	163.4	54.5	64.0	1940	12.1	12.1
5d wgn	96.5	157.1	58.3	63.9	2015	56.6	12.1

1984 Honda Civic 5-door

Honda

Engines	L/CID	BHP	MPG	AVAIL.
ohc I-4 3 bbl.	1.3/81	60	28–33	84–87
ohc I-4 3 bbl.	1.5/91	76	27–32	84–87
ohc I-4 FI	1.5/91	91	28–32	86–87

KEY: L/CID = liters/cubic inch displacement; **BHP** = brake horsepower; **MPG** = estimated average miles per gallon; **ohc** = overhead cam; **dohc** = double overhead cam; **ohv** = overhead valve; **I** = in-line engine; **V** = V engine; **flat** = horizontally opposed engine; **D** = diesel; **T** = turbocharged; **bbl.** = barrel (carburetor); **FI** = fuel injection.

RECALL HISTORY

1984: hood could open suddenly while car is moving because of faulty safety latch. **1984, 1986:** left side driveshaft could crack under high stress, causing sudden loss of power.

Honda Civic CRX 1984-87

1984 Honda Civic CRX 3-door

Honda's featherweight two-seat sport coupe manages to pack high mileage and peppy action into a low-cost package that handles like a sports car. CRX topped the EPA mileage race in 1984 and '85 with two different aluminum engines: first a 1.3-liter four with three valves per cylinder, next a 1.5 with the old CVCC cylinder head. Also available: a free-revving, high-output 1.5-liter four with the 12-valve head—the only engine used with automatic transmission. Wraparound bumpers, air dam, front fenders and lower body panels are lightweight impact-resistant plastic. A fuel-injected CRX Si arrived in mid-1985 with sunroof,

Honda

body-color spoiler and other extras. We haven't been able to match those EPA ratings (up to 49 mpg city), but CRX is very easy on gas even when you're not trying for economy. Road and exhaust noise can be annoying because of poor insulation. Firm suspension and short wheelbase add up to a jolting ride on rough pavement. But most of all, CRX is fun, especially in town where it can slither through traffic and zip around corners. Limited supply has kept prices high. CRX is the budget-buyer's answer to Pontiac Fiero and Toyota MR2. Note that the 12-valve engine is prone to valve problems and expensive to repair. Also, valve adjustment every 15,000 miles is essential on all CRXs to prevent problems. Restyled along with Civic for 1988, with revised engine lineup.

Price Range	GOOD	AVERAGE	POOR
1984 Civic CRX	$4800–5200	$4400–4800	$3900–4400
1985 Civic CRX	5900–6300	5400–5900	4700–5400
1986 Civic CRX	6800–7500	6300–7000	5700–6300
1987 Civic CRX	7800–8800	7200–8000	6700–7200

Dimensions	WHEEL-BASE, IN.	LGTH., IN.	HT., IN.	WIDTH, IN.	AVG. WT., LBS.	CARGO VOL., CU. FT.	FUEL TANK, GAL.
3d cpe	86.6	144.6	50.8	63.9	1713	20.2	10.8

Engines	L/CID	BHP	MPG	AVAIL.
ohc I-4 3 bbl.	1.3/81	60	28–33	84
ohc I-4 3 bbl.	1.5/91	58	29–34	85–87
ohc I-4 3 bbl.	1.5/91	76	27–33	84–87
ohc I-4 FI	1.5/91	91	27–32	85–87

1985 Honda Civic CRX Si 3-door

Honda

RECALL HISTORY

1984: hood could open suddenly while car is moving because of faulty safety latch.

Honda Prelude 1979-82

Tamed "adult" sports car runs with an Accord engine, but sits on the shorter Civic sedan/wagon floorpan. Cornering is sharper than Civic's, due to tighter suspension settings. Gas mileage and assembly quality are first-rate, as expected. Standard 5-speed manual transmission gives quiet cruising, but shorter-geared automatic is fussy at highway speeds. Back seat holds little more than a bit of cargo that won't fit in the small trunk. Repair history shows reliability/durability of average to well above, except for tendency of '79s to rust early. Also, flooding was a problem with some 1980–81 models due to defective carburetor floats and front disc brake rotor warpage was common, as was brake squeal. Valves should be adjusted every 15,000 miles to forestall engine problems. Preludes are packed with standard equipment. No, it's not a "real" sports car, but it is a sensible alternative for pleasant motoring in the '80s.

1981 Honda Prelude 2-door

Price Range	GOOD	AVERAGE	POOR
1979 Prelude	$2200–2500	$1800–2200	$1400–1800
1980 Prelude	2800–3100	2400–2800	2000–2400
1981 Prelude	3500–4000	3100–3500	2700–3100
1982 Prelude	4500–5000	4000–4500	3600–4000

Dimensions	WHEEL-BASE, IN.	LGTH., IN.	HT., IN.	WIDTH, IN.	AVG. WT., LBS.	CARGO VOL., CU. FT.	FUEL TANK, GAL.
2d cpe	91.3	161.4	51.0	64.4	2130	9.6	13.2

Engines	L/CID	BHP	MPG	AVAIL.
ohc I-4 3 bbl.	1.8/107	72–75	26–29	79–82

KEY: L/CID = liters/cubic inch displacement; **BHP** = brake horsepower; **MPG** = estimated average miles per gallon; **ohc** = overhead cam; **dohc** = double overhead cam; **ohv** = overhead valve; **I** = in-line engine; **V** = V engine; **flat** = horizontally opposed engine; **D** = diesel; **T** = turbocharged; **bbl.** = barrel (carburetor); **FI** = fuel injection.

RECALL HISTORY

1979: repair or replacement of front suspension components that could rust prematurely. **1980–81:** prolonged contact of undercarriage with road salt may, under certain conditions, cause eventual corrosion and weaken front and rear strut coil spring lower supports; components could break and cause loss of vehicle control.

Honda Prelude 1983-87

All-new second-generation sporty coupe rode a longer front-drive chassis, powered by a new 1.8-liter engine with three valves per cylinder and twin sidedraft carburetors. Loaded with standard equipment, it was a hit from the start and demand is still strong. That means dealers were able to charge more than suggested retail for their few Preludes, and they draw premium prices as used cars. Rear disc brakes, an adjustable steering column and variable-assist power steering (on manual-shift models) were added for '84. A performance Si model with fuel-injected 2.0-liter engine came late in the '85 model year, equipped with air, power windows, cruise control and decklid spoiler. Along with its smooth and "revvy" standard engine, the mid-80s Prelude offers tenacious handling, admirable mileage and performance, plus refinement well above most other sport coupes. Firm suspension grows stiff and jiggly on bumps, but not so bad as some rivals. Tall drivers won't like the tight cockpit and few grownups will want to squeeze into the back. Squealing brakes were a problem on some 1983

Honda

1983 Honda Prelude 2-door

models due to defective brake backing plates, and valves should be adjusted every 15,000 miles to prevent engine problems. Expensive? Sure, but Prelude is about as charming and classy a coupe as you'll ever find. Next (third) edition bowed in summer 1987 with new longer body/chassis—plus futuristic 4-wheel steering on the performance-oriented Si.

Price Range	GOOD	AVERAGE	POOR
1983 Prelude	$6700–7100	$6300–6700	$5800–6300
1984 Prelude	7800–8300	7200–7800	6700–7200
1985 Prelude	8700–9800	8200–9400	7800–8400
1986 Prelude	9700–11,500	9250–10,750	8600–9500
1987 Prelude	11,500–13,500	10,500–12,500	9500–11,000

1987 Honda Prelude Si 2-door

Dimensions	WHEEL-BASE, IN.	LGTH., IN.	HT., IN.	WIDTH, IN.	AVG. WT., LBS.	CARGO VOL., CU. FT.	FUEL TANK, GAL.
2d cpe	96.5	169.1	51.0	66.5	2266	10.3	15.8

Engines	L/CID	BHP	MPG	AVAIL.
ohc I-4 3 bbl.	1.8/113	100	20–26	83–87
ohc I-4 FI	2.0/119	110	20–26	85–87

KEY: L/CID = liters/cubic inch displacement; **BHP** = brake horsepower; **MPG** = estimated average miles per gallon; **ohc** = overhead cam; **dohc** = double overhead cam; **ohv** = overhead valve; **I** = in-line engine; **V** = V engine; **flat** = horizontally opposed engine; **D** = diesel; **T** = turbocharged; **bbl.** = barrel (carburetor); **FI** = fuel injection.

RECALL HISTORY

None to date.

Hyundai Excel 1986-88

1986 Hyundai Excel 4-door

South Korean subcompact shattered sales records for a first-year import, though it was available only in 31 states. Sales more than doubled in second season, making Hyundai the seventh best-selling car in the country. Low base price (starting at just $4995) with ample standard equipment has been its main attraction. A 3-door hatchback joined the original 4-door sedan and 5-door hatchback late in the first year. Built on the same platform as the Dodge/Plymouth Colt, it also shares that car's 1.5-liter engine, transmissions, and some suspension parts. Acceleration from a standing start is far from brisk, even with 5-speed manual shift; you'll have to hit the gas hard to keep up with traffic. Gas mileage is great. We averaged nearly 34

Hyundai

mpg in city/expressway driving. Handling is capable, ride comfortable for a small car. Top-line GLS, at least, was also a lot quieter under the hood than similar Colt models. Rear seat is cramped in the 3-door, though split rear seatbacks fold down for extra cargo space. Air flow through dash vents is weak. Assembly quality appears good; interior furnishings are a bit on the cheap side. All told, Excel offers a lot for a modest price. Hyundai is finally gaining nationwide distribution, which should make more secondhand models available before too long.

Price Range	GOOD	AVERAGE	POOR
1986 Excel	$4400–5300	$3900–5000	$3400–3900
1987 Excel	4900–6400	4500–5900	4000–4800
1988 Excel	5500–7200	5000–6750	—

Dimensions	WHEEL-BASE, IN.	LGTH., IN.	HT., IN.	WIDTH, IN.	AVG. WT., LBS.	CARGO VOL., CU. FT.	FUEL TANK, GAL.
3d sdn	93.7	160.9	54.1	63.1	2127	26.6	10.6
4d sdn	93.7	168.0	54.1	63.1	2150	11.2	10.6
5d sdn	93.7	160.9	54.1	63.1	2127	26.0	10.6

Engines	L/CID	BHP	MPG	AVAIL.
ohc I-4 2 bbl.	1.5/90	68	32–36	86–88

KEY: L/CID = liters/cubic inch displacement; **BHP** = brake horsepower; **MPG** = estimated average miles per gallon; **ohc** = overhead cam; **dohc** = double overhead cam; **ohv** = overhead valve; **I** = in-line engine; **V** = V engine; **flat** = horizontally opposed engine; **D** = diesel; **T** = turbocharged; **bbl.** = barrel (carburetor); **FI** = fuel injection.

RECALL HISTORY

1986: cotter pin in brake pedal to master cylinder linkage assembly may be missing; clevis pin may slide out, causing linkage to become disengaged and preventing brake application.

1986 Hyundai Excel 5-door

Lincoln Continental 1978-79

1977 Lincoln Continental 2-door

Last mammoth Lincoln grew eight inches since 1970-74, yet managed to shed a few pounds by this time. Style, size, ride and comfort are as impressive as you'd expect. So is that monstrous 7.5-liter V-8's vast appetite for fuel. Good repair record, but upkeep costs more than average. Ignition and electrical problems tend to crop up—no surprise with all the standard gadgets and power assists. Squeaks and leaks aren't uncommon either. Various optional designer trim packages and the limited-run 1979 "Collector's Series" appealed to a few hedonists of the day; and all of these luxury liners still fascinate some modern buyers. If you're one of them, be sure you have access to some huge parking spaces, and the patience to dock your dreamboat in position. Prices are a bit steep for the final biggies.

Price Range	GOOD	AVERAGE	POOR
1978 Continental	$2600–3200	$2200–2700	$1700–2200
1979 Continental	3400–3900	2900–3400	2400–2900

Dimensions	WHEEL-BASE, IN.	LGTH., IN.	HT., IN.	WIDTH, IN.	AVG. WT., LBS.	CARGO VOL. CU. FT.	FUEL TANK, GAL.
2d cpe	127.2	223.0	55.0	79.7	4867	21.1	24.2
4d sdn	127.2	223.0	55.2	80.0	4870	21.2	24.2

Lincoln

1978 Lincoln Continental 4-door

Engines	L/CID	BHP	MPG	AVAIL.
ohv V-8 2 bbl.	7.5/460	206	10–12	78–79

KEY: L/CID = liters/cubic inch displacement; **BHP** = brake horsepower; **MPG** = estimated average miles per gallon; **ohc** = overhead cam; **dohc** = double overhead cam; **ohv** = overhead valve; **I** = in-line engine; **V** = V engine; **flat** = horizontally opposed engine; **D** = diesel; **T** = turbocharged; **bbl.** = barrel (carburetor); **FI** = fuel injection.

RECALL HISTORY

1978: possible that secondary throttle lever may "hang up" on cast stop following wide-open throttle application, causing vehicle to accelerate to high speed; car may be halted by turning ignition off or placing gear selector in "neutral" and applying brakes. **1979:** possibility C-6 transmission may contain parking pawl actuating rods that were not heat-treated; cam surface could deform during use with resultant increase in shifting effort and difficulty in releasing parking pawl or, in some cases, engaging parking gear. **1979:** retaining pin connecting brake pushrod could fall off, resulting in loss of braking ability.

Lincoln
Continental Mark V 1978-79

Final version of the giant Mark is more luxurious than the prior Mark IV, especially in Designer Series trim. But beneath the more contemporary body, the chassis and running gear hadn't changed all that much. Smaller 400-cid

1979 Lincoln Continental Mark V 2-door

1979 Lincoln Continental Mark V 2-door

V-8 is still a guzzler. Back seat space is tight. Average 1978 repair record slips to below average for 1979, partly because the complex electrical system can be troublesome. Repairs cost more too, because fewer parts are shared with other FoMoCo cars. Collectors may crave these big boats, but Mark V is hardly a sensible choice for daily driving.

Price Range	GOOD		AVERAGE		POOR
1978 Mark V	$3100–3600		$2700–3100		$2200–2700
1979 Mark V	3900–4500		3400–3900		3000–3400

Dimensions	WHEEL-BASE, IN.	LGTH., IN.	HT., IN.	WIDTH, IN.	AVG. WT., LBS.	CARGO VOL., CU. FT.	FUEL TANK, GAL.
2d cpe	120.4	230.3	52.9	79.7	4775	18.1	25.0

Engines	L/CID	BHP	MPG	AVAIL.
ohv V-8 2 bbl.	6.6/400	166–181	12–15	78–79
ohv V-8 4 bbl.	7.5/460	208–210	10–12	78–78

Lincoln

KEY: L/CID = liters/cubic inch displacement; **BHP** = brake horsepower; **MPG** = estimated average miles per gallon; **ohc** = overhead cam; **dohc** = double overhead cam; **ohv** = overhead valve; **I** = in-line engine; **V** = V engine; **flat** = horizontally opposed engine; **D** = diesel; **T** = turbocharged; **bbl.** = barrel (carburetor); **FI** = fuel injection.

RECALL HISTORY

1978: possible that aluminum rear bumper reinforcement could become corroded by road salt and eventually detach from bumper. **1978 (460-cid engine):** secondary throttle lever may "hang up" on cast stop following wide-open throttle application, causing vehicle to accelerate to high speed; car may be halted by turning ignition off or placing gear selector in "neutral" and applying brakes. **1979:** replacement of transmission parking pawls that may be defective. **1979:** brake pushrod retaining pin could fall off, resulting in loss of braking ability.

Lincoln Continental Mark VI/Town Car 1980-88

1980 Lincoln Continental Mark VI 2-door

Downsized later than rival big cars, the Mark VI lineup included not only the expected coupe, but also (for the first time) a 4-door sedan. Like the lower-ranked Continental Town Coupe and Town Car sedan, the Mark sedan rode a 117.3-inch wheelbase, three inches longer than the Mark VI coupe. All are built on a stretched version of the "Panther" platform that began life with the 1979 Ford LTD. In fact, they're similar in running gear and body/chassis engineering. Both Mark VI models were dropped after 1983, replaced by a smaller Mark VII coupe and Continental sedan. The 4-door Town Car has remained as the "senior" Lincoln. Marks are known for their trunklid tire bulge, hidden headlamps, little oval opera windows, digital instruments and classy interiors. They're roomy and comfortable, riding quietly and smoothly. Handling is as heavy as expected on a luxury car, but better than the land yachts of the '70s. Fuel-injected 302-cid V-8, the only engine available after 1980, delivers adequate if unexceptional performance. Standard overdrive automatic transmission helps keep highway fuel mileage reasonable, though hardly admirable. Around town it can't help but guzzle. Lincoln's best-seller hasn't changed much over the years, except for Designer Series and other trim packages. Early 1988 restyle included new grille, taillamps and rear body panel, plus new interior fabrics. Verdict: sensible, traditional luxury cruiser rivals Cadillac DeVille and Brougham, but has grown a bit old-fashioned for the late '80s.

Price Range	GOOD	AVERAGE	POOR
1980 Town Car	$4500–4900	$4000–4500	$3500–4000
1980 Mark VI	5500–6700	5000–6200	4500–5100
1981 Town Car	5800–6100	5400–5800	4900–5400
1981 Mark VI	7600–8900	7100–8300	6500–7200
1982 Town Car	7300–7900	7000–7600	6300–7000
1982 Mark VI	9000–10,500	8500–10,000	7800–8500
1983 Town Car	8900–9800	8400–9200	7700–8400
1983 Mark VI	10,800–12,750	10,400–12,000	9800–10,500
1984 Town Car	10,500–11,200	10,000–10,700	9000–10,000
1985 Town Car	13,500–15,000	13,000–14,500	12,250–13,250
1986 Town Car	17,000–19,000	16,000–18,000	15,200–16,500
1987 Town Car	19,500–22,750	18,500–21,500	17,750–20,000
1988 Town Car	22,000–26,500	20,000–25,000	—

Dimensions	WHEEL-BASE, IN.	LGTH., IN.	HT., IN.	WIDTH, IN.	AVG. WT., LBS.	CARGO VOL., CU. FT.	FUEL TANK, GAL.
2d cpe	114.3	216.0	55.4	78.1	4010	22.4	18.0
2d cpe/4d sdn	117.3	219.0	56.1	78.1	4100	22.4	18.0

Engines	L/CID	BHP	MPG	AVAIL.
ohv V-8 FI	5.0/302	130–155	13–17	80–88
ohv V-8 2 bbl.	5.8/351	151	12–15	80

KEY: L/CID = liters/cubic inch displacement; BHP = brake horsepower; MPG = estimated average miles per gallon; ohc = overhead cam; dohc = double overhead cam; ohv = overhead valve; I = in-line engine; V = V engine; flat = horizontally opposed engine; D = diesel; T = turbocharged; bbl. = barrel (carburetor); FI = fuel injection.

Lincoln

1980 Lincoln Town Car 4-door

1987 Lincoln Town Car 4-door

RECALL HISTORY

1980: correction of potentially faulty instrument panel wiring, which could result in fire even when car is parked and key removed. **1980:** inspection and correction of potential stoplight failure. **1981:** neutral safety switch could be faulty, allowing car to be started with transmission in reverse gear. **1981:** possible that water could leak into electrical relays, resulting in overheating and risk of fire. **1982:** inadequate sealing between fuel filler pipe housing and collar assembly could allow fuel to overflow into right rear fender well, where it could be ignited by nearby electrical components. **1983:** retaining clips on automatic transmission selector may disengage, so gearshift indicator does not accurately show which gear transmission is in. **1983:** retainer pins in automatic transmission could break; parking pawl may not engage when selector is placed in "Park" position. **1984:** seatbelt anchors may not meet federal safety requirements. **1986:** aluminum casting flash on face of throttle body may break off and become trapped between throttle plate and bore; throttle may fail to return to idle position when gas pedal is released, which could result in loss of vehicle control. **1986:** incorrect bolts in automatic transmission linkage adjustment mechanism could cause selector lever to show wrong transmission function. **1986:** some fuel-injection tube assemblies may be bent, creating potential for fuel leakage and engine fire. **1986-88:** check retainer clips on fuel-line spring-lock couplings of fuel-injected engines. **1987:** main wiring harness in engine compartment may be misrouted and subject to damage, which could result in short circuit and possible fire, whether car is moving or parked. **1987:** steering centerlinks may break at bend location, diminishing control and allowing considerable free play in steering wheel. **1987:** idler arm brackets may fracture at threaded shafts, due to improper heat treatment, producing a clunking noise in turns and loose feel in steering wheel.

Lincoln Continental/ Mark VII 1982-88

1984 Lincoln Continental Mark VII 2-door

Mid-size Continental sedan, meant to rival the bustleback Cadillac Seville, contained two industry firsts: gas-pressurized shock absorbers and self-sealing tires, plus 4-wheel disc brakes. The sole engine, Ford's 302-cid (5.0-liter) V-8, gained fuel injection for 1983, sequential injection three years later. In 1984, a Mark VII coupe, more than a foot shorter and 400 pounds lighter than the prior Mark VI, joined the sedan. In addition to luxurious designer ver-

Lincoln

sions, a Mark VII LSC arrived with better-handling suspension and short final drive ratio for swifter pickup. Priced below BMW 633CSi and Mercedes 500SEC, the LSC still sold poorly. It gained a high-output V-8 with tubular exhaust headers for 1985, a tuned intake manifold in '86. Automatic-leveling electronic air suspension (occasionally troublesome) was standard for 1984 and a BMW turbodiesel engine became optional for just two seasons. Antilock braking became standard in 1985 on designer models and West Coast V-8s, then across the board the next year. Sensible size hasn't diminished Lincoln luxury one bit. Road manners are modern and competent; interior roomy enough. Verdict: good alternative to Seville, Eldorado and high-priced Europeans. Rear-drive Mark VII continues into 1988 with 25 added horsepower, but only in LSC touring coupe and Bill Blass Designer series, both with self-diagnosing anti-lock brakes. Continental gets a radical change to aero styling for '88 with "limo look" roofline, V-6 power and front-drive.

Price Range	GOOD	AVERAGE	POOR
1982 Continental	$8300–9000	$7800–8500	$6200–7800
1983 Continental	10,000–10,800	9400–10,400	8100–9400
1984 Continental	11,500–12,500	11,000–12,000	10,000–11,000
1984 Mark VII	12,000–13,000	11,000–12,000	10,000–11,000
1985 Continental	15,000–16,500	14,500–15,500	14,000–15,000
1985 Mark VII	15,000–16,000	14,000–15,000	13,000–14,000
1986 Continental	18,750–20,500	18,000–19,500	17,000–18,000
1986 Mark VII	18,000–19,000	17,000–18,000	16,000–17,000
1987 Continental	21,000–24,000	20,000–23,000	19,000–21,000
1987 Mark VII	20,500–22,000	19,000–20,500	18,000–19,000
1988 Mark VII	23,500–26,000	22,000–24,000	—

1984 Lincoln Continental 4-door

Lincoln

Dimensions	WHEEL-BASE, IN.	LGTH., IN.	HT., IN.	WIDTH, IN.	AVG. WT., LBS.	CARGO VOL., CU. FT.	FUEL TANK, GAL.
2d cpe	108.5	202.8	54.2	70.9	3615	14.7	22.1
4d sdn	108.5	200.7	55.6	73.6	3790	14.7	22.1

Engines	L/CID	BHP	MPG	AVAIL.
ohv V-8 2 bbl.	5.0/302	130	13–17	82
ohv V-8 FI	5.0/302	130–200	14–18	83–87
ohv V-8 FI	5.0/302	225	14–19	88
ohc I-6TD FI	2.4/149	115	22–28	84–85

KEY: **L/CID** = liters/cubic inch displacement; **BHP** = brake horsepower; **MPG** = estimated average miles per gallon; **ohc** = overhead cam; **dohc** = double overhead cam; **ohv** = overhead valve; **I** = in-line engine; **V** = V engine; **flat** = horizontally opposed engine; **D** = diesel; **T** = turbocharged; **bbl.** = barrel (carburetor); **FI** = fuel injection.

RECALL HISTORY

1982: inadequate sealing between fuel filler pipe housing and collar assembly could allow fuel to overflow into fender well, where it could be ignited by nearby electrical components. **1983:** retaining clips on automatic transmission selector may disengage, so indicator does not accurately show which gear transmission is in. **1983:** retainer pins in automatic transmission could break, with the result that parking pawl may not engage when selector is placed in "Park" position. **1984:** seatbelt anchors may not meet federal safety requirements. **1984:** steering column lock could be activated when ignition switch is off and shift lever in other than "Park" position. **1984 (Mark VII):** tire information placard may show incorrect weight/seating capacities. **1984 (diesel engine):** transmission parking pawl may not engage parking gear if selector is very gently moved from "Reverse" to "Park," or may not disengage reverse gear when moved from "Reverse" to "Neutral," due to excessive free play in linkage; car could roll or move backward. **1985:** malfunction in air suspension electronic control module could cause wire to overheat, creating fire potential, primarily when car is parked and key is removed. **1985–86:** under certain conditions, contacts in brake-system relay could remain closed, causing brake pump motor to run continuously, overheat and eventually fail; loss of power front assist and rear braking would increase stopping distance, but warning light should indicate problem. **1986:** aluminum casting flash on face of throttle body may break off and become trapped between throttle plate and bore; throttle may fail to return to idle position when gas pedal is released, which could result in loss of control. **1986:** electrical connections to master cylinder reservoir fluid level sensors may be reversed and fail to transmit signal to brake warning light; low fluid level could lead to loss of brake action. **1986-88:** check retainer clips on fuel-line spring-lock couplings.

Lincoln Versailles 1978-80

1979 Lincoln Versailles 4-door

When Cadillac brought out its Seville, Lincoln responded with this V-8 variant of the Ford Granada/Mercury Monarch sedan, adorned by tacky add-ons. Ranks with its cheaper parents in humdrum handling, gas mileage and interior room, but hardly in the same league as first Seville. Roadability is even worse, due to mushy suspension and extensive sound insulation. Average repair record, but low production and the use of special components means body repairs are costly. Electrical system problems were not uncommon, and the electronic engine control system was trouble-prone and difficult to service. Not popular when new, Versailles can't approach Seville as a used car today. Bustleback 1982 Continental, its successor as the "small" Lincoln, would be a much better choice.

1979 Lincoln Versailles 4-door

Price Range	GOOD	AVERAGE	POOR
1978 Versailles	$2800–3200	$2400–2800	$1900–2400
1979 Versailles	3500–3800	3000–3500	2500–3000
1980 Versailles	4100–4500	3700–4100	3100–3700

Dimensions	WHEEL-BASE, IN.	LGTH., IN.	HT., IN.	WIDTH, IN.	AVG. WT., LBS.	CARGO VOL., CU. FT.	FUEL TANK, GAL.
4d sdn	109.9	200.9	54.1	74.5	3916	14.1	19.2

Engines	L/CID	BHP	MPG	AVAIL.
ohv V-8 2 bbl.	5.0/302	133	13–17	78–80

KEY: L'CID = liters/cubic inch displacement; **BHP** = brake horsepower; **MPG** = estimated average miles per gallon; **ohc** = overhead cam; **dohc** = double overhead cam; **ohv** = overhead valve; **I** = in-line engine; **V** = V engine; **flat** = horizontally opposed engine; **D** = diesel; **T** = turbocharged; **bbl.** = barrel (carburetor); **FI** = fuel injection.

RECALL HISTORY

1979: brake pedal pushrod retaining pin could fall out, resulting in loss of braking.

Mazda GLC 1981-85

Mazda's subcompact has all the trademarks of modern small-car design: front drive, transverse-mounted engine, all-independent suspension, and unit construction. Typical basic Japanese body feels tinny, but GLC is easy to drive, offering fine mileage, good heating/ventilation and snappy performance (with manual shift). Highway ride is decent and relaxed, but can thump hard on certain bumps. Rear-drive wagon from prior GLC series offered through 1983.

1981 Mazda GLC 3-door

Mazda

New Luxury series replaced Sport as top model in '84. Fine repair record, except for breakdowns in automatic transmission and air conditioner, and oil leaks in the power steering pump on '84 models. Priced reasonably, GLC isn't a bad choice in a little used car.

Price Range	GOOD	AVERAGE	POOR
1981 GLC	$1900–2200	$1500–2000	$1200–1500
1982 GLC	2300–3000	2000–2700	1600–2000
1983 GLC	2900–3900	2600–3500	2100–2600
1984 GLC	3600–4400	3200–4000	2700–3200
1985 GLC	4500–5500	4000–5000	3500–4100

Dimensions	WHEEL-BASE, IN.	LGTH., IN.	HT., IN.	WIDTH, IN.	AVG. WT., LBS.	CARGO VOL., CU. FT.	FUEL TANK, GAL.
3d/5d sdn	93.1	159.1	54.1	64.2	1925	10.2	11.1
4d sdn	93.1	166.8	54.1	64.2	1935	13.6	11.1

Engines	L/CID	BHP	MPG	AVAIL.
ohc I-4 2 bbl.	1.5/91	68	30–35	81–85

KEY: L/CID = liters/cubic inch displacement; **BHP** = brake horsepower; **MPG** = estimated average miles per gallon; **ohc** = overhead cam; **dohc** = double overhead cam; **ohv** = overhead valve; **I** = in-line engine; **V** = V engine; **flat** = horizontally opposed engine; **D** = diesel; **T** = turbocharged; **bbl.** = barrel (carburetor); **FI** = fuel injection.

RECALL HISTORY

1981–83: seatbelt anchor bolts could loosen and eventually fall out. **1981–83:** idler arm pin may corrode, freeze and break after prolonged exposure to road salt (in certain high-salt areas), which causes dust seal to deteriorate; broken idler arm could result in loss of steering control. **1982:** tail lamps may not be intense enough. **1982:** cruise control fitting might bind, preventing throttle from returning properly and forcing driver to shift car into neutral.

1981 Mazda GLC 4-door

Mazda RX-7 1979-85

1982 Mazda RX-7 3-door

Mazda's high-winding rotary engine reappeared to power this slick two-seater sports coupe. Unlike previous rotaries, the RX-7 engine/driveline repair history rates average to well above, although the rotary engine does have a reputation for high oil consumption. A 4-speed overdrive automatic transmission became optional on GS and GSL models for 1984. In the same year, Mazda released a GSL-SE version with bigger engine, low-profile Pirelli tires and firmer suspension, priced $2000 above GSL. Well-built, fully equipped contemporary sports car delivers plenty of action, precise handling and agile cornering, fairly comfortable ride, and a refined feel. Fuel mileage disappoints, however. Cockpit is cramped for larger drivers and some interior trim looks cheap. Prices rose over the years, placing GSL and GSL-SE in the same region as Nissan's Z-cars and Toyota Supra. All models are expensive on the used-car lots, but we consider RX-7 the best sports car value on the market today.

Price Range	GOOD	AVERAGE	POOR
1979 RX-7	$3100–3400	$2700–3100	$2200–2700
1980 RX-7	3600–4000	3200–3700	2800–3200
1981 RX-7	4300–5200	4000–4800	3500–4000
1982 RX-7	5200–6100	4800–5600	4300–4900
1983 RX-7	6500–7500	6100–7000	5500–6200
1984 RX-7	7600–9500	7100–9000	6500–7100
1985 RX-7	9100–11,250	8600–10,500	8000–9000

Mazda

Dimensions	WHEEL-BASE, IN.	LGTH., IN.	HT., IN.	WIDTH, IN.	AVG. WT., LBS.	CARGO VOL., CU. FT.	FUEL TANK, GAL.
3d cpe	95.3	169.0	49.6	65.7	2380	17.0	16.4

Engines	L/CID	BHP	MPG	AVAIL.
2-rotor Wankel 4bbl.	1.1/70	101	16–20	79–85
2-rotor Wankel FI	1.3/80	135	15–19	84–85

KEY: L/CID = liters/cubic inch displacement; **BHP** = brake horsepower; **MPG** = estimated average miles per gallon; **ohc** = overhead cam; **dohc** = double overhead cam; **ohv** = overhead valve; **I** = in-line engine; **V** = V engine; **flat** = horizontally opposed engine; **D** = diesel; **T** = turbocharged; **bbl.** = barrel (carburetor); **FI** = fuel injection.

RECALL HISTORY

1979–83: idler arm pin may corrode, freeze and break after prolonged exposure to road salt (in certain high-salt areas), which causes dust seal to deteriorate; broken idler arm could result in loss of steering control.

1985 Mazda RX-7 GSL-SE 3-door

1985 Mazda RX-7 GSL-SE 3-door

Mazda RX-7 1986-88

1986 Mazda RX-7 GXL 3-door

Redesigned rotary-engine sports car added a 2+2 model to the basic two-seater, but retained rear-wheel drive. Dimensions are close to previous RX-7, but weight went up. Fuel-injected 1.3-liter rotary engine introduced for 1984 on the GLS-SE was made standard on the new version, with 5-speed manual or 4-speed automatic shift. Other improvements: four-wheel independent suspension and disc brakes. Headlamps are hidden, but little windows allow use of flash-to-pass with lights off. Electronic power-assisted steering on GXL adjusts effort to car speed and conditions. GXL also has Auto Adjusting Suspension, which changes shock absorber dampening either automatically or via an interior control. A turbocharged two-seater arrived in mid-1986. Anti-lock braking became optional for 1987 on Turbo and GXL. Normally aspirated version is strong enough, but the turbo's a scorcher, best enjoyed when coupled to manual gearbox. Handling is agile, though sharp bumps can lift the back wheels off the pavement and road feel is minimal at low speeds. Tall people barely fit up front, and one is about the limit in the rear seat of the 2+2. Performance models ride harshly on rough roads. Gas mileage isn't the rotary's strong point, though it's not out of line for a car of this caliber. Limited-production convertible is expected at mid-year. Our opinion: competent and complete sports car, with reliable rotary engine, offers good value despite high price.

Mazda

1986 Mazda RX-7 GX 3-door

Price Range	GOOD	AVERAGE	POOR
1986 RX-7	$10,500–11,500	$9500–10,500	$8500–9500
1986 GXL/Turbo	14,500–15,500	13,500–14,500	13,000–13,500
1987 RX-7	13,000–15,000	12,000–14,000	11,250–12,500
1987 GXL/Turbo	16,000–18,000	15,000–16,500	14,500–15,250
1988 RX-7	15,000–17,000	14,000–16,000	—
1988 GXL/Turbo	19,000–21,000	18,000–20,000	—

Dimensions	WHEEL-BASE, IN.	LGTH., IN.	HT., IN.	WIDTH, IN.	AVG. WT., LBS.	CARGO VOL., CU. FT.	FUEL TANK, GAL.
3d cpe	95.7	168.9	49.8	66.5	2625	19.5	16.6

Engines	L/CID	BHP	MPG	AVAIL.
2-rotor Wankel FI	1.3/80	146	15–19	86–88
2-rotor Wankel T FI	1.3/80	182	14–18	86–88

KEY: L/CID = liters/cubic inch displacement; **BHP** = brake horsepower; **MPG** = estimated average miles per gallon; **ohc** = overhead cam; **dohc** = double overhead cam; **ohv** = overhead valve; **I** = in-line engine; **V** = V engine; **flat** = horizontally opposed engine; **D** = diesel; **T** = turbocharged; **bbl.** = barrel (carburetor); **FI** = fuel injection.

RECALL HISTORY

None to date.

Mazda 323 1986-88

Subcompact front-drive replacement for the GLC is a little longer and heavier, with more spacious interior. Lineup includes a 3-door hatchback and 4-door sedan, plus a 5-door station wagon for 1987. With rear seats folded flat, the wagon has almost 57 cubic feet of cargo space, and even

1986 Mazda 323 4-door

the sedan has a deep, ample trunk. Performance is adequate with 5-speed manual shift, delivering over 30 mpg on the highway. New 1.6-liter fuel-injected engine is more powerful than before, though still loud and coarse at higher speeds. Exhaust noise also is excessive, even when cruising. Noise, economy and pickup suffer more yet with 3-speed automatic, or the 4-speed manual on base 3-doors. Even so, the capable 323 rates above average in performance, roominess and overall value. A 4-wheel-drive hatchback is expected during 1988, powered by an inter-cooled turbo engine.

1987 Mazda 323 5-door

Mazda

Price Range	GOOD	AVERAGE	POOR
1986 323	$5200–6600	$4700–6000	$4000–4900
1987 323	6000–7800	5500–7000	4800–5700
1988 323	7000–9000	6000–8000	—

Dimensions	WHEEL-BASE, IN.	LGTH., IN.	HT., IN.	WIDTH, IN.	AVG. WT., LBS.	CARGO VOL., CU. FT.	FUEL TANK, GAL.
3d sdn	94.5	161.8	54.7	64.8	2060	10.5	11.9
4d sdn	94.5	169.7	54.7	64.8	2115	14.7	11.9
5d wgn	94.5	169.7	55.5	64.8	2170	56.8	11.9

Engines	L/CID	BHP	MPG	AVAIL.
ohc I-4 FI	1.6/97	82	25–31	86–88

KEY: L/CID = liters/cubic inch displacement; **BHP** = brake horsepower; **MPG** = estimated average miles per gallon; **ohc** = overhead cam; **dohc** = double overhead cam; **ohv** = overhead valve; **I** = in-line engine; **V** = V engine; **flat** = horizontally opposed engine; **D** = diesel; **T** = turbocharged; **bbl.** = barrel (carburetor); **FI** = fuel injection.

RECALL HISTORY

None to date.

Mazda 626 1979-82

Standard Japanese rear-drive family car is pleasant to drive, well-trimmed and equipped, filled with nice touches. Overall design ranks slightly above Datsun 510 and Toyota Corolla. Somewhat harsh, unrefined 2.0-liter engine gets quite noisy at high rpm, but delivers adequate acceleration. Top-notch repair history is marred only by above-average brake and suspension repairs on 1979s and air conditioner ills on '80s. Replaced for 1983 by an all-new front-drive model, but this version is tough to beat for the price.

Price Range	GOOD	AVERAGE	POOR
1979 626	$1700–2000	$1400–1700	$1100–1400
1980 626	2200–2600	1900–2300	1500–1900
1981 626	2700–3300	2400–2900	2000–2400
1982 626	3750–4400	3300–4000	2800–3300

Dimensions	WHEEL-BASE, IN.	LGTH., IN.	HT., IN.	WIDTH, IN.	AVG. WT., LBS.	CARGO VOL., CU. FT.	FUEL TANK, GAL.
2d cpe	98.8	173.8	53.3	65.4	2485	11.4	14.5
4d sdn	98.8	173.8	54.5	65.4	2595	11.7	14.5

Engines	L/CID	BHP	MPG	AVAIL.
ohc I-4 2 bbl.	2.0/120	75	22–25	79–82

1979 Mazda 626 4-door

1982 Mazda 626 2-door

KEY: L/CID = liters/cubic inch displacement; **BHP** = brake horsepower; **MPG** = estimated average miles per gallon; **ohc** = overhead cam; **dohc** = double overhead cam; **ohv** = overhead valve; **I** = in-line engine; **V** = V engine; **flat** = horizontally opposed engine; **D** = diesel; **T** = turbocharged; **bbl.** = barrel (carburetor); **FI** = fuel injection.

RECALL HISTORY

1979–82: seatbelt anchor bolts could loosen and eventually fall out. **1979–82:** idler arm pin may corrode, freeze and break after prolonged exposure to road salt (in certain high-salt areas), which causes dust seal to deteriorate; broken idler arm could result in loss of steering control.

Mazda 626 1983-87

Popular compact switched to front-drive in 1983 redesign and has sold even better than the original. Coupe and 4-door bodies come in Deluxe or Luxury trim; the neat 5-door Touring Sedan only in Luxury dress. The 2.0-liter

Mazda

1983 Mazda 626 4-door

1983 Mazda 626 Touring Sedan 5-door

gas engine is a lot rougher and noisier than the Honda Accord's, but delivers fairly snappy pickup and good mileage with 5-speed manual shift. Port fuel injection was added for 1986, when the 626 body received a restyle. A sporty GT model with turbocharged four also joined the '86 lineup. Turbo performance is impressive. Diesel engine, offered only in the Luxury 4-door, sold few copies. Electronically adjustable shock absorbers with normal/firm/automatic settings were standard on Coupes and Touring Sedan through 1985, optional for '86; they do not wear well. In automatic, they adjust for car speed. Many Luxury models have digital instruments, which are hard to see in the sun. In all, a 626 offers a nice blend of comfort and performance, though head/leg room is limited. We rate it a little below Accord and Toyota Corolla. All-new third-generation lineup for 1988 includes MX-6 coupe (built in U.S.) plus Turbo sedan with 4-wheel steering.

Price Range	GOOD	AVERAGE	POOR
1983 626	$5100–5900	$4700–5500	$4000–4800
1984 626	6100–7000	5700–6500	5000–5800
1985 626	7000–8200	6600–7600	6000–6700
1986 626	8100–10,000	7600–9500	7000–8000
1987 626	9750–11,500	9000–10,500	8400–9200

Dimensions	WHEEL-BASE, IN.	LGTH., IN.	HT., IN.	WIDTH, IN.	AVG. WT., LBS.	CARGO VOL., CU. FT.	FUEL TANK, GAL.
2d cpe	98.8	177.8	53.7	66.5	2385	13.3	15.8
4d sdn	98.8	177.8	55.5	66.5	2410	13.7	15.8
5d sdn	98.8	177.8	53.7	66.5	2425	21.0	15.8

Engines	L/CID	BHP	MPG	AVAIL.
ohc I-4 2 bbl.	2.0/122	84	22–28	83–85
ohc I-4 FI	2.0/122	93	22–28	86–87
ohc I-4T FI	2.0/122	120	20–25	86–87
ohc I-4D FI	2.0/122	61	29–35	84–85

KEY: L/CID = liters/cubic inch displacement; **BHP** = brake horsepower; **MPG** = estimated average miles per gallon; **ohc** = overhead cam; **dohc** = double overhead cam; **ohv** = overhead valve; **I** = in-line engine; **V** = V engine; **flat** = horizontally opposed engine; **D** = diesel; **T** = turbocharged; **bbl.** = barrel (carburetor); **FI** = fuel injection.

RECALL HISTORY

1986: throttle angle sensor may contain nylon rotor that has not been heat treated; could cause throttle to stick open, which may result in loss of control.

1986 Mazda 626 Touring Sedan 5-door

Mercury Capri 1979-86

1979 Mercury Capri RS 3-door

Close cousin to the Ford Mustang came only in 3-door hatchback coupe form. Avoid the base 4-cylinder engine and early turbocharged four. Best choice is the 3.8-liter V-6 of 1983 and later. A V-8 is usually under the hood of a high-performance Capri RS, which also has firmer suspension and wider tires. Like Mustang's GT, the RS is the most costly Capri. Sequential fuel injection was added to the 5.0-liter V-8 for 1986, Capri's final year. With a V-8 underfoot, you're in the Z28/Trans Am league. See 1979–87 Mustang entry for comments.

Price Range	GOOD	AVERAGE	POOR
1979 Capri	$1700–2000	$1400–1700	$1100–1400
1980 Capri	2000–2300	1700–2100	1400–1700
1981 Capri	2300–3000	2000–2700	1700–2100
1982 Capri	3400–4400	2800–3900	2300–2900
1983 Capri	4200–5600	3700–4900	3000–3800
1984 Capri	5100–6500	4700–5800	3900–4700
1985 Capri	6100–7600	5600–6900	5000–5700
1986 Capri	7200–8700	6500–8200	6000–6800

Dimensions	WHEEL-BASE, IN.	LGTH., IN.	HT., IN.	WIDTH, IN.	AVG. WT., LBS.	CARGO VOL., CU. FT.	FUEL TANK, GAL.
3d cpe	100.5	179.3	52.1	69.1	2872	32.5	15.4

Engines	L/CID	BHP	MPG	AVAIL.
ohc I-4 1 bbl.	2.3/140	86–93	19–22	79–86
ohc I-4 T 2 bbl.	2.3/140	140	16–18	79–81
ohc I-4 T FI	2.3/140	145–155	17–20	83–84
ohv V-6 2 bbl.	2.8/171	109	18–21	79
ohv I-6 1 bbl.	3.3/200	88–91	18–21	80–82
ohv V-6 2 bbl.	3.8/232	105	16–19	83
ohv V-6 FI	3.8/232	120	16–20	84–86
ohv V-8 2 bbl.	4.2/255	111–118	15–18	80–82
ohv V-8 2 bbl.	5.0/302	140–155	13–16	79,82
ohv V-8 4 bbl.	5.0/302	175–210	12–15	83–85
ohv V-8 FI	5.0/302	165–200	13–16	84–86

KEY: L/CID = liters/cubic inch displacement; **BHP** = brake horsepower; **MPG** = estimated average miles per gallon; **ohc** = overhead cam; **dohc** = double overhead cam; **ohv** = overhead valve; **I** = in-line engine; **V** = V engine; **flat** = horizontally opposed engine; **D** = diesel; **T** = turbocharged; **bbl.** = barrel (carburetor); **FI** = fuel injection.

1980 Mercury Capri RS 3-door

1983 Mercury Capri 3-door

Mercury
RECALL HISTORY

1979: replacement of plastic fan guard, which may break if it comes in contact with fan. **1979:** improper steering coupling could impede steering functions. **1979:** brake pushrod retaining pin could fall off, resulting in loss of braking ability. **1979 (5.0-liter engine):** flexible blade cooling fan could crack at high engine speeds and break into fragments. **1981:** modify air injection if necessary to ensure acceptable emissions. **1981 (4.2- or 5.0-liter engine):** replace choke pull-down motor to ensure acceptable emissions. **1984:** seatbelt anchors may not meet federal safety requirements. **1984:** carburetor secondary throttle shaft, with accumulated mileage, may be susceptible to dirt contamination and wear of bearing coatings; could allow throttle plates to remain partly open after releasing gas pedal. **1984-85:** defective ignition module could make 2.3-liter engine hard to start, run poorly or stall. **1985 (3.8-liter engine):** rear shell of tandem brake booster may have thin wall that could crack after repeated brake use and come apart; braking ability would be totally lost without warning. **1986:** check retainer clips on fuel-line spring-lock couplings of fuel-injected engines.

Mercury Cougar 1978-79

Basic mid-size Mercury is similar to Ford LTD II, but specialty XR-7 coupe shared styling and features with Thunderbird. Check 1978-79 LTD II and T-Bird entries for details and comments, many of which are less than favorable. Cougar name also went on wagons during this period.

Price Range	GOOD	AVERAGE	POOR
1978 Cougar	$1300–1600	$1000–1300	$750–1000
1978 Cougar XR-7	1600–1900	1300–1600	1000–1300
1979 Cougar	1500–1800	1250–1550	950–1250
1979 Cougar XR-7	1900–2200	1600–1900	1300–1600

Dimensions	WHEEL-BASE, IN.	LGTH., IN.	HT., IN.	WIDTH, IN.	AVG. WT., LBS.	CARGO VOL., CU. FT.	FUEL TANK, GAL.
2d cpe	114.0	215.0	52.6	78.6	4154	15.1	26.5
4d sdn	118.0	219.0	53.3	78.6	4236	15.1	26.5
5d wgn	118.0	223.1	54.9	78.6	4540	NA	21.0

Engines	L/CID	BHP	MPG	AVAIL.
ohv V-8 2 bbl.	5.0/302	134	14–17	78–79
ohv V-8 2 bbl.	5.8/351	143–152	12–15	78–79
ohv V-8 2 bbl.	6.6/400	166	11–14	78

1979 Mercury Cougar XR-7 2-door

KEY: L/CID = liters/cubic inch displacement; **BHP** = brake horsepower; **MPG** = estimated average miles per gallon; **ohc** = overhead cam; **dohc** = double overhead cam; **ohv** = overhead valve; **I** = in-line engine; **V** = V engine; **flat** = horizontally opposed engine; **D** = diesel; **T** = turbocharged; **bbl.** = barrel (carburetor); **FI** = fuel injection.

RECALL HISTORY

1978: front outboard seatbelt assemblies may have shoulder harness retractors that do not lock; also, in some cases, retractors may not allow extraction of shoulder belt webbing due to prelocked condition. **1979:** possible that power steering gear could crack and render power steering ineffective.

Mercury Cougar 1981-82

New mid-size Cougar was similar to Ford Granada, sitting on "Fox" chassis from the compact Fairmont/Zephyr with 105.5-inch wheelbase. Check the 1981–82 Granada entry for comments. Base 4-cylinder engine is too feeble for a car of this size. The 200-cid (3.3-liter) inline six is a better choice. Neither performance nor fuel mileage is a strong point with the 3.8-liter V-6. Cougar isn't a bad car, but a Zephyr is cheaper and does about the same job.

Price Range	GOOD	AVERAGE	POOR
1981 Cougar	$2300–2800	$2000–2500	$1600–2000
1982 Cougar	3200–3700	2800–3300	2200–2800

Dimensions	WHEEL-BASE, IN.	LGTH., IN.	HT., IN.	WIDTH, IN.	AVG. WT., LBS.	CARGO VOL. CU. FT.	FUEL TANK, GAL.
2d sdn	105.5	196.5	52.9	71.0	2810	16.8	16.0
4d sdn	105.5	196.5	52.9	71.0	2865	16.8	16.0

Mercury

1981 Mercury Cougar 4-door

Engines	L/CID	BHP	MPG	AVAIL.
ohc I-4 2 bbl.	2.3/140	86–88	18–22	81–82
ohv I-6 1 bbl.	3.3/200	87–88	18–21	81–82
ohv V-6 2 bbl.	3.8/232	112	17–20	82
ohv V-8 2 bbl.	4.2/255	120	16–19	81

KEY: L/CID = liters/cubic inch displacement; **BHP** = brake horsepower; **MPG** = estimated average miles per gallon; **ohc** = overhead cam; **dohc** = double overhead cam; **ohv** = overhead valve; **I** = in-line engine; **V** = V engine; **flat** = horizontally opposed engine; **D** = diesel; **T** = turbocharged; **bbl.** = barrel (carburetor); **FI** = fuel injection.

1982 Mercury Cougar 5-door

RECALL HISTORY

1981: modify air injection as needed to ensure acceptable emissions. **1981 (4.2-liter engine):** replace choke pull-down motor to ensure acceptable emissions. **1982:** tire placards may show wrong tire sizes and inflation pressures.

Mercury Cougar XR-7 1980-82

1980 Mercury Cougar XR-7 2-door

Stylish but rather baroque mid-size coupe is close kin to Ford Thunderbird of like vintage, so see that entry for comments and repair history. Platform is a three-inch stretch of the Fairmont/Zephyr. Over-the-shoulder vision is minimal, especially with the optional Luxury Group trim offered in 1980–81. Engine choices include a 200-cid inline six (1981–82 only), a V-6, or two V-8 sizes. The 1980–81 V-8s seem to have more problems than the others.

Price Range	GOOD	AVERAGE	POOR
1980 Cougar XR-7	$2400–2700	$2100–2400	$1800–2100
1981 Cougar XR-7	3100–3500	2800–3200	2300–2800
1982 Cougar XR-7	3900–4500	3600–4200	3000–3600

Dimensions	WHEEL-BASE, IN.	LGTH., IN.	HT., IN.	WIDTH, IN.	AVG. WT., LBS.	CARGO VOL. CU. FT.	FUEL TANK, GAL.
2d cpe	108.4	200.4	53.2	74.1	3205	17.7	18.0

Mercury

1980 Mercury Cougar XR-7 2-door

Engines	L/CID	BHP	MPG	AVAIL.
ohv I-6 1 bbl.	3.3/200	88	18–21	81–82
ohv V-6 2 bbl.	3.8/232	112	16–20	82
ohv V-8 2 bbl.	4.2/255	111–120	17–20	80–82
ohv V-8 2 bbl.	5.0/302	131	16–19	80–81

KEY: L/CID = liters/cubic inch displacement; **BHP** = brake horsepower; **MPG** = estimated average miles per gallon; **ohc** = overhead cam; **dohc** = double overhead cam; **ohv** = overhead valve; **I** = in-line engine; **V** = V engine; **flat** = horizontally opposed engine; **D** = diesel; **T** = turbocharged; **bbl.** = barrel (carburetor); **FI** = fuel injection.

RECALL HISTORY

1980: possible that some cars have smaller rear brake assemblies intended for use on Mustangs. **1981 (4.2- or 5.0-liter engine):** replace choke pull-down motor to ensure acceptable emissions.

Mercury Cougar 1983-88

Rear-drive personal-luxury coupe differs from Ford Thunderbird mainly in Cougar's controversial roof design. Smaller and more aerodynamic than before, the latest Cougar comes in base and upscale dress. Standard 3.8-liter V-6 with 3-speed automatic does a competent job, but the optional 5.0-liter V-8 yields better performance with only a small sacrifice in mileage. Special XR-7 package from 1984-86 includes a 2.3-liter turbocharged four, performance tires and handling suspension. Even the base model offers capable road manners. Major 1987 restyle included aero headlamps, flush-fitting glass and full-width tail lamps, and XR-7 dropped the turbo four in favor of the 5.0 V-8. For 1988 the base V-6 gained 20 horsepower and a balance shaft, while V-8 Cougars added dual exhausts.

1984 Mercury Cougar XR-7 2-door

See 1983-88 Thunderbird entry for repair data and further comments.

Price Range	GOOD	AVERAGE	POOR
1983 Cougar	$5200–6000	$4800–5600	$4300–4800
1984 Cougar	6500–7400	6000–7000	5400–6000
1985 Cougar	7700–8900	7300–8400	6700–7400
1986 Cougar	9300–10,700	8900–10,000	8200–9000
1987 Cougar	11,000–13,000	10,000–12,000	9500–10,500
1988 Cougar	14,000–16,000	13,000–14,500	—

Dimensions	WHEEL-BASE, IN.	LGTH., IN.	HT., IN.	WIDTH, IN.	AVG. WT., LBS.	CARGO VOL., CU. FT.	FUEL TANK, GAL.
2d cpe	104.0	197.6	53.4	71.1	3084	14.6	20.6

1987 Mercury Cougar 2-door

Mercury

Engines

Engines	L/CID	BHP	MPG	AVAIL.
ohc I-4T FI	2.3/140	145–155	21–26	84–86
ohv V-6 2 bbl.	3.8/232	105	17–22	83
ohv V-6 FI	3.8/232	120–140	17–22	84–88
ohv V-8 FI	5.0/302	140–155	16–21	84–88

KEY: L/CID = liters/cubic inch displacement; **BHP** = brake horsepower; **MPG** = estimated average miles per gallon; **ohc** = overhead cam; **dohc** = double overhead cam; **ohv** = overhead valve; **I** = in-line engine; **V** = V engine; **flat** = horizontally opposed engine; **D** = diesel; **T** = turbocharged; **bbl.** = barrel (carburetor); **FI** = fuel injection.

RECALL HISTORY

1985: improperly anodized internal surfaces of master cylinder may accelerate wear of piston seal, rendering one portion of split-brake system ineffective. **1986-88:** check retainer clips on fuel-line spring-lock couplings of fuel-injected engines. **1987 "Silver Aero" promotional cars only:** headlamp covers were installed in error, so car does not comply with standard for safe operation in darkness or conditions of reduced visibility.

Mercury Lynx 1981-87

Subcompact front-drive successor to Bobcat is similar to Ford Escort. A 5-door sedan joined the original 3-door and wagon for 1982. The 1.6-liter CVH four got fuel injection in 1983 and was replaced by a new 1.9-liter four in mid-1985. That engine gained fuel injection for '87. Sporty XR3 hatchback appeared for 1986 with the same basic package as Escort GT: high-output engine, unique asymmetrical

1981 Mercury Lynx 3-door

grille, air dam, spoiler, and wheel spats. All Lynx models return fine gas mileage and handle with agility, though the 1.6 engine is awfully loud and slow with automatic. For repair data and comments, see Ford Escort entry. Escort continues as Ford's best-seller, but Lynx was replaced in spring 1987 by the new Mexican-built Tracer.

Price Range	GOOD	AVERAGE	POOR
1981 Lynx	$2000–2500	$1700–2300	$1200–1700
1982 Lynx	2500–3200	2200–2800	1800–2200
1983 Lynx	3100–3800	2700–3400	2200–2700
1984 Lynx	3600–4500	3200–4000	2700–3200
1985 Lynx	4500–5300	4000–4900	3500–4000
1986 Lynx	5200–6200	4700–5700	4100–4700
1987 Lynx	6000–7900	5500–6900	5000–6000

1985 Mercury Lynx 5-door wagon

1987 Mercury Lynx 5-door hatchback

Mercury

Dimensions	WHEEL-BASE, IN.	LGTH., IN.	HT., IN.	WIDTH, IN.	AVG. WT., LBS.	CARGO VOL., CU. FT.	FUEL TANK, GAL.
3d sdn	94.2	163.9	53.3	65.9	2082	32.2	10.0
5d sdn	94.2	163.9	53.4	65.9	2147	32.0	10.0
5d wgn	94.2	165.0	53.3	65.9	2173	58.8	13.0

Engines	L/CID	BHP	MPG	AVAIL.
ohc I-4 2 bbl.	1.6/98	69–72	27–32	81–85
ohc I-4 2 bbl.	1.6/98	80	26–30	83–85
ohc I-4 FI	1.6/98	88	26–30	83–84
ohc I-4T FI	1.6/98	120	22–27	84
ohc I-4 2 bbl.	1.9/114	86	26–31	85–86
ohc I-4 FI	1.9/114	90	25–30	87
ohc I-4 FI	1.9/114	108–115	22–26	85–87
ohc I-4D FI	2.0/121	52–58	28–35	84–87

KEY: L/CID = liters/cubic inch displacement; **BHP** = brake horsepower; **MPG** = estimated average miles per gallon; **ohc** = overhead cam; **dohc** = double overhead cam; **ohv** = overhead valve; **I** = in-line engine; **V** = V engine; **flat** = horizontally opposed engine; **D** = diesel; **T** = turbocharged; **bbl.** = barrel (carburetor); **FI** = fuel injection.

RECALL HISTORY

See Ford Escort 1981–88 entry for recall information.

Mercury Marquis/ Grand Marquis 1979-88

Nearly identical to Ford LTD, but slightly longer and more elaborate (even fussy) in body trim, the downsized full-size Mercury stood well ahead of its huge forerunner. Prices are higher, but drivetrains and body styles are same as LTD, in three trim levels: base, Marquis Brougham and Grand Marquis. When the smaller Marquis debuted for 1983 (see next entry), the Grand Marquis name went on this 114.3-inch wheelbase model. More modern styling arrived for 1988, when the 2-door was dropped. See 1979–88 Ford LTD/LTD Crown Victoria entry for comments on road manners, economy, performance and comfort. Grand Marquis has been Mercury's most popular model: one of the better big cars, in fact, a good alternative to Buick Electra or Olds Ninety-Eight. Repair record runs average to slightly better. Parts and service aren't a problem, but Mercury costs more than an LTD.

1979 Mercury Marquis Colony Park 5-door

Price Range	GOOD	AVERAGE	POOR
1979 Marquis	$2000–2600	$1600–2100	$1200–1600
1980 Marquis	2400–3400	2000–3000	1500–2000
1981 Marquis	2900–4100	2500–3700	2100–2600
1982 Marquis	3900–5200	3500–4700	3000–3500
1983 Grand Marquis	5700–6500	5400–6000	4700–5400
1984 Grand Marquis	7300–8000	6800–7500	6000–6800
1985 Grand Marquis	8900–9900	8500–9300	7600–8500
1986 Grand Marquis	10,900–11,900	10,250–11,400	9300–10,250
1987 Grand Marquis	13,000–14,500	12,000–13,500	11,000–12,000
1988 Grand Marquis	14,250–16,500	13,500–15,500	—

Dimensions	WHEEL-BASE, IN.	LGTH., IN.	HT., IN.	WIDTH, IN.	AVG. WT., LBS.	CARGO VOL., CU. FT.	FUEL TANK, GAL.
2d sdn	114.3	211.0	55.2	77.5	3758	22.4	18.0
4d sdn	114.3	211.0	55.2	77.5	3800	22.4	18.0
5d wgn	114.3	215.0	56.8	79.3	3967	89.5	18.5

Engines	L/CID	BHP	MPG	AVAIL.
ohv V-8 2 bbl.	4.2/255	120	15–18	81–82
ohv V-8 FI	5.0/302	130–155	15–18	83–88
ohv V-8 2 bbl.	5.0/302	130–133	14–17	79–82
ohv V-8 2 bbl.	5.8/351	135–145	13–16	79–81
ohv V-8 2 bbl.	5.8/351	151	13–16	79–80

KEY: L/CID = liters/cubic inch displacement; **BHP** = brake horsepower; **MPG** = estimated average miles per gallon; **ohc** = overhead cam; **dohc** = double overhead cam; **ohv** = overhead valve; **I** = in-line engine; **V** = V engine; **flat** = horizontally opposed engine; **D** = diesel; **T** = turbocharged; **bbl.** = barrel (carburetor); **FI** = fuel injection.

RECALL HISTORY

1979: possibility of 6.0-amp circuit breaker rather than 8.25-amp in windshield wiper/washer circuit; potential for circuit interruption under heavy loads, which may result in breaker failure. **1979:**

Mercury

front brake hoses may contact and chafe against edges of frame-mounted rebound bumper brackets; could result in hose wear and loss of brake fluid, and subsequent loss of front wheel braking, shown by warning light and increased pedal travel. **1979:** possible that cars have incorrect rear lamp sockets, causing tail and backup lamps to fail to comply with federal safety standard. **1979:** brake hose may contact front wheel or tire, chafe and rupture, leaking hydraulic fluid and posing fire hazard as well as loss of braking ability. **1979:** two rivet pins in lower steering shaft assembly could work loose, causing excessive free play in steering or loss of control. **1979:** brake pushrod pins could fall out, resulting in loss of braking ability. **1981:** faulty neutral safety switch could allow car to be started when transmission is in reverse gear. **1981:** possibility water could leak into electrical relays, causing overheating and potential for fire. **1983:** retaining pins in automatic overdrive transmissions could break; parking pawl may not then engage

1981 Mercury Marquis 4-door

1987 Mercury Grand Marquis 4-door

when selector lever is placed in "Park," allowing car to roll as if it were in neutral. **1984:** seatbelt anchors may not meet federal safety requirements. **1986–88:** check retainer clips on fuel-line spring-lock couplings of fuel-injected engines. **1987:** some fuel-injection tube assemblies may be bent, creating potential for fuel leakage and engine fire. **1987:** steering centerlinks may break at bend location, diminishing control and allowing considerable free play in steering wheel.

Mercury Marquis 1983-86

1983 Mercury Marquis 4-door

Roomy, comfortable, well-built compact/mid-size is nearly identical to Ford LTD in appearance and prices. Both evolved from the 1981–82 Granada/Cougar platform. Soft chassis doesn't help handling qualities. Base 2.3-liter four is too small, but the optional V-6 delivers adequate performance and economy. For 1986, the last model year for the Marquis, only the V-6 was available. (See the LTD entry for more details.) A 4-door sedan and 5-door wagon are available.

Price Range	GOOD	AVERAGE	POOR
1983 Marquis	$3800—4400	$3200—4000	$2800—3200
1984 Marquis	4600—5300	4200—4900	3600—4200
1985 Marquis	5700—6700	5300—6100	4600—5300
1986 Marquis	7000—8000	6600—7500	5800—6600

Dimensions	WHEEL-BASE, IN.	LGTH., IN.	HT., IN.	WIDTH, IN.	AVG. WT., LBS.	CARGO VOL., CU. FT.	FUEL TANK, GAL.
4d sdn	105.6	196.5	53.8	71.0	3001	15.1	16.0
5d wgn	105.6	196.5	54.4	71.0	3115	75.4	15.3

Mercury

1984 Mercury Marquis 4-door

Engines	L/CID	BHP	MPG	AVAIL.
ohc I-4 1 bbl.	2.3/140	88–93	17–21	83–85
ohc I-4 Propane	2.3/140	—	20–24	83–84
ohv I-6 1 bbl.	3.3/200	87	17–21	83
ohv V-6 2 bbl.	3.8/232	105	16–20	83
ohv V-6 FI	3.8/232	120	17–20	84–86
ohv V-8 FI	5.0/302	165	16–19	85

KEY: L/CID = liters/cubic inch displacement; **BHP** = brake horsepower; **MPG** = estimated average miles per gallon; **ohc** = overhead cam; **dohc** = double overhead cam; **ohv** = overhead valve; **I** = in-line engine; **V** = V engine; **flat** = horizontally opposed engine; **D** = diesel; **T** = turbocharged; **bbl.** = barrel (carburetor); **FI** = fuel injection.

RECALL HISTORY

1983: cars with 3.3-liter engine and C-5 automatic transmission, for possibility that vibrations over long period could cause leak in transmission oil cooler line. **1984:** seatbelt anchors may not meet federal safety requirements. **1984–85:** defective ignition module could make 2.3-liter engine hard to start, run poorly or stall. **1985:** rear shell of tandem power brake boosters on cars with 3.8- or 5.0-liter engine (except police/taxi) may have thin wall that could crack after repeated brake use and come apart; braking ability would be totally lost without warning.

Mercury Sable 1986-88

Daringly styled companion to the aerodynamic (and hot selling) Ford Taurus shares mechanical components, but no sedan sheetmetal. Wagons use Taurus metal from the windshield back, but Mercury's unique grille-free front

1987 Mercury Sable LS 4-door

end serves both bodies. Sables are powered by a 3.0-liter V-6 with 4-speed overdrive automatic transmission. Acceleration is decent, both from a standstill and when passing. A new 3.8-liter V-6 with balance shaft and multi-point fuel injection, optional for 1988, offers the same horsepower as the 3.0 but a lot more torque to boost low-speed pickup. The Taurus 4-cylinder engine is not available. Slick, modern styling has encouraged plenty of Sable sales, but added temptations lurk beneath the car's streamlined skin. Road manners are impressive, even with standard suspension, which is more comfortable than Taurus' over bumps. Firm, responsive steering lets the car zip around tight turns almost like an agile Eurosedan. Spacious interior holds four adults without cramping (one or two more could squeeze in). Controls are logically positioned and easy to use. Plush, tasteful furnishings add to comfortable feeling. Early models suffered from uneven idle and tended to die after cold starts. First heater outlets didn't deliver much warmth. We like Sable's look, feel and performance, though second-hand prices are hefty.

Price Range	GOOD	AVERAGE	POOR
1986 Sable	$9700–12,500	$9100–11,250	$8400–9200
1987 Sable	11,500–14,000	10,500–13,000	9500–11,000
1988 Sable	13,000–15,500	12,000–14,500	—

Dimensions	WHEEL-BASE, IN.	LGTH., IN.	HT., IN.	WIDTH, IN.	AVG. WT., LBS.	CARGO VOL., CU. FT.	FUEL TANK, GAL.
4d sdn	106.0	190.9	54.3	70.8	3054	18.5	16.0
5d wgn	106.0	191.9	55.1	70.7	3228	45.7	16.0

Mercury

1987 Mercury Sable LS 5-door

Engines	L/CID	BHP	MPG	AVAIL.
ohv V-6 FI	3.0/182	140	20–25	86–88
ohv V-6 FI	3.8/232	140	NA	88

KEY: L/CID = liters/cubic inch displacement; **BHP** = brake horsepower; **MPG** = estimated average miles per gallon; **ohc** = overhead cam; **dohc** = double overhead cam; **ohv** = overhead valve; **I** = in-line engine; **V** = V engine; **flat** = horizontally opposed engine; **D** = diesel; **T** = turbocharged; **bbl.** = barrel (carburetor); **FI** = fuel injection.

RECALL HISTORY

See Ford Taurus 1986–88 entry for recall information.

Mercury Topaz 1984-88

Aerodynamic front-drive sedan differs from Ford Tempo only in trim and option selection. Unusual "jellybean" styling is more distinctive than most rivals. Base 2.3-liter four was fuel-injected by 1985 and given multi-point injection (plus 12 more horsepower) for '88. High-output four was offered for 1985–86 (with 5-speed manual shift only) as part of GS Sports Group; later also with optional 4WD and automatic. Third choice: a Mazda-built diesel. New '88 sheetmetal includes a vertical-bar grille, while XR5 and LS Sport models replace the GS Sport. Check 1984-88 Ford Tempo entry for further comments. Both give you a lot of car for a moderate price.

1986 Mercury Topaz 2-door

Price Range	GOOD	AVERAGE	POOR
1984 Topaz	$3900–4400	$3500–4100	$2900–3500
1985 Topaz	5200–6100	4700–5500	4100–4700
1986 Topaz	6400–7300	5900–6500	5100–5800
1987 Topaz	7900–9000	7200–8200	6600–7400
1988 Topaz	9500–11,000	8500–10,000	—

Dimensions	WHEEL-BASE, IN.	LGTH., IN.	HT., IN.	WIDTH, IN.	AVG. WT., LBS.	CARGO VOL., CU. FT.	FUEL TANK, GAL.
2d sdn	99.9	176.5	52.7	68.3	2485	13.2	15.2
4d sdn	99.9	176.5	52.7	68.3	2507	12.9	15.2

Engines	L/CID	BHP	MPG	AVAIL.
ohv I-4 2 bbl.	2.3/141	84	22–27	84
ohv I-4 FI	2.3/141	86–98	22–27	85–88
ohv I-4 FI	2.3/141	94–100	22–26	85–88
ohc I-4D FI	2.0/121	52	32–36	84–86

KEY: L/CID = liters/cubic inch displacement; **BHP** = brake horsepower; **MPG** = estimated average miles per gallon; **ohc** = overhead cam; **dohc** = double overhead cam; **ohv** = overhead valve; **I** = in-line engine; **V** = V engine; **flat** = horizontally opposed engine; **D** = diesel; **T** = turbocharged; **bbl.** = barrel (carburetor); **FI** = fuel injection.

RECALL HISTORY

1984: front seatbelt webbing on cars without reclining seats could be cut or severed in a frontal crash. **1984:** forward bolt that partly attaches driver's seat back assembly to seat cushion frame may be subject to fatigue fracture; if bolt breaks, seat back will fall backward, which could result in driver losing control. **1984–85:** rear suspension control-arm-to-spindle attachment bolts may be subject to fracture during car use; rear spindle could then disengage, possibly resulting in loss of control. **1984–85:** defective igni-

Mercury

1984 Mercury Topaz 4-door

tion module could make 2.3-liter engine hard to start, run poorly or stall. **1985–86:** stiffness of thick rubber material that covers gearshift on manual transmission may push shift lever out of gear and toward neutral, when operated in cold weather (under 40°F). **1986:** on cars with 2.3-liter engine (non-California) and automatic transmission, intermittent timing in the electronic engine control processor may cause throttle to remain partly open, resulting in unexpected increase in engine speed. **1987:** disturbance in electronic control module of 2.3-liter engine (manual shift) may cause high idling speed, loss of power and, eventually, engine may stop running.

Mercury Zephyr 1978-83

Sensible rear-drive compact on "Fox" platform is virtually identical to Ford Fairmont, except for grille and trim. Avoid the weak, noisy base 4-cylinder engine, which is no more economical than the 200-cid six. For better pickup (but less gas mileage) look for a V-8. Zephyr is a worthy family car, not so much different from the more luxurious 1981–82 Cougar and 1983–86 Marquis. But before you buy, check Fairmont entry for further comments and long recall list.

Price Range	GOOD	AVERAGE	POOR
1978 Zephyr	$1000–1300	$750—1000	$450–750
1979 Zephyr	1200–1500	950–1200	600–950
1980 Zephyr	1700–2000	1250–1700	1000–1250
1981 Zephyr	1900–2400	1500–2000	1100–1500
1982 Zephyr	2400–2900	2000–2600	1600–2000
1983 Zephyr	2900–3400	2600–3100	2200–2600

CONSUMER GUIDE®

1978 Mercury Zephyr 2-door

1979 Mercury Zephyr 4-door

Dimensions	WHEEL-BASE, IN.	LGTH., IN.	HT., IN.	WIDTH, IN.	AVG. WT., LBS.	CARGO VOL. CU. FT.	FUEL TANK, GAL.
2d cpe/sdn	105.5	195.5	52.9	71.0	2750	16.8	14.0
4d sdn	105.5	195.5	52.9	71.0	2800	16.8	14.0
5d wgn	105.5	195.5	54.2	71.0	2900	79.5	14.0

Engines	L/CID	BHP	MPG	AVAIL.
ohc I-4 2 bbl.	2.3/140	88–93	18–22	78–83
ohv I-6 1 bbl.	3.3/200	85–91	18–21	78–83
ohv V-8 2 bbl.	4.2/255	119	16–19	80–81
ohv V-8 2 bbl.	5.0/302	139–140	15–18	78–79

KEY: L/CID = liters/cubic inch displacement; **BHP** = brake horsepower; **MPG** = estimated average miles per gallon; **ohc** = overhead cam; **dohc** = double overhead cam; **ohv** = overhead valve; **I** = in-line engine; **V** = V engine; **flat** = horizontally opposed engine; **D** = diesel; **T** = turbocharged; **bbl.** = barrel (carburetor); **FI** = fuel injection.

RECALL HISTORY

See Ford Fairmont 1978–83 entry for complete recall information.

Mitsubishi Cordia/Tredia 1983-88

1983 Mitsubishi Cordia L 3-door

These sporty, upscale front-drive cars were Mitsubishi's volume models for most of these years, so they should be the easiest of this brand to find on used-car lots. Cordia comes only as a 3-door hatchback, while Tredia comes only as a 4-door sedan. Under the skin, they're the same, sharing engines, transmissions and suspensions. Judged by overall length, they're compact cars; judged by their modest 96.3-inch wheelbase and cramped interiors, they're subcompacts. The 1983 models come only with an 82-horsepower 1.8-liter four. That engine grew to 2.0 liters and 88 horsepower for 1984, when a 116-horsepower turbo 1.8 also arrived. The turbo comes only with a 5-speed manual, while the naturally aspirated engines come with manual or 3-speed automatic transmissions. Later models have longer factory warranties (five years on rust; three years on electronic components) that can be transferred to second owners. These cars have generally good repair records, but they've consistently been among the worst for injury claims, according to insurance industry statistics.

Price Range	GOOD	AVERAGE	POOR
1983 Cordia	$4000–4500	$3500–4000	$3000–3500
1983 Tredia	3600–4000	3200–3600	2800–3200
1984 Cordia	5000–5600	4200–5000	3600–4200
1984 Tredia	4500–5100	4000–4500	3500–4000

Price Range	GOOD	AVERAGE	POOR
1985 Cordia	5300–5700	4900–5300	4600–4900
1985 Tredia	5400–5800	4800–5400	4400–4800
1986 Cordia	6900–7400	6400–6900	5900–6400
1986 Tredia	6500–7000	6000–6500	5500–6000
1987 Cordia	8600–9200	8000–8600	7400–8000
1987 Tredia	7800–8200	7400–7800	7000–7400
1988 Cordia	10,000–10,900	9300–10,000	—
1988 Tredia	9500–10,200	9000–9500	—

Dimensions	WHEEL-BASE, IN.	LGTH., IN.	HT., IN.	WIDTH, IN.	AVG. WT., LBS.	CARGO VOL., CU. FT.	FUEL TANK, GAL.
3d cpe	96.3	173.0	49.4	65.4	2325	NA	12.8
4d sdn	96.3	172.4	51.6	65.4	2365	13.6	12.8

1986 Mitsubishi Cordia L 3-door

1986 Mitsubishi Tredia Turbo 4-door

Mitsubishi

Engines	L/CID	BHP	MPG	AVAIL.
ohc I-4 2 bbl.	1.8/110	82	27–32	83
ohc I-4 2 bbl.	2.0/122	88	25–30	84–88
ohc I-4T FI	1.8/110	116	23–28	84–88

KEY: L/CID = liters/cubic inch displacement; **BHP** = brake horsepower; **MPG** = estimated average miles per gallon; **ohc** = overhead cam; **dohc** = double overhead cam; **ohv** = overhead valve; **I** = in-line engine; **V** = V engine; **flat** = horizontally opposed engine; **D** = diesel; **T** = turbocharged; **bbl.** = barrel (carburetor); **FI** = fuel injection.

RECALL HISTORY

1983: throttle could remain open on some models with automatic transmission because of interference from a cotter-pin retainer.

Mitsubishi Galant 1985-87

1985 Mitsubishi Galant 4-door

The front-drive Galant is a "near-luxury" sedan that Mitsubishi positioned against the Nissan Maxima and Toyota Cressida. Galant was priced well below Nissan's and Toyota's luxury cars, but came only with a 2.4-liter 4-cylinder engine (Maxima and Cressida have 6-cylinder engines). Horsepower jumped to 110 from 101 in 1986 with a change to multi-point fuel injection from single-point injection. Nearly all Galants came with a 4-speed overdrive automatic transmission with electronic shift controls. In 1987, a 5-speed manual transmission was offered, but few were sold. With automatic, there's adequate acceleration and decent fuel economy. Electronics abound in the fully equipped Galant: All models have power windows, locks and mirrors; cruise control; and electronically tuned stereo systems with power antennas. In addition to the automatic transmission, the power steering and climate control systems are electronically controlled, plus some models have the optional ECS Package (electronically controlled suspension). We'd avoid the ECS Package since it does little to improve ride and handling, but can be expensive to fix if it breaks. A 3-year/36,000-mile warranty covering major electronic components became standard for 1987 and is transferable to second owners. With so many electronic components standard or optional, it would be prudent to find a Galant still under warranty.

Price Range	GOOD	AVERAGE	POOR
1985 Galant	$8000–8300	$7600–8000	$7100–7600
1986 Galant	9400–10,000	8800–9400	8400–8800
1987 Galant	10,600–11,500	10,000–10,600	—

Dimensions	WHEEL-BASE, IN.	LGTH., IN.	HT., IN.	WIDTH, IN.	AVG. WT., LBS.	CARGO VOL., CU. FT.	FUEL TANK, GAL.
4d sdn	102.4	183.1	51.6	66.7	2795	NA	15.9

Engines	L/CID	BHP	MPG	AVAIL.
ohc I-4 FI	2.4/143	101–110	20–25	85–87

KEY: L/CID = liters/cubic inch displacement; BHP = brake horsepower; MPG = estimated average miles per gallon; ohc = overhead cam; dohc = double overhead cam; ohv = overhead valve; I = in-line engine; V = V engine; flat = horizontally opposed engine; D = diesel; T = turbocharged; bbl. = barrel (carburetor); FI = fuel injection.

RECALL HISTORY

None to date.

1986 Mitsubishi Galant 4-door

Mitsubishi Mirage/Precis 1985-88

1985 Mitsubishi Mirage Turbo 3-door

These front-drive compacts are of similar design, but differ in sheetmetal and in country of manufacture. Mirage is built by Mitsubishi in Japan. Also sold as the Dodge/Plymouth Colt, it debuted under the Mitsubishi banner in 1985. Precis is built for Mitsubishi by Hyundai in Korea. It was designed by Mitsubishi and introduced in 1987. Hyundai also sells it as the Excel. Mirage is available as a 3-door hatchback or 4-door notchback, Precis as a 3- or 5-door hatchback. Both come standard with a carbureted

1987 Mitsubishi Precis 3-door

1.5-liter 4-cylinder. A 1.6-liter turbocharged engine is available in the Mirage. Mileage is high, but the normally aspirated engines give weak acceleration, especially with automatic transmission. The Mitsubishis handle pretty well, and the turbocharged Mirage is a budget hot rod. Interiors on the hatchbacks are cramped, but the sedan is fairly comfortable for four adults. Good build quality and reliability make these attractive used-car buys in the economy sector.

Price Range	GOOD	AVERAGE	POOR
1985 Mirage	$3900–5200	$3700–4800	$3100–3800
1986 Mirage	4900–6100	4400–5400	3600–4500
1987 Mirage	5900–7350	5300–6600	4800–5400
1987 Precis	5500–6000	5000–5500	4500–5000
1988 Mirage	6800–8900	6100–8100	—
1988 Precis	6200–6800	5600–6200	5000–5600

Dimensions	WHEEL-BASE, IN.	LGTH., IN.	HT., IN.	WIDTH, IN.	AVG. WT., LBS.	CARGO VOL., CU. FT.	FUEL TANK, GAL.
Mirage 3d sdn	93.7	157.3	53.5	63.8	2018	11.7	11.9
Mirage 4d sdn	93.7	169.1	64.4	53.5	2059	10.9	11.9
Precis 3d sdn	93.7	160.9	63.1	54.1	2161	13.2	10.6
Precis 5d sdn	93.7	160.9	63.1	54.1	2161	12.9	10.6

Engines	L/CID	BHP	MPG	AVAIL.
ohc I-4 2 bbl.	1.5/90	68	26–38	85–88
ohc I-4T FI	1.6/97	102–105	24–28	85–88

KEY: L/CID = liters/cubic inch displacement; **BHP** = brake horsepower; **MPG** = estimated average miles per gallon; **ohc** = overhead cam; **dohc** = double overhead cam; **ohv** = overhead valve; **I** = in-line engine; **V** = V engine; **flat** = horizontally opposed engine; **D** = diesel; **T** = turbocharged; **bbl.** = barrel (carburetor); **FI** = fuel injection.

RECALL HISTORY

None to date.

Mitsubishi Starion 1983-88

Turbocharged rear-drive 3-door coupe, the star performer in Mitsubishi's stable, first came in three levels: standard LS, luxury LE and sporty ES (with standard anti-lock rear brakes since '84). The 2.6-liter four is noisy when pushed hard, but delivers swift acceleration. Fully independent suspension gives capable handling. Performance got an even bigger boost with the mid-1985 debut of an intercooled

Mitsubishi

1983 Mitsubishi Starion ES 3-door

ESI model. Next year the LS was dropped but the super-hot ESI-R arrived. Automatic transmission has been offered only on the LE, which departed after 1987, and the latest ESI-R. For '88, both the new basic ESI and top-line ESI-R carry 188-horsepower intercooled turbos. Starion has an impressive record in showroom-stock endurance races, but shines less brightly in gas mileage. Road noise is annoying; interior space limited. Competing with such blazing performers as Nissan 300ZX, Toyota Supra and Mustang GT, Starion ranks high and is cheaper than most. If all this sounds tempting but you can't spot a Starion, look for a Dodge/Plymouth Conquest; it's the same car. Watch for signs of hard usage either way, and note that regular valve adjustment is essential to prevent engine problems.

1987 Mitsubishi Starion ESI-R 3-door

Price Range	GOOD	AVERAGE	POOR
1983 Starion	$5800–6400	$5400–6000	$4800–5400
1984 Starion	7000–7900	6600–7300	6000–6600
1985 Starion	8400–9600	7900–8800	7000–7900
1986 Starion	10,750–12,500	10,250–11,750	9500–10,500
1987 Starion	12,500–14,500	11,750–13,500	11,000–12,000
1988 Starion	16,000–18,000	14,500–17,000	—

Dimensions	WHEEL-BASE, IN.	LGTH., IN.	HT., IN.	WIDTH, IN.	AVG. WT., LBS.	CARGO VOL., CU. FT.	FUEL TANK, GAL.
3d cpe	95.9	173.2	50.2	66.3	2828	19.0	19.8

Engines	L/CID	BHP	MPG	AVAIL.
ohc I-4T FI	2.6/156	145	18–22	83–87
ohc I-4T FI	2.6/156	170–188	17–22	86–88

KEY: L/CID = liters/cubic inch displacement; **BHP** = brake horsepower; **MPG** = estimated average miles per gallon; **ohc** = overhead cam; **dohc** = double overhead cam; **ohv** = overhead valve; **I** = in-line engine; **V** = V engine; **flat** = horizontally opposed engine; **D** = diesel; **T** = turbocharged; **bbl.** = barrel (carburetor); **FI** = fuel injection.

RECALL HISTORY

None to date.

Nissan Maxima 1985-88

Premium sedan switched to front-wheel drive with a transverse-mounted 3.0-liter V-6 engine--the powerplant used in the 300ZX sports car. The 4-door sedan comes in GL or sporty SE trim; wagon in GL only. Aiming to compete with Euro-style sport sedans, the SE had only 5-speed manual shift until '87, while GL models carry overdrive automatic. A new GXE series replaced the GL for '87. Standard luxury touches include a sophisticated six-speaker sound system, keyless entry and, starting in '86, a theft-deterrent system. Road manners are capable with 4-wheel independent suspension, aided by driver-adjustable shock absorbers in the SE. Big news for 1988: a high-tech suspension with sonar-like sensor that matches ride characteristics to road conditions. Refined, powerful V-6 delivers fine performance, though fuel mileage disappoints. Interior space could be better. Five adults fit only in a pinch, but trunk is large. Maximas carry a big load of equipment for the luxury-minded buyer, and may become a good value as more reach the used-car market.

Nissan

1985 Nissan Maxima SE 4-door

Price Range	GOOD	AVERAGE	POOR
1985 Maxima	$9800–10,500	$9200–10,000	$8600–9200
1986 Maxima	11,750–12,500	11,000–11,750	10,000–11,000
1987 Maxima	14,000–15,500	13,000–14,500	12,000–13,000
1988 Maxima	16,000–17,500	15,000–16,750	—

Dimensions	WHEEL-BASE, IN.	LGTH., IN.	HT., IN.	WIDTH, IN.	AVG. WT., LBS.	CARGO VOL., CU. FT.	FUEL TANK, GAL.
4d sdn	100.4	181.7	55.1	66.5	3060	14.5	15.9
5d wgn	100.4	184.6	56.1	66.5	3296	NA	15.9

Engines	L/CID	BHP	MPG	AVAIL.
ohc V-6 FI	3.0/181	152	17–22	85–88

KEY: L/CID = liters/cubic inch displacement; **BHP** = brake horsepower; **MPG** = estimated average miles per gallon; **ohc** = overhead cam; **dohc** = double overhead

1985 Nissan Maxima GL 5-door

cam; **ohv** = overhead valve; **I** = in-line engine; **V** = V engine; **flat** = horizontally opposed engine; **D** = diesel; **T** = turbocharged; **bbl.** = barrel (carburetor); **FI** = fuel injection.

RECALL HISTORY

1985–86: may be insufficient adhesive between windshield bottom and car body; windshield may come loose during an accident, allowing car occupants to be ejected from car.

Nissan Pulsar 1983-86

1983 Nissan Pulsar 5-door

Rebodied variant of the front-drive Sentra, meant to replace the earlier 310, shares Sentra's running gear and all-independent suspension. Hatchback sedans lasted only a year, and only the sporty NX notchback coupe survived after 1983. NX is a strange looking beast with a vertical backlight and pop-up headlamps. Performance lacks zip (especially with automatic), but the 1.6-liter four makes a lot of noise while trying. Gas mileage is Pulsar's strong point: expect 30 mpg even in the city, with a 5-speed. A turbocharged engine lasted only through part of the '84 model year. Seats are poorly padded in a cheap-looking interior. Grownups won't like the back seat. You get a lot of standard features, but Pulsar is cramped and crude, not up to the usual Japanese quality. Redesigned for 1987 as a versatile and attractive 3-door hatchback coupe.

Nissan

Price Range	GOOD	AVERAGE	POOR
1983 Pulsar	$3500–4300	$3100–3900	$2500–3100
1984 Pulsar	5100–5500	4700–5200	4100–4700
1985 Pulsar	6100–6500	5700–6200	5000–5700
1986 Pulsar	6900–7400	6500–7000	6000–6500

Dimensions	WHEEL-BASE, IN.	LGTH., IN.	HT., IN.	WIDTH, IN.	AVG. WT., LBS.	CARGO VOL., CU. FT.	FUEL TANK, GAL.
2d cpe	95.1	162.4	53.3	63.8	2008	10.3	13.2
3d sdn	95.0	162.0	54.3	63.7	1895	NA	13.2
5d sdn	95.0	162.0	54.3	63.7	1907	NA	13.2

Engines	L/CID	BHP	MPG	AVAIL.
ohc I-4 2 bbl.	1.6/97	69	27–32	83–86
ohc I-4T FI	1.5/91	100	24–27	84

KEY: L/CID = liters/cubic inch displacement; **BHP** = brake horsepower; **MPG** = estimated average miles per gallon; **ohc** = overhead cam; **dohc** = double overhead cam; **ohv** = overhead valve; **I** = in-line engine; **V** = V engine; **flat** = horizontally opposed engine; **D** = diesel; **T** = turbocharged; **bbl.** = barrel (carburetor); **FI** = fuel injection.

RECALL HISTORY

1983–84: operating hood latch lever in incorrect direction with extremely strong force could damage assembly and eventually result in separation of secondary hood latch; if primary latch were not fully engaged, hood could open unexpectedly. **1984:** impure lubricant in headlight switch could contaminate one or more contact points, possibly causing loss or delay of light operation.

Nissan Pulsar 1987-88

Radical restyle, emanating from California design studio, altered Pulsar from an economical eyesore with mediocre performance to a "flexible" flyer with plenty of potential. Front-drive 3-door hatchback coupe only seats two, but a tiny bench seat in back is okay for kids and emergencies. T-bar roof has removable steel panels, and the hatchback lid comes off to add cargo space. Base 1.6-liter four, now fuel-injected, retains the prior Pulsar's economy but adds nothing to performance since the new model is heavier. Rather, it's the 16-valve, dual overhead cam version that turns Pulsar into a moving machine. Standard in the SE, that engine grew from 1.6 to 1.8 liters for 1988. First offered only with 5-speed manual transmission, the SE is available with a 4-speed overdrive automatic for 1988. Latest Pulsar

1987 Nissan Pulsar NX SE

is both practical and fun to drive, especially with roof panels to let the air flow through. Air conditioner is inadequate, though, and cuts into available power. Handling and roadholding are good, but expect a fair amount of noise, not unlike those memorable old British sports cars.

Price Range	GOOD	AVERAGE	POOR
1987 Pulsar	$10,250–11,250	$9500–10,500	$9000–9500
1988 Pulsar	11,750–13,000	11,000–12,000	—

Dimensions	WHEEL-BASE, IN.	LGTH., IN.	HT., IN.	WIDTH, IN.	AVG. WT., LBS.	CARGO VOL., CU. FT.	FUEL TANK, GAL.
3d cpe	95.7	166.5	50.8	65.7	2380	NA	13.2

1987 Nissan Pulsar NX SE

Nissan

Engines	L/CID	BHP	MPG	AVAIL.
ohc I-4 FI	1.6/97	70	25–30	87–88
dohc I-4 FI	1.6/97	113	22–27	87
dohc I-4 FI	1.8/110	125	21–26	88

KEY: L/CID = liters/cubic inch displacement; **BHP** = brake horsepower; **MPG** = estimated average miles per gallon; **ohc** = overhead cam; **dohc** = double overhead cam; **ohv** = overhead valve; **I** = in-line engine; **V** = V engine; **flat** = horizontally opposed engine; **D** = diesel; **T** = turbocharged; **bbl.** = barrel (carburetor); **FI** = fuel injection.

RECALL HISTORY

None to date.

Nissan Sentra 1982-86

1983 Nissan Sentra 4-door

Front-drive subcompact successor to the Datsun 210 managed to become the best-selling imported car. Initial 1.5-liter four was enlarged to 1.6 liters for 1983. Diesel optional 1983–85. Durability/reliability record has been fine, maintaining Nissan's admirable reputation. More modern than 210, Sentra delivers excellent mileage and a pretty good ride. Performance is hardly exciting as the coarse engine strains loudly at higher rpm. Handling is flawed by too much body roll in hard cornering, wind/road noise is strong, and sheetmetal sounds tinny. Small interior is nicely laid out, if tackily trimmed. Capably engineered and well equipped, an easygoing Sentra offers good value in a used econobox. Redesigned 1987 Sentra is a bit longer, wider and heavier, available in 4WD wagon form.

Price Range	GOOD	AVERAGE	POOR
1982 Sentra	$2200–3100	$1900–2700	$1400–2000
1983 Sentra	2900–3800	2600–3500	2100–2800
1984 Sentra	3500–4800	3200–4300	2700–3500
1985 Sentra	4300–5900	3900–5400	3400–4300
1986 Sentra	5100–7200	4700–6700	4000–5200

Dimensions	WHEEL-BASE, IN.	LGTH., IN.	HT., IN.	WIDTH, IN.	AVG. WT., LBS.	CARGO VOL., CU. FT.	FUEL TANK, GAL.
2d sdn	94.5	165.3	54.5	63.8	1918	11.3	13.2
3d cpe	94.5	165.6	53.3	63.8	2028	16.5	13.2
4d sdn	94.5	165.3	54.5	63.8	1939	11.3	13.2
5d wgn	94.5	170.2	53.5	63.8	2024	23.5	13.2

Engines	L/CID	BHP	MPG	AVAIL.
ohc I-4 2 bbl.	1.5/91	67	28–33	82
ohc I-4 2 bbl.	1.6/97	69	27–32	83–86
ohc I-4D FI	1.7/103	55	32–38	83–85

KEY: L/CID = liters/cubic inch displacement; **BHP** = brake horsepower; **MPG** = estimated average miles per gallon; **ohc** = overhead cam; **dohc** = double overhead cam; **ohv** = overhead valve; **I** = in-line engine; **V** = V engine; **flat** = horizontally opposed engine; **D** = diesel; **T** = turbocharged; **bbl.** = barrel (carburetor); **FI** = fuel injection.

RECALL HISTORY

1982–83: windshield wiper blade could catch on radio antenna bracket, damaging wiper arm and preventing proper operation.

1984 Nissan Sentra 3-door

Nissan Sentra 1987-88

1987 Nissan Sentra SE Sport Coupe 3-door

Nissan's most popular U.S. model gained some weight but grew only slightly when redesigned as an early '87. The 1.6-liter carbureted engine was the same as before, but the new 3-door sport coupe and 4WD wagon (and all '88 models) have a fuel-injected version. A dashboard switch engages the wagon's 4-wheel drive "on the fly." The sporty SE coupe is a lot more athletic than any previous Sentra, cornering capably and hugging the road in wet weather. Performance rates only adequate, though, even with man-

1987 Nissan Sentra XE 3-door

ual shift. Economy is much more impressive; we averaged 30 mpg around the city. Back seat space in the coupe (really a 2 + 2) is narrow; other models are better, if hardly spacious. This latest Sentra has a much more solid, substantial—even upscale—feel, not so flimsy as before. Insulation has improved, too, though engine and road noise still can grow annoying. Some sedans are built in Tennessee. For dependable low-budget transportation, Sentra remains an excellent choice.

Price Range	GOOD	AVERAGE	POOR
1987 Sentra	$5900–8500	$5400–8000	$4700–6500
1988 Sentra	6400–10,000	5900–9000	—

Dimensions	WHEEL-BASE, IN.	LGTH., IN.	HT., IN.	WIDTH, IN.	AVG. WT., LBS.	CARGO VOL. CU. FT.	FUEL TANK, GAL.
3d cpe	95.7	166.5	52.2	65.6	2258	NA	13.2
2d sdn	95.7	168.7	54.3	64.6	2200	NA	13.2
3d sdn	95.7	162.4	55.3	64.6	2238	NA	13.2
4d sdn	95.7	168.7	54.3	64.6	2231	NA	13.2
5d wgn	95.7	172.2	54.3	64.6	2304	NA	13.2

Engines	L/CID	BHP	MPG	AVAIL.
ohc I-4 2 bbl.	1.6/97	70	26–31	87
ohc I-4 FI	1.6/97	70	27–32	87–88

KEY: L/CID = liters/cubic inch displacement; **BHP** = brake horsepower; **MPG** = estimated average miles per gallon; **ohc** = overhead cam; **dohc** = double overhead cam; **ohv** = overhead valve; **I** = in-line engine; **V** = V engine; **flat** = horizontally opposed engine; **D** = diesel; **T** = turbocharged; **bbl.** = barrel (carburetor); **FI** = fuel injection.

RECALL HISTORY

None to date.

1987 Nissan Sentra GXE 4-door

Nissan Stanza 1982-86

1982 Nissan Stanza 5-door

1986 Nissan Stanza 4WD wagon

Mid-level front-drive model took over the 510's spot in the Nissan lineup. Peppy 2.0-liter four, fuel injected since '84, offers spunky performance and good mileage with a 5-speed, and isn't so bad even with automatic. Original 3- and 5-door hatchbacks, in base Deluxe or upscale XE trim, were joined during 1983 by a plush GL 4-door sedan. Deluxe hatchbacks departed the next year and in '85 the 3-door was dropped. A front-drive wagon, longer in wheelbase and 10 inches taller than the sedan, joined the roster late in the 1985 model year. A wagon with pillarless side styling appeared for '86 in 2- and 4-wheel-drive versions.

Stanza is agile enough, but soft suspension produces a lot of bounce and sway. Front seats roomy; two adults fit in back. Though assembly quality seems very good, we're less certain about durability of the lightweight sheetmetal. Still, Stanza has impressed us favorably and should provide good service as a secondhand compact. Bigger 1987 version was restyled along Maxima lines.

Price Range	GOOD	AVERAGE	POOR
1982 Stanza	$2900–3200	$2600–3000	$2100–2600
1983 Stanza	3800–4400	3500–4100	3000–3500
1984 Stanza	5100–5700	4800–5400	4300–4800
1985 Stanza	6500–7000	6000–6500	5400–6000
1986 Stanza	8000–8800	7600–8400	7000–7600

Dimensions	WHEEL-BASE, IN.	LGTH., IN.	HT., IN.	WIDTH, IN.	AVG. WT., LBS.	CARGO VOL., CU.FT.	FUEL TANK, GAL.
3d sdn	97.2	170.9	53.9	65.6	2300	18.3	14.3
4d sdn	97.2	173.4	54.7	65.2	2325	11.4	14.3
5d sdn	97.2	173.4	54.7	65.2	2302	19.3	14.3
5d wgn	99.0	170.3	64.2	65.6	2809	80.0	15.9

Engines	L/CID	BHP	MPG	AVAIL.
ohc I-4 2 bbl.	2.0/120	88	24–29	82–83
ohc I-4 FI	2.0/120	97	24–29	84–86

KEY: L/CID = liters/cubic inch displacement; **BHP** = brake horsepower; **MPG** = estimated average miles per gallon; **ohc** = overhead cam; **dohc** = double overhead cam; **ohv** = overhead valve; **I** = in-line engine; **V** = V engine; **flat** = horizontally opposed engine; **D** = diesel; **T** = turbocharged; **bbl.** = barrel (carburetor); **FI** = fuel injection.

RECALL HISTORY

1982: brake pedal height may have been adjusted lower than specified, which could result in longer stopping distances under certain conditions. **1986 wagon (2WD):** in a certain type of rear-end collision, the edge of a welded bracket may pierce fuel filler pipe, causing fuel leakage; cover should be installed.

Nissan Stanza 1987-88

Compact family sedans were redesigned along luxury Maxima lines, atop its longer front-drive platform, for debut in spring 1986. Size grew only a few inches, but weight shot up 450 pounds. The 2.0-liter four comes from the previous Stanza, offered with standard 5-speed manual gearbox or optional 4-speed overdrive automatic. The 4-door

Nissan

1987 Nissan Stanza XE 5-door

sedan comes in E or upscale GXE trim; XE 5-door hatchback was dropped after the first year due to weak sales. Five-door wagon has entirely different styling: upright and boxy, nearly 10 inches taller than the sedan but on a shorter wheelbase. Sliding doors on both sides make the spacious wagon unusually easy to enter, and it's available with part-time ("shift-on-the-fly") 4-wheel drive. Sedan's trunk is deep and rear seatback folds down for extra cargo space. Both models are underpowered; the familiar Stanza engine struggles harder than ever to pull the increased weight. Stanza handles capably and rides comfortably, though the tires tend to squeal around corners. The tall wagon leans a bit in turns and gets tossed about by crosswinds. Fluid levels are easy to check. Stanza has a lot to offer for a moderate price. If only that engine had a little more power, we'd like it even better.

1987 Nissan Stanza GXE 4-door

Price Range	GOOD	AVERAGE	POOR
1987 Stanza	$9300–10,800	$8800–10,200	$8000–9500
1988 Stanza	10,300–12,750	9800–12,000	—

Dimensions	WHEEL-BASE, IN.	LGTH., IN.	HT., IN.	WIDTH, IN.	AVG. WT. LBS.	CARGO VOL., CU. FT.	FUEL TANK, GAL.
4d sdn	100.4	177.8	54.9	66.5	2770	12.0	16.1
5d sdn	100.4	176.2	54.9	66.5	2845	22.0	16.1
5d wgn	99.0	170.3	64.2	65.6	2950	80.0	15.9

Engines	L/CID	BHP	MPG	AVAIL.
ohc I-4 FI	2.0/120	97	21–27	87–88

KEY: L/CID = liters/cubic inch displacement; **BHP** = brake horsepower; **MPG** = estimated average miles per gallon; **ohc** = overhead cam; **ohv** = overhead valve; **I** = in-line engine; **V** = V engine; **flat** = horizontally opposed engine; **D** = diesel; **T** = turbocharged; **bbl.** = barrel (carburetor); **FI** = fuel injection.

RECALL HISTORY

None to date.

(Nissan) Datsun 200-SX 1980-83

1981 Datsun 200-SX SL 2-door

Sporty coupe based on rear-drive 510 chassis is powered by fuel-injected version of its 2.0-liter four-cylinder engine (enlarged to 2.2 liters for 1982). More pleasant than late '70s edition, it's easy and relaxed to drive with good low-speed flexibility, nice dash, fine visibility. Road manners average; light back end could lose traction on corners in

Nissan

1982 Datsun 200-SX 3-door

the rain. Well-equipped, especially in SL (Sport Luxury) trim, but poor ventilation. Three-door carries much more than 2-door notchback with tiny trunk. Repair history very good for 1980–81, except for brake problems. Later 2.2 engine is rougher, and workmanship seems less careful. Good choice, but hardly the best of the imports.

Price Range	GOOD	AVERAGE	POOR
1980 200-SX	$2400–2600	$2100–2400	$1800–2100
1981 200-SX	2800–3200	2500–3000	2100–2500
1982 200-SX	3500–3800	3100–3600	2700–3100
1983 200-SX	4400–4750	4100–4500	3500–4100

Dimensions	WHEEL-BASE, IN.	LGTH., IN.	HT., IN.	WIDTH, IN.	AVG. WT., LBS.	CARGO VOL. CU. FT.	FUEL TANK, GAL.
2d cpe	94.5	176.4	51.6	66.1	2565	8.0	14.0
3d cpe	94.5	176.4	51.6	66.1	2635	24.0	14.0

Engines	L/CID	BHP	MPG	AVAIL.
ohc I-4 FI	2.0/119	100	25–29	80–81
ohc I-4 FI	2.2/133	102	24–29	82–83

KEY: L/CID = liters/cubic inch displacement; **BHP** = brake horsepower; **MPG** = estimated average miles per gallon; **ohc** = overhead cam; **dohc** = double overhead cam; **ohv** = overhead valve; **I** = in-line engine; **V** = V engine; **flat** = horizontally opposed engine; **D** = diesel; **T** = turbocharged; **bbl.** = barrel (carburetor); **FI** = fuel injection.

RECALL HISTORY

1980: moisture could condense and freeze in emission-control system in sub-zero weather, causing throttle to stick open before engine is warmed up.

Nissan 200SX 1984-88

1984 Nissan 200SX 2-door

Nissan's reworked rear-drive sport coupe sat on a new platform, but was still offered in 2-door and hatchback bodies as before. Standard fuel-injected 2.0-liter four is from the front-drive Stanza, with a turbocharged 1.8-liter four optional through 1986. A 3.0-liter V-6, taken from the 300ZX sports car, became standard in the SE hatchback for '87. Unlike previous 200-SX, the Turbo version goes as fast as it looks. Handling is capable, too, since Turbos were given independent rear suspension (off the 300ZX), rear disc brakes and 15-inch tires, plus an air dam and spoiler. Others gained the independent suspension and larger wheels for 1985. Nicely equipped even in base form, the XE and Turbo are usually loaded. An '84 might have a digital instrument package with cassette player and sunroof, which cost up to $1400 new. Base engine performance isn't bad. Rear seat room minimal, as expected. Repair data skimpy. Not many recent 200SX models are likely to be offered, but it's worth a close look if you happen to spot one.

Price Range	GOOD	AVERAGE	POOR
1984 200SX	$6400–6900	$5800–6500	$5100–5800
1985 200SX	7400–8100	6800–7600	6200–6900
1986 200SX	8800–10,500	8200–9500	7500–8400
1987 200SX	10,200–13,000	9800–12,250	9000–11,000
1988 200SX	11,000–14,000	10,500–13,500	—

Nissan

1987 Nissan 200SX SE 3-door

Dimensions	WHEEL-BASE, IN.	LGTH., IN.	HT., IN.	WIDTH, IN.	AVG. WT., LBS.	CARGO VOL., CU. FT.	FUEL TANK, GAL.
2d cpe	95.5	174.4	52.4	65.4	2508	9.0	14.5
3d cpe	95.5	174.4	52.4	65.4	2712	19.0	14.5

Engines	L/CID	BHP	MPG	AVAIL.
ohc I-4 FI	2.0/120	102	23–29	84–88
ohc I-4T FI	1.8/110	120	22–27	84–86
ohc V-6 FI	3.0/181	160	19–24	87–88

KEY: L/CID = liters/cubic inch displacement; **BHP** = brake horsepower; **MPG** = estimated average miles per gallon; **ohc** = overhead cam; **dohc** = double overhead cam; **ohv** = overhead valve; **I** = in-line engine; **V** = V engine; **flat** = horizontally opposed engine; **D** = diesel; **T** = turbocharged; **bbl.** = barrel (carburetor); **FI** = fuel injection.

RECALL HISTORY

None to date.

(Nissan) Datsun 210 1979-82

Live-axle rear suspension with coil springs gives far better ride and handling than predecessor's leaf springs. Small 4-cylinder engine in lightweight body gives high mileage, too, but can barely handle air conditioning or automatic transmission. Interior looks pleasant (especially later models with SL package), but space is marginal for four adults. Good choice of body styles includes a sharp 5-door wagon. High assembly standards brought first-rate reliability, except for troublesome air conditioning. Watch for body rust and disc brake squeal on 1979-81 models, due to brake pad vibration. Replaced by front-drive Nissan Sentra during 1982, but a well-maintained 210 should still deliver many miles of solid service.

1981 Datsun 210 SL 5-door

1982 Datsun 210 Deluxe 4-door

Price Range	GOOD	AVERAGE	POOR
1979 210	$1250–1500	$1000–1250	$700–1000
1980 210	1600–1850	1200–1600	900–1200
1981 210	1900–2200	1400–1900	1200–1500
1982 210	2000–2800	1750–2500	1500–1800

Dimensions	WHEEL-BASE, IN.	LGTH., IN.	HT., IN.	WIDTH, IN.	AVG. WT., LBS.	CARGO VOL., CU. FT.	FUEL TANK, GAL.
2d sdn	92.1	165.0	52.6	62.2	2035	11.0	13.2
3d cpe	92.1	165.0	52.6	62.2	2035	21.9	13.2
4d sdn	92.1	165.0	53.7	62.2	2060	11.0	13.2
5d wgn	92.1	167.3	53.7	62.2	2115	39.4	13.2

Engines	L/CID	BHP	MPG	AVAIL.
ohv I-4 2 bbl.	1.2/75	52–58	28–32	80–82
ohv I-4 2 bbl.	1.4/85	65	28–31	79–82
ohv I-4 2 bbl.	1.5/91	67	28–32	80–82

Nissan

KEY: L/CID = liters/cubic inch displacement; **BHP** = brake horsepower; **MPG** = estimated average miles per gallon; **ohc** = overhead cam; **dohc** = double overhead cam; **ohv** = overhead valve; **I** = in-line engine; **V** = V engine; **flat** = horizontally opposed engine; **D** = diesel; **T** = turbocharged; **bbl.** = barrel (carburetor); **FI** = fuel injection.

RECALL HISTORY

1979–80: tail and brake lamp sockets could be defective, making lamps inoperative. **1980:** possible that seatbelt could come unlatched without being disengaged by the user.

(Nissan) Datsun 280ZX 1979-83

1979 Datsun 280ZX 3-door

Second-generation Z-car is similar to forerunners in style and concept, but more like Corvette in character. It's better built, more luxurious, quieter and softer riding—but heavier and less agile. Fuel-injected 2.8-liter straight six, available with turbocharger from 1981 on, powers two-seat and 2 + 2 hatchbacks. Handling is steady if ponderous, pickup brisk even without the turbo, but ride jiggly and noisy in oddly nondescript seats. Mileage only fair. Repair record good, except for cooling system ills on '79 models. Workmanship, other than patchy paint, is better than before, but watch for rust. Neat engine bay allows good service access. In sum: gentleman's sports car combines performance with reliability.

Nissan

1983 Datsun 280ZX 3-door

Price Range	GOOD	AVERAGE	POOR
1979 280ZX	$3500–4000	$3200–3700	$2500–3200
1980 280ZX	4000–4600	3600–4200	3100–3600
1981 280ZX	4700–5500	4100–5100	3600–4300
1981 280ZX Turbo	5900–6500	5400–5900	5000–5400
1982 280ZX	6200–6700	5700–6300	5200–5700
1982 280ZX Turbo	7000–7500	6500–7000	6000–6500
1983 280ZX	7600–8300	7200–7900	6500–7200
1983 280ZX Turbo	8600–9200	8200–8700	7500–8200

Dimensions	WHEEL-BASE, IN.	LGTH., IN.	HT., IN.	WIDTH, IN.	AVG. WT., LBS.	CARGO VOL. CU. FT.	FUEL TANK, GAL.
3d cpe	91.3	174.0	51.0	66.5	2840	15.6	21.1
2 + 2 3d cpe	99.2	181.9	51.4	66.5	2940	18.2	21.1

Engines	L/CID	BHP	MPG	AVAIL.
ohc I-6 FI	2.8/168	132–145	19–23	79–83
ohc I-6T FI	2.8/168	180	17–21	81–83

KEY: L/CID = liters/cubic inch displacement; **BHP** = brake horsepower; **MPG** = estimated average miles per gallon; **ohc** = overhead cam; **dohc** = double overhead cam; **ohv** = overhead valve; **I** = in-line engine; **V** = V engine; **flat** = horizontally opposed engine; **D** = diesel; **T** = turbocharged; **bbl.** = barrel (carburetor); **FI** = fuel injection.

RECALL HISTORY

1979: possibility of excessively high idle speeds in cold weather due to moisture condensing in fuel injection unit; car could be hazardous to operate on icy or snowy roads before engine is fully warmed up and idle returns to normal. **1981:** exhaust gas sensor may be deteriorating prematurely due to exposure to lead in gas (non-California cars only).

Nissan 300ZX 1984-88

1984 Nissan 300ZX 3-door

All-new Z-car was the first Japanese import sold in the U.S. with a V-6. That overhead-cam engine comes in normally aspirated or turbocharged form. More aerodynamic than the previous 280ZX, the new one has a sharper nose, smaller windshield and integrated front bumpers. As before, 2-seat and 2+2 coupes are available. Flared fenders and rocker panel extensions were added for '86; an integrated hood, bumper and air dam the next year. Performance rivals Corvette's, but with more refinement and a smoother, quieter ride. Mileage isn't the finest. Electronics are everywhere: microcomputers control the engine, transmission, stereo, air conditioning and theft alarm. Shock absorbers on turbo models adjust electronically. Even base models are loaded; but for the ultimate, look for a 1984 50th Anniversary two-seater, which added removable T-bar roof panels, pneumatic seat, "Body Sonic" sound and a leather/digital equipment package. But add $8000– $10,000 to the prices listed below. Lockable T-tops became standard for 1985, but left the base model next year. Most used examples tend to be packed with options that jack up the price.

Price Range	GOOD	AVERAGE	POOR
1984 300ZX	$9500–10,200	$9000–9600	$8400–9000
1984 300ZX Turbo	10,500–11,300	10,000–10,500	9500–10,000
1985 300ZX	11,500–12,250	10,750–11,500	10,000–10,750

1985 Nissan 300ZX Turbo 3-door

Price Range

	GOOD	AVERAGE	POOR
1985 300ZX Turbo	13,000–13,500	12,500–13,000	11,500–12,500
1986 300ZX	13,500–15,000	12,750–14,000	12,000–13,000
1986 300ZX Turbo	16,000–17,000	15,000–16,000	14,000–15,000
1987 300ZX	16,000–17,000	15,000–16,500	14,000–15,000
1987 300ZX Turbo	18,000–19,000	17,000–18,000	16,250–17,000
1988 300ZX	18,500–20,000	17,500–19,000	—
1988 300ZX Turbo	21,000–22,000	20,000–21,000	—

Dimensions

	WHEEL-BASE, IN.	LGTH., IN.	HT., IN.	WIDTH, IN.	AVG. WT., LBS.	CARGO VOL., CU. FT.	FUEL TANK, GAL.
3d cpe	91.3	170.7	49.7	67.9	3071	14.7	19.0
2 + 2 3d cpe	99.2	178.5	49.7	67.9	3139	20.3	19.0

Engines

	L/CID	BHP	MPG	AVAIL.
ohc V-6 FI	3.0/181	160–165	18–24	84–88
ohc V-6T FI	3.0/181	200–205	16–20	84–88

KEY: L/CID = liters/cubic inch displacement; **BHP** = brake horsepower; **MPG** = estimated average miles per gallon; **ohc** = overhead cam; **dohc** = double overhead cam; **ohv** = overhead valve; **I** = in-line engine; **V** = V engine; **flat** = horizontally opposed engine; **D** = diesel; **T** = turbocharged; **bbl.** = barrel (carburetor); **FI** = fuel injection.

RECALL HISTORY

1984: improperly installed "C" clip in brake master cylinder could become disengaged, causing fluid leak and loss of braking ability.
1984: impure lubricant in headlight switch could contaminate one or more contact points, possibly causing loss or delay of light operation.

(Nissan) Datsun 310 1979-82

1979 Datsun 310 GX 3-door

Second Datsun fling at front-wheel drive, powered by crosswise-mounted engine from the rear-drive 210, handles a bit better than F-10 predecessor and delivers fine mileage. Weak points include ride, room, noise and overall utility. Interior trim leans toward tacky plastic. Five-door sedan offered from mid-1980 on is the most practical body. Upkeep cost is lower than average; repair record admirable, except for 1979–81 brake and air conditioner troubles. Dodge Colt and Honda Civic rate as better values.

Price Range	GOOD	AVERAGE	POOR
1979 310	$1250–1500	$1000–1250	$700–1000
1980 310	1500–1800	1200–1500	1000–1200
1981 310	1700–2000	1400–1800	1100–1400
1982 310	2000–2500	1800–2200	1400–1800

Dimensions	WHEEL-BASE, IN.	LGTH., IN.	HT., IN.	WIDTH, IN.	AVG. WT., LBS.	CARGO VOL., CU. FT.	FUEL TANK, GAL.
3d cpe	94.3	160.6	52.0	63.8	2015	19.6	13.2
3d sdn	94.3	160.6	53.5	63.8	2025	18.0	13.2
5d sdn	94.3	160.6	53.5	63.8	2025	20.5	13.2

Engines	L/CID	BHP	MPG	AVAIL.
ohv I-4 2 bbl.	1.4/85	65	29–33	79–80
ohc I-4 2 bbl.	1.5/91	65–67	29–33	81–82

KEY: L/CID = liters/cubic inch displacement; **BHP** = brake horsepower; **MPG** = estimated average miles per gallon; **ohc** = overhead cam; **dohc** = double overhead cam; **ohv** = overhead valve; **I** = in-line engine; **V** = V engine; **flat** = horizontally opposed engine; **D** = diesel; **T** = turbocharged; **bbl.** = barrel (carburetor); **FI** = fuel injection.

1980 Datsun 310 GX 5-door

RECALL HISTORY

1980: possible that transmission main shaft could come loose, causing difficulty in shifting and, in extreme cases, making transmission inoperable. **1980:** potential seatbelt defect may cause belt to become unlatched without being disengaged by wearer.

(Nissan) Datsun 510 1978-81

Midrange rear-drive Datsun delivers good mileage with clear visibility and capable, if uninspired, roadability. Noisy except at highway speed, with poor ventilation. Cylinder head designed to improve emissions in 1980 didn't help erratic engine behavior. Five-door hatchback replaced the 3-door and 4-door models for 1980. Fine workmanship helps put repair record far above average, apart from cooling and air conditioning troubles on 1978–79 models (which also had driveability ills), and disc brake squeal on 1979–81 models that was caused by brake-pad vibration. Good choice in a used econobox.

Price Range	GOOD	AVERAGE	POOR
1978 510	$1250–1500	$1000–1250	$750–1000
1979 510	1500–1750	1250–1500	900–1200
1980 510	1800–2100	1500–1800	1200–1500
1981 510	2000–2400	1750–2100	1500–1750

Nissan

1978 Datsun 510 5-door wagon

Dimensions	WHEEL-BASE, IN.	LGTH., IN.	HT., IN.	WIDTH, IN.	AVG. WT., LBS.	CARGO VOL., CU. FT.	FUEL TANK, GAL.
2d sdn	94.5	169.9	54.7	63.0	2265	10.1	13.0
3d cpe	94.5	169.9	54.7	63.0	2265	18.5	13.0
4d sdn	94.5	169.9	54.7	63.0	2330	10.1	13.0
5d sdn	94.5	169.9	54.7	63.0	2330	18.5	13.0
5d wgn	94.5	172.1	55.3	63.0	2410	55.2	13.0

Engines	L/CID	BHP	MPG	AVAIL.
ohc I-4 2 bbl.	2.0/119	92	27–30	78–81

KEY: L/CID = liters/cubic inch displacement; **BHP** = brake horsepower; **MPG** = estimated average miles per gallon; **ohc** = overhead cam; **dohc** = double overhead cam; **ohv** = overhead valve; **I** = in-line engine; **V** = V engine; **flat** = horizontally opposed engine; **D** = diesel; **T** = turbocharged; **bbl.** = barrel (carburetor); **FI** = fuel injection.

1981 Datsun 510 5-door hatchback

RECALL HISTORY

1979–81: seatbelts could be defective, preventing webbing from being pulled out of seatbelt retractor.

Datsun 810 1978-80

1979 Datsun 810 5-door

Datsun's finest wasn't a huge seller, but it's a fine value as a used car. Reliability record is excellent apart from the 1978 cooling system. Interior is well-appointed, road manners a pleasant surprise. First versions had insufficient seat padding and gave only a fair ride; but upgraded trim and chassis changes improved the 1979–80 models, which are also quieter. Intermediate in size outside, the 810 has a compact interior. Visibility isn't the best because of low seats and high beltline. Next year's 810/Maxima is more modern, but these will do nicely (if you can find one).

Price Range	GOOD	AVERAGE	POOR
1978 810	$1600–1900	$1300–1600	$1000–1300
1979 810	2000–2300	1750–2100	1400–1750
1980 810	2800–3200	2400–2800	1900–2400

Dimensions	WHEEL-BASE, IN.	LGTH., IN.	HT., IN.	WIDTH, IN.	AVG. WT., LBS.	CARGO VOL., CU. FT.	FUEL TANK, GAL.
2d sdn	104.3	183.5	54.9	64.8	2756	9.4	15.6
4d sdn	104.3	183.5	54.9	64.8	2780	9.4	15.6
5d wgn	104.3	184.6	55.6	64.8	2878	51.0	14.6

Nissan

Engines	L/CID	BHP	MPG	AVAIL.
ohc I-6 FI	2.4/146	118–120	19–23	78–80

KEY: L/CID = liters/cubic inch displacement; **BHP** = brake horsepower; **MPG** = estimated average miles per gallon; **ohc** = overhead cam; **dohc** = double overhead cam; **ohv** = overhead valve; **I** = in-line engine; **V** = V engine; **flat** = horizontally opposed engine; **D** = diesel; **T** = turbocharged; **bbl.** = barrel (carburetor); **FI** = fuel injection.

RECALL HISTORY

1978: possibility of premature hose deterioration due to high fuel oxidation levels; could lead to potential fire hazard. **1978–79:** may have defective fuel injection system that idles excessively high in cold weather due to moisture condensation in the unit; car could be hazardous to operate on icy or snow-covered roads before engine is fully warmed up and idle returns to normal.

1978 Datsun 810 4-door

1979 Datsun 810 2-door

(Nissan) Datsun 810/ Maxima 1981-84

1981 Datsun 810 Maxima 5-door

Luxury model was fully revamped for 1981 in an attempt to lure prestige import buyers. Square-cut styling looks more modern. Sedan and wagon in two trim levels were offered at first, but only the upper-ranked Maxima carried on after '81. Fuel-injected gas six from earlier 810 was joined in mid-1981 by a diesel (dropped after '83). Gas engine is smooth, quiet, fairly lively and economical with 5-speed; most used Maximas probably have automatic, which lags in mileage and performance. Driveline tunnel in well-trimmed interior cuts passenger space. Headroom limited, especially with power sunroof. Good repair record won many future customers for Nissan. Workmanship might not quite match a Toyota Cressida, but these capable cars offer plenty of luxury and value.

Price Range	GOOD	AVERAGE	POOR
1981 810	$3000–3500	$2700–3100	$2000–2700
1981 Maxima	4200–4500	3800–4200	3300–3800
1982 Maxima	5000–5400	4500–5000	4000–4500
1983 Maxima	5700–6000	5200–5700	4700–5200
1984 Maxima	7000–7500	6500–7100	6000–6500

Dimensions	WHEEL-BASE, IN.	LGTH., IN.	HT., IN.	WIDTH, IN.	AVG. WT., LBS.	CARGO VOL., CU.FT.	FUEL TANK, GAL.
4d sdn	103.4	183.3	54.5	65.2	2880	10.7	16.4
5d wgn	103.4	183.3	55.7	65.2	3040	63.1	15.9

Nissan • Oldsmobile

1984 Datsun Maxima 4-door

Engines	L/CID	BHP	MPG	AVAIL.
ohc I-6 FI	2.4/146	120	19–24	81–84

KEY: L/CID = liters/cubic inch displacement; **BHP** = brake horsepower; **MPG** = estimated average miles per gallon; **ohc** = overhead cam; **dohc** = double overhead cam; **ohv** = overhead valve; **I** = in-line engine; **V** = V engine; **flat** = horizontally opposed engine; **D** = diesel; **T** = turbocharged; **bbl.** = barrel (carburetor); **FI** = fuel injection.

RECALL HISTORY

1981: exhaust gas sensor may be deteriorating prematurely due to exposure to lead in gas (non-California cars only).

Oldsmobile Calais/ Cutlass Calais 1985-88

Stylish, compact front-drive luxury coupe, like the similar N-body Buick Somerset Regal and Pontiac Grand Am, attracts upscale buyers. A 4-door sedan was added for 1986, as were ES (sedan) and GT (coupe) sport/handling packages that include FE3 suspension. Plush interior seats five, with standard front buckets and console. Base 2.5-liter engine performs feebly even with 5-speed manual shift. Generation II version of 1987 adds 6 horsepower, but isn't much stronger. This car needs the more potent 3.0-liter V-6, even though it comes only with automatic. The 1988 edition, now called Cutlass Calais, steps way up in performance potential with optional 150-horsepower Quad-4 engine. A

1985 Oldsmobile Calais Supreme 2-door

1987 Oldsmobile Calais Supreme 2-door

sporty '88 International Series also replaces the GT's equipment package. Calais isn't cheap with typical options, but has many luxury touches. See Buick Somerset Regal report for additional comments.

Price Range	GOOD	AVERAGE	POOR
1985 Calais	$6800–7600	$6600–7200	$6000–6600
1986 Calais	8000–8700	7500–8200	7000–7500
1987 Calais	9400–10,250	8700–9700	8400–8800
1988 Calais	10,000–11,000	9500–10,500	—

Dimensions	WHEEL-BASE, IN.	LGTH., IN.	HT., IN.	WIDTH, IN.	AVG. WT. LBS.	CARGO VOL. CU. FT.	FUEL TANK, GAL.
2d cpe	103.4	178.8	53.3	66.9	2502	13.3	13.6
4d sdn	103.4	178.8	53.3	66.9	2530	13.3	13.6

Oldsmobile

Engines	L/CID	BHP	MPG	AVAIL.
dohc I-4 FI	2.3/138	150	22–27	88
ohv I-4 FI	2.5/151	92–98	22–25	85–88
ohv V-6 FI	3.0/181	125	18–22	85–88

KEY: L/CID = liters/cubic inch displacement; **BHP** = brake horsepower; **MPG** = estimated average miles per gallon; **ohc** = overhead cam; **dohc** = double overhead cam; **ohv** = overhead valve; **I** = in-line engine; **V** = V engine; **flat** = horizontally opposed engine; **D** = diesel; **T** = turbocharged; **bbl.** = barrel (carburetor); **FI** = fuel injection.

RECALL HISTORY

1985: throttle return spring on 2.5-liter engine may fail, preventing throttle from returning to closed (idle) position when accelerator pedal is released. **1985–86:** misalignment or binding of latch assembly may cause hood to open unexpectedly while car is in motion. **1985-86:** small cracks may develop in body pillar around door striker bolt hole, which could make door hard to close and allow it to open during collision; install reinforcement plates.

Oldsmobile
Custom Cruiser 1986-88

1987 Oldsmobile Custom Cruiser 5-door

Full-size holdover wagon from old rear-drive Delta 88 lineup is similar to Buick Estate, Chevrolet Caprice and Pontiac Safari wagons. Hard to beat for towing brawn and cargo-hauling potential, Cruiser is powered by an Olds 5.0-liter V-8 with 4-speed overdrive automatic transmission. Six passengers ride comfortably; two can share the optional rear-facing third seat. Large families might love

1986 Oldsmobile Custom Cruiser 5-door

1986 Oldsmobile Custom Cruiser 5-door

the roominess. Those who need to haul a boat or trailer (up to 5000 pounds) may want to have a look. But Cruiser's huge size and weight (by today's standards) bring a penalty in maneuverability and economy. Ride is mushy, handling nearly boatlike. Unless you really must have this kind of space, think about a mid-size wagon or compact van instead.

Price Range	GOOD	AVERAGE	POOR
1986 Custom Cruiser	$10,500–11,500	$9800–10,500	$9200–9800
1987 Custom Cruiser	12,750–14,000	11,800–13,000	11,300–12,000
1988 Custom Cruiser	14,500–16,000	13,500–15,000	—

Dimensions	WHEEL-BASE, IN.	LGTH., IN.	HT., IN.	WIDTH, IN.	AVG. WT., LBS.	CARGO VOL., CU. FT.	FUEL TANK, GAL.
5d wgn	115.9	220.3	58.5	79.8	4085	87.2	22.0

Engines	L/CID	BHP	MPG	AVAIL.
ohv V-8 4 bbl.	5.0/307	140	15–18	86–88

Oldsmobile

RECALL HISTORY

None to date.

Oldsmobile Cutlass Ciera 1982-88

1982 Oldsmobile Cutlass Ciera 4-door

Sensibly modern mid-size shares basic design and engines with Buick Century (see that report for more details). Both are similar to Chevrolet Celebrity and Pontiac 6000, the other GM A-body front-drives. Recent S and SL coupes have unique shorter, rounded roofs. Base "Iron Duke" four is too feeble; 2.8- or 3.0-liter V-6 is better, but hardly stunning performer. Big 3.8 V-6, standard with ES and GT sport packages, goes (and guzzles) almost like a V-8. As usual, we don't recommend the trouble-prone diesel. New International Series of '88 includes much of GT's equipment, while 4-cylinder engine adds twin balance shafts. Spacious inside and in the trunk, Cutlass Ciera is a pleasant, quiet family car, well worth considering.

Price Range	GOOD	AVERAGE	POOR
1982 Cutlass Ciera	$3800–4500	$3400–4100	$2800–3400
1983 Cutlass Ciera	4800–5500	4400–5100	3800–4400

Price Range

	GOOD	AVERAGE	POOR
1984 Cutlass Ciera	5700–6400	5300–6000	4700–5300
1985 Cutlass Ciera	6800–7500	6400–7000	5700–6400
1986 Cutlass Ciera	8000–8900	7500–8300	6900–7700
1987 Cutlass Ciera	9700–11,000	9000–10,200	8200–9000
1988 Cutlass Ciera	11,000–12,500	10,000–11,500	—

Dimensions

	WHEEL-BASE, IN.	LGTH., IN.	HT., IN.	WIDTH, IN.	AVG. WT., LBS.	CARGO VOL., CU. FT.	FUEL TANK, GAL.
2d cpe	104.9	190.3	54.1	69.5	2710	15.8	16.6
4d sdn	104.9	190.3	54.1	69.5	2748	15.8	16.6
5d wgn	104.9	194.4	54.5	69.5	2912	74.4	16.6

Engines

	L/CID	BHP	MPG	AVAIL.
ohv I-4 FI	2.5/151	82–98	20–25	82–88
ohv V-6 FI	2.8/173	112–125	18–24	86–88
ohv V-6 2 bbl.	3.0/181	110	17–23	82–85
ohv V-6 FI	3.8/231	125–150	16–23	84–88
ohv V-6D FI	4.3/262	85	23–29	82–85

KEY: L/CID = liters/cubic inch displacement; **BHP** = brake horsepower; **MPG** = estimated average miles per gallon; **ohc** = overhead cam; **dohc** = double overhead cam; **ohv** = overhead valve; **I** = in-line engine; **V** = V engine; **flat** = horizontally opposed engine; **D** = diesel; **T** = turbocharged; **bbl.** = barrel (carburetor); **FI** = fuel injection.

RECALL HISTORY

1982: brake hoses may not meet federal standards for strength, which could result in loss of fluid and partial loss of braking ability. **1982:** hose clamps on fuel tank filler pipe could fracture, causing leaks and potential for fire. **1983:** brake proportioning valve could break and separate from master cylinder, causing fluid leak and partial loss of braking ability. **1984:** 2-door models

1986 Oldsmobile Cutlass Ciera GT 2-door

Oldsmobile

with optional bucket seats may have seatback locks that don't meet federal safety requirements. **1984 (2.5-liter engine):** fuel may leak at injection feed pipe connection, which could result in under-hood fire that may spread to passenger compartment. **1986:** on cars with luggage rack and opera lamp options, an incorrect wiring harness may cause the center high-mounted stop lamp to remain lit when headlights or parking lights are on; and opera lamps may come on when brakes are applied. **1987:** windshield on a few cars may be poorly bonded to mounting, and could separate during a frontal crash.

Oldsmobile Cutlass Salon/ Cutlass Supreme 1978-88

1978 Oldsmobile Cutlass Salon 2-door

Nearly as spacious inside as its big predecessor, mid-size Cutlass actually gained trunk space in 1978 downsizing. Handling is fairly nimble, ride pleasant with soft standard suspension. Gas mileage isn't bad (at least with Buick V-6). Supreme coupes were a separate line at first, distinct from Salon fastback sedans and Cruiser wagons. Salon 2-doors departed after 1980 and 4-doors switched to notch-back styling. By 1982, the Supreme name covered all these rear-drives, to avoid confusion with the new front-drive Cutlass Ciera line. The wagon was dropped after '83. For 1985 the legendary 4-4-2 package returned, and a sporty Salon coupe appeared. Only base and Brougham rear-drive coupes remain for 1988, under the Cutlass Supreme Classic label. An all-new front-drive Supreme coupe, related to Buick Regal, is expected at mid-year. Rear-drive versions remain one of the best mid-size buys: quiet, refined and comfortable, with strong resale value. Reliability has rated average or better (except for diesel engines), with upkeep costs lower than normal. Watch for models equipped with the undersized Turbo Hydra-matic 200C transmission, which has a record of early failure. For some reason, 1981 V-6 models have one of the worst records, especially for fuel and brake problems.

Price Range	GOOD	AVERAGE	POOR
1978 Cut. Salon	$1400–1600	$1100–1400	$800–1100
1978 Cut. Supreme	1900–2100	1500–1900	1200–1500
1979 Cut. Salon	1700–2000	1400–1700	1000–1300
1979 Cut. Supreme	2200–2500	1800–2200	1500–1800
1980 Cut. Salon	1800–2100	1500–1800	1200–1500
1980 Cut. Supreme	2500–2900	2000–2500	1500–2000
1981 Cut. Supreme	3100–3900	2700–3500	2100–2700
1982 Cut. Supreme	4200–5000	3800–4600	3100–3800
1983 Cut. Supreme	5200–5900	4800–5500	4100–4800
1984 Cut. Supreme	6200–7000	5800–6600	5000–5800
1985 Cut. Supreme	7600–8400	7200–8000	6500–7200
1986 Cut. Supreme	9000–10,000	8500–9500	7800–8500
1987 Cut. Supreme	10,500–11,750	9750–11,000	9000–9750
1988 Cut. Classic	12,000–13,000	11,000–12,000	—

Dimensions	WHEEL-BASE, IN.	LGTH., IN.	HT., IN.	WIDTH, IN.	AVG. WT., LBS.	CARGO VOL., CU. FT.	FUEL TANK, GAL.
2d cpe	108.1	200.1	53.7	71.6	3075	16.1	17.4
2d sdn	108.1	197.7	53.7	71.6	3075	16.1	17.4
4d sdn	108.1	197.7	54.5	71.9	3125	16.1	17.4
5d wgn	108.1	197.6	54.9	71.9	3250	72.4	18.2

Engines	L/CID	BHP	MPG	AVAIL.
ohv V-6 2 bbl.	3.8/231	105–115	18–21	78–87
ohv V-8 2 bbl.	4.3/260	100–110	16–19	78–82
ohv V-8 D	4.3/260	95	22–24	79
ohv V-6 D	4.3/262	85–90	25–28	82–83
ohv V-8 2 bbl.	5.0/307	145	15–18	78
ohv V-8 4 bbl.	5.0/307	140–180	14–17	78–88
ohv V-8 4 bbl.	5.7/350	160	12–15	78–79
ohv V-8 D FI	5.7/350	105–125	23–27	79–85

KEY: L/CID = liters/cubic inch displacement; BHP = brake horsepower; MPG = estimated average miles per gallon; ohc = overhead cam; dohc = double overhead cam; ohv = overhead valve; I = in-line engine; V = V engine; flat = horizontally opposed engine; D = diesel; T = turbocharged; bbl. = barrel (carburetor); FI = fuel injection.

Oldsmobile

1986 Oldsmobile Cutlass Supreme 4-door

1986 Oldsmobile Cutlass Salon 2-door

RECALL HISTORY

1978: fan blade spider (hub portion) may fatigue and break apart, allowing two-blade segment to be thrown off. **1978:** faulty wheel bearings could damage front wheel spindles and, in extreme cases, result in loss of control. **1978–80:** rear axle shafts may have thin end buttons or buttons that could wear excessively; may result in separation of wheel from axle shaft, and loss of control. **1978–80:** excessive enlargement of wheel cylinder pilot hole in rear brake backing plate could allow cylinder to rotate, causing loss of brake fluid which leads to loss of rear brake action. **1978–81:** replacement of two bolts in lower control arms of rear suspension that could break from corrosion. **1979:** brake lights could become inoperative and cruise control could remain engaged after brakes are released. **1982 (diesel V-8):** injection pump governor could fail, preventing throttle from returning to idle or engine from being shut off. **1983:** brake master cylinder pipe could develop a leak from rubbing on air cleaner resonator bracket, causing loss of rear-wheel braking capability. **1984:** 2-door models with optional bucket seats may have seatback locks that fail to meet federal safety requirements. **1985:** tie rods on some models may have loose adjuster clamps, which could allow tie rod to loosen and separate, with loss of steering control. **1986:** on cars with removable hatchroof, left-hand driver's side shoulder belt anchor plate may be upside-down in lock pillar; in case of crash, anchor bolt may pull loose, increasing likelihood of injury.

Oldsmobile Delta 88 1978-85

1980 Oldsmobile Delta 88 4-door

Popular full-size B-bodied family car is a close twin to Buick LeSabre. Most comments and repair data for LeSabre apply here. Engine choices include a base V-6 that delivers fair mileage and performance, or V-8s for power. We recommend the 5.0-liter V-8 and warn against the diesel. Spacious and quiet, a Delta 88 lags in handling and economy, but is great for families that need space. For 1986, the name found a new home on a smaller front-drive model.

1985 Oldsmobile Custom Cruiser 5-door

Oldsmobile

Price Range	GOOD	AVERAGE	POOR
1978 Delta 88	$1600–2000	$1300–1600	$950–1300
1979 Delta 88	2000–2500	1500–2000	1100–1500
1980 Delta 88	2500–3000	2000–2700	1600–2000
1981 Delta 88	3100–3800	2700–3400	2200–2700
1982 Delta 88	4200–5100	3700–4600	3100–3700
1983 Delta 88	5200–6100	4800–5600	4100–4800
1984 Delta 88	6700–7900	6200–7400	5500–6200
1985 Delta 88	8300–9500	7800–9000	7000–7800

Dimensions	WHEEL-BASE, IN.	LGTH., IN.	HT., IN.	WIDTH, IN.	AVG. WT., LBS.	CARGO VOL., CU. FT.	FUEL TANK, GAL.
2d cpe	115.9	218.1	56.0	76.3	3492	20.8	27.0
4d sdn	115.9	218.1	56.7	76.3	3531	20.8	27.0
5d wgn	115.9	220.3	58.5	79.8	4085	87.2	22.0

Engines	L/CID	BHP	MPG	AVAIL.
ohv V-6 2 bbl.	3.8/231	105–115	16–18	78–85
ohv V-8 2 bbl.	4.3/260	100–110	15–17	79–82
ohv V-8 2 bbl.	4.9/301	135	15–17	79
ohv V-8 4 bbl.	5.0/307	140–150	14–17	80–85
ohv V-8 4 bbl.	5.7/350	160–170	14–16	79
ohv V-8D FI	5.7/350	105–125	23–27	78–85
ohv V-8 4 bbl.	6.6/403	185	11–14	78

KEY: **L/CID** = liters/cubic inch displacement; **BHP** = brake horsepower; **MPG** = estimated average miles per gallon; **ohc** = overhead cam; **dohc** = double overhead cam; **ohv** = overhead valve; **I** = in-line engine; **V** = V engine; **flat** = horizontally opposed engine; **D** = diesel; **T** = turbocharged; **bbl.** = barrel (carburetor); **FI** = fuel injection.

RECALL HISTORY

1978: fan blade spider (hub portion) may fatigue and break apart, throwing off two-blade segment. **1979 (301-cid engine):** emissions may be excessive. **1979:** brake lights could become inoperative and cruise control remain engaged after brakes are released. **1979–80:** possibility outboard front seatbelt anchor bolts could

1985 Oldsmobile Delta 88 Royale 4-door

CONSUMER GUIDE®

break off during normal use. **1981:** some models with gas engines have wrong brake pedal support bracket, which could reduce braking effectiveness. **1982 (diesel V-8):** injection pump governor could fail, preventing throttle from returning to idle or engine from being shut off. **1984:** models with hydroboost brakes may have incorrect brake pedal bracket, placing pedal in lower position than normal so it doesn't allow full travel for brake application if fluid loss occurred in either half of dual-brake system. **1985:** tire placard on a few cars may show higher maximum loading than allowed.

Oldsmobile Delta 88 1986-88

1987 Oldsmobile Delta 88 Royale 4-door

Front-drive Delta 88 revision, like the similar Buick LeSabre, is smaller and lighter than forerunners. Chassis evolves from the front-drive Ninety-Eight, which debuted earlier. Four passengers ride comfortably; six require a bit of squeezing, though head and leg room are ample. High seats and low beltine combine to offer an open, airy feeling, plus good driver's view. Simple dash carries easy-to-reach controls. Trunk is adequate, though hardly huge. Initial base 3.0-liter V-6 is anemic. Optional 3.8 V-6, made standard for 1987, performs much better. GM's new "3800" V-6, with 15 more horsepower, becomes optional on '88 models. All engines drive a 4-speed overdrive automatic transmission. Coupe and sedan bodies come in base Royale or upscale Royale Brougham trim. Tempting list of standard equipment includes air conditioning. Suspension remains rather soft for traditional Olds ride, but handling

Oldsmobile

1986 Oldsmobile Delta 88 Royale 4-door

is notably better than before. Far different from predecessors, today's Delta 88 makes a pretty good family car that approaches full-size spaciousness.

Price Range	GOOD	AVERAGE	POOR
1986 Delta 88	$10,250–11,250	$9700–10,700	$9000–9700
1987 Delta 88	12,000–13,000	11,000–12,000	10,500–11,000
1988 Delta 88	13,000–14,750	12,000–13,500	—

Dimensions	WHEEL-BASE, IN.	LGTH., IN.	HT., IN.	WIDTH, IN.	AVG. WT., LBS.	CARGO VOL., CU. FT.	FUEL TANK, GAL.
2d cpe	110.8	196.1	54.7	72.4	3080	16.4	18.0
4d sdn	110.8	196.1	55.5	72.4	3121	16.4	18.0

Engines	L/CID	BHP	MPG	AVAIL.
ohv V-6 FI	3.0/181	125	16–21	86
ohv V-6 FI	3.8/231	150–165	17–21	86–88

KEY: L/CID = liters/cubic inch displacement; **BHP** = brake horsepower; **MPG** = estimated average miles per gallon; **ohc** = overhead cam; **dohc** = double overhead cam; **ohv** = overhead valve; **I** = in-line engine; **V** = V engine; **flat** = horizontally opposed engine; **D** = diesel; **T** = turbocharged; **bbl.** = barrel (carburetor); **FI** = fuel injection.

1987 Oldsmobile Delta 88 Royale 2-door

RECALL HISTORY

1986: possible that inadequately tightened rear suspension parts could eventually break and separate, resulting in loss of vehicle control. **1987:** fusible link could melt under high-resistance load and ignite plastic windshield washer bracket, causing underhood fire; replace with nonflammable bracket.

Oldsmobile Ninety-Eight 1978-84

1978 Oldsmobile Ninety-Eight 4-door

Full-size, rear-drive Olds remained roomy, but was much smaller and lighter after 1977 downsizing. Like the similar Buick Electra, it's not known for economy, even with a V-6. Most examples have a V-8 engine, which is thirstier yet. Diesel V-8 is economical, but unreliable. Some models were equipped with the undersized Turbo Hydra-matic 200C transmission, which is known for premature failure. Overall durability and reliability rank high, but for similar comfort with a bit less luxury, a smaller Delta 88 might serve as well. See Electra report for additional comments.

Price Range	GOOD	AVERAGE	POOR
1978 Ninety-Eight	$2200–2500	$1800–2200	$1500–1800
1979 Ninety-Eight	2700–3200	2300–2700	1800–2300
1980 Ninety-Eight	3400–4000	3100–3700	2600–3100
1981 Ninety-Eight	4100–4900	3700–4400	3200–3700
1982 Ninety-Eight	5700–6400	5400–5900	4500–5400
1983 Ninety-Eight	7200–8000	6700–7500	5900–6700
1984 Ninety-Eight	8900–9800	8500–9300	7700–8500

Oldsmobile

1978 Oldsmobile Ninety-Eight Regency 4-door

1982 Oldsmobile Ninety-Eight 4-door

Dimensions	WHEEL-BASE, IN.	LGTH., IN.	HT., IN.	WIDTH, IN.	AVG. WT., LBS.	CARGO VOL., CU. FT.	FUEL TANK, GAL.
2d cpe	119.0	221.0	57.2	76.3	3811	20.5	25.0
4d sdn	119.0	221.0	57.2	76.3	3888	20.5	25.0

Engines	L/CID	BHP	MPG	AVAIL.
ohv V-6 4 bbl.	4.1/252	125	15–18	81–83
ohv V-8 4 bbl.	5.0/307	140–150	14–17	80–84
ohv V-8 4 bbl.	5.7/350	160–170	15–16	78–80
ohv V-8D FI	5.7/350	105–125	23–27	78–84
ohv V-8 4 bbl.	6.6/403	175–190	12–14	78–79

KEY: L/CID = liters/cubic inch displacement; **BHP** = brake horsepower; **MPG** = estimated average miles per gallon; **ohc** = overhead cam; **dohc** = double overhead cam; **ohv** = overhead valve; **I** = in-line engine; **V** = V engine; **flat** = horizontally opposed engine; **D** = diesel; **T** = turbocharged; **bbl.** = barrel (carburetor); **FI** = fuel injection.

CONSUMER GUIDE®

RECALL HISTORY

1978: fan blade spider (hub portion) may fatigue and break apart, throwing off two-blade segment. **1979:** possibility stoplights could become inoperative and cruise control remain engaged after brake is released. **1978–80:** outboard front seatbelt anchor bolts could break off during normal use. **1982 (diesel V-8):** injection pump governor could fail, preventing throttle from returning to idle or engine from being shut off. **1983:** catalytic converter may be faulty; if partly blocked, could cause loss of power and acceleration, or engine might not start at all.

Oldsmobile Ninety-Eight 1985-88

1985 Oldsmobile Ninety-Eight 4-door

Dramatically different front-drive Olds is again related to Buick Electra (see that report for more comments). Reduced size with fully independent suspension improves maneuverability, mileage, and winter traction. Ride is still luxuriously soft; trunk and interior smaller, yet comfortable for four. At first, a 3.0-liter V-6 was standard on the Regency; a fuel-injected 3.8 V-6 on the Brougham, with diesel optional. By 1986, only the 3.8 remained. Performance is lively enough, but mileage disappoints. For improved handling, the FE3 suspension was optional in '86. A sporting Touring Sedan with FE3, front air dam, anti-lock brakes and Euro-look ribbed rocker moldings debuted

Oldsmobile

1985 Oldsmobile Ninety-Eight 4-door

in 1987. For 1988 a new standard "3800" V-6 with balance shaft gives 15 more horsepower, and the 2-door coupe leaves the lineup. Our opinion: reasonable size makes the modern Ninety-Eight a good late-model choice.

Price Range	GOOD	AVERAGE	POOR
1985 Ninety-Eight	$10,200–11,000	$9700–10,600	$9000–9700
1986 Ninety-Eight	12,500–13,600	11,800–13,000	11,000–12,000
1987 Ninety-Eight	14,750–16,000	14,000–15,250	13,000–14,000
1988 Ninety-Eight	17,000–18,500	16,000–17,500	

Dimensions	WHEEL-BASE, IN.	LGTH., IN.	HT., IN.	WIDTH, IN.	AVG. WT., LBS.	CARGO VOL., CU. FT.	FUEL TANK, GAL.
2d cpe	110.8	196.1	55.0	71.4	3261	16.7	18.0
4d sdn	110.8	196.1	55.0	71.4	3298	16.7	18.0

Engines	L/CID	BHP	MPG	AVAIL.
ohv V-6 2 bbl.	3.0/181	110	16–20	85
ohv V-6 FI	3.8/231	125–150	17–21	85–87
ohv V-6 FI	3.8/231	165	17–21	88
ohv V-6D FI	4.3/262	85	20–24	85

KEY: L/CID = liters/cubic inch displacement; **BHP** = brake horsepower; **MPG** = estimated average miles per gallon; **ohc** = overhead cam; **dohc** = double overhead cam; **ohv** = overhead valve; **I** = in-line engine; **V** = V engine; **flat** = horizontally opposed engine; **D** = diesel; **T** = turbocharged; **bbl.** = barrel (carburetor); **FI** = fuel injection.

RECALL HISTORY

1986: power steering hose could overheat and rupture, due to insufficient clearance from exhaust manifold, possibly causing underhood fire. **1986-87:** fluid may seep from anti-lock brake system onto pump motor and certain relays may have been exposed to water contamination; could result in total loss of rear brakes and loss of power assist to front brakes. **1987:** fusible link could melt under high-resistance load and ignite plastic windshield washer bracket, causing underhood fire; replace with nonflammable bracket.

Oldsmobile Omega 1980-84

1980 Oldsmobile Omega Brougham 4-door

One of the notorious X-car bunch, Omega is similar to Buick Skylark, Chevrolet Citation and Pontiac Phoenix. Praised at first, the group soon became most noted for recalls, repair needs, and flawed workmanship. Engine choices include the "Iron Duke" four or more potent V-6. Omega was abandoned after 1984, but Buick's version hung on one more year. See Skylark report for further comments and the complete list of safety recalls. Not a desirable choice, even though '81 and later models improved.

Price Range	GOOD	AVERAGE	POOR
1980 Omega	$1800–2100	$1400–1800	$1100–1400
1981 Omega	2200–2600	1800–2300	1500–1800
1982 Omega	2700–3100	2300–2900	1900–2300
1983 Omega	3400–3900	3000–3500	2500–3000
1984 Omega	4100–4700	3700–4300	3100–3700

Dimensions	WHEEL-BASE, IN.	LGTH., IN.	HT., IN.	WIDTH, IN.	AVG. WT., LBS.	CARGO VOL., CU. FT.	FUEL TANK, GAL.
2d cpe	104.9	182.8	54.8	69.8	2510	14.3	14.6
4d sdn	104.9	182.8	54.8	69.8	2510	14.3	14.2

Engines	L/CID	BHP	MPG	AVAIL.
ohv I-4 2 bbl.	2.5/151	84–90	21–24	80–81
ohv I-4 FI	2.5/151	82–92	22–25	82–84
ohv V-6 2 bbl.	2.8/173	112–115	20–22	80–84
ohv V-6 2 bbl.	2.8/173	130–135	18–21	81–84

Oldsmobile

1981 Oldsmobile Omega ES 4-door

KEY: L/CID = liters/cubic inch displacement; **BHP** = brake horsepower; **MPG** = estimated average miles per gallon; **ohc** = overhead cam; **dohc** = double overhead cam; **ohv** = overhead valve; **I** = in-line engine; **V** = V engine; **flat** = horizontally opposed engine; **D** = diesel; **T** = turbocharged; **bbl.** = barrel (carburetor); **FI** = fuel injection.

RECALL HISTORY

See Buick Skylark 1980–85 for full recall information.

Oldsmobile Toronado 1979-85

Though still big and heavy, thus thirsty at the gas pumps, the Olds front-drive personal-luxury coupe is a lot smaller than pre-1979 version. Fully independent suspension gives smooth ride but is overly soft, allowing too much sway and bounce. Handling is weak and numb. Best engine bets: Buick-built 4.1-liter V-6 (dropped in 1985) or 5.0-liter V-8, which performs pretty well. Stay away from the diesel. Toro is similar in construction and appearance to Buick Riviera, which went front-drive in '79 (see that entry for more comments). Verdict: not your worst choice in a quiet, traditional luxury cruiser.

Price Range	GOOD	AVERAGE	POOR
1979 Toronado	$3400–3700	$2900–3400	$2500–2900
1980 Toronado	4200–4500	3800–4200	3300–3800
1981 Toronado	5000–5400	4500–5000	4000–4500
1982 Toronado	6200–6800	5800–6400	5100–5800

1979 Oldsmobile Toronado 2-door

Price Range	GOOD		AVERAGE		POOR
1983 Toronado	8000–8500		7500–8000		6900–7500
1984 Toronado	9700–10,250		9300–9800		8400–9300
1985 Toronado	11,750–12,500		11,000–12,000		10,500–11,000

Dimensions	WHEEL-BASE, IN.	LGTH., IN.	HT., IN.	WIDTH, IN.	AVG. WT., LBS.	CARGO VOL., CU. FT.	FUEL TANK, GAL.
2d cpe	114.0	206.0	54.6	71.4	3742	15.2	22.8

Engines	L/CID	BHP	MPG	AVAIL.
ohv V-6 4 bbl.	4.1/252	125	14–17	81–84
ohv V-8 4 bbl.	5.0/307	140–150	14–18	80–85
ohv V-8 4 bbl.	5.7/350	160–165	13–18	79–80
ohv V-8D FI	5.7/350	105–125	23–27	79–84

1980 Oldsmobile Toronado 2-door

Oldsmobile

RECALL HISTORY

1980 (diesel engine): possible that a wire in EGR harness could be pinched, causing electrical short that may result in fire. **1981:** possible that left front upper control arm could loosen and come off, reducing steering control; could result in vehicle crash. **1982 (diesel engine):** injection pump governor may fail and throttle valve could stick, preventing engine from returning to idle speed or being shut off. **1983:** catalytic converter may be faulty; if partly blocked, could cause loss of power and acceleration, or engine might not start at all.

Oldsmobile Toronado 1986-88

All-new descendant of personal-luxury Olds coupe, still front-drive, has been a big sales disappointment. Traditional Toro buyers apparently disliked the shrunken styling, which too closely resembles other GM models—a common recent complaint. Close kin include Buick Riviera and Cadillac Eldorado. A sporty Trofeo edition for 1987-88 carries interior leather with bucket seats and FE3 sport suspension. A 3.8-liter V-6 with 4-speed overdrive automa-

1986 Oldsmobile Toronado 2-door

CONSUMER GUIDE®

tic provides quick pickup because of the car's weight loss. The new "3800" version for 1988 adds 15 horsepower. Trimmed-down Toro is agile and responsive, but expect ample body roll in turns. Light steering lacks road feel. Passenger space is almost as ample as before, but trunk is shallow. Though supposedly a six-passenger, only two grownups fit reasonably in the back seat. First dashboard was cluttered with tiny lookalike controls, but later version is better. Conclusion: definitely improved, but bland styling doesn't warrant hefty price as a used car.

Price Range	GOOD	AVERAGE	POOR
1986 Toronado	$14,000–15,000	$13,000–14,000	$12,000–13,000
1987 Toronado	16,000–17,000	15,000–16,000	14,250–15,000
1988 Toronado	19,000–21,500	18,000–20,500	—

Dimensions	WHEEL-BASE, IN.	LGTH., IN.	HT., IN.	WIDTH, IN.	AVG. WT., LBS.	CARGO VOL., CU. FT.	FUEL TANK, GAL.
2d cpe	108.0	187.5	53.0	70.7	3265	14.1	18.0

1986 Oldsmobile Toronado 2-door

1987 Oldsmobile Toronado 2-door

Oldsmobile • Plymouth

Engines	L/CID	BHP	MPG	AVAIL.
ohv V-6 FI	3.8/231	140–165	18–22	86–88

KEY: L/CID = liters/cubic inch displacement; **BHP** = brake horsepower; **MPG** = estimated average miles per gallon; **ohc** = overhead cam; **dohc** = double overhead cam; **ohv** = overhead valve; **I** = in-line engine; **V** = V engine; **flat** = horizontally opposed engine; **D** = diesel; **T** = turbocharged; **bbl.** = barrel (carburetor); **FI** = fuel injection.

RECALL HISTORY

1986: some console front compartment doors may not remain closed in a crash. **1986-87:** engine oil pressure warning system could fail and give false low reading.

Plymouth Caravelle 1985-88

1985 Plymouth Caravelle 4-door

Intermediate family sedan on extended K-car chassis is basically the former Chrysler E Class, revised slightly for 1985 and given a new Plymouth nameplate. Front-drive design is roomy and comfortable, with good trunk space. Performance from the base 2.2-liter four or optional Mitsubishi 2.6 is uninspiring but adequate. With a turbo, you'll move out in a hurry but the loud exhaust seems incongruous in a modest sedan. A new 2.5-liter four was made optional for '86. Only a premium SE version was offered for 1985, but a base model was added the next year. See Chrysler New Yorker and Dodge 600 entries for more details. Conclusion: good basic transportation at a reasonable price.

1986 Plymouth Caravelle 4-door

1986 Plymouth Caravelle 4-door

Price Range	GOOD	AVERAGE	POOR
1985 Caravelle	$6000–6500	$5500–6000	$5000–5500
1986 Caravelle	7200–7900	6700–7500	6000–6800
1987 Caravelle	8500–9400	7900–8800	7300–8000
1988 Caravelle	10,250–11,000	9250–10,250	—

Dimensions	WHEEL-BASE, IN.	LGTH., IN.	HT., IN.	WIDTH, IN.	AVG. WT., LBS.	CARGO VOL., CU. FT.	FUEL TANK, GAL.
4d sdn	103.3	187.2	53.1	68.5	2527	17.0	14.0

Engines	L/CID	BHP	MPG	AVAIL.
ohc I-4 FI	2.2/135	93–99	20–25	85–88
ohc I-4T FI	2.2/135	146	18–24	85–88
ohc I-4 FI	2.5/153	96–100	20–25	86–88
ohc I-4 2 bbl.	2.6/156	101	19–24	85

KEY: L/CID = liters/cubic inch displacement; **BHP** = brake horsepower; **MPG** = estimated average miles per gallon; **ohc** = overhead cam; **dohc** = double overhead cam; **ohv** = overhead valve; **I** = in-line engine; **V** = V engine; **flat** = horizontally opposed engine; **D** = diesel; **T** = turbocharged; **bbl.** = barrel (carburetor); **FI** = fuel injection.

Plymouth
RECALL HISTORY

1985 (2.2-liter Turbo): fuel hose routed to pressure regulator may have inadequately tightened hose clamp; hose could leak and possibly result in engine compartment fire.

Plymouth Gran Fury 1982-88

1982 Plymouth Gran Fury 4-door

Since 1982, Gran Fury has been nearly identical to Dodge Diplomat (see that entry for more comments). Its 112.7-inch wheelbase falls between mid- and full-size. Early models came with a 225-cid six, which lacks strength for its job. Since 1983, only the 318-cid (5.2-liter) V-8 has been offered. Riding an old-fashioned chassis with soft suspension, Gran Fury hasn't sold well except for taxi and police fleets. Smooth, reliable drivetrain is tempting, but gas mileage and outmoded handling make us say no.

Price Range	GOOD	AVERAGE	POOR
1982 Gran Fury	$2700–3000	$2400–2700	$2000–2400
1983 Gran Fury	3400–3800	3100–3500	2700–3100
1984 Gran Fury	4600–5000	4100–4700	3500–4100
1985 Gran Fury	5900–6400	5400–6000	4800–5400
1986 Gran Fury	7000–7600	6600–7100	6000–6600
1987 Gran Fury	8000–8500	7400–8000	6900–7500
1988 Gran Fury	10,000–11,000	9250–10,250	—

1984 Plymouth Gran Fury 4-door

Dimensions	WHEEL-BASE, IN.	LGTH., IN.	HT., IN.	WIDTH, IN.	AVG. WT., LBS.	CARGO VOL., CU. FT.	FUEL TANK, GAL.
4d sdn	112.7	205.7	55.3	74.2	3492	15.6	18.0

Engines	L/CID	BHP	MPG	AVAIL.
ohv I-6 1 bbl.	3.7/225	90	15–19	82–83
ohv V-8 2 bbl.	5.2/318	120–140	15–19	82–88
ohv V-8 4 bbl.	5.2/318	165	14–17	82

KEY: L/CID = liters/cubic inch displacement; **BHP** = brake horsepower; **MPG** = estimated average miles per gallon; **ohc** = overhead cam; **dohc** = double overhead cam; **ohv** = overhead valve; **I** = in-line engine; **V** = V engine; **flat** = horizontally opposed engine; **D** = diesel; **T** = turbocharged; **bbl.** = barrel (carburetor); **FI** = fuel injection.

RECALL HISTORY

1986: battery cap vents may be partially or completely blocked with plastic flashing; buildup of internal gas pressure, especially while charging, could result in case rupture and release of gases and/or acid, which might cause injury.

1986 Plymouth Gran Fury 4-door

Plymouth Horizon 1978-88

1978 Plymouth Horizon 5-door

Chrysler's first front-drive subcompact, identical to Dodge Omni, hasn't changed its 5-door hatchback body much, but has gone through a series of engines. First came a 1.7-liter four derived from VW's Rabbit. A Chrysler 2.2 four became optional in 1981; then a 1.6-liter Peugeot became the base engine during '83. High-output 2.2 was a 1984-86 option. Like Omni, standardized 1987-88 Horizon America comes only with a 2.2-liter four (fuel injected for '88) and limited option choices. For performance, pick a 2.2, which packs a lot more punch without burning much more fuel. With 5-speed manual shift, it can take off like some sporty cars. Repair record after 1980 is average or better, though workmanship has been inconsistent. Four adults fit with a bit of squeezing, but driving position isn't tops. Check Omni entry for more comments and full safety recall data. All told, Horizon is a solid little car with a modest price tag. Current versions are built in Wisconsin, following Chrysler's takeover of AMC.

Price Range	GOOD	AVERAGE	POOR
1978 Horizon	$900–1100	$700–900	$450–700
1979 Horizon	1100–1300	850–1100	600–850
1980 Horizon	1300–1600	1100–1400	900–1100

Plymouth

Price Range

	GOOD	AVERAGE	POOR
1981 Horizon	1700–2000	1400–1800	1100–1400
1982 Horizon	2100–2700	1800–2300	1500–1800
1983 Horizon	2700–3100	2400–2800	2000–2400
1984 Horizon	3400–3800	3000–3400	2500–3000
1985 Horizon	4100–4500	3800–4200	3300–3800
1986 Horizon	4800–5300	4400–5000	3900–4400
1987 Horizon America	5300–5700	4800–5300	4300–4800
1988 Horizon America	5800–6200	5300–5800	—

Dimensions

	WHEEL-BASE, IN.	LGTH., IN.	HT., IN.	WIDTH, IN.	AVG. WT., LBS.	CARGO VOL., CU. FT.	FUEL TANK, GAL.
5d sdn	99.1	164.8	53.0	63.8	2094	33.0	13.0

Engines

	L/CID	BHP	MPG	AVAIL.
ohc I-4 2 bbl.	1.7/105	70	25–30	78–83
ohv I-4 2 bbl.	1.6/98	62–64	25–30	83–86
ohc I-4 2 bbl.	2.2/135	84–96	24–29	81–87
ohc I-4 FI	2.2/135	93	23–28	88
ohc I-4 2 bbl.	2.2/135	110	22–28	84–86

1984 Plymouth Horizon 5-door

1986 Plymouth Horizon 5-door

Plymouth

KEY: L/CID = liters/cubic inch displacement; **BHP** = brake horsepower; **MPG** = estimated average miles per gallon; **ohc** = overhead cam; **dohc** = double overhead cam; **ohv** = overhead valve; **I** = in-line engine; **V** = V engine; **flat** = horizontally opposed engine; **D** = diesel; **T** = turbocharged; **bbl.** = barrel (carburetor); **FI** = fuel injection.

RECALL HISTORY

See Dodge Omni 1978–88 entry for recall information.

Plymouth Reliant 1981-88

1981 Plymouth Reliant Custom 4-door

Both Reliant and its K-car twin, the Dodge Aries, sold well from the start, with fewer first-year bugs than most cars. Functional, roomy design with spacious trunk makes them popular as family and company cars. Base 2.2-liter engine is noisier and less potent than the optional Mitsubishi 2.6, but a bit more economical. Optional for 1986–88 is a new 2.5-liter four that's smooth and peppy. One of many running improvements was the redesigned dash of 1984, which added temperature and voltage gauges along with a trip odometer. Restyling for 1985 gave the car a more European look. Sensible front-drive design isn't exactly thrilling, but with a modest price tag, Reliant is ready for reliable low-budget motoring. Most comments for Dodge Aries apply here, so see that entry. Look for an '83 or later to get the best chance of long, trouble-free life. Reliant shrinks to only one series for 1988, the low-cost America with fewer option choices.

1985 Plymouth Reliant 4-door

Price Range	GOOD	AVERAGE	POOR
1981 Reliant	$1700–2300	$1400–2000	$1100–1400
1982 Reliant	2400–3100	1900–2700	1500–1900
1983 Reliant	3100–3800	2700–3400	2300–2800
1984 Reliant	4000–4800	3400–4200	2900–3400
1985 Reliant	4700–5800	4300–5100	3700–4300
1986 Reliant	5800–7000	5300–6300	4800–5500
1987 Reliant	6900–7900	6300–7300	5900–6400
1988 Reliant America	7000–7500	6500–7000	—

Dimensions	WHEEL-BASE, IN.	LGTH., IN.	HT., IN.	WIDTH, IN.	AVG. WT., LBS.	CARGO VOL., CU. FT.	FUEL TANK, GAL.
2d sdn	100.3	176.1	52.5	68.4	2317	15.0	14.0
4d sdn	100.3	176.1	52.5	68.4	2323	15.0	14.0
5d wgn	100.3	176.1	53.1	68.4	2432	67.7	14.0

1986 Plymouth Reliant 2-door

Plymouth

Engines	L/CID	BHP	MPG	AVAIL.
ohc I-4 2 bbl.	2.2/135	84–96	22–28	81–85
ohc I-4 FI	2.2/135	93–97	22–27	86–88
ohc I-4 FI	2.5/153	96–100	21–26	86–88
ohc I-4 2 bbl.	2.6/156	93–101	20–26	81–85

KEY: L/CID = liters/cubic inch displacement; **BHP** = brake horsepower; **MPG** = estimated average miles per gallon; **ohc** = overhead cam; **dohc** = double overhead cam; **ohv** = overhead valve; **I** = in-line engine; **V** = V engine; **flat** = horizontally opposed engine; **D** = diesel; **T** = turbocharged; **bbl.** = barrel (carburetor); **FI** = fuel injection.

RECALL HISTORY

1981: faulty stoplight switch could prevent brake lights from working when brake is applied. **1981:** automatic speed control switch could stick in "resume" position, preventing system from being deactivated by normal brake pedal application. **1982:** bolts used to attach front suspension ball joints to steering knuckles could eventually crack, allowing ball joint to separate from knuckle. **1983:** brake fluid hose could leak from rubbing against exhaust bracket, resulting in partial loss of braking capability. **1984–85 (2.2-liter engine):** fuel reservoir may leak at seam and inlet hose connection, which could cause engine compartment fire. **1986:** battery cap vents may be partially or completely blocked with plastic flashing; buildup of internal gas pressure, especially while charging, could result in case rupture and release of gases and/or acid, which might cause injury.

Plymouth TC3/Turismo 1979-87

Snappy front-drive sport coupe is based on Plymouth Horizon/Dodge Omni subcompact chassis. Comments for the identical Dodge 024/Charger apply (see separate report), except for Dodge's super-swift Shelby version. First called TC3, then TC3 Turismo, the Turismo name has stuck since 1983. Styling improved with a 1984 redesign. Best engine choice is the economical 2.2-liter, offered since 1981 (in high-performance tune from 1984–86). Though on the crude side, both offer plenty of zip. Performance fans should look for a Turismo 2.2, which delivers eye-opening pickup and has firmer suspension and wide tires for better handling. Ride gets rough, though, and the loud exhaust can be annoying. Turismo can move well but lacks refinement compared to a Honda Prelude or Datsun 200SX. Driving

1981 Plymouth TC3 3-door

1984 Plymouth Turismo 2.2 3-door

position and controls also lag behind rivals. Rear space is tight, though no worse than some. The 1979–81 models have had the most problems, and any model might be sloppily assembled. Turismo was dropped after 1987, leaving only the basic Omni/Horizon America sedan.

Price Range	GOOD	AVERAGE	POOR
1979 TC3	$1200–1500	$950–1200	$700–950
1980 TC3	1600–1900	1300–1600	1000–1300
1981 TC3	1900–2250	1500–1900	1200–1500
1982 TC3	2400–2700	2000–2400	1700–2000
1982 TC3 Turismo	2700–3000	2300–2700	2000–2300
1983 Turismo	3100–3500	2700–3100	2300–2700

Plymouth

Price Range	GOOD	AVERAGE	POOR
1984 Turismo	3800–4300	3500–4000	3000–3500
1985 Turismo	4700–5300	4400–4900	3900–4400
1986 Turismo	5500–6100	5100–5700	4500–5100
1987 Turismo	6500–7000	6000–6500	5500–6000

Dimensions	WHEEL-BASE, IN.	LGTH., IN.	HT., IN.	WIDTH, IN.	AVG. WT., LBS.	CARGO VOL. CU.FT.	FUEL TANK, GAL.
3d cpe	96.6	174.8	50.7	65.9	2155	32.4	13.0

Engines	L/CID	BHP	MPG	AVAIL.
ohc I-4 2 bbl.	1.7/105	70	25–30	79–83
ohv I-4 2 bbl.	1.6/98	62–64	25–30	83–86
ohc I-4 2 bbl.	2.2/135	84–96	24–28	81–87
ohc I-4 2 bbl.	2.2/135	110	21–26	84–86

KEY: L/CID = liters/cubic inch displacement; **BHP** = brake horsepower; **MPG** = estimated average miles per gallon; **ohc** = overhead cam; **dohc** = double overhead cam; **ohv** = overhead valve; **I** = in-line engine; **V** = V engine; **flat** = horizontally opposed engine; **D** = diesel; **T** = turbocharged; **bbl.** = barrel (carburetor); **FI** = fuel injection.

RECALL HISTORY

See Dodge Omni 1978–88 for recall history.

Plymouth Voyager 1984-88

New-wave front-drive compact van has become a hot item, offering plenty of passenger/cargo space in a small vehicle that handles like a car. Dodge Caravan is identical, so check that report. Ride is steady and comfortable. Noisy base 2.2-liter engine will suffice with manual shift, but is sluggish with automatic. Optional 2.6-liter four has history of stalling and rough ride. For peak performance, an optional Mitsubishi 3.0-liter V-6 (only with 3-speed automatic) came along in spring 1987. So did a lengthened Grand Voyager. Latest base engine is a 2.5-liter four. With any powerplant, we rate this pair tops among modern vans. Demand has outstripped supply lately, so prices are likely to remain hefty, both new and secondhand.

Price Range	GOOD	AVERAGE	POOR
1984 Voyager	$7300–8000	$6800–7600	$6000–6800
1985 Voyager	8900–9400	8100–8900	7500–8100
1986 Voyager	9750–10,750	9100–10,250	8500–9200
1987 Voyager	11,000–12,000	10,100–11,000	9500–10,250
1988 Voyager	11,750–13,000	11,000–12,000	—

1984 Plymouth Voyager

Dimensions	WHEEL-BASE, IN.	LGTH., IN.	HT., IN.	WIDTH, IN.	AVG. WT., LBS.	CARGO VOL., CU. FT.	FUEL TANK, GAL.
4d van	112.0	175.9	64.2	69.6	2911	125.0	15.0
4d van*	119.1	190.5	65.0	69.6	3304	150.0	15.0

*Grand Voyager.

Engines	L/CID	BHP	MPG	AVAIL.
ohc I-4 2 bbl.	2.2/135	95–101	17–20	84–87
ohc I-4 2 bbl.	2.6/156	104	16–20	84–87
ohc I-4 FI	2.5/153	96–102	18–22	88
ohc V-6 FI	3.0/187	136–144	16–20	87–88

1986 Plymouth Voyager

Plymouth • Pontiac

RECALL HISTORY

1984–85: roadway stones could become lodged in weight-sensing brake proportioning valve, which might change brake "feel" and increase stopping distance during hard braking; protective cover should be installed. **1984–85 (2.2-liter engine):** fuel supply tube between fuel pump and filter may be subject to vibration fatigue, cracking at fuel pump end, which could cause fuel leakage and potential for fire. **1986 7–8 passenger van:** first rear seats were installed with incorrect left side riser; in case of accident, seats may become detached, causing serious injuries.

Pontiac Bonneville/ Catalina 1978-81

1979 Pontiac Bonneville 4-door

Downsized yet sizable B-body duo didn't sell as well as other GM full-size cars: Buick LeSabre, Chevrolet Caprice/ Impala, and Olds Delta 88. Both disappeared after 1981. Demand for big cars revived shortly thereafter, so they returned to life as the 1983 Parisienne. Gas-engine models have above-average repair record for 1978; just average in later years (including paint and rust problems). Avoid 1980-81 models with the unreliable Olds-built diesel V-8. Catalina, powered by a Buick V-6, delivers decent gas

Pontiac

mileage for its class. Early version is a better choice than full-size rivals, and 1979-81s rate a bit higher than Ford LTD/Mercury Marquis. Equivalent GM models are just about as desirable, but Pontiacs may be a little cheaper.

Price Range	GOOD	AVERAGE	POOR
1978 Bonneville	$1800–2200	$1500–1800	$1100–1500
1978 Catalina	1400–1700	1100–1400	900–1100
1979 Bonneville	2200–2600	1800–2200	1400–1800
1979 Catalina	1700–2000	1300–1700	1000–1300
1980 Bonneville	2700–3100	2300–2800	1800–2300
1980 Catalina	2200–2500	1800–2200	1400–1800
1981 Bonneville	3300–3800	2800–3400	2300–2800
1981 Catalina	2700–3000	2300–2700	1900–2300

Dimensions	WHEEL-BASE, IN.	LGTH., IN.	HT., IN.	WIDTH, IN.	AVG. WT., LBS.	CARGO VOL., CU. FT.	FUEL TANK, GAL.
2d cpe	116.0	214.3	54.9	78.0	3650	18.8	20.7
4d sdn	116.0	214.3	57.3	78.0	3800	18.8	20.7
5d wgn	116.0	215.1	57.3	78.0	4150	98.4	22.0

Engines	L/CID	BHP	MPG	AVAIL.
ohv V-6 2 bbl.	3.8/231	105–115	16–18	78–81
ohv V-8 2 bbl.	4.3/265	120	15–17	80–81
ohv V-8 2 bbl.	4.9/301	130–140	15–17	78–80
ohv V-8 4 bbl.	5.0/307	145	14–17	81
ohv V-8 4 bbl.	5.7/350	155–170	13–16	78–79
ohv V-8 D FI	5.7/350	125	23–27	80–81
ohv V-8 4 bbl.	6.6/400	180	11–14	78

KEY: L/CID = liters/cubic inch displacement; **BHP** = brake horsepower; **MPG** = estimated average miles per gallon; **ohc** = overhead cam; **dohc** = double overhead cam; **ohv** = overhead valve; **I** = in-line engine; **V** = V engine; **flat** = horizontally opposed engine; **D** = diesel; **T** = turbocharged; **bbl.** = barrel (carburetor); **FI** = fuel injection.

1981 Pontiac Catalina 4-door

CONSUMER GUIDE®

Pontiac
RECALL HISTORY

1978: fan blade spider (hub portion) may fatigue and break apart, allowing two-blade segment to be thrown off. **1978 (301-cid engine):** replacement of front seat anchor bolts. **1979–80:** front outboard seatbelt anchor bolts could break off during normal use, increasing chances of injury.

Pontiac Bonneville 1987-88

1987 Pontiac Bonneville LE 4-door

Famous Pontiac badge now adorns a sporty full-size, front-wheel-drive 4-door sedan that shares its H-body platform with Buick LeSabre and Olds Delta 88. Unlike Buick and Olds, Pontiac offers no 2-door coupe. Sole drivetrain is a 3.8-liter V-6 with 4-speed overdrive automatic transmission. The "3800" version for '88 added a balance shaft and 15 horsepower. Base and luxury LE editions were offered at first, plus a sporty SE package that includes a body-color grille, floor shift console, and firmer suspension. In second season, the base model departed but a new, aggressively styled SSE model joined the lineup, sporting aero ground-effects components, Road Car performance suspension, and anti-lock brakes. Though basically a family sedan, Bonneville performs capably, handles responsively, and is quite agile for its size. Ride is stable and nicely controlled. SE version has even better road manners, if less riding comfort. Low-speed pickup is strong, highway passing brisk, and the V-6 emits a pleasing, muted sound during hard acceleration. On the minus side, brake response is

1987 Pontiac Bonneville SE 4-door

mushy and power steering too light. Also, our test car often
stalled when idling in gear. Couchlike seats are soft yet
comfortable. Head and leg room are ample for everyone.
Large trunk with wide, flat floor holds plenty. We prefer
Pontiac's version of this smaller full-size family sedan, and
you might too.

Price Range	GOOD	AVERAGE	POOR
1987 Bonneville	$12,000–13,000	$11,500–12,500	$10,750–11,500
1988 Bonneville	13,500–15,000	12,800–14,000	–

Dimensions	WHEEL-BASE, IN.	LGTH., IN.	HT., IN.	WIDTH, IN.	AVG. WT., LBS.	CARGO VOL., CU. FT.	FUEL TANK, GAL.
4d sdn	110.8	198.7	55.5	72.1	3316	15.5	18.0

Engines	L/CID	BHP	MPG	AVAIL.
ohv V-6 FI	3.8/231	150	20–24	87–88
ohv V-6 FI	3.8/231	165	19–24	88

KEY: L/CID = liters/cubic inch displacement; **BHP** = brake horsepower; **MPG** =
estimated average miles per gallon; **ohc** = overhead cam; **dohc** = double overhead
cam; **ohv** = overhead valve; **I** = in-line engine; **V** = V engine; **flat** = horizontally
opposed engine; **D** = diesel; **T** = turbocharged; **bbl.** = barrel (carburetor); **FI** = fuel
injection.

RECALL HISTORY

1987: fusible link could melt under high-resistance load and ignite
plastic windshield washer bracket, causing underhood fire; replace
with nonflammable bracket.

Pontiac Fiero 1984-88

Racy plastic mid-engine sportster found an unprecedented
100,000 buyers in its opening season, though sales have
slackened lately. Striking low-slung design was the main

Pontiac

1984 Pontiac Fiero 2-door

attraction, since the 2.5-liter "Iron Duke" engine couldn't deliver performance to match the car's appealing looks. A 4-cylinder Fiero is little more than a sharply styled econocar. Fuel-injected V-6, first offered on 1985½ models, produces action more appropriate to the slick shape. Performance GT, introduced as a 1986½, sports distinctive swept-back pillars plus standard V-6 with Getrag-designed 5-speed gearbox. Rear-drive chassis has all-independent suspension and disc brakes all around. Performance suspension, standard on upper-level SE and GT and optional on others, gives best handling but roughens the ride quite a bit. Fully revised suspension for 1988 is supposed to turn Fiero into a "true" sports car—agile, smooth riding, easy to steer. We wouldn't bet on that. Corrosion-resistant plastic body panels attach to a space frame, but Fiero's no lightweight, especially with a V-6. Passenger/luggage space is limited. Low roof and tall center console produce a cramped interior. Power steering wasn't scheduled to become available until mid-1988, so plenty of muscle is needed to turn the wheel at low speeds on earlier models. Fiero looks great but has many faults; cooling systems have been troublesome, rear wheel misalignment and stiff steering are common, and the V-6 is difficult to service in tight engine compartment. An '84 may appeal to collectors, and latest GT or Formula model may be tempting, but we don't recommend any Fiero for ordinary driving.

1986 Pontiac Fiero GT 2-door

Price Range	GOOD	AVERAGE	POOR
1984 Fiero	$4800–5700	$4400–5200	$3700–4400
1985 Fiero	6000–7600	5400–7000	4800–5800
1986 Fiero	6900–8800	6400–8200	5800–7000
1987 Fiero	8000–10,000	7500–9500	6800–8000
1988 Fiero	9750–13,000	9000—12,000	—

Dimensions	WHEEL-BASE, IN.	LGTH., IN.	HT., IN.	WIDTH, IN.	AVG. WT., LBS.	CARGO VOL., CU. FT.	FUEL TANK, GAL.
2d cpe	93.4	160.7	46.9	68.9	2464	5.8	10.2

Engines	L/CID	BHP	MPG	AVAIL.
ohv I-4 FI	2.5/151	92–98	21–26	84–88
ohv V-6 FI	2.8/173	130–140	19–25	85–88

KEY: L/CID = liters/cubic inch displacement; **BHP** = brake horsepower; **MPG** = estimated average miles per gallon; **ohc** = overhead cam; **dohc** = double overhead cam; **ohv** = overhead valve; **I** = in-line engine; **V** = V engine; **flat** = horizontally opposed engine; **D** = diesel; **T** = turbocharged; **bbl.** = barrel (carburetor); **FI** = fuel injection.

RECALL HISTORY

None to date.

Pontiac Firebird 1978-81

Second-generation ponycar shares basic body/chassis design with Chevy Camaro, but has different nose and tail styling plus wider choice of engines. In addition to sleek shape, you get tenacious handling/roadholding and tough

1978 Pontiac Firebird Turbo Trans Am 2-door

1980 Pontiac Firebird Trans Am 2-door

performance (with bigger V-8s). You also get rotten gas mileage, a minimal back seat and puny trunk. Poor paint and rust resistance, along with squeaks and rattles, are main trouble spots. Turbocharged engines are more vulnerable to problems than the regular versions. Clutch repairs are needed more often than average for 1978–79. Think twice about hot-performing Trans Am and Formula versions, many of which have been driven roughly. Base and Esprit models are a better (and cheaper) bet.

Price Range	GOOD	AVERAGE	POOR
1978 Firebird	$1800–2000	$1400–1800	$1000–1400
1978 Trans Am/Formula	2400–2700	2000–2400	1600–2000
1979 Firebird	2000–2300	1700–2000	1200–1700
1979 Trans Am/Formula	2700–3100	2400–2700	1900–2400
1980 Firebird	2500–3000	2200–2700	1700–2200
1980 Trans Am/Formula	3200–4000	2900–3700	2250–3000
1981 Firebird	3200–3900	2800–3500	2200–2900
1981 Trans Am/Formula	4100–4900	3700–4500	3000–3900

Dimensions	WHEEL-BASE, IN.	LGTH., IN.	HT., IN.	WIDTH, IN.	AVG. WT., LBS.	CARGO VOL., CU. FT.	FUEL TANK, GAL.
2d cpe	108.2	198.1	50.3	73.0	3400	9.2	21.0

Engines	L/CID	BHP	MPG	AVAIL.
ohv V-6 2 bbl.	3.8/231	105–115	18–21	78–81
ohv V-8 2 bbl.	4.3/265	120	16–18	80–81
ohv V-8 4 bbl.	4.9/301	135–155	14–16	79–81
ohv V-8T 4 bbl.	4.9/301	210	12–15	80–81
ohv V-8 4 bbl.	5.0/305	145	14–16	78–81
ohv V-8 4 bbl.	5.7/350	170–200	12–15	78
ohv V-8 4 bbl.	6.6/400	170–200	11–14	78–79
ohv V-8 4 bbl.	6.6/403	185	11–14	79

KEY: L/CID = liters/cubic inch displacement; **BHP** = brake horsepower; **MPG** = estimated average miles per gallon; **ohc** = overhead cam; **dohc** = double overhead cam; **ohv** = overhead valve; **I** = in-line engine; **V** = V engine; **flat** = horizontally opposed engine; **D** = diesel; **T** = turbocharged; **bbl.** = barrel (carburetor); **FI** = fuel injection.

RECALL HISTORY

1978: fan blade spider (hub portion) may fatigue and break apart, allowing two-blade segment to be thrown off. **1979:** brake lights could become inoperative and cruise control could remain engaged after brakes are released, because of incorrect lubricant used in assembly. **1980:** lower ball joints may not have been sufficiently tightened at steering knuckle, and could separate from knuckle. **1981:** possible that rear seatbelt retractors would not restrain smaller passengers in a crash.

Pontiac Firebird 1982-88

Latest rear-drive ponycar is smaller, lighter, more practical—and closer to its Chevy Camaro cousin, except for differences in body metal, chassis tuning, dashboard, trim and equipment. Hatchback coupe comes in base, SE, or hot Formula and Trans Am form. Nearly all engine choices are shared with Camaro, so check that report. Optional

Pontiac

1982 Pontiac Firebird 3-door

5.0-liter V-8 with twin throttle-body fuel injectors (a la Corvette) was supposed to be the hot one for 1982-83, but Trans Ams carrying it couldn't keep up with Mustang GTs or Toyota Supras. A high-output (190 horsepower) carbureted V-8 has performed better. For 1985 a new 5.0 V-8 option arrived, with port fuel injection and 205 horsepower. Trans Ams and Formulas for 1987-88 could even have a 5.7-liter Corvette V-8, offered only with automatic. Four-cylinder Firebirds finally departed after '86. A muscular Trans Am is the logical choice for performance fans, if you can find one that hasn't been abused—a tall order. A V-6 version (fuel injected since 1985) delivers better mileage and softer ride, yet moves well enough for most drivers.

1985 Pontiac Firebird Trans Am 3-door

Y99 Rally Tuned Suspension improves handling of V-6 and V-8 'birds from 1986. Only base and Trans Am editions survive into 1988, but with new Formula and GTA packages. Traditional 2 + 2 styling means the "2" in back are squeezed tightly. A potent Firebird can be hard to handle on icy roads, so northern buyers might want to think about a front-drive coupe instead. Watch for clutch chatter on some 1982-83 models.

Price Range	GOOD	AVERAGE	POOR
1982 Firebird	$3900–4500	$3500–4100	$2900–3500
1982 Trans Am/SE	4900–5800	4500–5400	3900–4700
1983 Firebird	4600–5200	4200–4800	3500–4200
1983 Trans Am/SE	6100–7000	5700–6600	5000–5800
1984 Firebird	5500–6000	4900–5500	4000–4900
1984 Trans Am/SE	7200–8200	6800–7700	6000–6900
1985 Firebird	6300–7000	5900–6700	5000–5900
1985 Trans Am/SE	8500–9400	8000–9000	7200–8000
1986 Firebird	7700–8500	7300–8100	6700–7300
1986 Trans Am/SE	9600–11,250	9000–10,750	8500–9500
1987 Firebird	9250–11,250	8800–10,500	8000–9000
1987 Trans Am	12,250–13,500	11,500–12,500	10,500–11,500
1988 Firebird	10,500–12,000	9500–11,000	—
1988 Trans Am	13,500–15,000	12,500–13,500	—

Dimensions	WHEEL-BASE, IN.	LGTH., IN.	HT., IN.	WIDTH, IN.	AVG. WT., LBS.	CARGO VOL., CU. FT.	FUEL TANK, GAL.
3d cpe	101.1	189.9	49.7	72.0	2929	31.2	15.9

Engines	L/CID	BHP	MPG	AVAIL.
ohv I-4 FI	2.5/151	88–90	19–23	82–86
ohv V-6 2 bbl.	2.8/173	107–112	17–21	82–83
ohv V-6 2 bbl.	2.8/173	135	16–19	83–84
ohv V-6 FI	2.8/173	135	17–21	85–88
ohv V-8 4 bbl.	5.0/305	150–190	13–16	82–87
ohv V-8 FI	5.0/305	170	15–19	88
ohv V-8 FI	5.0/305	165–175	12–15	82–83
ohv V-8 FI	5.0/305	190–215	15–19	85–87
ohv V-8 FI	5.7/350	210–225	15–18	87–88

KEY: L/CID = liters/cubic inch displacement; BHP = brake horsepower; MPG = estimated average miles per gallon; ohc = overhead cam; dohc = double overhead cam; ohv = overhead valve; I = in-line engine; V = V engine; flat = horizontally opposed engine; D = diesel; T = turbocharged; bbl. = barrel (carburetor); FI = fuel injection.

RECALL HISTORY

1982: thermal vacuum switch in evaporative emission control system of carbureted 5.0-liter V-8 engine may be broken. **1982:** Trans Ams with fuel-injected engines could have faulty fuel vent

1986 Pontiac Firebird Trans Am 3-door

valve that might force fuel out of filler neck if cap was removed while the tank was more than ¾ full. **1982:** rear seatbelts may not meet federal safety standards. **1983–85:** dislocation of a spring cover will not allow shoulder seatbelt to retract after being extended; extra slack could increase injuries in the event of an accident. **1984:** optional bucket seats may have seatback inertia locks that don't meet federal safety requirements. **1984:** certain brake hoses fail to conform to standard and might separate from fittings, resulting in loss of fluid and partial loss of braking. **1984–85:** hub area of cast aluminum wheels may be subject to fracture; wheel could separate from car, causing loss of control.

Pontiac Grand Am 1985-88

Front-drive N-body compact is mechanically similar to Buick Somerset Regal and Olds Calais, but looks more aggressive. BMW-like grille didn't arrive by accident, either. Grand Am first came in coupe form, with a sedan added for 1986. Top-line SE, another '86 arrival, enhances Pontiac's sporty image with standard fuel-injected V-6 plus air dam, side skirts, aero headlamps and more. Extras like that don't come cheap, so a used SE is likely to be expensive. Economical 4-cylinder engine is a bit feeble, and the V-6 comes only with automatic. Late 1987 brought an SE turbo with 165-horsepower four. Big news for '88: GM's new Quad 4 engine replaces the V-6 as an option. See Buick Somerest/Skylark entry for additional comments.

1985 Pontiac Grand Am 2-door

Price Range

Price Range	GOOD	AVERAGE	POOR
1985 Grand Am	$7100–7700	$6700–7400	$6000–6700
1986 Grand Am	8200–8800	7800–8400	7000–7800
1986 Grand Am SE	9500–10,000	9000–9500	8500–9000
1987 Grand Am	9200–10,200	8700–9800	8000–9000
1987 Grand Am SE	11,250–12,000	10,500–11,500	10,000–10,750
1988 Grand Am	10,000–11,000	9500–10,500	—
1988 Grand Am SE	12,250–13,500	11,500–12,500	

Dimensions	WHEEL-BASE, IN.	LGTH., IN.	HT., IN.	WIDTH, IN.	AVG. WT., LBS.	CARGO VOL. CU. FT.	FUEL TANK, GAL.
2d cpe	103.4	177.5	52.5	66.9	2492	13.1	13.6
4d sdn	103.4	177.5	52.5	66.5	2565	13.1	13.6

1986 Pontiac Grand Am SE 4-door

Pontiac

Engines	L/CID	BHP	MPG	AVAIL.
ohc I-4T FI	2.0/121	165	18–23	87–88
dohc I-4 FI	2.3/138	150	22—27	88
ohv I-4 FI	2.5/151	92–98	22–25	85–88
ohv V-6 FI	3.0/181	125	18–22	85–87

KEY: L/CID = liters/cubic inch displacement; **BHP** = brake horsepower; **MPG** = estimated average miles per gallon; **ohc** = overhead cam; **dohc** = double overhead cam; **ohv** = overhead valve; **I** = in-line engine; **V** = V engine; **flat** = horizontally opposed engine; **D** = diesel; **T** = turbocharged; **bbl.** = barrel (carburetor); **FI** = fuel injection.

RECALL HISTORY

1985: throttle return spring on 2.5-liter engine may fail, preventing throttle from returning to closed (idle) position when accelerator pedal is released. **1985-86:** small cracks may develop in body pillar around door striker bolt hole, which could make door hard to close and allow it to open during collision; install reinforcement plates.

Pontiac Grand Prix 1978-87

1978 Pontiac Grand Prix 2-door

Formerly one of Pontiac's best-sellers, Grand Prix faded somewhat in final years. Rear-drive intermediate luxury coupe is closely related to G-body Chevy Monte Carlo, Buick Regal, and Olds Cutlass Supreme. Early versions used mainly Pontiac engines, but 1985-87 models carry a Chevrolet V-6 or V-8. A 2+2 sport model appeared in mid-1986, with fastback roofline and standard 5.0-liter

V-8. Built on LeMans/Bonneville sedan's chassis, the curvaceous body cuts interior space down to a comfortable 4-seater. Repair history is average; not as good as Regal/Cutlass. Some models were equipped with undersized Turbo Hydra-matic 200C transmission, which has a record of early failure. You can expect quiet, relaxed motoring but mediocre gas mileage. We can't recommend Grand Prix, which usually sells for more than an equivalent Monte Carlo. All-new Grand Prix, built on same GM10 front-drive platform as Buick Regal and Oldsmobile Cutlass Supreme, arrives late in 1988 model year.

Price Range	GOOD	AVERAGE	POOR
1978 Grand Prix	$1800–2100	$1500–1800	$1100–1500
1979 Grand Prix	2100–2500	1700–2100	1300–1700
1980 Grand Prix	2400–3000	2000–2700	1500–2000
1981 Grand Prix	3300–3900	2900–3600	2400–2900
1982 Grand Prix	4200–5000	3800–4500	3000–3800
1983 Grand Prix	5100–5900	4700–5400	3900–4700
1984 Grand Prix	6200–7000	5700–6400	4900–5700
1985 Grand Prix	7300–8000	6900–7600	6000–6900
1986 Grand Prix	8600–9700	8200–9300	7500–8500
1987 Grand Prix	10,000–11,000	9500–10,500	8800–9500

Dimensions	WHEEL-BASE, IN.	LGTH., IN.	HT., IN.	WIDTH, IN.	AVG. WT., LBS.	CARGO VOL., CU. FT.	FUEL TANK, GAL.
2d cpe	108.1	201.9	54.7	72.3	3231	16.4	18.1

Engines	L/CID	BHP	MPG	AVAIL.
ohv V-6 2 bbl.	3.8/231	105–115	18–21	78–87
ohv V-6 4 bbl.	4.1/252	125	17–20	82
ohv V-6 FI	4.3/262	140	18–21	87
ohv V-8 2 bbl.	4.4/265	120	16–19	80–81
ohv V-8 2 bbl.	4.9/301	135–140	15–18	78–80
ohv V-8 4 bbl.	5.0/305	150–165	16–19	83–87
ohv V-8 4 bbl.	5.0/305	150–155	13–16	78–80
ohv V-8 D FI	5.7/350	105	23–27	81–84

KEY: L/CID = liters/cubic inch displacement; **BHP** = brake horsepower; **MPG** = estimated average miles per gallon; **ohc** = overhead cam; **dohc** = double overhead cam; **ohv** = overhead valve; **I** = in-line engine; **V** = V engine; **flat** = horizontally opposed engine; **D** = diesel; **T** = turbocharged; **bbl.** = barrel (carburetor); **FI** = fuel injection.

RECALL HISTORY

1978: front bench seats may have incorrect head restraints that do not conform to federal safety standard; in event of accident, could result in head injury to rear seat passenger. **1978:** fan blade spider (hub portion) may fatigue and break apart, throwing off two-blade segment. **1978:** faulty wheel bearings could damage

Pontiac

1986 Pontiac Grand Prix 2-door

1987 Pontiac Grand Prix 2+2 2-door

front wheel spindles and result, in extreme cases, in loss of control. **1978-80:** some rear axle shafts have end buttons that are thin or wear excessively, which could result in separation of axle shaft and wheel, leading to loss of control. **1978-80:** enlarged wheel cylinder pilot hole in rear brake backing plate could allow cylinder to rotate, causing loss of fluid that could lead to loss of rear brake action. **1978-81:** replacement of two bolts in lower control arms of rear suspension that could break from corrosion, resulting in loss of control. **1979:** brake lights may become inoperative and cruise control could remain engaged after brakes are released. **1979-80:** front brake pipe may come in contact with edge of oil pan, causing rupture and resulting in loss of braking ability. **1982:** injection pump governor on diesel V-8 could fail, preventing engine from returning to idle or being shut off. **1983:** brake master cylinder pipe could develop a leak from rubbing on air cleaner resonator bracket, causing loss of rear-wheel braking capability. **1984:** models with optional bucket seats may have seatback locks that fail to meet federal safety requirements. **1985-86 LE/ Brougham:** power door-lock switch on driver's side may separate during use, exposing the electrical terminal; short circuit could occur, leading to overheating and possible fire. **1986:** tire label on a few cars contains incorrect tire size information. **1986:** contacts on push-pull headlight switch may be intermittent, causing headlamps to flicker or go out suddenly.

Pontiac LeMans/ Bonneville 1978-86

1980 Pontiac Grand LeMans Safari 5-door

Mid-size Pontiac shared G-body design with Chevy Malibu/ Monte Carlo, Buick Century/Regal, and Olds Cutlass/Cutlass Supreme. LeMans-styled Bonneville became the company's "full-size" model for 1982, after the big B-body Bonneville/Catalina bit the dust. Bonneville badge went on new front-drive sedan for '87. Average repair record except for 1981 models, which rate worse (V-6s) to much worse (V-8s). V-8 models also suffer overheating, suspension failures, and imperfect paint finish. Gas mileage isn't bad with one of the smaller engines, which have no particular trouble spots. Avoid the troubled diesel. Handles better than most intermediates and seats five adults in comfort. Verdict: easy to like, but an equivalent Buick or Olds should be less troublesome.

Price Range	GOOD	AVERAGE	POOR
1978 LeMans	$1500–1750	$1200–1500	$900–1200
1979 LeMans	1700–2000	1400–1700	1000–1400
1980 LeMans	2000–2400	1700–2100	1400–1700

Pontiac

Price Range	GOOD	AVERAGE	POOR
1981 LeMans	2500–3200	2200–2900	1700–2200
1982 Bonneville	3700–4300	3400–4000	2800–3400
1983 Bonneville	4700–5500	4300–5000	3700–4300
1984 Bonneville	5600–6300	5300–5900	4600–5300
1985 Bonneville	6700–7300	6300–7000	5600–6300
1986 Bonneville	8000–8800	7500–8300	6800–7600

Dimensions	WHEEL-BASE, IN.	LGTH., IN.	HT., IN.	WIDTH, IN.	AVG. WT., LBS.	CARGO VOL., CU. FT.	FUEL TANK, GAL.
2d cpe	108.1	198.5	54.4	71.6	3150	16.6	18.1
4d sdn	108.1	198.5	54.4	71.6	3300	16.6	18.1
5d wgn	108.1	197.8	54.8	71.6	3500	72.4	18.2

Engines	L/CID	BHP	MPG	AVAIL.
ohv V-6 2 bbl.	3.8/229	115	18–21	80
ohv V-6 2 bbl.	3.8/231	105–115	18–21	78–79, 81–86
ohv V-8 2 bbl.	4.3/265	120	16–19	80–82
ohv V-8 2 bbl.	4.9/301	135–140	15–18	78–80

1981 Pontiac LeMans 2-door

1985 Pontiac Bonneville 4-door

Engines	L/CID	BHP	MPG	AVAIL.
ohv V-8 4 bbl.	4.9/301	150–155	14–17	78–81
ohv V-8 4 bbl.	5.0/305	150–163	14–18	83–86
ohv V-8 D FI	5.7/350	105	23–27	82–84

KEY: L/CID = liters/cubic inch displacement; **BHP** = brake horsepower; **MPG** = estimated average miles per gallon; **ohc** = overhead cam; **dohc** = double overhead cam; **ohv** = overhead valve; **I** = in-line engine; **V** = V engine; **flat** = horizontally opposed engine; **D** = diesel; **T** = turbocharged; **bbl.** = barrel (carburetor); **FI** = fuel injection.

RECALL HISTORY

1978: fan blade spider (hub portion) may fatigue and break apart, allowing two-blade segment to be thrown off. **1978:** front bench seats may have incorrect head restraint that fails to conform to federal safety standard and could result in injury during a crash. **1978:** faulty wheel bearing could damage front wheel spindle and, in extreme cases, result in loss of control. **1978 (301-cid engine):** replacement of front seat anchor bolts. **1978–80:** enlargement of wheel cylinder pilot hole in rear brake backing plate could allow wheel cylinder to rotate, causing loss of brake fluid. **1978–80:** rear axle shafts on certain cars have end buttons that are too thin or could wear excessively, possibly causing shaft/wheel assembly to separate from vehicle. **1978–81:** replacement of two bolts in lower control arms of rear suspension that could break from corrosion, resulting in loss of vehicle control. **1982 (diesel V-8):** injection pump governor could fail, preventing throttle from returning to idle or engine from being shut off. **1983:** brake master cylinder pipe could develop a leak from rubbing on air cleaner resonator bracket, causing loss of braking capability at rear wheels. **1984:** 2-door models with optional bucket seats may have seatback locks that fail to meet federal safety requirements. **1985:** tie rods on some models have loose adjuster clamps, which allow tie rod to loosen and separate, with loss of steering control. **1985:** pulse wiper systems may have 2-speed switches and pulse motors, and operate at nearly same speed in Hi or Lo. **1986:** contacts on push-pull headlight switch may be intermittent, causing headlamps to flicker or go out suddenly.

Pontiac Parisienne/ Safari 1983-88

Two years after the full-size B-body Bonneville disappeared from Pontiac's lineup, it reappeared as the Parisienne (a name formerly used in Canada). Differing

Pontiac

1984 Pontiac Parisienne 4-door

1987 Pontiac Safari 5-door

from Chevrolet Caprice only in minor styling touches at first, it received a new back-end look for '85, using old Bonneville quarter panels, deck lid and taillights. Sedan departed after 1986, but wagon continued under Safari name, V-8 powered only. Engines and other parts are identical to Caprice/Impala, so check that report for comments. Main difference: Parisienne has snazzier furnishings inside and a higher price tag.

Price Range	GOOD	AVERAGE	POOR
1983 Parisienne	$5200–5900	$4900–5500	$4200–4900
1984 Parisienne	6500–7200	6200–6800	5500–6200
1985 Parisienne	8000–8800	7500–8200	7000–7600
1986 Parisienne	9500–10,300	9000–9900	8400–9000
1987 Safari	11,750–12,500	11,000–11,750	10,000–11,000
1988 Safari	13,000–14,000	12,400–13,400	—

Dimensions	WHEEL-BASE, IN.	LGTH., IN.	HT., IN.	WIDTH, IN.	AVG. WT., LBS.	CARGO VOL., CU.FT.	FUEL TANK, GAL.
4d sdn	116.0	212.3	56.6	76.4	3675	20.9	25.0
5d wgn	116.0	215.0	57.4	79.3	4225	87.9	22.0

Engines	L/CID	BHP	MPG	AVAIL.
ohv V-6 2 bbl.	3.8/231	110	17–21	83–84
ohv V-6 FI	4.3/262	130–140	17–20	85–86
ohv V-8 4 bbl.	5.0/305	140–165	15–19	83–86
ohv V-8 4 bbl.	5.0/307	140	15–19	87–88
ohv V-8 D FI	5.7/350	105	21–25	83–85

KEY: L/CID = liters/cubic inch displacement; **BHP** = brake horsepower; **MPG** = estimated average miles per gallon; **ohc** = overhead cam; **dohc** = double overhead cam; **ohv** = overhead valve; **I** = in-line engine; **V** = V engine; **flat** = horizontally opposed engine; **D** = diesel; **T** = turbocharged; **bbl.** = barrel (carburetor); **FI** = fuel injection.

RECALL HISTORY

1984: tire information label on cars with rally tuned suspension may have incorrect tire size information. **1985:** a hose in fuel feed and return pipe assemblies may contact pointed end of radiator shroud attaching screw, which could cause gasoline leak and risk of underhood fire. **1985:** battery cable on cars with 4.3-liter V-6 engine may contact upper control arm or exhaust manifold shield, which could eventually wear through insulation; could result in underhood fire. **1986:** contacts on push-pull headlight switch may be intermittent, causing headlamps to flicker or go out suddenly.

Pontiac Phoenix 1980-84

Pontiac's version of the infamous GM X-car, furnished more comfortably than the similar Chevrolet Citation. All progressed quickly from plaudits to complaints after long list of first-year recalls. See Citation report for repair data and comments. Available in coupe or 5-door form, Phoenix was dropped at the end of 1984, a year before Citation. Later models are better than the 1980s, but we still say these are cars to be avoided.

Price Range	GOOD	AVERAGE	POOR
1980 Phoenix	$1600–1900	$1250–1600	$1000–1250
1981 Phoenix	1900–2200	1500–1900	1200–1500
1982 Phoenix	2300–3000	1900–2600	1500–1900
1983 Phoenix	2900–3700	2600–3300	2100–2600
1984 Phoenix	3700–4400	3300–4000	2800–3300

Pontiac

1980 Pontiac Phoenix 5-door

Dimensions	WHEEL-BASE, IN.	LGTH., IN.	HT., IN.	WIDTH, IN.	AVG. WT., LBS.	CARGO VOL., CU. FT.	FUEL TANK, GAL.
2d cpe	104.9	176.7	53.1	68.3	2504	14.3	14.0
5d sdn	104.9	179.3	53.4	69.6	2543	41.3	14.0

Engines	L/CID	BHP	MPG	AVAIL.
ohv I-4 2 bbl.	2.5/151	84–90	21–24	80–81
ohv I-4 FI	2.5/151	90–92	22–25	82–84
ohv V-6 2 bbl.	2.8/173	112–115	20–22	80–84
ohv V-6 2 bbl.	2.8/173	130–135	18–21	81–84

KEY: L/CID = liters/cubic inch displacement; **BHP** = brake horsepower; **MPG** = estimated average miles per gallon; **ohc** = overhead cam; **dohc** = double overhead cam; **ohv** = overhead valve; **I** = in-line engine; **V** = V engine; **flat** = horizontally opposed engine; **D** = diesel; **T** = turbocharged; **bbl.** = barrel (carburetor); **FI** = fuel injection.

1980 Pontiac Phoenix 5-door

CONSUMER GUIDE®

RECALL HISTORY

1980: rear brakes tend to lock in moderate to hard braking, which can cause car to spin unexpectedly. **1980:** clutch control cable could interfere with brake pipe and eventually cause pipe to break, causing fluid loss and partial loss of braking capability. **1980:** fuel hose could contact right drive axle boot, which may wear a hole in the hose, causing fuel leaks and possibility of engine fire. **1980:** longitudinal body bars at rear control arm may not have been adequately welded and could damage brake or fuel lines, resulting in separation of control arm. **1980:** front coil spring may be too large in diameter and could be forced over lower seat of strut assembly, which could damage brake hose and suspension. **1980:** automatic transmission cooler line hoses could fail under certain conditions, creating potential for fire. **1980:** steering gear mounting plate could crack after high mileage, which would allow gear attachment to come loose; under certain conditions, could result in crash. **1981 (V-6 engines):** may have incorrectly routed power steering hose that could deteriorate and leak, possibly causing fire. **1981:** engine ground cable could break and reduce performance of electrical system, dimming headlights and slowing wipers. **1982:** possible that brake hoses don't meet federal standards for strength; loss of fluid could result in partial loss of braking capability. **1982:** hose clamps on fuel tank filler and vent pipe could fracture, causing fuel leaks that may create possibility of fire. **1983:** brake proportioning valve could break and separate from master cylinder, causing fluid leak and partial loss of braking ability. **1984 (2.5-liter engine):** fuel may leak at injection feed pipe connection, which could result in underhood fire. **1984:** 2-door models with optional bucket seats may have seatback inertia locks that fail to meet federal safety requirements.

1980 Pontiac Phoenix 2-door

Pontiac Sunbird 1978-80

1977 Pontiac Sunbird 2-door

Subcompact coupes and wagon, descended from old Chevy
Vega/Pontiac Astre, are similar to Chevrolet Monza. Fairly
smooth, quiet engines deliver mediocre gas mileage. Passenger room is fair, ride passable, but luggage space puny
on notchback coupe. Repair record below par, with frequent
problems in suspension, clutch and manual transmission.
Watch for squeaks and rattles, poor paint, and tendency
to rust. Front suspension and alignment problems were
common, due to sagging chassis cross support. With so
many flaws, why take a chance?

Price Range	GOOD	AVERAGE	POOR
1978 Sunbird	$900–1150	$700–900	$500–700
1979 Sunbird	1200–1400	1000–1200	700–1000
1980 Sunbird	1400–1600	1200–1400	1000–1200

Dimensions	WHEEL-BASE, IN.	LGTH., IN.	HT., IN.	WIDTH, IN.	AVG. WT., LBS.	CARGO VOL., CU. FT.	FUEL TANK, GAL.
2d cpe	97.0	179.2	49.6	65.4	2700	6.6	10.7
3d cpe	97.0	179.2	49.6	65.4	2900	27.8	13.3
3d wgn	97.0	178.0	51.8	65.4	3075	46.6	16.6

Engines	L/CID	BHP	MPG	AVAIL.
ohv I-4 2 bbl.	2.5/151	85–90	20–22	78–80
ohv V-6 2 bbl.	3.8/231	105–115	17–19	78–80
ohv V-8 2 bbl.	5.0/305	130–145	15–17	78–79

Pontiac

KEY: L/CID = liters/cubic inch displacement; **BHP** = brake horsepower; **MPG** = estimated average miles per gallon; **ohc** = overhead cam; **dohc** = double overhead cam; **ohv** = overhead valve; **I** = in-line engine; **V** = V engine; **flat** = horizontally opposed engine; **D** = diesel; **T** = turbocharged; **bbl.** = barrel (carburetor); **FI** = fuel injection.

RECALL HISTORY

1978: replacement of left engine mount bracket, which may deform and interfere with steering linkage. **1978:** steering intermediate shaft coupling may have been machined oversize where it attaches to steering gear shaft, which might prevent coupling from tightening properly on shaft when clamp and pinch bolt were installed; could result in loss of steering control. **1979:** replacement of carburetor fuel feed hose, which may chafe against EGR valve causing rupture, leakage of fuel, and possible fire hazard. **1980:** possible that rear seatbelt retractors would not restrain smaller passengers in a crash.

1979 Pontiac Sunbird 3-door wagon

1979 Pontiac Sunbird 2-door

Pontiac J2000/Sunbird 1982-88

1982 Pontiac J2000 3-door

Pontiac ran through a trio of names for its front-drive subcompact J-car, but Sunbird has stuck since 1985. Like Chevrolet Cavalier, it comes in five body styles (including a convertible since '84), but with different engines. Both began with a feeble 1.8-liter four, soon enlarged to 2.0 liters. Pontiac made that one optional, turning instead to a 1.8-liter overhead-cam four from GM of Brazil as base powerplant. A turbocharged 1.8 became standard on the sporty SE for '84, optional on other models. New, more

1985 Pontiac Sunbird Turbo convertible

powerful overhead-cam 2.0-liter fours have been sole choices for 1987-88. Both the turbo SE and newer turbo GT, introduced for 1986 with spoiler and rally suspension, deliver their share of thrills. Handling impresses, too, though ride gets stiff. Non-turbos lack zest, especially with automatic transmission. Mileage with the smaller engines is below par. Grownups won't enjoy the back seat. Rear end was restyled for 1988, and 3-door hatchback was dropped. Watch for engine/transaxle vibrations caused by deterioration of the upper engine torque strap. Turbocharged engines tend to have more problems than non-turbos. Repair record lags behind Japanese rivals, but Sunbird is a fairly attractive (and cheaper) alternative to a Honda Accord or Toyota Corolla.

Price Range	GOOD	AVERAGE	POOR
1982 J2000	$2400–3100	$2100–2700	$1600–2100
1983 2000	3400–4100	3000–3700	2500–3000
1984 2000 Sunbird	4400–5300	3900–4800	3300–3900
1984 Convertible	7000–7500	6500–7000	5800–6500
1985 Sunbird	5500–6400	5000–5800	4300–5000
1985 Convertible	8000–8900	7500–8100	6900–7600
1986 Sunbird	6300–7800	5900–7200	5100–6000
1986 Convertible	10,000–11,000	9000–10,000	8500–9250
1987 Sunbird	7500–9500	7000–8900	6400–7700
1987 Convertible	12,000–13,000	11,000–12,000	10,000–11,000
1988 Sunbird	8500–10,500	7800–9800	—
1988 Convertible	15,000–16,000	14,000–15,000	—

Dimensions	WHEEL-BASE, IN.	LGTH., IN.	HT., IN.	WIDTH, IN.	AVG. WT., LBS.	CARGO VOL. CU. FT.	FUEL TANK, GAL.
2d cpe	101.2	173.7	51.9	65.9	2353	12.6	13.6
2d conv.	101.2	173.7	52.7	65.9	2585	10.4	13.6

1986 Pontiac Sunbird Turbo GT 3-door

Pontiac

Dimensions	WHEEL-BASE, IN.	LGTH., IN.	HT., IN.	WIDTH, IN.	AVG. WT., LBS.	CARGO VOL., CU. FT.	FUEL TANK, GAL.
3d cpe	101.2	173.7	51.9	66.6	2413	38.5	13.6
4d sdn	101.2	175.7	53.8	66.2	2412	13.5	13.6
5d wgn	101.2	175.8	54.1	66.2	2487	66.4	13.6

Engines	L/CID	BHP	MPG	AVAIL.
ohv I-4 2 bbl.	1.8/112	88	22–27	82
ohv I-4 FI	2.0/122	86	22–27	83–85
ohc I-4 FI	1.8/112	82–84	23–28	83–86
ohc I-4T FI	1.8/112	150	20–25	84–86
ohc I-4 FI	2.0/121	96	23–28	87–88
ohc I-4T FI	2.0/121	165	20–25	87–88

KEY: L/CID = liters/cubic inch displacement; **BHP** = brake horsepower; **MPG** = estimated average miles per gallon; **ohc** = overhead cam; **dohc** = double overhead cam; **ohv** = overhead valve; **I** = in-line engine; **V** = V engine; **flat** = horizontally opposed engine; **D** = diesel; **T** = turbocharged; **bbl.** = barrel (carburetor); **FI** = fuel injection.

RECALL HISTORY

1982: hose clamps on fuel tank filler pipe and vent pipe could break, creating possibility of fire. **1983:** brake proportioning valve could break and separate from master cylinder, causing fluid leak and partial loss of braking ability. **1983–84:** metal floor pan anchor bar of manually adjustable driver's seat could fatigue and break, allowing seat to tip backward without warning. **1984:** 2-door models with optional bucket seats may have seatback locks that fail to meet federal safety requirements. **1986:** contacts on push-pull headlight switch may be intermittent, causing headlamps to flicker or go out suddenly.

Pontiac 6000 1982-88

Pontiac considers its version of the A-body intermediate to be more European in flavor than its GM cousins: Chevrolet Celebrity, Buick Century, and Olds Cutlass Ciera. A 5-door wagon joined the twin sedans in 1984. Topping the lineup, though, is the sport-luxury STE sedan, introduced in 1983 to lure buyers of Audis, BMWs, and similar European sedans. Fully equipped and driven by a high-output V-6 engine, the STE has been a huge success. The STE received new front-end styling with aero headlamps for 1986. Generation II engines were extensively reworked for 1987, and STE added anti-lock braking. Base "Iron Duke" 2.5-liter four isn't as good a choice as the optional 2.8-liter V-6, which has more power but consumes only slightly more fuel. Watch for V-6 oil leaks, plus camshaft

1985 Pontiac 6000 LE 5-door

problems in STE's high-output version. Some STEs also suffered wheel vibration troubles. Engine/transaxle vibrations could be caused by deterioration of the upper engine torque strap. Avoid the imperfect diesel V-6. A-cars have much better repair records than the troubled X-cars from which they evolved, but they're hardly flawless. STEs are loaded with power accessories waiting to fail. Road manners are capable and pleasant; interior and trunk quite spacious. During the 1986 model year, Pontiac unveiled an S/E series of sedans and wagons, offering a standard 2.8 and sport suspension at lower prices than STE. Full-time 4-wheel-drive will arrive for STE at mid-year '88 (the first GM passenger car to offer 4WD), along with a new 3.1-liter V-6. Front-drive can cost more in upkeep, but its winter traction may be well worth the price. Compare reports on similar Chevy, Buick and Olds A-cars before you buy.

Price Range	GOOD	AVERAGE	POOR
1982 6000	$3700–4000	$3250–3700	$2800–3250
1983 6000	4400–5000	4000–4600	3500–4000
1983 6000 STE	6500–7000	6000–6500	5400–6000
1984 6000	5200–5900	4800–5400	4000–4800
1984 6000 STE	7700–8200	7200–7700	6600–7200
1985 6000	6400–7300	6000–6800	5400–6100
1985 6000 STE	9500–10,200	9000–9700	8300–9000
1986 6000	7700–8500	7200–8000	6500–7200
1986 6000 STE	11,250–12,500	10,500–11,500	9900–10,750

Pontiac

Price Range	GOOD		AVERAGE		POOR	
1987 6000	9400–11,000		8800–10,500		8000–9000	
1987 6000 STE	14,000–15,000		13,000–14,000		12,000–13,000	
1988 6000	10,750–13,000		10,000–11,750		—	
1988 6000 STE	17,000–18,500		16,000–17,500		—	

Dimensions	WHEEL-BASE, IN.	LGTH., IN.	HT., IN.	WIDTH, IN.	AVG. WT., LBS.	CARGO VOL., CU. FT.	FUEL TANK, GAL.
2d cpe	104.9	188.8	53.3	72.0	2660	16.2	15.7
4d sdn	104.9	188.8	53.8	72.0	2700	16.2	15.7
5d wgn	104.9	193.2	54.1	72.0	2860	74.4	15.7

Engines	L/CID	BHP	MPG	AVAIL.
ohv I-4 FI	2.5/151	90–98	20–24	82–88
ohv V-6 2 bbl.	2.8/173	112–135	19–23	82–86
ohv V-6 FI	2.8/173	125–130	19–23	85–88
ohv V-6D FI	4.3/262	85	24–29	82–85

KEY: L/CID = liters/cubic inch displacement; **BHP** = brake horsepower; **MPG** = estimated average miles per gallon; **ohc** = overhead cam; **dohc** = double overhead

1986 Pontiac 6000 STE 4-door

1987 Pontiac 6000 S/E 5-door

cam; **ohv** = overhead valve; **I** = in-line engine; **V** = V engine; **flat** = horizontally opposed engine; **D** = diesel; **T** = turbocharged; **bbl.** = barrel (carburetor); **FI** = fuel injection.

RECALL HISTORY

1982: hose clamps on fuel tank filler pipe and vent pipe could break, creating possibility of fire. **1982:** brake hoses might not meet federal standards for strength; loss of brake fluid could result in partial loss of braking capability. **1983:** brake proportioning valve could break and separate from master cylinder, causing fluid leak and partial loss of braking ability. **1984:** 2-door models with optional bucket seats may have seatback locks that fail to meet federal safety requirements. **1984 (2.5-liter engine):** fuel may leak at injection feed pipe connection, with potential for fire that could spread to passenger compartment. **1984:** remote tailgate lock release on small number of station wagons could be deactivated while vehicle is moving, allowing tailgate to open. **1985 (2.8-liter fuel-injected V-6):** throttle linkage retaining clip might interfere with throttle body casting, causing throttle to remain open after driver has released gas pedal. **1986:** contacts on push-pull headlight switch may be intermittent, causing headlamps to flicker or go out suddenly. **1986–87:** fluid may seep from anti-lock brake system onto pump motor and certain relays may have been exposed to water contamination; could result in total loss of rear brakes and loss of power assist to front brakes. **1987:** windshield on a few cars may be poorly bonded, and could separate during frontal crash.

Renault Alliance/Encore 1983-87

French-designed, American-made Alliance notchback front-drive sedan, derived from European Renault, scored well for AMC right away. Next year came the mechanically identical Encore, in 3-door and 5-door hatchback form. Encore name disappeared after 1986; final models were called Alliance hatchbacks. Ancient little 1.4-liter four produces terrific gas mileage but barely passable performance, even with manual shift. A 1.7-liter overhead-cam four, optional since '85, isn't much peppier but a far better choice with automatic transmission. Sporty '87 GTA has 2.0-liter engine and sport suspension for snappy pickup, capable handling. Ride is excellent for this league. Both models are stable on the highway and agile around town. Though

Renault

1983 Renault Alliance Limited 2-door

fine for commuting, cramped back seat won't do for large families. Early models suffered inconsistent assembly quality. Doors and body metal sound tinny and flimsy plastic adorns the interior. We wouldn't bet on long life of the tiny 1.4 engine or automatic transmission. Idle speed control motor and MAP sensor need frequent replacement. Overheating has been a problem too, sometimes causing head gasket failure. Rear torsion bar bushings wear quickly; brake squeal and rapid rear brake wear have been common. Slackened sales in final years make used-car prices temptingly low, but don't buy until your mechanic checks it out. Ragtop fans might go for the Alliance convertible. Renault models halted production at Kenosha plant before the '88 model year began, as a result of Chrysler takeover.

Price Range	GOOD	AVERAGE	POOR
1983 Alliance	$2500–3200	$2200–2900	$1700–2200
1984 Alliance	3000–3600	2700–3300	2200–2700
1984 Encore	2900–3500	2600–3200	2100–2600
1985 Alliance	3800–4400	3300–4000	2800–3300
1985 Convertible	6100–6700	5500–6200	5000–5500
1985 Encore	3700–4500	3200–4000	2700–3300
1986 Alliance	4500–5300	4000–4800	3500–4000
1986 Convertible	7300–8000	6800–7500	6200–6900
1986 Encore	4600–5300	4100–4900	3600–4100
1987 Alliance	5400–7000	4800–6400	4000–5000
1987 Convertible	9500–10,500	8800–9800	7800–8800

1984 Renault Encore 3-door

Dimensions	WHEEL-BASE, IN.	LGTH., IN.	HT., IN.	WIDTH, IN.	AVG. WT., LBS.	CARGO VOL., CU. FT.	FUEL TANK, GAL.
2d sdn	97.8	163.8	54.5	65.0	1969	13.0	12.5
2d conv.	97.8	163.8	53.1	65.0	2184	7.5	12.5
4d sdn	97.8	163.8	54.5	65.0	2000	13.0	12.5
3d sdn	97.8	160.6	54.5	65.0	2010	32.0	12.5
5d sdn	97.8	160.6	54.5	65.0	2044	32.4	12.5

Engines	L/CID	BHP	MPG	AVAIL.
ohv I-4 FI	1.4/85	56	24–31	83–87
ohc I-4 FI	1.7/105	77–78	23–30	85–87
ohc I-4 FI	2.0/120	95	22–28	87

KEY: L/CID = liters/cubic inch displacement; **BHP** = brake horsepower; **MPG** = estimated average miles per gallon; **ohc** = overhead cam; **dohc** = double overhead

1985 Renault Alliance L convertible

Renault ● Saab

cam; **ohv** = overhead valve; **I** = in-line engine; **V** = V engine; **flat** = horizontally opposed engine; **D** = diesel; **T** = turbocharged; **bbl.** = barrel (carburetor); **FI** = fuel injection.

RECALL HISTORY

1983–85: manual steering gear may become corroded due to heavy use of road salt, making vehicle difficult or impossible to steer (expecially while turning), resulting in loss of control; protective splash shield should be installed. **1983–85:** five fuel hoses for 1.4-liter engine with multi-point fuel injection could deteriorate over time, allowing fuel leakage and possible underhood fire.

Saab 900/Turbo 1979-88

1981 Saab 900S 4-door

Upscale Swedish sedan, long known for front-drive traction, comes with or without a turbocharger on its well-proven 2.0-liter 4-cylinder engine. Dual camshafts with four valves per cylinder added considerable power to the turbo for 1985. The non-turbo four in the mid-level 900S gained a similar 16-valve head for '86, boosting its previously mediocre acceleration. Front-drive helps ride and handling rate above average. Four adults sit comfortably in upright position, with plenty of room for luggage. Workmanship is very good, repair rate average. Some Saabs may have problems with main wiring harness; 1979 models have frequent engine, overheating, and exhaust system troubles. We rank the Turbo one of the best around, but since many owners push them hard, they may not last long. The '88 version is water-cooled. Turbo models also cost even more to buy and maintain. Turbo convertible arrived in spring 1986, but few are likely to be available secondhand. Like BMW and Volvo, Saabs are favored by many affluent young professionals, but priced high both new and used.

Price Range	GOOD	AVERAGE	POOR
1979 900	$2600–3000	$2200–2600	$1700–2200
1979 900 Turbo	3200–3500	2900–3200	2500–2900
1980 900	3400–3800	3000–3500	2500–3000
1980 900 Turbo	4200–4600	3800–4200	3300–3800
1981 900	4100–4700	3700–4300	3100–3700
1981 900 Turbo	5200–5700	4800–5400	4300–4800
1982 900	4800–5800	4500–5400	3800–4600
1982 900 Turbo	6300–7000	5900–6500	5400–5900
1983 900	6100–6900	5700–6400	5000–5700
1983 900 Turbo	8200–8700	7800–8300	6900–7800
1984 900	7200–8300	6800–7800	6000–6800
1984 900 Turbo	9500–10,300	9000–9600	8500–9000
1985 900	8700–10,500	8100–9800	7400–8400
1985 900 Turbo	11,600–12,500	11,200–11,800	10,300–11,200
1986 900	10,000–12,000	9500–11,000	8800–10,000
1986 900 Turbo	14,250–15,250	13,500–14,500	12,500–13,500
1987 900	12,250–15,000	11,500–14,500	10,750–13,000
1987 900 Turbo	17,000–18,500	16,000–17,500	15,000–16,500
1987 900 Turbo Conv.	23,000–25,000	22,000–24,000	21,000–22,000
1988 900	14,500–18,000	14,000–17,000	—
1988 Turbo	20,000–21,000	19,000—20,000	—
1988 900 Turbo Conv.	26,000—28,000	25,000–27,000	—

1981 Saab Turbo 3-door

Saab

1987 Saab 900S 4-door

Dimensions	WHEEL-BASE, IN.	LGTH., IN.	HT., IN.	WIDTH, IN.	AVG. WT., LBS.	CARGO VOL., CU. FT.	FUEL TANK, GAL.
3d/5d sdn	99.1	186.6	56.1	66.5	2710	56.5	16.6
2d/4d sdn	99.1	186.6	56.1	66.5	2761	53.0	16.6

Engines	L/CID	BHP	MPG	AVAIL.
ohc I-4 FI	2.0/121	110–115	22–25	79–88
ohc I-4T FI	2.0/121	135	20–24	79–84
dohc I-4T FI	2.0/121	160–165	20–24	85–88
dohc I-4 FI	2.0/121	125	21–25	86–88

KEY: L/CID = liters/cubic inch displacement; **BHP** = brake horsepower; **MPG** = estimated average miles per gallon; **ohc** = overhead cam; **dohc** = double overhead cam; **ohv** = overhead valve; **I** = in-line engine; **V** = V engine; **flat** = horizontally opposed engine; **D** = diesel; **T** = turbocharged; **bbl.** = barrel (carburetor); **FI** = fuel injection.

RECALL HISTORY

1979 (Turbo): replacement of positive battery cable, which may melt because of exposure to high heat; and possible installation of new insulation and/or heat shields on battery and cables. **1979 (non-turbo):** possible that ice could build up on throttle plate in extremely cold weather, preventing plate from closing fully and returning to idle when gas pedal is released. **1979–80:** gradual loss of transmission oil could lead to transmission lock-up. **1980:** possible that electric fuel pump (submerged in fuel tank) could partially detach, creating potential for fuel leaks. **1981–82:** electric fuel pump could stop operating, causing car to stall. **1983–84:** battery-to-alternator cable could be damaged by rubbing against brake pipe, causing short circuit and possibility of fire. **1984:** starter-to-alternator cable can rub against brake fluid pipe attached to left inner wheelhouse; damaged insulation may result in short circuit, which could cause fire. **1985 (Turbo with air condition-**

ing): flexible fuel hose may have sharp bend or twist near one fitting, which could lead to hose rupture, fuel leakage and possibility of fire. **1986:** bolt in upper steering column U-joint of a few cars may have been over-torqued and could break, allowing steering shaft to pull out of joint and result in loss of control. **1986-87:** fuel hose in engine compartment between pressure regulator and injector fuel rail may rupture due to stress, resulting in leakage and possible fire.

Saab 9000 1986-88

1986 Saab 9000 Turbo 5-door

First all-new Saab since 1969 is longer in wheelbase but shorter overall than the 900. Larger passenger space gives it EPA ranking as a full-size car. Hatchback design looks more like a notchback sedan. Initial engine was a 16-valve turbo 2.0-liter four (from the 900 Turbo), transversely mounted. Non-turbo 9000S arrived for 1987, along with wider availability of 4-speed overdrive automatic transmissions. Only a 5-speed manual shift was offered at first. Turbo edition is a well-designed sport sedan with breathtaking performance, fine handling, generous passenger/cargo space. Split rear seatbacks fold flat for extra cargo area. The 9000S lags somewhat in go-power, but offers all the other Saab front-drive virtues. Both versions are loaded with useful comfort/convenience features. Our only objection: the electronic climate control wants to work automatically, even when you make a manual adjustment. Antilock brakes became standard for 1988. Priced high, as expected, Saab's new 9000 offers upscale buyers a lot of car

Saab

1986 Saab 9000 Turbo 5-door

1987 Saab 9000S 5-door

for the money. We like the turbo engine, but it's more costly to maintain and doesn't always last so long.

Price Range	GOOD	AVERAGE	POOR
1986 9000 Turbo	$19,000–20,000	$18,000–19,000	$17,000–18,000
1987 9000S	19,500–20,500	18,500–19,500	17,000–18,500
1987 9000 Turbo	22,000–22,800	21,000–22,000	20,000–21,000
1988 9000S	22,000–23,000	21,000–22,000	—
1988 9000 Turbo	25,000–27,000	24,000–26,000	—

Dimensions	WHEEL-BASE, IN.	LGTH., IN.	HT., IN.	WIDTH, IN.	AVG. WT., LBS.	CARGO VOL., CU. FT.	FUEL TANK, GAL.
5d sdn	105.2	181.9	55.9	69.4	3007	56.5	17.9

Engines	L/CID	BHP	MPG	AVAIL.
dohc I-4 FI	2.0/121	125	19–23	87–88
dohc I-4T FI	2.0/121	160	18–23	86–88

KEY: L/CID = liters/cubic inch displacement; **BHP** = brake horsepower; **MPG** = estimated average miles per gallon; **ohc** = overhead cam; **dohc** = double overhead cam; **ohv** = overhead valve; **I** = in-line engine; **V** = V engine; **flat** = horizontally opposed engine; **D** = diesel; **T** = turbocharged; **bbl.** = barrel (carburetor); **FI** = fuel injection.

RECALL HISTORY

1986: wiring harness may chafe against windshield wiper motor bracket, possibly causing short circuit and fire.

Subaru 1980-84

1981 Subaru GL 4WD 3-door

Subcompact Subaru, offered in a variety of body styles, carries a water-cooled, flat (horizontally opposed) 4-cylinder engine in choice of two sizes. Four-wheel-drive versions are popular with outdoor types who drive in rough weather. By 1984, 4WD was available on all models, after appearing on the wagon and short-wheelbase 3-door hatchback years earlier. A turbocharged engine was offered on the 4WD wagon for 1983, the 4WD sedan the next year. Pick the bigger 1.8-liter engine if you want reasonable acceleration. Both engines are rather gruff and coarse, though—definitely not star performers. Tight interior looks a bit cut-rate on most models. Early repair record is good; 1982-84 very good. Subarus are known for solid durability, but received a surprising number of recalls for a Japanese car. Most owners seem to love their Subes, and you might too.

Subaru

Price Range	GOOD	AVERAGE	POOR
1980 Subaru	$1300–2000	$1000–1700	$600–1200
1981 Subaru	1500–2700	1200–2300	900–1500
1982 Subaru	2000–3300	1700–2800	1300–2100
1983 Subaru	2800–4000	2400–3500	1900–2600
1984 Subaru	3500–5500	3000–4800	2500–3500

Dimensions	WHEEL-BASE, IN.	LGTH., IN.	HT., IN.	WIDTH, IN.	AVG. WT., LBS.	CARGO VOL., CU. FT.	FUEL TANK, GAL.
2d cpe	96.9	168.1	53.2	63.4	2113	13.0	13.2
3d sdn	93.7	156.9	53.7	63.4	2055	11.9	11.9
4d sdn	96.9	168.1	53.7	63.4	2136	13.0	13.2
5d wgn	96.7	168.3	54.7	63.4	2236	58.0	13.2

Engines	L/CID	BHP	MPG	AVAIL.
ohv flat-4 2 bbl.	1.6/97	67–69	23–27	80–84
ohv flat-4 2 bbl.	1.8/109	71–73	22–26	80–84
ohv flat-4T FI	1.8/109	95	20–26	83–84

1981 Subaru GL 4-door

1981 Subaru GL 5-door

KEY: L/CID = liters/cubic inch displacement; BHP = brake horsepower; MPG = estimated average miles per gallon; ohc = overhead cam; dohc = double overhead cam; ohv = overhead valve; I = in-line engine; V = V engine; flat = horizontally opposed engine; D = diesel; T = turbocharged; bbl. = barrel (carburetor); FI = fuel injection.

RECALL HISTORY

1980: protective boot could slip off steering rack and excessive corrosion could result in hard steering or seizure of the steering system. **1980:** replacement of master link in windshield wiper system to prevent wiper motor from freezing and becoming inoperable; also, if wiper motor is switched on when wiper blades are frozen to windshield, motor could become inoperative. **1980:** driver's seatback frame could break and separate through normal use. **1980–81:** headlight fuse could melt, causing an open circuit that results in inoperative headlights. **1981:** fast idle control lever could bind, preventing throttle from returning to idle. **1981–82:** steering wheel nut could loosen, allowing wheel to separate from its shaft. **1981–82:** insulation on main wiring harness could be chafed and the exposed wires could short out, creating possibility of fire. **1982–84:** accelerator cable on Hitachi cruise control system may fray from wear on cable housing, which leads to throttle sticking in open position and possible loss of control.

Subaru 1985-88

Extensively restyled sedan and wagon are longer outside, roomier inside—better looking than their parents. New 1.8-liter overhead-cam flat four is smoother, quieter, more potent than overhead-valve predecessor. Offered first in carbureted, fuel-injected or turbocharged form, all had fuel injection by 1988 and the turbo was dropped. Dual Range 5-speed shift is optional on the 4-wheel-drive Turbo sedan, which also has computer-controlled air spring suspension. For 1986, that suspension went on 4WD Turbo wagons with automatic. 3-door coupe arrived during 1986. Full-time 4WD became available on '87 coupe and sedan, then on wagon a year later. Sleek XT Coupe is the real eye-catcher; XT6 version for '88 carries new flat 6-cylinder engine and electronic power steering. Sedans are roomy and comfortable, have adequate cargo space, and maneuver nicely. Flashy electronic instruments are hard to read, though, and brakes on 1985 turbocharged models may squeal due to brake pad vibration. Small 3-door hatchback is identical to pre-1985 style, carrying lower-powered 1.6

Subaru

1985 Subaru GL-10 4-door

or 1.8 four. Verdict: lots of high-tech in a diverse series of small front-drive cars that command strong owner loyalty.

Price Range	GOOD	AVERAGE	POOR
1985 Subaru	$4000–7500	$3600–6300	$3000–5000
1986 Subaru	4700–9000	4300–8200	3700–7000
1987 Subaru	5200–10,000	4800–8500	4200–7500
1988 Subaru	5700–14,000	5200–12,500	—

Dimensions	WHEEL-BASE, IN.	LGTH., IN.	HT., IN.	WIDTH, IN.	AVG. WT., LBS.	CARGO VOL., CU. FT.	FUEL TANK, GAL.
2d cpe	97.1	175.2	49.4	66.5	2280	9.8	15.9
3d cpe	97.2	174.6	51.8	65.4	2240	39.8	15.9
3d sdn	93.7	157.9	53.7	63.6	2120	33.9	13.2
4d sdn	97.2	172.0	52.5	65.4	2145	14.9	15.8
5d wgn	97.0	173.6	53.0	65.4	2290	70.3	15.9

1985 Subaru RX 4WD Turbo 4-door

Engines	L/CID	BHP	MPG	AVAIL.
ohv I-3 2 bbl.	1.2/73	66	32–37	87–88
ohv flat-4 2 bbl.	1.6/97	69	23–36	85–88
ohv flat-4 2 bbl.	1.8/109	73	22–28	85–88
ohc flat-4 2 bbl.	1.8/109	82–84	24–28	85–87
ohc flat-4 FI	1.8/109	90–94	23–29	85–88
ohc flat-4T FI	1.8/109	111–115	20–26	85–88
ohc flat-6 FI	2.7/163	145	18–24	88

KEY: L/CID = liters/cubic inch displacement; **BHP** = brake horsepower; **MPG** = estimated average miles per gallon; **ohc** = overhead cam; **dohc** = double overhead cam; **ohv** = overhead valve; **I** = in-line engine; **V** = V engine; **flat** = horizontally opposed engine; **D** = diesel; **T** = turbocharged; **bbl.** = barrel (carburetor); **FI** = fuel injection.

RECALL HISTORY

1985 XT Coupe: inadequate spot welding between bumper bracket rail and right front frame of rear side member may have created a gap; in case of rear impact, bumper could break loose and damage air vent hose, which may cause fuel to leak and contribute to fire hazard.

1986 Subaru XT Turbo 2-door

Toyota Camry 1983-86

Not much time passed before this front-drive successor to the popular Corona became a top seller. Since high demand and limited supply encouraged dealers to push prices well above suggested retail, secondhand examples aren't cheap either. Both the 4-door sedan and 5-door Liftback are unusually roomy and airy inside, with ample cargo area. Fuel-injected 2.0-liter four performs well and goes easy on

Toyota

1983 Toyota Camry 5-door

gas, even with 4-speed overdrive automatic. Few of the turbodiesel engines have found buyers. Fully independent suspension eases over bumps and ruts, and Camry cruises quietly. Throw in Toyota's reputation for reliability/durability and you're looking at one of the best compact family sedans on the market. Note, however, that oil pump gaskets on 1983–84 engines can fail at high mileage, and that the ignition module has had a high failure rate for the same years. Problems with the automatic transmission have been common. All in all, the capable Camry is one of our favorites. Aero headlamps and new grille gave '85s an altered look, but the same high quality.

Price Range	GOOD	AVERAGE	POOR
1983 Camry	$5900–6800	$5400–6200	$4800–5500
1984 Camry	6900–7800	6500–7300	5900–6700
1985 Camry	8000–9000	7500–8500	6900–7500
1986 Camry	9300–10,500	8800–10,000	8000–8800

Dimensions	WHEEL-BASE, IN.	LGTH., IN.	HT., IN.	WIDTH, IN.	AVG. WT., LBS.	CARGO VOL., CU. FT.	FUEL TANK, GAL.
4d sdn	102.4	175.6	54.9	66.5	2414	13.6	13.8
5d sdn	102.4	175.6	53.9	66.5	2458	41.3	13.8

Engines	L/CID	BHP	MPG	AVAIL.
ohc I-4 FI	2.0/122	92–95	25–30	83–86
ohc I-4TD FI	1.8/112	73	28–34	84–85
ohc I-4TD FI	2.0/121	79	28–34	86

KEY: L/CID = liters/cubic inch displacement; **BHP** = brake horsepower; **MPG** = estimated average miles per gallon; **ohc** = overhead cam; **dohc** = double overhead cam; **ohv** = overhead valve; **I** = in-line engine; **V** = V engine; **flat** = horizontally opposed engine; **D** = diesel; **T** = turbocharged; **bbl.** = barrel (carburetor); **FI** = fuel injection.

1983 Toyota Camry 5-door

1984 Toyota Camry 4-door

RECALL HISTORY

1983–84: voltage regulator could fail, allowing battery to overcharge, which could result in engine misfiring or stalling.

Toyota Camry 1987-88

Toyota's second best-seller became No. 1 following restyle that carries a strong hint of luxury Cressida's lines. Wheelbase didn't change, but overall length and weight went up. New 5-door station wagon replaces the prior 5-door Liftback; its rear seatbacks fold flat to produce 65 cubic feet of cargo space. New 2.0-liter 4-cylinder engine has dual-overhead cams and 16 valves, churning out 20 more horsepower than previous Camry powerplant. That

Toyota

1987 Toyota Camry LE 4-door

suggests livelier movement when starting off, as well as for passing, but increased car weight offsets some of the extra power. Coarse, growling engine detracts from the pleasure too, especially when accelerating. Deluxe models have standard 5-speed manual shift; plusher LE carries only 4-speed overdrive automatic, electronically controlled with Economy or Power shift mode. Front-drive design offers capable handling and absorbent ride. Few-frills Standard sedan debuted during the 1987 model year, and a new All Trac sedan with permanent 4-wheel-drive (manual shift only) arrived for '88. Roomy sedan trunk has low liftover for easy loading. Interior also offers a bit more leg room, comfortable all around, ranking with Honda Accord. High new-car prices mean secondhand examples won't be cheap, but resale value should be terrific.

1987 Toyota Camry LE 5-door

Price Range	GOOD	AVERAGE	POOR
1987 Camry	$11,000–13,000	$10,000–12,000	$9500–11,000
1988 Camry	12,000–14,500	11,000–13,500	

Dimensions	WHEEL-BASE, IN.	LGTH., IN.	HT., IN.	WIDTH, IN.	AVG. WT., LBS.	CARGO VOL., CU. FT.	FUEL TANK, GAL.
4d sdn	102.4	182.1	54.1	67.3	2734	15.4	15.9
5d sdn	102.4	183.1	54.5	67.3	2855	65.1	15.9

Engines	L/CID	BHP	MPG	AVAIL.
dohc I-4 FI	2.0/122	115	24–29	87–88

KEY: L/CID = liters/cubic inch displacement; **BHP** = brake horsepower; **MPG** = estimated average miles per gallon; **ohc** = overhead cam; **dohc** = double overhead cam; **ohv** = overhead valve; **I** = in-line engine; **V** = V engine; **flat** = horizontally opposed engine; **D** = diesel; **T** = turbocharged; **bbl.** = barrel (carburetor); **FI** = fuel injection.

RECALL HISTORY

None to date.

Toyota Celica/ Celica Supra 1978-81

1978 Toyota Celica GT 2-door

Second-generation, 4-cylinder Celica was joined in its second year by longer-wheelbase Supra, carrying 6-cylinder engine. Visibility and passenger space are better than before, but back seat is minimal for adults. Notchback coupe has skimpy trunk. Soft suspension gives acceptable ride but weaker handling, partly because luxury trappings add

Toyota

weight. Four-cylinder gas mileage disappoints. Supra six is more potent and nearly as economical. Both engines grew in size for final season. Excellent repair record shows most ratings above average, none below. Regular valve adjustment is essential to prevent engine problems. Celica styling didn't last long and Supra sold poorly, but Celicas deliver sports car flair in a practical package. We recommend both for their sound design and proven reliability.

Price Range	GOOD	AVERAGE	POOR
1978 Celica	$1800–2200	$1400–1800	$1100–1400
1979 Celica	2200–2500	1800–2200	1400–1800
1979 Celica Supra	2800–3200	2400–2800	2000–2400
1980 Celica	2700–3100	2400–2700	2000–2400
1980 Celica Supra	3700–4200	3200–3700	2700–3200
1981 Celica	3500–3900	3200–3600	2800–3200
1981 Celica Supra	5000–5500	4600–5100	4000–4600

1979 Toyota Celica Supra 3-door

1979 Toyota Celica GT 3-door

Dimensions	WHEEL-BASE, IN.	LGTH., IN.	HT., IN.	WIDTH, IN.	AVG. WT., LBS.	CARGO VOL., CU. FT.	FUEL TANK, GAL.
2d cpe	98.4	175.5	51.2	64.6	2490	14.0	16.1
3d cpe	98.4	175.5	50.8	64.6	2530	28.0	16.1
Supra 3d cpe	103.5	181.7	51.8	65.0	2855	28.0	16.1

Engines	L/CID	BHP	MPG	AVAIL.
ohc I-4 2 bbl.	2.2/134	90–95	21–24	78–80
ohc I-4 2 bbl.	2.4/144	96	22–25	81
ohc I-6 2 bbl.	2.6/156	116–121	19–22	79–80
ohc I-6 FI	2.8/168	116	20–23	81

KEY: L/CID = liters/cubic inch displacement; **BHP** = brake horsepower; **MPG** = estimated average miles per gallon; **ohc** = overhead cam; **dohc** = double overhead cam; **ohv** = overhead valve; **I** = in-line engine; **V** = V engine; **flat** = horizontally opposed engine; **D** = diesel; **T** = turbocharged; **bbl.** = barrel (carburetor); **FI** = fuel injection.

RECALL HISTORY

1980: replacement of alternator pulley, which may break causing the car to overheat and battery to drain. **1981:** defective parts in computerized cruise control system could cause sudden acceleration.

Toyota Celica 1982-85

Popular rear-drive sporty coupe kept its earlier four-cylinder drivetrain through massive changes in style and engineering. Good looking, well-equipped and nice to drive, Celica is one of the most reliable (and desirable) cars on

1982 Toyota Celica GT 2-door

Toyota

the road today. Performance lags well behind the flashy facade, however, and rear seats hold only tiny people. Special GT-S package with Supra-type independent rear suspension arrived in '82. Prices are rather steep on the used-car lots, especially for the GT-S convertible, which cost over $17,000 for its 1985 debut. Minimally equipped base ST isn't easy to locate. If you're looking for a sporty yet dependable car that keeps on cruising with minimal maintenance, Celica is hard to beat, but remember to adjust the valves regularly to forestall engine problems. Replaced by front-drive version for 1986.

Price Range	GOOD	AVERAGE	POOR
1982 Celica	$4300–4900	$3900–4500	$3300–3900
1983 Celica	5200–6700	4800–6200	4100–5000

1982 Toyota Celica GT 2-door

1984 Toyota Celica GT-S 2-door

Price Range	GOOD	AVERAGE	POOR
1984 Celica	6300–8000	5800–7500	5200–6200
1985 Celica	7400–9000	6900–8400	6200–7100
1985 Convertible	14,000–15,000	13,000–14,000	12,000–13,000

Dimensions	WHEEL-BASE, IN.	LGTH., IN.	HT., IN.	WIDTH, IN.	AVG. WT., LBS.	CARGO VOL., CU. FT.	FUEL TANK, GAL.
2d cpe	98.4	176.2	52.0	65.5	2496	10.6	16.1
3d cpe	98.4	176.6	52.0	65.5	2566	25.8	16.1
2d conv.	98.4	176.6	52.9	65.5	2975	9.9	16.1

Engines	L/CID	BHP	MPG	AVAIL.
ohc I-4 2 bbl.	2.4/144	96	21–24	82–83
ohc I-4 FI	2.4/144	105–116	22–25	83–85

KEY: L/CID = liters/cubic inch displacement; **BHP** = brake horsepower; **MPG** = estimated average miles per gallon; **ohc** = overhead cam; **dohc** = double overhead cam; **ohv** = overhead valve; **I** = in-line engine; **V** = V engine; **flat** = horizontally opposed engine; **D** = diesel; **T** = turbocharged; **bbl.** = barrel (carburetor); **FI** = fuel injection.

RECALL HISTORY

1982–83: defective parts in computerized cruise control system could cause sudden acceleration. **1984:** voltage regulator could fail, allowing battery to overcharge, which could result in engine misfiring or stalling.

Toyota Celica 1986-88

Popular Japanese sporty coupe and liftback switched to front drive, rounded styling and new 2.0-liter engines. Twin-cam version replaced the initial 97-horsepower four on mid-level GT and base ST in second season, boosting performance to match Celica's sporty look. A convertible arrived for 1987, in GT trim only. Enthusiast's top-line GT-S carries a high-revving 16-valve four that delivers plenty of action up to 6700-rpm redline. Rising exhaust noise has less appeal, however. Neither engine qualifies as refined, though GT-S is noisier. Independent suspension and variable-assist power steering help Celica handle nimbly. Front-wheel drive offers good rain/snow traction. As expected, rear seat is for kids. New turbo hatchback coupe for '88 has full-time viscous 4-wheel-drive and optional anti-lock brakes. No Celica is cheap, but in addition to performance, handling and fine gas mileage, you get plenty of standard equipment plus Toyota's reputation for durability.

Toyota

1986 Toyota Celica GT 2-door

Price Range	GOOD	AVERAGE	POOR
1986 Celica	$8500–10,500	$8000–9700	$7300–8500
1987 Celica	10,250–12,750	9400–12,000	8900–10,500
1987 Convertible	15,000–16,000	14,000–15,000	13,000–14,000
1988 Celica	11,000–14,000	10,250–13,000	—
1988 Convertible	16,000–17,000	15,000–16,000	—

Dimensions	WHEEL-BASE, IN.	LGTH., IN.	HT., IN.	WIDTH, IN.	AVG. WT., LBS.	CARGO VOL., CU. FT.	FUEL TANK, GAL.
2d cpe	99.4	173.6	49.8	67.3	2455	120	15.9
2d conv.	99.4	173.6	50.8	67.3	2700	NA	15.9
3d cpe	99.4	171.9	49.8	67.3	2555	25.2	15.9

1986 Toyota Celica 3-door

CONSUMER GUIDE®

Engines	L/CID	BHP	MPG	AVAIL.
ohc I-4 FI	2.0/122	97	24–28	86
dohc I-4 FI	2.0/122	115	25–29	87–88
dohc I-4 FI	2.0/122	135	22–26	86–88
dohc I-4T FI	2.0/122	190	19–23	88

KEY: L/CID = liters/cubic inch displacement; **BHP** = brake horsepower; **MPG** = estimated average miles per gallon; **ohc** = overhead cam; **dohc** = double overhead cam; **ohv** = overhead valve; **I** = in-line engine; **V** = V engine; **flat** = horizontally opposed engine; **D** = diesel; **T** = turbocharged; **bbl.** = barrel (carburetor); **FI** = fuel injection.

RECALL HISTORY

None to date.

Toyota Celica Supra 1982-86

1983 Toyota Celica Supra L Type 3-door

Six-cylinder edition of the Celica sport coupe got a boost in its performance image for 1982, along with restyled body. Fuel-injected in-line engine received new twin over-head-cam cylinder head, and fully independent rear suspension replaced the old rigid axle. Acceleration matches that of rival sport/GT coupes and Supra handles confidently, yet comfort and refinement are impressive. Loaded with convenience features, it's easy and fun to drive daily. Popular from day one, used Supras are expensive but give a lot for your money, although the rear brakes can be troublesome and difficult to repair. Most of the highly

Toyota

1984 Toyota Celica Supra 3-door

1984 Toyota Celica Supra 3-door

favorable comments for the basic Celica also apply here. With Toyota's admirable reliability and durability, Supra equals value in a high-performance coupe.

Price Range	GOOD	AVERAGE	POOR
1982 Celica Supra	$6200–6900	$5700–6300	$5100–5700
1983 Celica Supra	7300–8200	6800–7300	6000–8000
1984 Celica Supra	9000–9700	8500–9000	8000–8500
1985 Supra	10,750–11,750	10,000–11,000	9000–10,000
1986 Supra	14,000–16,000	13,000–15,000	11,750–13,500

Dimensions	WHEEL-BASE, IN.	LGTH., IN.	HT., IN.	WIDTH, IN.	AVG. WT., LBS.	CARGO VOL., CU. FT.	FUEL TANK, GAL.
3d cpe	103.0	183.5	52.0	67.7	2970	21.0	16.1

Engines	L/CID	BHP	MPG	AVAIL.
dohc I-6 FI	2.8/168	145–150	18–23	82–86

KEY: L/CID = liters/cubic inch displacement; **BHP** = brake horsepower; **MPG** = estimated average miles per gallon; **ohc** = overhead cam; **dohc** = double overhead cam; **ohv** = overhead valve; **I** = in-line engine; **V** = V engine; **flat** = horizontally opposed engine; **D** = diesel; **T** = turbocharged; **bbl.** = barrel (carburetor); **FI** = fuel injection.

RECALL HISTORY

1982–83: defective parts in computerized cruise control system could cause sudden acceleration. **1983–84:** faulty oil pressure sender gauge could break under high temperatures and high engine oil pressure, causing oil leakage and possible engine seizure. **1984:** voltage regulator could fail, allowing battery to overcharge, which could result in engine misfiring or stalling.

Toyota Corolla 1980-83

Toyota's best-seller, riding on a mechanically simple rear-drive chassis, gained visibility and interior room with new body. Adults won't like the back seat, though. Hatchback Sport Coupe is a more practical choice. Repair record suggests long, dependable service, with above-average ratings except for brakes on 1980 models. Valves must be adjusted regularly to prevent engine problems. An optional 4-speed overdrive automatic transmission arrived for '82. A slightly smaller engine was used in final year. Small families and singles who want reliable, worry-free transportation can hardly beat a Corolla.

1980 Toyota Corolla 3-door

Toyota

1980 Toyota Corolla 3-door

Price Range	GOOD	AVERAGE	POOR
1980 Corolla	$2100–2500	$1700–2200	$1400–1700
1981 Corolla	2600–3200	2200–2800	1700–2300
1982 Corolla	3300–4000	2900–3600	2300–2900
1983 Corolla	4100–5000	3700–4600	3000–3800

Dimensions	WHEEL-BASE, IN.	LGTH., IN.	HT., IN.	WIDTH, IN.	AVG. WT., LBS.	CARGO VOL., CU. FT.	FUEL TANK, GAL.
2d sdn	94.5	166.3	53.0	64.0	2090	11.0	13.2
4d sdn	94.5	166.3	53.0	64.0	2140	11.0	13.2
2d/3d cpe/wgn	94.5	168.3	50.8	64.0	2180	33.0	13.2
5d wgn	94.5	168.9	53.0	64.0	2225	40.1	13.2

Engines	L/CID	BHP	MPG	AVAIL.
ohv I-4 2 bbl.	1.7/108	70–75	26–30	80–82
ohc I-4 2 bbl.	1.6/97	70	26–31	83

KEY: L/CID = liters/cubic inch displacement; **BHP** = brake horsepower; **MPG** = estimated average miles per gallon; **ohc** = overhead cam; **dohc** = double overhead cam; **ohv** = overhead valve; **I** = in-line engine; **V** = V engine; **flat** = horizontally opposed engine; **D** = diesel; **T** = turbocharged; **bbl.** = barrel (carburetor); **FI** = fuel injection.

1980 Toyota Corolla 4-door

RECALL HISTORY

1980: replacement of alternator pulley, which may break causing the car to overheat and battery to drain. **1983:** defective ignition-control module could cause car to stall after startup, or not start.

Toyota Corolla/FX 1984-88

1984 Toyota Corolla 4-door

After a long history as a top-selling Toyota, the popular Corolla switched to front drive for 1984. Corolla Sport (see next report) continued the old rear-drive chassis a few more years. The 1.6-liter four comes from '83 Corolla, but is mounted transversely here. Gas mileage is good but acceleration is feeble. A 1.8-liter diesel was offered through 1985. Four-speed overdrive automatic transmission, optional for '85 on LE and plush Limited models, allows relaxed highway cruising. Front-drive traction and ride are good, handling unimpressive. Sedan and 5-door hatchback are roomier in back than rear-drive predecessors. Sporty FX16 3-door hatchback for '87, powered by twin-cam, 16-valve four, is made in California; so is FX hatchback with 8-valve engine. Others hail from Japan. Little repair data is available, but some early models had automatic transmission breakdowns and ignition modules on '84 engines had a high failure rate. Keep the valves ad-

Toyota

justed to prevent engine problems. Design is the same as the current joint-venture Chevrolet Nova, with Toyota's reputation for reliability. FX and FX16 continue into 1988, but Corolla lineup is all new and more powerful, including a 5-door station wagon.

Price Range	GOOD	AVERAGE	POOR
1984 Corolla	$5300–5700	$4800–5400	$4300–4800
1985 Corolla	6000–6800	5700–6300	5200–5800
1986 Corolla	7000–8000	6500–7500	6000–6700
1987 Corolla/FX	8000–8900	7400–8400	6900–7700
1987 FX16	9000–10,250	8300–9500	7800–8500
1988 FX	8000–8500	7700–8100	—
1988 FX16	10,000–11,500	9250–10,500	—

Dimensions	WHEEL-BASE, IN.	LGTH., IN.	HT., IN.	WIDTH, IN.	AVG. WT., LBS.	CARGO VOL., CU. FT.	FUEL TANK, GAL.
FX16 3d cpe	95.7	160.0	52.8	65.2	2141	30.0	13.2
4d sdn	95.7	166.3	53.0	64.4	2081	12.7	13.2
5d sdn	95.7	166.3	52.8	64.4	2109	26.0	13.2

Engines	L/CID	BHP	MPG	AVAIL.
ohc I-4 2 bbl.	1.6/97	70–74	26–31	84–88
dohc I-4 FI	1.6/97	108–110	22–27	87–88
ohc I-4D FI	1.8/112	56	28–34	84–85

KEY: **L/CID** = liters/cubic inch displacement; **BHP** = brake horsepower; **MPG** = estimated average miles per gallon; **ohc** = overhead cam; **dohc** = double overhead cam; **ohv** = overhead valve; **I** = in-line engine; **V** = V engine; **flat** = horizontally opposed engine; **D** = diesel; **T** = turbocharged; **bbl.** = barrel (carburetor); **FI** = fuel injection.

RECALL HISTORY

1984: voltage regulator could fail, allowing battery to overcharge, which could result in engine misfiring or stalling. **1984–86:** defective ignition-control module could cause car to stall after startup, or not start.

1987 Toyota Corolla FX16 GT-S 3-door

Toyota
Corolla Sport 1984-87

1984 Toyota Corolla Sport SR5 3-door

Rear-drive version of Corolla, carried over from 1983 but with new 2-door coupe and 3-door hatchback styling, offered only in sporty SR5 trim. The 1.6-liter overhead-cam gas engine is identical to that in the front-drive Corolla, but mounted longitudinally. Though just as economical, it's noisier in this layout. Road noise is annoying too, and ride is jumpy, but economy and maneuverability rate high. A high-performance GT-S appeared for 1985 with a dual-overhead-cam 16-valve engine (same as in the MR2 two-

1985 Toyota Corolla Sport GT-S 2-door

Toyota

seater) that produces 112 horsepower and can rev to 7500 rpm. Stiffer GT-S suspension makes ride even rougher, though it has rear disc brakes and 14-inch tires. 3-door dropped after 1986. Corolla Sport has a more stylish, sporty image than the front drive, but less space in back. You also benefit from Corolla's admirable reputation for reliability, although the ignition module had a high failure rate on the '84s, and regular valve adjustment is necessary to prevent engine problems. Totally new SR5 and GT-S models for 1988 are front-drive, with double-overhead-cam engines.

Price Range	GOOD	AVERAGE	POOR
1984 Corolla Sport	$5900–6300	$5500–5900	$5000–5500
1985 Corolla Sport	6700–7500	6300–6900	5800–6400
1986 Corolla Sport	7600–8700	7100–8200	6500–7300
1987 Corolla Sport	9000–10,000	8500–9500	8000–8700

Dimensions	WHEEL-BASE, IN.	LGTH., IN.	HT., IN.	WIDTH, IN.	AVG. WT., LBS.	CARGO VOL., CU. FT.	FUEL TANK, GAL.
2d cpe	94.5	168.7	52.6	64.0	2196	9.0	13.2
3d cpe	94.5	168.7	52.6	64.0	2204	12.2	13.2

Engines	L/CID	BHP	MPG	AVAIL.
ohc I-4 2 bbl.	1.6/97	70–74	24–30	84–87
dohc I-4 FI	1.6/97	112	22–28	85–87

KEY: L/CID = liters/cubic inch displacement; **BHP** = brake horsepower; **MPG** = estimated average miles per gallon; **ohc** = overhead cam; **dohc** = double overhead cam; **ohv** = overhead valve; **I** = in-line engine; **V** = V engine; **flat** = horizontally opposed engine; **D** = diesel; **T** = turbocharged; **bbl.** = barrel (carburetor); **FI** = fuel injection.

RECALL HISTORY

1984: voltage regulator could fail, allowing battery to overcharge, which could result in engine misfiring or stalling.

Toyota Corona 1979-82

Second-rung Toyota model, ranked just below the luxurious Cressida, was restyled and upgraded to make room in the lineup for a bigger 1980 Corolla. Offered in sedan, 5-door hatchback and wagon. Same drivetrains as prior Coronas, but greater weight and tighter emission controls reduce fuel economy. Enlarging the 4-cylinder engine to 2.4 liters for 1981 didn't alter performance or mileage much. Less popular than earlier versions, Corona was re-

1980 Toyota Corona 5-door

1982 Toyota Corona 4-door

placed by the new front-drive '83 Camry. Toyota's usual high quality helps keep repair record nearly spotless, but regular valve adjustment is essential to prevent engine problems. Sturdy and reliable, their conventional design nicely developed, the final Coronas are excellent values as used cars.

Price Range	GOOD	AVERAGE	POOR
1979 Corona	$1800–2100	$1500–1800	$1200–1500
1980 Corona	2400–2800	2100–2500	1800–2100
1981 Corona	3300–4000	2800–3600	2400–2900
1982 Corona	4400–4900	4000–4500	3500–4000

Toyota

Dimensions	WHEEL-BASE, IN.	LGTH., IN.	HT., IN.	WIDTH, IN.	AVG. WT., LBS.	CARGO VOL., CU. FT.	FUEL TANK, GAL.
4d sdn	99.4	175.0	53.9	65.2	2514	11.0	16.1
5d sdn	99.4	175.0	53.0	65.2	2549	27.7	16.1
5d wgn	99.4	178.7	54.3	65.2	2574	63.0	15.6

Engines	L/CID	BHP	MPG	AVAIL.
ohc I-4 2 bbl.	2.2/134	98	20–24	79–80
ohc I-4 2 bbl.	2.4/144	96	21–24	81–82

KEY: L/CID = liters/cubic inch displacement; **BHP** = brake horsepower; **MPG** = estimated average miles per gallon; **ohc** = overhead cam; **dohc** = double overhead cam; **ohv** = overhead valve; **I** = in-line engine; **V** = V engine; **flat** = horizontally opposed engine; **D** = diesel; **T** = turbocharged; **bbl.** = barrel (carburetor); **FI** = fuel injection.

RECALL HISTORY

1980: replacement of alternator pulley, which may break causing car to overheat and battery to drain.

Toyota Cressida 1981-84

Crisp, contemporary styling highlights the early '80s luxury Toyota, powered by an engine just a bit bigger than predecessor. Major changes for 1983, including a dual-cam cylinder head, independent rear suspension and rear disc brakes, aided the battle against Audi, BMW, and similar upscale European sedans. A 5-speed manual shift was also offered. (Station wagons got only the new head.) Thus modified, Cressida added capable road manners and impressive performance to its pleasant demeanor. Rear-drive layout isn't the most efficient, so interior space is marginal for a

1981 Toyota Cressida 4-door

mid-size. Driving position might be cramped for tall people. Reliability and durability conform to Toyota's high standards. A nicely balanced blend of performance and comfort, marred only by high price as a used car.

Price Range	GOOD	AVERAGE	POOR
1981 Cressida	$5300–5600	$4900–5300	$4400–4900
1982 Cressida	6000–6500	5500–6000	5000–5500
1983 Cressida	6800–7400	6400–6800	6000–6400
1984 Cressida	8300–8900	7800–8300	7300–7800

Dimensions	WHEEL-BASE, IN.	LGTH., IN.	HT., IN.	WIDTH, IN.	AVG. WT., LBS.	CARGO VOL., CU. FT.	FUEL TANK, GAL.
4d sdn	104.1	186.2	54.3	66.5	2998	12.4	17.2
5d wgn	104.1	186.6	55.5	66.5	3007	67.3	17.2

Engines	L/CID	BHP	MPG	AVAIL.
ohc I-6 FI	2.8/168	116	20–24	81–82
dohc I-6 FI	2.8/168	143–156	20–24	83–84

KEY: L/CID = liters/cubic inch displacement; **BHP** = brake horsepower; **MPG** = estimated average miles per gallon; **ohc** = overhead cam; **dohc** = double overhead cam; **ohv** = overhead valve; **I** = in-line engine; **V** = V engine; **flat** = horizontally opposed engine; **D** = diesel; **T** = turbocharged; **bbl.** = barrel (carburetor); **FI** = fuel injection.

RECALL HISTORY

1981: improper wire routing could result in failure of emergency locking retractor of driver's side automatic seatbelt. **1981–83:** defective parts in computerized cruise control system could cause sudden acceleration. **1983–84:** faulty oil pressure sender gauge could break under high temperatures and high oil pressure, causing oil leakage and possible engine seizure. **1984:** voltage regulator could fail, allowing battery to overcharge, which could result in engine misfiring or stalling.

Toyota Cressida 1985-88

Latest, slightly enlarged redesign of Toyota's luxury sedan retains rear-drive layout. Styling is more aerodynamic with Euro-style headlamps and front spoiler, but similar to prior version. A station wagon was available until '88. Smooth, powerful twin-cam 6-cylinder engine added 12 horsepower, enhancing Cressida's fine performance. Suspension is soft, yet offers good highway stability and pre-

Toyota

1985 Toyota Cressida 5-door

dictable handling, aided by new rack-and-pinion steering. Some sedans have electronic shock absorber control with Normal/Sport selector on the console. Some add digital instruments to the large standard array of gadgets. Latest electronically controlled overdrive automatic transmissions have Normal or Power Shift mode. Roomy and comfortable, Cressida offers Toyota's laudable reliability, but gas mileage isn't the best and secondhand prices are steep.

Price Range	GOOD	AVERAGE	POOR
1985 Cressida	$10,800–11,500	$10,000–10,800	$9400–10,000
1986 Cressida	13,250–14,250	12,500–13,500	11,800–12,500
1987 Cressida	17,000–18,500	16,000–17,500	15,000–16,000
1988 Cressida	19,500–20,500	18,500–20,000	—

Dimensions	WHEEL-BASE, IN.	LGTH., IN.	HT., IN.	WIDTH, IN.	AVG. WT., LBS.	CARGO VOL. CU. FT.	FUEL TANK, GAL.
4d sdn	104.5	187.8	54.1	66.5	3214	13.0	18.5
5d wgn	104.5	187.8	54.1	66.5	3240	70.2	18.5

Engines	L/CID	BHP	MPG	AVAIL.
dohc I-6 FI	2.8/168	156	17–23	85–88

KEY: L/CID = liters/cubic inch displacement; **BHP** = brake horsepower; **MPG** = estimated average miles per gallon; **ohc** = overhead cam; **dohc** = double overhead cam; **ohv** = overhead valve; **I** = in-line engine; **V** = V engine; **flat** = horizontally opposed engine; **D** = diesel; **T** = turbocharged; **bbl.** = barrel (carburetor); **FI** = fuel injection.

RECALL HISTORY

None to date.

Toyota Starlet 1981-84

1981 Toyota Starlet 3-door

Basic, conventional rear-drive minicar sold overseas for three years before it appeared in the U.S. as a 3-door sedan in one trim level. Sole drivetrain is a 1.3-liter 4-cylinder engine hooked to manual gearbox: 5-speed standard through 1982, 4-speed later (with 5-speed optional). Tiny size and weight allow easy parking and slinking through traffic, but ride is jumpy, snow/ice traction poor. Steering wheel and pedals may be too close for tall drivers. Few Starlets sold in final year as the new front-drive Tercel took over the U.S. market. For economical urban commuting, Starlet does its job well and is worth checking out.

Price Range	GOOD	AVERAGE	POOR
1981 Starlet	$1800–2100	$1500–1800	$1200–1500
1992 Starlet	2300–2700	2000–2400	1600–2000
1983 Starlet	2900–3300	2600–3000	2200–2600
1984 Starlet	3600–4000	3300–3600	2900–3300

1983 Toyota Starlet 3-door

Toyota

Dimensions	WHEEL-BASE, IN.	LGTH., IN.	HT., IN.	WIDTH, IN.	AVG. WT., LBS.	CARGO VOL., CU. FT.	FUEL TANK, GAL.
3d sdn	90.6	152.2	54.3	60.0	1730	23.7	10.6

Engines	L/CID	BHP	MPG	AVAIL.
ohv I-4 2 bbl.	1.3/79	58	30–35	81–82
ohv I-4 FI	1.3/79	58	30–35	83–84

KEY: L/CID = liters/cubic inch displacement; **BHP** = brake horsepower; **MPG** = estimated average miles per gallon; **ohc** = overhead cam; **dohc** = double overhead cam; **ohv** = overhead valve; **I** = in-line engine; **V** = V engine; **flat** = horizontally opposed engine; **D** = diesel; **T** = turbocharged; **bbl.** = barrel (carburetor); **FI** = fuel injection.

RECALL HISTORY

None to date.

Toyota Supra 1986½-88

Redesigned performance coupe debuted in mid-year, weighing in at a whopping 3450 pounds. Standing-start acceleration suffered but the base dual-cam, 24-valve six delivers good torque for brisk pickup when passing and rolling along. The 1987–88 Turbo edition, with air-to-air intercooler and 30 more horsepower, moves swifter yet, sending in a burst of power when it's needed. Optional anti-lock brakes for '87 make Supra's good braking even better. Turbos include a rear deck spoiler, tougher 4-speed automatic transmission, 3-coil ignition, plus Sports pack-

1986 1/2 Toyota Supra 3-door

age with electronically adjustable suspension and limited-slip differential. Well-shaped front seats are comfortable on long trips. Driver's seat adjusts to please just about anyone. Rear seat is tiny. Fuel mileage, while adequate on the highway, drops to marginal around town. Though not as nimble as some, Supra handles well and is a good choice for enjoyable cruising and daily driving.

Price Range	GOOD	AVERAGE	POOR
1986½ Supra	$16,000–18,000	$15,000–17,000	$14,000–15,500
1987 Supra	18,000–20,000	17,000–19,000	16,000–17,000
1988 Supra	21,000–23,000	20,000–21,500	—

Dimensions	WHEEL-BASE, IN.	LGTH., IN.	HT., IN.	WIDTH, IN.	AVG. WT., LBS.	CARGO VOL. CU. FT.	FUEL TANK, GAL.
3d cpe	102.2	181.9	51.6	68.7	3450	12.8	18.5

Engines	L/CID	BHP	MPG	AVAIL.
dohc I-6 FI	3.0/180	200	17–22	86–88
dohc I-6T FI	3.0/180	230	16–22	87–88

KEY: L/CID = liters/cubic inch displacement; **BHP** = brake horsepower; **MPG** = estimated average miles per gallon; **ohc** = overhead cam; **dohc** = double overhead cam; **ohv** = overhead valve; **I** = in-line engine; **V** = V engine; **flat** = horizontally opposed engine; **D** = diesel; **T** = turbocharged; **bbl.** = barrel (carburetor); **FI** = fuel injection.

RECALL HISTORY

None to date.

1986 1/2 Toyota Supra 3-door

Toyota Tercel 1980-82

1980 Toyota Tercel SR-5 3-door

Toyota's first front-drive offering was named Corolla Tercel, yet bears little resemblance to the rear-drive Corolla. Front seat isn't really spacious, but grownups won't complain as they would in back. Gas mileage and visibility are excellent; notchback sedan's tiny trunk is not. Workmanship is up to high standard, though traces of bare metal create a cheap look. Repair history excellent—as good as any Toyota, but valves must be adjusted regularly to prevent engine problems. Changes for 1981 included a different (same size) engine, minor facelift, and new 4-door sedan. Tercel may not be as modern as some Europeans, but it's just as pleasant and far less trouble-prone. One more top-notch Toyota value.

Price Range	GOOD	AVERAGE	POOR
1980 Tercel	$1700–2000	$1200–1600	$900–1200
1981 Tercel	2000–2400	1600–2000	1200–1600
1982 Tercel	2500–3000	2100–2500	1700–2100

Dimensions	WHEEL-BASE, IN.	LGTH., IN.	HT., IN.	WIDTH, IN.	AVG. WT., LBS.	CARGO VOL., CU. FT.	FUEL TANK, GAL.
2d/4d sdn	98.4	161.4	52.8	61.0	1895	9.3	11.9
3d sdn	98.4	161.4	52.8	61.0	1895	25.6	11.9

Engines	L/CID	BHP	MPG	AVAIL.
ohc I-4 2 bbl.	1.5/89	62	28–31	80–82

KEY: L/CID = liters/cubic inch displacement; **BHP** = brake horsepower; **MPG** = estimated average miles per gallon; **ohc** = overhead cam; **dohc** = double overhead

cam; **ohv** = overhead valve; **I** = in-line engine; **V** = V engine; **flat** = horizontally opposed engine; **D** = diesel; **T** = turbocharged; **bbl.** = barrel (carburetor); **FI** = fuel injection.

RECALL HISTORY

1980–82: lower rear control arms are subject to corrosion in regions where a large amount of road salt is used; corrosion failure could result in loss of vehicle control.

Toyota Tercel 1983-86

Wearing fresh sheetmetal on a new chassis, the second-generation front-drive subcompact rode a shorter wheelbase than before. Toyota claimed the 3- and 5-door hatchback interiors were bigger because of a more compact rear suspension, but four passengers will lack elbow room. Tall 5-door wagon is enormous inside for a vehicle this size, easy to enter, with ample headroom for six-footers in front or rear. First offered only with on-demand 4-wheel drive and unique 6-speed manual shift, the wagon could have front drive for 1984, with either automatic or 5-speed manual transmission. Carbureted 1.5-liter four delivers high mileage. Performance passable on manual-shift hatchback, slow with automatic. Ignition modules on 1983-84 engines also had a high failure rate. Hatchbacks tend to be reasonably priced; wagons (especially 4WD) are higher.

1983 Toyota Tercel 4WD 5-door

Toyota

1983 Toyota Tercel 5-door hatchback

Price Range	GOOD	AVERAGE	POOR
1983 Tercel	$3200–4700	$2700–4000	$2300–3000
1984 Tercel	3800–5600	3400–5000	2900–3800
1985 Tercel	4700–6500	4200–6000	3600–4800
1986 Tercel	5300–7200	4800–6500	4300–5500

Dimensions	WHEEL-BASE, IN.	LGTH., IN.	HT., IN.	WIDTH, IN.	AVG. WT., LBS.	CARGO VOL., CU. FT.	FUEL TANK, GAL.
3d sdn	95.7	158.7	54.5	63.6	1990	29.0	11.9
5d sdn	95.7	158.7	54.5	63.6	2040	29.3	11.9
5d wgn	95.7	169.7	59.1	63.6	2140	59.8	13.2

Engines	L/CID	BHP	MPG	AVAIL.
ohc I-4 2 bbl.	1.5/88	60–62	28–34	83–86

KEY: L/CID = liters/cubic inch displacement; **BHP** = brake horsepower; **MPG** = estimated average miles per gallon; **ohc** = overhead cam; **dohc** = double overhead cam; **ohv** = overhead valve; **I** = in-line engine; **V** = V engine; **flat** = horizontally opposed engine; **D** = diesel; **T** = turbocharged; **bbl.** = barrel (carburetor); **FI** = fuel injection.

RECALL HISTORY

1983–86: defective ignition-control module could cause car to stall after startup, or not start.

Toyota Tercel 1987-88

Latest front-drive Liftback subcompacts have minimal ties to earlier Tercels. Aerodynamic look stems from sloped nose, raked windshield and aero-halogen headlamps, plus lower beltline and taller glass area. New overhead-cam engine is the same size as before (1.5 liters), but has three valves per cylinder and a variable-venturi carburetor. It's

1987 Toyota Tercel Deluxe 3-door

mounted transversely in the new version. Front-drive and 4WD wagons got only modest styling changes and kept the old, longitudinally mounted 1.5 four, with 14 fewer horsepower; only the 4WD edition survived into 1988. Halfway through the opening season, a new coupe and EZ 3-door hatchback arrived. Powerplant delivers much livelier performance than before, at least with 5-speed. Automatic is sluggish: Wagons with the old underpowered engine are weaker yet, even with 6-speed manual shift. Tercel cruises comfortably even at high engine speeds and handles capably enough to satisfy most drivers. Optional sunroof cuts into headroom; back seat legroom less than ample (coupe nearly impossible) for grownups. Behind-the-seat cargo space isn't bad. Hatchback rear seats fold flat to add cargo area. Road noise isn't as bad as on prior Tercels. All told, a reasonable, rather refined, but unexceptional rival to Honda Civic, Omni/Horizon and Hyundai Excel, with Toyota's well-known reputation for durability.

Price Range	GOOD	AVERAGE	POOR
1987 Tercel	$5900–8500	$5400–7500	$4900–6500
1988 Tercel	6000–10,000	5500–9000	—

Dimensions	WHEEL-BASE, IN.	LGTH., IN.	HT., IN.	WIDTH, IN.	AVG. WT., LBS.	CARGO VOL., CU. FT.	FUEL TANK, GAL.
3d sdn	93.7	157.3	52.6	64.0	1970	36.2	11.9
5d sdn	93.7	157.3	52.8	64.0	2015	37.8	11.9
5d wgn	93.7	169.7	56.1	63.6	2207	63.7	13.2

Engines	L/CID	BHP	MPG	AVAIL.
ohc I-4 1 bbl.	1.5/89	76–78	27–33	87–88
ohc I-4 2 bbl.	1.5/89	62	28–34	87–88

Toyota

1987 Toyota Tercel Standard 2-door

KEY: L/CID = liters/cubic inch displacement; **BHP** = brake horsepower; **MPG** = estimated average miles per gallon; **ohc** = overhead cam; **dohc** = double overhead cam; **ohv** = overhead valve; **I** = in-line engine; **V** = V engine; **flat** = horizontally opposed engine; **D** = diesel; **T** = turbocharged; **bbl.** = barrel (carburetor); **FI** = fuel injection.

RECALL HISTORY

None to date.

Toyota Van 1984-88

First of the new-wave compact vans hit the U.S. market a few months ahead of Chrysler's. Rear-drive layout is unusual for mid-engine placement of its 2.0-liter four, between the front seats. Appearance is also unusual, with the shortest wheelbase of the modern mini-vans. The ride is bouncy with lots of pitching on the highway and body lean around turns. Rear and middle seats remove easily, creating great passenger/cargo room. You can't move from front to back past the engine, however, and must raise the driver's seat to get at the engine even for fluid checks. The 1700-pound payload and one-ton towing limit are lower than Chevy Astro or Ford Aerostar. A larger, more powerful engine arrived for 1986, yet performance is weak. Also new for '86 were rack-and-pinion steering and a captain's chair option on the top LE model. Part-time 4WD, optional for 1987–88, improves snow/rain traction. A 2-seat cargo

1984 Toyota Van LE

van also is available. Even with fine workmanship and space for seven adults, we can't call the Toyota Van one of our favorites.

Price Range	GOOD	AVERAGE	POOR
1984 Van	$6400–7300	$5900–6700	$5400–6000
1985 Van	7600–8500	7000–7900	6500–7200
1986 Van	8700–9700	8200–9200	7500–8400
1987 Van	10,700–13,700	10,000–13,000	9000–11,500
1988 Van	12,250–16,500	11,500–15,000	—

Dimensions	WHEEL-BASE, IN.	LGTH., IN.	HT., IN.	WIDTH, IN.	AVG. WT., LBS.	CARGO VOL., CU. FT.	FUEL TANK, GAL.
4d van/wgn	88.0	175.4	70.1	66.3	2985	149.8	15.9

Engines	L/CID	BHP	MPG	AVAIL.
ohv I-4 FI	2.0/122	90	20–25	84–85
ohv I-4 FI	2.2/137	101	20–24	86–88

KEY: L/CID = liters/cubic inch displacement; **BHP** = brake horsepower; **MPG** = estimated average miles per gallon; **ohc** = overhead cam; **dohc** = double overhead cam; **ohv** = overhead valve; **I** = in-line engine; **V** = V engine; **flat** = horizontally opposed engine; **D** = diesel; **T** = turbocharged; **bbl.** = barrel (carburetor); **FI** = fuel injection.

RECALL HISTORY

1983–86: defective ignition-control module could cause car to stall after startup, or not start. **1984–85:** on vehicles with power steering, center control arm of steering linkage may develop crack if steering wheel is repeatedly operated while parked; arm breakage would result in complete loss of steering control.

Volkswagen Golf/Jetta 1985-88

1985 Volkswagen Jetta 4-door

Both the hatchback Golf (which replaces the old Rabbit) and notchback Jetta are larger than before, with 25 percent more cargo volume. In fact, the EPA switched them from subcompact to compact status. Shared front-drive chassis has a 2.6-inch longer wheelbase and new torsion beam rear axle. Golf may look familiar, yet uses no Rabbit body parts. As before, 3- and 5-door Golfs are American-made, Jetta sedans imported from Germany. (Some 1987-88 Jettas made in U.S.) Cabriolet convertible carries on the previous Rabbit design, with a higher-powered version of the Golf/Jetta 1.8-liter engine. Both may instead have a 1.6-liter diesel; 1985-86 Jetta GL, a turbodiesel. All are fairly thrifty and the potent gas fours deliver brisk pickup. Performance fans might look for a Golf GTI or Jetta GLI, both of which moved up to a 123-horsepower 16-valve engine late in 1987. For 1988, the base four added 15 horsepower, Cabriolets dressed up in new aero-look styling details, and Jetta gained a fully loaded Carat model. Impressive road manners come from a nicely tuned chassis. Ride is firm yet compliant, steering crisp. Five-passenger interiors are roomy if austere, Jetta's trunk quite spacious. Road noise can be nasty, especially on rough pavement. Repair records are sketchy, but noisy front disc brake pads are a common flaw.

Volkswagen

Price Range	GOOD	AVERAGE	POOR
1985 Golf	$5400–6800	$5000–6300	$4400–5400
1985 Jetta	6600–8000	6200–7500	5500–6400
1985 Cabriolet	9000–9600	8600–9100	8000–8600
1986 Golf	6300–7800	5900–7000	5200–6200
1986 Jetta	7500–9200	7000–8500	6500–7500
1986 Cabriolet	10,200–11,000	9800–10,500	9200–9900
1987 Golf	7500–9000	7000–8500	6500–7600
1987 Jetta	8900–11,300	8300–10,500	7700–8900
1987 Cabriolet	11,700–12,500	11,000–12,000	10,500–11,200
1988 Golf	8200–12,000	7800–11,000	—
1988 Jetta	9500–12,500	9000–11,000	—
1988 Cabriolet	13,250–14,000	12,500–13,250	—

Dimensions	WHEEL-BASE, IN.	LGTH., IN.	HT., IN.	WIDTH, IN.	AVG. WT., LBS.	CARGO VOL., CU. FT.	FUEL TANK, GAL.
3d/5d sdn	97.3	158.0	55.7	65.5	2172	17.9	14.5
2d/4d sdn	97.3	171.7	55.7	65.5	2300	16.6	14.5
2d conv.	94.5	159.3	55.6	64.2	2214	6.2	13.8

Engines	L/CID	BHP	MPG	AVAIL.
ohc I-4 FI	1.8/109	85–105	22–27	85–88
dohc I-4 FI	1.8/109	123	20–24	87–88
ohc I-4D FI	1.6/97	52	36–42	85–87
ohc I-4TD FI	1.6/97	68	36–40	85–86

KEY: L/CID = liters/cubic inch displacement; **BHP** = brake horsepower; **MPG** = estimated average miles per gallon; **ohc** = overhead cam; **dohc** = double overhead cam; **ohv** = overhead valve; **I** = in-line engine; **V** = V engine; **flat** = horizontally opposed engine; **D** = diesel; **T** = turbocharged; **bbl.** = barrel (carburetor); **FI** = fuel injection.

1988 Volkswagen Golf GT 5-door

Volkswagen

RECALL HISTORY

1985 Golf: master cylinder's primary and secondary piston cups may have been interchanged during assembly, reducing effectiveness in one brake circuit and increasing stopping distance. **1985:** front seatbelt retractors on 2-door models may not lock properly during sudden heavy brake application or impact. **1985 Cabriolet:** fuel supply hose connected to transfer pump (in fuel tank) could loosen from its connection, interrupting fuel supply. **1985 Jetta:** one plastic clip holding brake line could melt as a result of abnormally high temperature of nearby exhaust pipe, after prolonged engine idling; dripping of plastic onto hot pipe may cause fire. **1985–86:** excessive fuel may escape from fuel tank; in event of accident, fuel spillage may result in fire. **1985–87:** fuel pump inside tank could seize during high ambient temperature because an extremely fine-mesh filter restricts the fuel flow, causing engine stall. **1987 Golf:** left front lug nuts on cars with alloy wheels may have been improperly tightened, which could allow wheel to loosen over a period of time and eventually separate.

Volkswagen Rabbit/Jetta 1978-84

Trend-setting front-drive Rabbit debuted in 1975 with 3- and 5-door hatchback bodies. Jetta, its companion since 1980, is structurally similar but carries a roomy trunk. Rabbits sold here since 1979 are American-made. Jettas and convertibles come from Germany. Though dated in

1984 Volkswagen Jetta GLI 4-door

basic subcompact design, this pair rivals many newer models. Front seat and luggage space are good, handling agile, gas-engine pickup snappy. Mileage is nice with gas, sensational from diesels. Drawbacks include tight back seat, plastic interior, and too much noise. A high-performance 3-door GTI helped boost sagging Rabbit sales in 1983–84. Jetta's early repair record is good. Rabbits have always been more trouble-prone, with problems through 1980 in electrical and fuel systems, plus oil leakage and oil burning. Engine problems include premature valve guide wear, cylinder head warpage and cam bearing wear. The aluminum radiators have a history of premature failure, and in the snowbelt beware of severe underbody corrosion which can dangerously weaken rear suspension. Diesel Rabbits do better except for mechanical, cooling and exhaust failures. Air conditioners are neither effective nor reliable. Rabbit workmanship lags behind Japanese rivals and service can be costly. We wouldn't buy one without a full mechanical check.

Price Range	GOOD	AVERAGE	POOR
1978 Rabbit	1200–1500	900–1200	600–900
1979 Rabbit	1300–1700	1000–1300	750–1000
1980 Rabbit	1800–2100	1350–1800	1000–1350
1980 Convertible	4800–5100	4400–4800	4000–4400
1980 Jetta	2500–2800	2200–2500	1900–2200
1981 Rabbit	2000–2500	1600–2100	1200–1600
1981 Convertible	5200–5500	4800–5200	4400–4800
1981 Jetta	3000–3300	2600–3000	2200–2600
1982 Rabbit	2700–3200	2300–2800	1800–2300
1982 Convertible	6000–6300	5600–6000	5200–5600
1982 Jetta	3700–4100	3400–3800	3000–3400
1983 Rabbit	3400–4300	3000–3900	2500–3100
1983 Convertible	6500–7000	6100–6500	5700–6100
1983 Jetta	4300–4700	4000–4400	3600–4000
1984 Rabbit	4000–5200	3600–4800	3100–3900
1984 Convertible	7800–8200	7400–7800	6800–7500
1984 Jetta	5300–6100	4900–5600	4200–5000

Dimensions	WHEEL-BASE, IN.	LGTH., IN.	HT., IN.	WIDTH, IN.	AVG. WT., LBS.	CARGO VOL., CU. FT.	FUEL TANK, GAL.
2d/4d sdn	94.5	167.8	55.5	63.4	2175	13.3	10.6
3d/5d sdn	94.5	153.3	55.5	63.4	2000	22.6	10.0
2d conv.	94.5	159.3	55.6	64.2	2215	6.2	10.6

Engines	L/CID	BHP	MPG	AVAIL.
ohc I-4 2 bbl.	1.5/89	62	26–30	80
ohc I-4 FI	1.5/89	70–71	27–31	78–79

Volkswagen

1978 Volkswagen Rabbit L 3-door

Engines	L/CID	BHP	MPG	AVAIL.
ohc I-4D FI	1.5/90	48	45–50	78–80
ohc I-4 FI	1.6/97	76–78	26–30	80
ohc I-4D FI	1.6/97	52	45–50	81–84
ohc I-4TD FI	1.6/97	68	45–50	83–84
ohc I-4 2 bbl./FI	1.7/105	65–74	25–28	81–84
ohc I-4 FI	1.8/110	90	22–25	83–84

KEY: L/CID = liters/cubic inch displacement; **BHP** = brake horsepower; **MPG** = estimated average miles per gallon; **ohc** = overhead cam; **dohc** = double overhead cam; **ohv** = overhead valve; **I** = in-line engine; **V** = V engine; **flat** = horizontally opposed engine; **D** = diesel; **T** = turbocharged; **bbl.** = barrel (carburetor); **FI** = fuel injection.

RECALL HISTORY

1978–79: corrosion could cause leaks in brake lines located in passenger compartment, causing one or both brake circuits to fail. **1978–79:** water leaks in cars with automatic transmission may cause starter to activate accidentally, exhausting battery and preventing restarting. **1978–79:** possible that electrical defect could result in car with standard transmission starting and moving without driver turning on ignition. **1978–80:** accelerator cable on fuel-injected models with automatic transmission could malfunction, causing high engine idle speed and hesitation during acceleration. **1978–82:** electrical connector in fuse panel could overload and malfunction, interrupting supply of electricity to fuel pump, causing car to stall or preventing it from starting. **1980–81:** possibility of fuel spilling from fuel tank, creating potential for fire; corrected by installing restrictor valve in fuel pipe. **1981:** outer tie rod ends may crack and separate from ball socket. **1981:** inner ball joint lock nuts may not have been properly torqued, which could allow tie rod to separate from steering assembly. **1982–84 Rabbit:** throttle shaft in carburetor may crack and eventually break due to excessive vibration; throttle would not return to idle so engine would continue to race, possibly resulting in loss of control. **1983–84 Jetta and convertible:** outer rubber layer of brake hoses may become brittle under adverse weather conditions and develop cracks, which could lead to loss of brake fluid and increased stopping distance.

Volkswagen Scirocco 1982-88

1982 Volkswagen Scirocco 3-door

New rounded body, slightly longer, tops previous Scirocco's chassis and drivetrain. Larger it is, but still a 2 + 2, which means scant space in back for adults and minimal headroom up front. Though slightly quieter and softer-feeling than before, Scirocco is a lively driver with swift pickup, eager handling, a taut chassis for flat cornering, and confident front-drive traction. Loud exhaust can dim driving pleasure and lack of power steering (until '87) demands muscle while parking. During 1983, the Rabbit GTI's potent 1.8-liter engine and close-ratio 5-speed were added, in an effort to spark sales. That helped some, but Scirocco hasn't sold briskly, partly because the current GTI is both faster and cheaper. New 16V with 16-valve, 123-horsepower engine arrived during '86.

Price Range	GOOD	AVERAGE	POOR
1982 Scirocco	$3900–4200	$3600–4000	$3200–3600
1983 Scirocco	5000–5400	4700–5000	4200–4700
1984 Scirocco	5900–6400	5500–6000	5000–5500
1985 Scirocco	7400–7800	7000–7500	6400–7000

Volkswagen • Volvo

Price Range	GOOD	AVERAGE	POOR
1986 Scirocco	8700–9100	8200–8700	7700–8200
1987 Scirocco	10,100–11,500	9600–11,000	9000–10,000
1988 Scirocco	11,200–13,500	10,500–12,500	—

Dimensions	WHEEL-BASE, IN.	LGTH., IN.	HT., IN.	WIDTH, IN.	AVG. WT., LBS.	CARGO VOL., CU. FT.	FUEL TANK, GAL.
3d cpe	94.5	165.7	51.4	64.0	2181	23.7	10.6

Engines	L/CID	BHP	MPG	AVAIL.
ohc I-4 FI	1.7/105	74	23–26	82–83
ohc I-4 FI	1.8/109	90	22–26	84–87
ohc I-4 FI	1.8/109	123	21–25	86–88

KEY: L/CID = liters/cubic inch displacement; **BHP** = brake horsepower; **MPG** = estimated average miles per gallon; **ohc** = overhead cam; **dohc** = double overhead cam; **ohv** = overhead valve; **I** = in-line engine; **V** = V engine; **flat** = horizontally opposed engine; **D** = diesel; **T** = turbocharged; **bbl.** = barrel (carburetor); **FI** = fuel injection.

RECALL HISTORY

1982: electrical connector in fuse panel could overload and malfunction, interrupting supply of electricity to fuel pump, causing the car to stall or preventing it from starting. **1985:** fuel supply hose connected to transfer pump (in gas tank) could loosen from its connection, interrupting fuel supply to engine and causing vehicle to stall abruptly; also, fuel pump could fail during high ambient temperatures, interrupting fuel supply. **1985–87:** fuel pump inside tank could seize during high ambient temperature because an extremely fine-mesh filter restricts the fuel flow, causing engine to stall.

Volvo 240/260 1978-88

Well-built, popular rear-drive Swedes carry modern overhead-cam 4-cylinder or V-6 engines. Handling and cornering are much better than prior series, steering lighter, road manners competent. Six-cylinder 260 series and GLE share wheelbase and body styles with the 240. Starting in 1984, the base DL and mid-level GL came closer in price and equipment. Along with 1986 front-end restyling came a return of the 240 nameplate (after official absence of several years), as the diesel and turbo departed. Four-cylinder models lack vigor, except for the turbocharged version added for 1981; but their repair record is much better than average, apart from early exhaust system failures. The V-6 models rate average overall, but have more trouble

1981 Volvo GLT 5-door

with electrical, ignition, cooling, fuel and brake systems. Diesel reliability falls in between, while the complex turbo is likely to be more troublesome. Parts and service are expensive. Top-shelf GLE (replaced by new 760 GLE in 1983), turbos and cavernous station wagon carry highest price, but no Volvo comes cheap. Functional, fad-free design and high-quality materials have kept sales strong. Volvos are built to last. We recommend the 4-speed manual shift with electric overdrive (5-speed starting in '87) over an automatic.

Price Range	GOOD	AVERAGE	POOR
1978 240 Series	$2900–3300	$2500–2900	$2000–2500
1978 260 Series	3100–3500	2800–3100	2300–2800
1979 240 Series	3600–4100	3100–3500	2600–3100
1979 260 Series	3900–4400	3400–3800	2900–3400
1980 240 (DL/GL)	4500–5200	4000–4800	3500–4200
1980 GLE	5500–6000	5000–5500	4500–5000
1981 240 (DL/GL)	5100–6600	4600–5900	4000–5000
1981 GLE	6500–7000	6000–6500	5400–6000
1982 240 (DL/GL)	6500–8000	5800–7400	5100–6500
1982 GLE	7900–8300	7400–7900	6900–7400
1983 240 (DL/GL)	7700–9500	7100–8900	6500–7600
1984 240 (DL/GL)	9000–11,000	8500–10,500	7800–9000
1985 240 (DL/GL)	10,700–13,000	10,100–12,000	9400–11,000
1986 240	12,600–14,800	12,000–14,000	11,000–13,000
1987 240	14,200–16,500	13,500–15,500	12,700–14,000
1988 240	16,000–19,000	15,000–18,000	—

Volvo

Dimensions	WHEEL-BASE, IN.	LGTH., IN.	HT., IN.	WIDTH, IN.	AVG. WT., LBS.	CARGO VOL., CU. FT.	FUEL TANK, GAL.
2d sdn	104.3	192.6	56.5	67.1	3030	13.7	15.8
4d sdn	104.3	192.6	56.5	67.1	3130	13.9	15.8
5d wgn	104.3	190.7	57.5	67.1	3180	76.0	15.8

Engines	L/CID	BHP	MPG	AVAIL.
ohc I-4 FI	2.1/130	102–107	19–22	78–82
ohc I-4T FI	2.1/130	127–162	17–20	81–85
ohc I-4 FI	2.3/141	107–114	20–24	83–88
ohc I-6D FI	2.4/145	76–80	25–29	80,82–85
ohc V-6 FI	2.7/163	125–130	16–19	78–80
ohc V-6 FI	2.8/174	130–134	17–20	81–83

KEY: L/CID = liters/cubic inch displacement; **BHP** = brake horsepower; **MPG** = estimated average miles per gallon; **ohc** = overhead cam; **dohc** = double overhead cam; **ohv** = overhead valve; **I** = in-line engine; **V** = V engine; **flat** = horizontally opposed engine; **D** = diesel; **T** = turbocharged; **bbl.** = barrel (carburetor); **FI** = fuel injection.

RECALL HISTORY

1978: rear wheel bearings may have been inadequately lubricated, which could eventually lead to bearing seizure and rear axle reaching shearing point. **1981 DL:** high voltage peaks in distributor can cause ignition misfiring or intermittent stalling. **1981–84 GLT Turbo:** alternator-to-starter wire could be chafed by heat shield, causing short circuit that can drain the battery, melt or burn the wiring harness and, under certain conditions, cause a fire. **1982 DL, GL:** increased resistance in ignition system wiring connectors can cause misfiring or intermittent stalling. **1985–86:** after low-speed frontal collision, throttle cable sleeve could be pulled out of original position, increasing engine speed and making car difficult to control.

1983 Volvo Diesel 5-door

Volvo 740/760 GLE 1983-88

1985 Volvo 740 GLE 4-door

Replacement for top-rung 260 GLE uses the same alloy V-6 gas engine, hooked to 4-speed overdrive automatic transmission. Wheelbase is almost 5 inches longer than 240-series, but length about the same. Upright angular styling resembles recent GM cars. Refined V-6 runs smoothly and quietly and gives good performance. Turbocharged inline 6-cylinder diesel might cost less, but it's loud and less potent. A turbocharged 2.3-liter four joined the lineup in 1984 and a new 740 series, with intercooled turbo or normally aspirated 4-cylinder engine, appeared for '85. Turbo models are noisier and stiffer riding, though quicker. A 5-door wagon joined the original sedan as a 1985½ model. Anti-lock brakes became standard on 760 sedan for '87, as the diesel disappeared; 740 got the brakes a year later. Latest 760 has restyled front end and new multi-link independent rear suspension. You get a lot of luxury in an upper Volvo: roomy, comfortable interior, nice handling, and absorbent suspension for a smooth, pleasant ride. You also have to pay plenty for secondhand examples.

Price Range	GOOD	AVERAGE	POOR
1983 760 GLE	$9500–10,200	$9000–9600	$8400–9000
1984 760 GLE	11,600–12,500	11,000–12,000	10,300–11,300
1985 740 GLE	13,200–15,000	12,500–14,000	12,000–13,000

Volvo

Price Range	GOOD	AVERAGE	POOR
1985 760 GLE	14,300–16,000	13,800–15,500	13,000–14,500
1986 740 GLE	15,700–17,300	15,000–16,750	14,000–15,800
1986 760 GLE	17,200–18,750	16,500–18,000	15,500–17,000
1987 740 GLE	18,250–20,000	17,750–19,500	17,000–18,500
1987 760 GLE	22,500–24,000	21,500–22,500	20,800–21,500
1988 740 GLE	21,000–23,000	20,000–22,000	—
1988 760 GLE	29,000–31,000	27,500–30,000	—

Dimensions	WHEEL-BASE, IN.	LGTH., IN.	HT., IN.	WIDTH, IN.	AVG. WT., LBS.	CARGO VOL., CU. FT.	FUEL TANK, GAL.
4d sdn	109.1	188.4	55.5	68.9	2904	17.2	15.8
5d wgn	109.1	188.4	56.5	69.3	3049	76.0	15.8

Engines	L/CID	BHP	MPG	AVAIL.
ohc I-4 FI	2.3/141	111–114	20–25	85–88
ohc I-4T FI	2.3/141	157–160	19–25	84–88
ohc V-6 FI	2.8/174	134–145	18–24	83–88
ohc I-6TD FI	2.4/145	106	24–30	83–86

1985 Volvo 740 Turbo 5-door

1988 Volvo 760 GLE 4-door

CONSUMER GUIDE®

KEY: L/CID = liters/cubic inch displacement; **BHP** = brake horsepower; **MPG** = estimated average miles per gallon; **ohc** = overhead cam; **dohc** = double overhead cam; **ohv** = overhead valve; **I** = in-line engine; **V** = V engine; **flat** = horizontally opposed engine; **D** = diesel; **T** = turbocharged; **bbl.** = barrel (carburetor); **FI** = fuel injection.

RECALL HISTORY

1983: brake fluid could leak during pedal applications without activating the brake failure warning light, resulting in loss of braking power without warning. **1985:** certain water pump pulleys are defective and could break; pieces may be thrown inside engine compartment, causing damage and potential for injury. **1985-87 740 GLE, 740/760 Turbo:** engine wiring harness could chafe against air conditioning pipe and short-circuit the electrical system. **1986 wagon:** child-proof tailgate can be opened from inside vehicle while lock is engaged.

Yugo 1986-88

1986 Yugo GV 3-door

Tiny Yugoslavian-built hatchback was billed as the cheapest (and smallest) car sold in the U.S. when it debuted in summer of '85. Base price was only $3990, length well under 12 feet. Early buyer interest faded a bit, as first-year sales lagged behind predictions. Lately, it tends to draw more snickers than raves, almost becoming the car that people love to hate. Extensive reports of mechanical problems haven't helped Yugo's reputation, nor has insurance industry criticism that the car fared poorly in crash tests.

Yugo

1988 Yugo GVL 3-door

Sales during 1987 show a healthy increase. Front-drive chassis derives from the old Fiat 128. A 1.1-liter overhead-cam four with 4-speed manual shift was the sole drivetrain, until the sportier GVX arrived for '88 with a 1.3 four and 5-speed. Yugos are now available in nearly every state, which should help sales and service. Our recommendation: drive one for a distance before you buy. Not too many have hit used-car lots yet, though one dealer we spoke to wished he had a few to offer. Hardly a gem, but secondhand prices may prove irresistible for urban commuters.

Price Range	GOOD	AVERAGE	POOR
1986 GV	$2700–3000	$2400–2700	$2100–2400
1987 GV	3400–3900	3000–3500	2600–3000
1988 GV/GVL/GVX	3800–4600	3600–4400	—

Dimensions	WHEEL-BASE, IN.	LGTH., IN.	HT., IN.	WIDTH, IN.	AVG. WT., LBS.	CARGO VOL., CU. FT.	FUEL TANK, GAL.
3d sdn	84.6	139.0	54.7	60.7	1832	27.5	8.5

Engines	L/CID	BHP	MPG	AVAIL.
ohc I-4 2 bbl.	1.1/68	52–55	28–34	86–88
ohc I-4 2 bbl.	1.3/79	64	27–34	88

KEY: L/CID = liters/cubic inch displacement; **BHP** = brake horsepower; **MPG** = estimated average miles per gallon; **ohc** = overhead cam; **dohc** = double overhead cam; **ohv** = overhead valve; **I** = in-line engine; **V** = V engine; **flat** = horizontally opposed engine; **D** = diesel; **T** = turbocharged; **bbl.** = barrel (carburetor); **FI** = fuel injection.

RECALL HISTORY

1986: front seatbelt retractors, center common seatbelt mount, and rear inboard seat anchors were improperly installed; passengers may not be properly restrained in event of accident.